GANs & AI Creativity: Building Synthetic Intelligence

Gilbert Gutiérrez

Artificial intelligence is no longer confined to rule-based systems and predictive analytics—modern AI is creative, generative, and capable of producing stunningly realistic images, music, and even literature. At the forefront of this revolution is Generative Adversarial Networks (GANs), a groundbreaking deep learning architecture that has transformed AI's ability to create synthetic data, mimic human creativity, and revolutionize industries ranging from art and entertainment to healthcare and cybersecurity.

In **GANs & AI Creativity: Building Synthetic Intelligence**, the 12th book in the "*AI from Scratch*" series, Gilbert Gutiérrez takes readers on a comprehensive, step-by-step journey into the world of GANs, their underlying mechanisms, and how they power the next wave of AI-generated content. Whether you're a beginner eager to grasp the foundations of GANs or an experienced AI researcher looking to refine your understanding, this book serves as a complete guide to mastering synthetic intelligence.

Why This Book?

GANs are among the most exciting innovations in AI, but they are also notorious for being difficult to train and understand. Many books on deep learning skim over the complexities of GANs, leaving readers with a theoretical overview but little practical guidance. This book is different—it provides a step-by-step approach that moves from fundamental concepts to hands-on implementation, ensuring that readers not only understand GANs in theory but can also build, train, and optimize their own GAN models in practice.

Each chapter includes clear explanations, real-world applications, and coding tutorials, making this book an invaluable resource for AI enthusiasts, data scientists, and developers.

What You'll Learn

This book is divided into five comprehensive parts, covering everything from the basics of GANs to cutting-edge AI creativity applications.

◆ Part 1: Foundations of GANs

Before diving into implementation, it's essential to understand what GANs are and how they work. This section introduces the concept of adversarial learning, where two neural networks—the generator and the discriminator—compete against each other to produce highly realistic synthetic data.

You'll explore:

✅ The history of GANs and why they revolutionized AI creativity

✅ The fundamental architecture of GANs and how they train

✅ The key mathematical concepts, including probability distributions and optimization

✅ Different types of GANs and their real-world applications

◆ Part 2: Building GANs from Scratch

Once you grasp the fundamentals, it's time to get hands-on. This section provides a step-by-step guide to implementing GANs in Python, using TensorFlow and PyTorch.

You'll learn:

✅ How to set up your deep learning environment and choose the right framework

✅ How to write the generator and discriminator networks from scratch

✅ How to train a simple GAN and evaluate its performance

✅ Common training challenges like mode collapse and vanishing gradients—and how to fix them

✅ How to fine-tune hyperparameters for optimal results

◆ Part 3: GANs in Creative AI

GANs have made AI-generated art, music, and storytelling a reality. This section explores how GANs are reshaping creative industries, from deepfake technology to AI-assisted video game development.

You'll discover:

✅ How GANs create hyper-realistic artwork (StyleGAN, DeepDream)

✅ How AI generates music and sound effects (MuseGAN, WaveGAN)

✅ The power of text-based GANs for storytelling, chatbots, and creative writing

✅ The use of GANs in game design, NPC generation, and level creation

✅ The ethical implications of AI-generated content

◆ Part 4: Advanced GAN Architectures & Techniques

This section dives into cutting-edge GAN architectures, including StyleGAN, CycleGAN, and 3D GANs. If you want to go beyond basic GANs and explore state-of-the-art techniques, this section is for you.

You'll learn:

✅ How StyleGAN produces photorealistic images

✅ How CycleGAN enables image-to-image translation without paired data

✅ How text-to-image GANs (like DALL·E) generate stunning AI-generated artwork

✅ How 3D GANs are being used for metaverse and VR world-building

✅ How GANs contribute to scientific research and healthcare applications

◆ Part 5: Ethics, Challenges, and the Future of Synthetic Intelligence

GANs are powerful, but they come with risks. This final section addresses the ethical concerns, legal issues, and future of AI-generated content.

You'll explore:

✅ The rise of deepfakes and how to detect them

✅ Bias in AI-generated content and how to mitigate it

✅ The legal status of AI-generated art—who owns the copyright?

✅ How GANs are being used for medical advancements, climate science, and robotics

✅ The future of synthetic intelligence and its role in AGI (Artificial General Intelligence)

Who Is This Book For?

This book is designed for:

✅ AI Beginners who want an accessible yet thorough introduction to GANs

✓ Machine Learning Engineers & Data Scientists looking to implement GANs in real-world projects

✓ Developers & Programmers eager to experiment with AI creativity

✓ Artists & Content Creators curious about AI-generated art, music, and storytelling

✓ AI Ethics Enthusiasts interested in the legal and ethical aspects of AI creativity

Whether you're a self-learner, student, researcher, or AI professional, this book will equip you with the knowledge and practical skills to master GANs and explore the frontiers of AI creativity.

Why GANs Matter

GANs are more than just a niche area of AI—they are reshaping the entertainment, marketing, cybersecurity, and scientific industries. From AI-generated faces indistinguishable from real humans to realistic voice synthesis that can clone anyone's speech, GANs are paving the way for a new era of AI-driven creativity.

However, with great power comes great responsibility. The ability to generate fake yet convincing content brings challenges related to privacy, misinformation, and AI ethics. Understanding GANs isn't just about learning how to build them—it's about understanding how they impact society and how we can use them responsibly.

This book provides a balanced perspective—teaching both the technical skills to build GANs and the wisdom to navigate their ethical implications.

Final Thoughts

With GANs & AI Creativity: Building Synthetic Intelligence, you'll gain a deep understanding of one of the most exciting fields in AI today. You'll move from fundamental concepts to practical coding, explore real-world applications, and dive into the future of AI creativity.

Are you ready to unlock the power of synthetic intelligence and become a part of the AI revolution? Let's get started! 🚀

1. Introduction to Generative Adversarial Networks (GANs)

Artificial Intelligence has made incredible strides, but one of its most revolutionary breakthroughs is the ability to generate entirely new data—from lifelike images and music to deepfake videos and synthetic voices. At the heart of this innovation lies Generative Adversarial Networks (GANs), a deep learning architecture where two neural networks— the generator and the discriminator—compete against each other to create increasingly realistic outputs. This chapter introduces the core concept of GANs, explores their origins, and explains why they have transformed fields like art, gaming, healthcare, and AI research. Whether you're new to machine learning or an experienced practitioner, understanding GANs is a crucial step toward mastering AI-driven creativity and synthetic intelligence. 🚀

1.1 The Evolution of Generative Models

Generative models have played a crucial role in the advancement of artificial intelligence (AI), enabling machines to create new data rather than just analyzing existing patterns. These models have evolved significantly over the years, from early probabilistic methods to modern deep learning approaches like Generative Adversarial Networks (GANs), Variational Autoencoders (VAEs), and Transformers. This chapter explores the historical progression of generative models, highlighting key breakthroughs and their impact on AI-driven creativity, synthetic media, and real-world applications.

Early Generative Models: The Foundation

Before the rise of deep learning, generative models relied on statistical and probabilistic methods to create new data based on observed distributions. Some of the earliest generative approaches include:

1. Bayesian Networks

One of the first generative approaches, Bayesian Networks, used probabilistic graphical models to represent complex distributions of data. These networks captured relationships between variables and were applied in fields like medical diagnosis, speech recognition, and predictive modeling.

However, Bayesian Networks had limitations in handling high-dimensional data, making them less effective for complex generative tasks like image or text generation.

2. Markov Models and Hidden Markov Models (HMMs)

Markov models, particularly Hidden Markov Models (HMMs), became widely used for sequence generation in areas such as natural language processing (NLP) and speech synthesis. HMMs generated data based on probabilistic state transitions, making them effective for tasks like text prediction and phoneme generation in speech processing.

Despite their success, HMMs struggled with capturing long-term dependencies and complex structures, making them inadequate for generating highly realistic data.

3. Restricted Boltzmann Machines (RBMs) and Deep Belief Networks (DBNs)

In the early 2000s, Geoffrey Hinton and colleagues introduced Restricted Boltzmann Machines (RBMs) and Deep Belief Networks (DBNs), which marked the transition from classical probabilistic models to deep learning-based generative approaches. RBMs were capable of learning representations in an unsupervised manner, making them useful for dimensionality reduction, feature learning, and generative tasks.

However, training RBMs and DBNs was computationally expensive, and they lacked the scalability required for generating high-quality images, audio, or text.

The Rise of Deep Learning in Generative Models

With the emergence of deep learning, generative models underwent a major transformation. Neural networks enabled AI to learn hierarchical representations, leading to the development of models capable of generating realistic and complex data.

4. Autoencoders: The Birth of Representation Learning

Autoencoders became one of the first deep learning-based generative models. These neural networks consisted of two parts:

- **Encoder**: Compresses input data into a lower-dimensional latent representation.
- **Decoder**: Reconstructs the original data from this compressed representation.

Autoencoders paved the way for Variational Autoencoders (VAEs), which introduced probabilistic modeling to generate new samples by sampling from a learned distribution.

VAEs were widely used in image generation, anomaly detection, and latent space exploration.

Despite their success, VAEs often produced blurry images due to limitations in modeling fine details. This led to the need for more powerful generative techniques.

5. Generative Adversarial Networks (GANs): The Game-Changer

In 2014, Ian Goodfellow introduced Generative Adversarial Networks (GANs), a groundbreaking framework that revolutionized generative modeling. Unlike previous methods, GANs used a game-theoretic approach, consisting of two neural networks:

- **Generator**: Creates synthetic data.
- **Discriminator**: Evaluates whether the data is real or fake.

These two networks engage in an adversarial process, improving their capabilities iteratively. GANs quickly became the leading approach for image synthesis, deepfake generation, and AI-driven creativity. Unlike VAEs, GANs were able to produce sharp, high-quality images that closely resembled real-world data.

However, training GANs was challenging due to instability, mode collapse, and sensitivity to hyperparameters. Researchers responded by developing advanced variants such as DCGANs, WGANs, and StyleGANs, each improving training stability and output quality.

Beyond GANs: Modern Advances in Generative AI

6. Transformer-Based Generative Models

While GANs dominated image generation, the field of text generation saw a breakthrough with Transformers, particularly models like GPT (Generative Pre-trained Transformer). Introduced by OpenAI, GPT-3 and GPT-4 demonstrated how self-attention mechanisms could generate human-like text, enabling AI to compose stories, poetry, and even code.

The transformer architecture was later extended to multimodal AI systems like DALL·E, which combined text and image generation. Unlike traditional GANs, DALL·E used diffusion-based models to create highly detailed, semantically accurate images from textual descriptions.

7. Diffusion Models: The New Frontier

Recently, Diffusion Models have emerged as a promising alternative to GANs. These models, such as Stable Diffusion and Imagen, generate images by gradually denoising a random noise vector, similar to a reverse process of diffusion in physics.

Advantages of diffusion models over GANs:

- Higher diversity and realism without mode collapse.
- More stable training without the need for adversarial optimization.
- Ability to handle complex multimodal tasks (e.g., text-to-image generation).

Diffusion models have gained traction in AI-generated art, video synthesis, and medical imaging, marking a new phase in generative AI research.

The Future of Generative Models

As generative AI continues to evolve, several key trends are shaping the future:

1. AI-Powered Creativity

Generative models are redefining creativity in art, music, fashion, and design, allowing AI to collaborate with humans in unprecedented ways. Future developments will enhance user control and personalization in AI-generated content.

2. Real-Time Generation

New architectures are pushing towards real-time generative models, which will revolutionize gaming, virtual reality, and interactive AI applications. GANs and diffusion models will enable on-the-fly 3D world generation for the metaverse.

3. Ethical and Legal Challenges

As AI-generated media becomes indistinguishable from real content, issues related to deepfakes, misinformation, and intellectual property will require robust AI ethics and regulation.

4. Hybrid Models

Future research is likely to integrate GANs, transformers, and diffusion models into hybrid architectures, leveraging the strengths of each approach. This could lead to more powerful, controllable, and interpretable generative AI systems.

The evolution of generative models—from Bayesian networks and HMMs to GANs, VAEs, transformers, and diffusion models—has dramatically transformed AI's ability to create realistic and innovative content. Each breakthrough has addressed previous limitations, bringing us closer to synthetic intelligence capable of human-like creativity. As research continues, generative models will play an increasingly vital role in artificial intelligence, creativity, and real-world problem-solving. 🚀

1.2 The Birth of GANs – Ian Goodfellow's Breakthrough

The development of Generative Adversarial Networks (GANs) in 2014 by Ian Goodfellow marked one of the most significant advancements in the field of artificial intelligence (AI) and deep learning. Before GANs, generative models struggled with producing high-quality synthetic data, often suffering from blurry outputs, lack of realism, and training inefficiencies. Goodfellow's breakthrough introduced a novel adversarial training mechanism that enabled AI to generate high-resolution, photorealistic images, videos, and even deepfake content. This chapter explores the story behind the invention of GANs, their core architecture, working principles, and early impact on AI research.

The Challenge of Generative Models Before GANs

Before GANs, deep learning researchers primarily relied on Autoencoders, Variational Autoencoders (VAEs), and Restricted Boltzmann Machines (RBMs) for generative tasks. While these methods were effective in some domains, they struggled with:

- **Generating High-Resolution Images** – VAEs, for instance, often produced blurry outputs due to their probabilistic nature.
- **Capturing Complex Data Distributions** – Many generative models failed to learn intricate details of real-world images, limiting their usefulness.
- **Stable Training** – Training generative models was computationally expensive and prone to failure.

Researchers sought a new approach that could overcome these limitations and push generative AI forward—and that's where Ian Goodfellow's GANs changed the game.

The Birth of GANs – The Late-Night Idea

In 2014, Ian Goodfellow was a PhD student at the University of Montreal, working under the supervision of Yoshua Bengio, one of the pioneers of deep learning. One evening, while discussing generative models with colleagues, Goodfellow proposed a radical new approach based on game theory—a system where two neural networks would compete against each other.

As the story goes, Goodfellow left the conversation, went home, and within a few hours, he coded the first version of a Generative Adversarial Network (GAN). After running initial tests, he discovered that the model produced surprisingly realistic results compared to traditional generative models. This breakthrough led to the publication of his now-famous paper:

📖 **"Generative Adversarial Networks" (2014)** – Presented at the NeurIPS conference, this paper introduced the GAN framework and demonstrated its potential to generate photorealistic images.

How GANs Work – The Adversarial Game

GANs are based on a unique adversarial training mechanism, where two neural networks are pitted against each other in a zero-sum game:

Generator (G):

- Learns to create realistic synthetic data (e.g., images, text, or music).
- Starts with random noise and gradually improves by fooling the Discriminator.

Discriminator (D):

- Learns to distinguish between real data and fake data generated by the Generator.
- Provides feedback to the Generator, pushing it to improve.

The Training Process

- The Generator creates fake samples and sends them to the Discriminator.
- The Discriminator evaluates the samples and labels them as "real" or "fake".
- If the Discriminator correctly detects a fake, the Generator adjusts its parameters to improve.
- This process repeats iteratively until the Generator fools the Discriminator consistently, producing highly realistic data.

This adversarial process is inspired by game theory, where both networks improve through competition. Over time, the Generator becomes so effective that it can create indistinguishable replicas of real-world data.

Early Challenges and Limitations of GANs

Despite their promise, the first versions of GANs faced several challenges:

- **Training Instability** – Since both networks are constantly improving, GANs were difficult to train, often leading to mode collapse (where the Generator produces repetitive outputs instead of diverse samples).
- **Vanishing or Exploding Gradients** – The adversarial nature made gradient updates unstable, requiring careful hyperparameter tuning.
- **Computationally Expensive** – GANs required significant computational resources, limiting their accessibility in early research.

Goodfellow and other researchers responded by introducing improvements, leading to modern GAN architectures such as:

✓ **Deep Convolutional GANs (DCGANs)** – Introduced convolutional layers for better image generation.
✓ **Wasserstein GANs (WGANs)** – Addressed training instability by modifying the loss function.
✓ **StyleGAN** – Allowed fine-grained control over image synthesis, leading to photorealistic AI-generated faces.

The Impact of GANs on AI Research

The introduction of GANs had a transformative effect on AI research and real-world applications:

1. AI-Generated Art and Creativity 🎨

- GANs enabled AI-generated paintings, sculptures, and digital artwork, leading to the rise of AI-assisted creativity.
- Projects like DeepArt and RunwayML have allowed artists to collaborate with AI.

2. Deepfake Technology 🎭

- GANs made it possible to synthesize realistic human faces and voices, leading to deepfake videos.
- This raised ethical concerns around misinformation, requiring advancements in deepfake detection.

3. AI in Medical Imaging ⊕

- GANs improved MRI scans, X-ray synthesis, and medical image enhancement, aiding in early disease detection.
- Researchers used GANs for data augmentation, generating high-quality synthetic medical data for training AI models.

4. Gaming and Virtual Reality 🎮

- GANs helped create realistic textures, landscapes, and 3D models for video games and VR simulations.
- AI-powered game development tools now use GANs for procedural content generation.

5. Super-Resolution and Image Enhancement 📷

- GANs allowed for image upscaling, improving the quality of old photos and low-resolution videos.
- Tools like ESRGAN (Enhanced Super-Resolution GAN) are widely used in film restoration and photography.

Ian Goodfellow's Legacy and Future of GANs

Ian Goodfellow's breakthrough with GANs has inspired a new era of AI-driven creativity and machine learning innovation. After publishing his paper, Goodfellow continued working on deep learning at Google Brain and later joined Apple as a key AI researcher.

Key Contributions:

📌 Introduced GANs, revolutionizing generative AI.
📌 Contributed to deep learning research at Google, Apple, and OpenAI.
📌 Helped shape AI ethics discussions around deepfakes and misinformation.

The Future of GANs

- **Hybrid Models** – Combining GANs with diffusion models and transformers for more advanced generative AI.
- **Real-Time AI Generation** – GANs in metaverse, gaming, and real-time content creation.
- **Ethical AI** – Developing safeguards to prevent misuse of deepfake and synthetic media.

Ian Goodfellow's development of Generative Adversarial Networks (GANs) reshaped the landscape of AI creativity, image synthesis, and machine learning. By introducing a competitive learning framework, GANs enabled AI to generate highly realistic data, leading to groundbreaking applications in art, entertainment, healthcare, and beyond.

Despite early challenges, GANs continue to evolve, driving innovation in deep learning and artificial intelligence. As AI research advances, the legacy of Goodfellow's breakthrough will continue shaping the future of synthetic intelligence and generative AI.
🚀

1.3 Why GANs Are Revolutionary in AI

Generative Adversarial Networks (GANs) have been hailed as one of the most revolutionary breakthroughs in artificial intelligence (AI), fundamentally transforming how machines learn to generate realistic and creative content. Unlike traditional AI models that focus on classification, recognition, or prediction, GANs enable AI to create entirely new data—whether images, videos, music, or even text.

Since their introduction by Ian Goodfellow in 2014, GANs have reshaped industries ranging from art and entertainment to healthcare and cybersecurity. But what makes GANs so revolutionary? In this chapter, we'll explore why GANs are considered a game-changer in AI, examining their unique learning process, their impact on deep learning research, and their ability to push the boundaries of machine creativity.

1. GANs Introduced Adversarial Learning – A New Paradigm

Before GANs, most AI models relied on supervised learning, where machines were trained on labeled datasets to recognize patterns and make predictions. However, GANs introduced a new approach called adversarial learning, where two neural networks—the Generator and Discriminator—compete in a game-like scenario.

How Adversarial Learning Works

- The Generator (G) tries to create fake but realistic data (e.g., an AI-generated image of a human face).
- The Discriminator (D) attempts to detect whether the data is real or generated.

Both networks improve over time as they learn from each other—the Generator gets better at fooling the Discriminator, and the Discriminator gets better at detecting fakes.

♦ **Why This is Revolutionary**: Traditional AI models required large amounts of labeled data, which was time-consuming and expensive to curate. GANs removed the need for labeled data by learning in an unsupervised manner, making them more powerful for data synthesis and augmentation.

2. GANs Can Generate Completely New, High-Quality Data

GANs go beyond analyzing data—they create new, never-before-seen data that looks and feels real. This is a significant leap from traditional AI models, which could only classify or manipulate existing data.

Key Examples of GAN-Generated Content:

✓ **Photorealistic Faces** – AI-generated human faces that don't exist in real life (e.g., ThisPersonDoesNotExist.com).

✓ **Art and Design** – AI-created paintings, fashion designs, and even music compositions.

✓ **3D Models & Virtual Environments** – GANs generate lifelike 3D objects and landscapes for gaming and VR.

✓ **Medical Imaging** – Synthetic MRI and CT scans for AI training in healthcare.

♦ **Why This is Revolutionary**: GANs blur the line between real and synthetic content, allowing AI to produce creative and innovative outputs that rival human-generated work.

3. GANs Solve the Data Problem – The Power of Data Augmentation

A major challenge in AI is the need for vast amounts of high-quality training data. Many AI applications, especially in fields like medicine, self-driving cars, and security, struggle with insufficient or biased datasets.

How GANs Help:

◆ **Generate Synthetic Data** – GANs can create realistic training samples, such as synthetic medical images for AI models in radiology.

◆ **Balance Biased Datasets** – GANs help correct biases in AI models by generating underrepresented samples (e.g., diverse human faces in facial recognition AI).

◆ **Reduce the Need for Expensive Data Collection** – GAN-generated data lowers costs and accelerates AI development.

◆ **Why This is Revolutionary**: With GANs, AI can generate infinite amounts of high-quality data, eliminating the dependency on real-world datasets and making AI more accessible, scalable, and unbiased.

4. GANs Revolutionized Image & Video Synthesis

GANs transformed digital content creation, enabling AI to edit, enhance, and synthesize images and videos in ways that were previously impossible.

Key Innovations in GAN-Based Image & Video Processing:

✓ **Deepfake Technology** – GANs power deepfake videos, allowing for realistic face-swapping and voice synthesis.

✓ **AI-Powered Photo Editing** – Apps like FaceApp and Photoshop's AI-powered tools use GANs for style transfer, image enhancement, and aging effects.

✓ **Super-Resolution Imaging** – GANs upscale low-resolution images to high-definition quality (e.g., ESRGAN).

✓ **AI-Generated Animations** – GANs create synthetic avatars, animated characters, and lifelike digital humans.

◆ **Why This is Revolutionary**: GANs eliminate the boundaries between real and artificial visuals, making AI a powerful tool for photography, film, and digital content creation.

5. GANs Enable AI Creativity – Machine-Generated Art & Music

Before GANs, AI struggled to generate creative content in the way humans do. However, GANs unlocked machine creativity, allowing AI to paint, compose music, and even write stories.

Examples of AI-Generated Creativity with GANs:

🎨 **AI-Painted Art** – GANs generated paintings that sold for thousands of dollars (e.g., "Portrait of Edmond de Belamy" by Obvious).

🎼 **AI-Composed Music** – GAN-powered AI creates original songs, symphonies, and electronic music.

📖 **AI-Written Stories & Poetry** – GAN-based text models can generate fiction, poetry, and screenplays.

♦ **Why This is Revolutionary**: GANs expand the boundaries of creativity, enabling AI to collaborate with humans in art, music, and storytelling.

6. GANs Have Transformed Scientific Research & Healthcare

Beyond art and media, GANs are impacting real-world fields like medicine, drug discovery, and climate science.

Key Scientific & Healthcare Applications of GANs:

✚ **Medical Image Synthesis** – GANs generate synthetic MRI, CT, and X-ray scans for AI-based diagnostics.

🔬 **Drug Discovery & Molecular Design** – AI-powered GANs help design new drug molecules for faster pharmaceutical research.

☐ **Climate Modeling & Satellite Imaging** – GANs improve weather forecasting, ocean mapping, and environmental monitoring.

♦ **Why This is Revolutionary**: GANs accelerate scientific discovery by simulating real-world data without requiring expensive physical experiments.

7. The Future of AI – GANs & Synthetic Intelligence

GANs have paved the way for a new era of AI—one where machines can not only recognize patterns but also create, imagine, and innovate.

Future Trends in GANs & AI:

🌐 **AI-Generated Virtual Worlds** – GANs will power realistic virtual environments for the metaverse.

☐ **AI-Powered Digital Humans** – GANs will create lifelike AI avatars for customer service, gaming, and social media.

⚡ **Fusion with Other AI Models** – GANs will integrate with Transformers & Diffusion Models for next-generation AI creativity.

🏛 **Ethical & Regulatory Challenges** – The rise of GANs will require new laws to regulate deepfakes, AI art ownership, and misinformation.

◆ **Why This is Revolutionary**: GANs are pushing AI toward synthetic intelligence, where machines can learn, create, and evolve like human beings.

Generative Adversarial Networks (GANs) have revolutionized AI by enabling machines to generate new, high-quality data, expanding AI's role in creativity, entertainment, healthcare, and scientific research. Their ability to create realistic synthetic content has transformed art, media, and industry applications, making AI not just a tool for automation but a partner in innovation.

As GANs continue to evolve, they will shape the future of synthetic intelligence, where AI will become increasingly creative, lifelike, and seamlessly integrated into human life. 🚀

1.4 Real-World Applications of GANs

Generative Adversarial Networks (GANs) have rapidly evolved from a groundbreaking AI concept into one of the most powerful tools in machine learning. Their ability to generate high-quality synthetic data, enhance images, and even create realistic human-like content has made them invaluable across multiple industries. From art and entertainment to medicine and cybersecurity, GANs are reshaping the way we interact with technology.

In this chapter, we will explore real-world applications of GANs and how they are revolutionizing fields such as image synthesis, deepfake technology, gaming, medical imaging, and more.

1. Image Synthesis and Enhancement

One of the most well-known applications of GANs is image generation and enhancement. GANs can create photorealistic images, modify existing images, and even restore old or damaged visuals.

A. AI-Generated Human Faces

- GANs can generate hyper-realistic human faces that do not exist in real life.

- Websites like ThisPersonDoesNotExist.com use StyleGAN to create fake, yet incredibly realistic, portraits.
- These faces are used in virtual avatars, marketing, and media.

B. Image Super-Resolution

- GANs like ESRGAN (Enhanced Super-Resolution GAN) can upscale low-resolution images into high-definition quality.
- This is widely used in photo restoration, security footage enhancement, and gaming graphics.

C. AI-Powered Photo Editing

- GAN-based tools in Adobe Photoshop, FaceApp, and DeepArt allow users to modify facial expressions, apply artistic styles, and enhance photos.
- AI-powered style transfer lets users transform images into the styles of famous artists like Picasso or Van Gogh.

◆ **Impact**: GANs have made image processing and editing more powerful than ever, benefiting photographers, designers, and content creators.

2. Deepfake Technology & Synthetic Media

GANs are the driving force behind deepfake videos, where AI can swap faces, mimic voices, or generate entirely new videos.

A. Deepfake Videos & Face Swapping

- Apps like Zao, Reface, and DeepFaceLab use GANs to create ultra-realistic face swaps.
- This is used in entertainment, social media, and even filmmaking (e.g., bringing back actors posthumously in movies).

B. AI-Generated Voice Cloning

- GANs can synthesize human-like voices, allowing text-to-speech (TTS) models to sound natural.
- This technology is used in virtual assistants, audiobooks, and accessibility tools.

C. Misinformation & Ethical Concerns

- While deepfakes have creative applications, they also raise serious ethical concerns about fake news, political propaganda, and identity theft.
- AI researchers are working on deepfake detection methods to counter misinformation.

♦ **Impact**: GANs are transforming the entertainment industry, but they also pose ethical challenges regarding the spread of false information.

3. Gaming and Virtual Reality (VR)

The gaming industry is one of the biggest beneficiaries of GAN technology, using it for procedural content generation, character animation, and virtual world creation.

A. AI-Generated Game Environments

- GANs help generate realistic landscapes, textures, and objects for games.
- NVIDIA's GameGAN created a playable version of Pac-Man by watching video gameplay.

B. Realistic NPCs & AI-Driven Characters

- GANs enable lifelike non-playable characters (NPCs) that can learn and evolve based on player interactions.
- AI-generated character faces and animations improve realism in AAA games like The Last of Us and Cyberpunk 2077.

C. Virtual Reality & AI-Powered Avatars

- GANs are used to create realistic 3D avatars in VR applications and the Metaverse.
- AI-generated facial expressions make virtual humans more natural and engaging.

♦ **Impact**: GANs are making gaming and VR worlds more immersive, realistic, and interactive than ever before.

4. Medical Imaging & Healthcare

GANs have made significant contributions to medicine and healthcare, improving the quality of medical imaging and aiding in drug discovery.

A. AI-Generated Medical Scans

- GANs generate high-resolution MRI, CT, and X-ray scans to help train AI models.
- This reduces the need for large datasets while improving disease detection models.

B. AI-Based Disease Diagnosis

- GANs help doctors detect diseases like cancer, Alzheimer's, and retinal disorders.
- AI-powered tools analyze patient scans to provide faster, more accurate diagnoses.

C. Drug Discovery & Molecular Synthesis

- GANs like MoleculeGAN help design new drug compounds for faster pharmaceutical research.
- AI-generated molecular structures accelerate vaccine development and personalized medicine.

⬥ **Impact**: GANs are improving healthcare accessibility, medical research, and early disease detection, potentially saving lives.

5. AI-Powered Fashion & Design

The fashion industry has embraced GANs for design automation, personalized clothing, and trend forecasting.

A. AI-Designed Clothing & Textiles

- Brands like Zalando and H&M use GANs to generate new clothing designs.
- AI helps predict fashion trends and create customized apparel.

B. Virtual Try-On & Smart Shopping

- GANs power virtual fitting rooms, allowing customers to see how clothes look on them before purchasing.
- AI-generated models can wear clothing samples without requiring human photoshoots.

◆ **Impact**: GANs are revolutionizing e-commerce by providing personalized shopping experiences and AI-assisted fashion design.

6. Cybersecurity & Fraud Detection

GANs play a crucial role in cybersecurity, biometric authentication, and fraud prevention.

A. AI-Generated CAPTCHA Solvers & Cyber Defense

- GANs help detect security vulnerabilities by mimicking hacker attacks.
- AI-driven CAPTCHA solvers test system defenses and enhance cybersecurity measures.

B. Deepfake Detection

- Since GANs can create deepfakes, they are also used to develop AI models that detect fake videos and images.
- Tech companies like Microsoft and Facebook are deploying GAN-based deepfake detection tools.

◆ **Impact**: GANs are being used both offensively and defensively in cybersecurity, improving fraud detection and system security.

7. AI in Film, Music & Content Creation

GANs are reshaping media production, filmmaking, and content creation by enabling AI-generated visuals, music, and scripts.

A. AI-Generated Movie Effects

- Hollywood studios use GANs for special effects, digital de-aging, and CGI character creation.
- Movies like Rogue One (Star Wars) used GANs to recreate actor Peter Cushing's likeness.

B. AI-Composed Music & Soundtracks

- GANs create original music scores and background tracks for movies and games.
- OpenAI's Jukebox generates AI-written songs with realistic singing voices.

C. AI-Written Screenplays & Books

- GAN-based models assist in screenwriting, poetry generation, and automated storytelling.
- AI-generated novels and scripts are now being experimented with in entertainment and publishing.

✦ **Impact**: GANs are making filmmaking, music production, and content creation more innovative and accessible.

GANs are one of the most revolutionary AI technologies, enabling machines to generate high-quality, creative, and useful content across various industries. From deepfake videos to medical imaging, gaming, and fashion, their impact is undeniable and far-reaching.

As GANs continue to evolve, they will push the boundaries of synthetic intelligence, transforming how AI interacts with creativity, security, and human life. 🚀

1.5 Limitations and Challenges

Generative Adversarial Networks (GANs) have revolutionized AI by enabling machines to generate realistic images, videos, music, and text. From deepfake technology to AI-generated art, GANs have found applications in numerous industries, including entertainment, healthcare, and cybersecurity. However, despite their remarkable capabilities, GANs are far from perfect.

In this chapter, we will explore the limitations and challenges of GANs, including their training difficulties, instability, ethical concerns, and computational demands. Understanding these limitations is crucial for researchers and developers to improve GAN technology and mitigate its risks.

1. Training Instability & Mode Collapse

One of the biggest challenges in GANs is their unstable training process. Since GANs rely on an adversarial game between two networks (the Generator and Discriminator), training them to reach equilibrium is difficult.

A. Mode Collapse – When GANs Get Stuck

- Mode collapse occurs when the Generator learns to produce only a limited variety of outputs, instead of generating diverse, high-quality samples.
- For example, in an image generation task, the GAN might only generate faces with similar expressions instead of varied, unique portraits.
- This happens because the Generator finds a "shortcut" to fool the Discriminator with repetitive patterns rather than improving diversity.

B. Non-Converging Training

- GAN training is notoriously unstable, often requiring careful hyperparameter tuning.
- Since both networks are improving simultaneously, one can overpower the other, leading to failed training.
- Finding the right balance between the Generator and Discriminator is complex and requires trial and error.

◆ **Impact**: Mode collapse and unstable training make GANs difficult to deploy in real-world applications, requiring advanced techniques like progressive growing, minibatch discrimination, and spectral normalization to improve stability.

2. Computational Power & Resource Intensiveness

GANs demand significant computational resources, making them expensive and challenging to train.

A. High GPU/TPU Requirements

- GANs require powerful GPUs or TPUs for effective training.
- High-resolution models like StyleGAN or BigGAN take weeks to train on expensive hardware.

B. Energy Consumption

- Training a single large-scale GAN model can consume as much energy as several households use in a year.
- AI researchers are working on energy-efficient GAN architectures, but power consumption remains a major concern.

◆ **Impact**: The high computational cost limits accessibility, making GANs less practical for individuals and small organizations without cloud computing resources.

3. Data Dependence & Bias in GANs

GANs are only as good as the data they are trained on. If the dataset is biased or limited, the generated outputs will reflect those flaws.

A. Bias in AI-Generated Content

- If a GAN is trained on a dataset with racial, gender, or cultural biases, it will generate biased outputs.
- **Example**: AI-generated human faces often struggle with diversity, favoring lighter skin tones if trained on an unbalanced dataset.

B. Overfitting to Training Data

- GANs sometimes memorize their training data rather than learning to generate new variations.
- This reduces originality and can cause legal issues if the generated content is too similar to real data.

◈ **Impact**: To reduce bias, GAN developers must use diverse, well-balanced datasets and implement fairness-aware training methods.

4. Ethical Concerns – Deepfakes & Misinformation

GANs have given rise to deepfake technology, which has both creative and malicious applications.

A. The Rise of Deepfakes

- Deepfake videos can swap faces in videos, generate fake news, and impersonate public figures.
- This has led to concerns about political misinformation, identity theft, and fraud.

B. AI-Generated Misinformation

- GANs can generate realistic-looking fake documents, social media profiles, and even fake scientific research.
- The ability to create synthetic images, audio, and video raises concerns about trust and authenticity online.

Impact: Governments and tech companies are working on deepfake detection tools, but ethical concerns surrounding GANs remain a growing issue.

5. Lack of Control Over GAN Outputs

GANs lack precise control over the outputs they generate, making it difficult to fine-tune specific features.

A. Challenges in Customization

- Unlike other AI models, GANs cannot be easily directed to generate highly specific outputs.
- **Example**: If asked to generate a cat with green eyes and striped fur, a GAN may struggle to meet all conditions precisely.

B. Difficulty in Interpretability

- GANs function as black boxes, meaning it's hard to understand why they generate certain outputs.
- This limits their use in applications where explainability is essential, such as healthcare and law enforcement.

Impact: Researchers are developing conditional GANs (cGANs) and latent space manipulation techniques to improve control, but the challenge remains.

6. Legal & Copyright Issues

GAN-generated content raises complex legal and intellectual property (IP) questions.

A. Who Owns AI-Generated Content?

- If an AI creates a painting, a song, or a book, who owns the copyright?
- Current laws do not fully address AI-generated works, leading to legal uncertainty.

B. AI Plagiarism Risks

- GANs trained on copyrighted material may generate outputs that closely resemble original works.
- This raises ethical concerns about artistic ownership and fair use.

◆ **Impact**: As AI-generated content becomes more widespread, governments will need to develop new copyright laws to address ownership and plagiarism concerns.

7. Difficulty in Scaling GANs for Real-World Use

While GANs work well in research and experimental settings, scaling them for large-scale real-world applications remains a challenge.

A. Issues with Deployment

- Many GAN models require massive datasets and high computing power, making deployment expensive.
- GAN-generated content may require human oversight to ensure quality and accuracy.

B. Consistency & Reliability Issues

- GANs do not always produce consistent results, making them less reliable for applications requiring precision.
- **Example**: A GAN generating medical images may create inaccurate abnormalities, leading to misdiagnosis risks.

◆ **Impact**: More robust training techniques and hybrid AI models combining GANs with rule-based systems are needed to improve reliability.

GANs have transformed artificial intelligence, enabling machines to create realistic and innovative content. However, they still face significant challenges, including training instability, high computational costs, ethical concerns, and legal uncertainties.

To maximize their potential while minimizing risks, researchers must work on improving GAN training methods, reducing bias, increasing interpretability, and addressing ethical issues. With continued advancements, GANs will become more stable, controllable, and widely applicable in the future. 🚀

2. The Anatomy of a GAN

At its core, a Generative Adversarial Network (GAN) consists of two competing neural networks—the generator and the discriminator—locked in a dynamic battle of improvement. The generator aims to create realistic synthetic data, while the discriminator attempts to distinguish between real and fake samples. This chapter breaks down the internal architecture of GANs, explaining how these networks interact, learn, and refine their outputs through an adversarial process. We'll explore key components like loss functions, optimization techniques, and training dynamics, providing a clear blueprint for understanding how GANs achieve their remarkable ability to generate lifelike content. 🚀

2.1 Understanding the Generator and Discriminator

At the heart of Generative Adversarial Networks (GANs) lies a powerful yet simple concept: a competition between two neural networks—the Generator and the Discriminator. These two networks engage in a zero-sum game, where one tries to create realistic data, while the other learns to distinguish between real and fake data. Through this adversarial process, both networks improve over time, leading to the creation of highly realistic synthetic content.

In this chapter, we will break down how these two components work, their roles, and how they interact to make GANs function effectively.

1. The Generator: Creating Synthetic Data

A. What is the Generator?

The Generator (G) is a neural network that creates fake data by learning to map random noise into meaningful outputs. It tries to produce samples that resemble real data so well that the Discriminator cannot tell the difference.

Think of the Generator as an artist who is learning to paint realistic human faces without ever having seen a real one—only through feedback from a critic (the Discriminator).

B. How Does the Generator Work?

Starts with Random Noise:

- The Generator takes a random input (z) from a probability distribution (e.g., Gaussian noise).
- This ensures diversity in the generated samples.

Transforms Noise into a Structured Output:

- The noise is passed through layers of a neural network, which learn to generate realistic data.
- Over multiple iterations, the Generator learns patterns, textures, and structures from real data.

Tries to Fool the Discriminator:

- The output of the Generator is a fake sample that looks like real data.
- It is passed to the Discriminator, which will decide whether it's real or fake.
- If the Discriminator correctly identifies it as fake, the Generator receives feedback and improves.

◆ **Goal**: The Generator aims to produce high-quality, realistic data that is indistinguishable from real-world samples.

2. The Discriminator: The AI Critic

A. What is the Discriminator?

The Discriminator (D) is a binary classifier that distinguishes between real data (from a dataset) and fake data (from the Generator).

Imagine the Discriminator as an art expert who is trained to identify real paintings from counterfeits. As the Generator improves, the expert also gets better at spotting fakes.

B. How Does the Discriminator Work?

Receives Two Inputs:

- **Real Data**: Samples from an actual dataset.
- **Fake Data**: Samples generated by the Generator.

Assigns a Probability Score:

The Discriminator outputs a probability D(x) → [0,1], where:

- 1 (or close to it) = Real sample
- 0 (or close to it) = Fake sample

Learns to Differentiate:

- If the Discriminator classifies real samples as real and fake samples as fake, it receives a reward (positive feedback).
- If it fails to detect a fake, it adjusts its weights to improve in the next iteration.

◈ **Goal**: The Discriminator aims to become a perfect detector, correctly distinguishing real from fake data 100% of the time.

3. The Adversarial Game: How GANs Learn

The Generator and Discriminator are engaged in a continuous learning loop, where:

- The Generator improves at creating realistic data.
- The Discriminator improves at detecting fake data.

This creates a dynamic process where both networks push each other to perform better, leading to the generation of highly realistic synthetic data.

A. The Training Process

- Generator creates fake data → Discriminator evaluates it.
- Discriminator provides feedback to the Generator.
- Generator adjusts its parameters to produce more realistic outputs.
- Discriminator adjusts its parameters to better detect fake samples.
- The process repeats until the Generator creates data so realistic that the Discriminator can no longer reliably distinguish between real and fake samples.

At this point, the GAN has reached equilibrium, meaning the Generator is producing high-quality, indistinguishable outputs.

4. Mathematical Representation

The Generator and Discriminator are optimized using a loss function based on a min-max game:

$$\min_{G} \max_{D} V(D, G) = E_{x \sim P_{data}(x)}[\log D(x)] + E_{z \sim P_z(z)}[\log(1 - D(G(z)))]$$

Where:

- $D(x)$ is the probability that the Discriminator correctly identifies a real sample.
- $D(G(z))$ is the probability that the Discriminator correctly identifies a fake sample from the Generator.
- The Generator **minimizes** this function (tries to fool the Discriminator).
- The Discriminator **maximizes** this function (tries to detect fakes).

This adversarial loss function ensures that both networks continuously improve until they reach an optimal state.

5. Challenges in GAN Training

Despite their power, training GANs is notoriously difficult due to:

A. Mode Collapse

- The Generator produces limited variations instead of diverse samples.
- **Solution**: Techniques like minibatch discrimination and feature matching.

B. Vanishing Gradients

- If the Discriminator becomes too strong, the Generator stops learning because gradients vanish.
- **Solution**: Adjusting learning rates, using Wasserstein loss, and employing improved architectures like WGANs.

C. Overfitting

- The Discriminator may memorize real samples instead of learning general patterns.
- Solution: Regularization techniques and diverse training data.

6. Real-World Applications

A. Image & Video Generation

- StyleGAN creates realistic human faces.
- DeepFake technology enables AI-generated video content.

B. Super-Resolution & Image Enhancement

- ESRGAN enhances low-resolution images to high-definition quality.

C. AI-Powered Design & Content Creation

- AI-generated fashion designs, digital art, and music composition.

◆ **Impact**: The Generator and Discriminator dynamic has led to some of the most powerful AI breakthroughs in history.

The Generator and Discriminator are the two fundamental components of GANs, engaged in a constant battle to create and distinguish between real and fake data. Through this adversarial process, GANs improve over time, leading to groundbreaking applications in art, design, gaming, healthcare, and beyond.

Understanding how these networks interact is essential for anyone looking to build and optimize GANs effectively. As researchers continue to refine GAN training methods, we can expect even more powerful AI-generated content in the future. 🚀

2.2 How GANs Learn Through Adversarial Training

At the core of Generative Adversarial Networks (GANs) is a fascinating and game-theoretic learning process called adversarial training. Unlike traditional machine learning models, GANs use two competing neural networks—the Generator and the Discriminator—that continuously improve by challenging each other. This adversarial dynamic is what enables GANs to generate realistic and high-quality synthetic data.

In this chapter, we will explore how adversarial training works, break down the learning process step by step, and discuss the challenges that arise in training GANs effectively.

1. The Core Concept of Adversarial Training

GANs consist of two neural networks:

- **The Generator (G):** Creates fake data.
- **The Discriminator (D):** Determines whether the data is real or fake.

These two models are engaged in a zero-sum game, meaning one model's gain is the other's loss. The Generator improves only if it can fool the Discriminator, while the Discriminator improves by better detecting fake data.

This adversarial process continues until the Generator produces samples that are so realistic that the Discriminator can no longer distinguish them from real ones.

♦ **Analogy**: Imagine a counterfeiter (Generator) trying to create fake banknotes, while a bank security expert (Discriminator) learns to detect counterfeit money. As the counterfeiter improves, the expert must also refine their skills to detect fakes more accurately. Eventually, the fake money becomes indistinguishable from real money.

2. Step-by-Step Learning Process in GANs

The adversarial training of a GAN involves several key steps:

Step 1: Initialize Networks

- The Generator (G) and Discriminator (D) are initialized with random weights.
- At this stage, both networks are untrained and perform poorly.

Step 2: Training the Discriminator

- The Discriminator is first trained independently using real data from a dataset.
- It learns to classify real images as real (label = 1) and random noise as fake (label = 0).
- This step ensures that the Discriminator has a strong baseline before the Generator starts challenging it.

Step 3: Training the Generator

- The Generator creates fake data using random noise as input.
- These fake samples are passed to the Discriminator for classification.

- The Generator's goal is to fool the Discriminator into believing the fake samples are real.
- If the Discriminator correctly identifies them as fake, the Generator adjusts its weights to produce more realistic outputs.

Step 4: Updating Both Networks

- The Discriminator continuously refines its ability to detect real vs. fake data.
- The Generator continuously improves its ability to generate more convincing data.
- This back-and-forth competition forces both networks to improve over time.

Step 5: Repeat Until Convergence

- The process is repeated for thousands or millions of iterations.
- Eventually, the Generator produces highly realistic outputs, and the Discriminator can no longer distinguish real from fake with certainty.

◆ **Result**: The GAN reaches a state of equilibrium, where the Generator's outputs are so realistic that the Discriminator's accuracy is around 50% (random guessing).

3. The Mathematical Foundation of Adversarial Training

GANs optimize a min-max objective function based on game theory. This function represents a competition between the Generator and the Discriminator:

$$\min_{G} \max_{D} V(D,G) = E_{x \sim P_{data}(x)}[\log D(x)] + E_{z \sim P_z(z)}[\log(1 - D(G(z)))]$$

Where:

- $D(x)$ is the probability that the Discriminator classifies real data x as real.
- $G(z)$ is the Generator's fake output given random noise z.
- The Discriminator aims to **maximize** this function (becoming better at distinguishing real vs. fake).
- The Generator aims to **minimize** this function (making fake data indistinguishable from real data).

The Learning Process

- The Discriminator is updated using gradient ascent to maximize its ability to differentiate real vs. fake data.
- The Generator is updated using gradient descent to minimize the Discriminator's ability to detect fake data.
- This adversarial learning pushes both networks to improve, creating high-quality synthetic outputs.

4. Key Challenges in Adversarial Training

Despite its effectiveness, adversarial training is notoriously difficult due to several challenges:

A. Mode Collapse

- The Generator repeatedly produces the same type of output instead of generating diverse samples.
- **Example**: If training a GAN on human faces, the Generator might only create one type of face rather than multiple unique faces.
- **Solution**: Use minibatch discrimination, feature matching, or adding randomness to training.

B. Training Instability

- If one network (Generator or Discriminator) becomes too strong, the training process collapses.
- If the Discriminator is too powerful, it easily detects fakes, and the Generator stops learning.
- If the Generator is too strong, the Discriminator becomes ineffective.
- **Solution**: Use Wasserstein GANs (WGANs), gradient penalty methods, and regularization techniques.

C. Vanishing Gradients

- If the Discriminator is too confident, the gradient updates for the Generator become too small, preventing learning.
- Solution: Modify the loss function (e.g., Wasserstein loss instead of traditional binary cross-entropy).

D. Computational Cost

- GANs require extensive computational power, especially for high-resolution outputs (e.g., StyleGAN, BigGAN).
- Training can take days or weeks on powerful GPUs.
- Solution: Use progressive growing, parallel computing, or cloud-based training.

5. Practical Techniques to Improve Adversarial Training

To improve GAN training, researchers have developed several techniques:

A. Label Smoothing

- Instead of using binary labels (0 for fake, 1 for real), use soft labels like 0.9 for real and 0.1 for fake.
- This prevents the Discriminator from becoming too confident and improves stability.

B. Feature Matching

- Instead of training the Generator solely based on fooling the Discriminator, match its features to those of real data.
- Helps avoid mode collapse.

C. Wasserstein GAN (WGAN)

- Uses a different loss function to reduce training instability and prevent vanishing gradients.
- Works well for high-quality image generation.

D. Spectral Normalization

- Regularizes the Discriminator to prevent it from overpowering the Generator.

Helps in stabilizing GAN training.

Adversarial training is the core mechanism behind GANs, enabling them to generate highly realistic synthetic content. By continuously competing and improving, the Generator learns to create near-perfect outputs, while the Discriminator sharpens its classification skills.

Despite its challenges, adversarial training remains one of the most powerful AI learning techniques, leading to groundbreaking applications in AI-generated art, deepfakes, data augmentation, and more. With continued advancements in GAN optimization and stabilization, the future of synthetic intelligence looks more promising than ever. 🚀

2.3 The Loss Function in GANs – Minimax Game

At the core of Generative Adversarial Networks (GANs) is a minimax game, where two neural networks—the Generator and the Discriminator—compete against each other. This competition is driven by a loss function that determines how both networks update their parameters during training. Unlike traditional machine learning models that optimize a single objective, GANs involve a dynamic system where one model's success leads to the other's failure.

In this chapter, we will explore the minimax loss function, understand its role in GAN training, and analyze the challenges and improvements made to stabilize training.

1. Understanding the Minimax Game in GANs

GANs are formulated as a two-player game, where:

- **The Generator** (G) tries to create fake samples that look as realistic as possible.
- **The Discriminator** (D) tries to correctly classify real and fake samples.

This adversarial setup results in a minimax optimization problem, where:

- The Discriminator tries to maximize the probability of correctly distinguishing real from fake data.
- The Generator tries to minimize the Discriminator's ability to detect fake data.

Mathematically, the minimax objective function for GANs is:

$$\min_{G} \max_{D} V(D, G) = E_{x \sim P_{data}(x)}[\log D(x)] + E_{z \sim P_z(z)}[\log(1 - D(G(z)))]$$

Where:

- $x \sim P_{data}(x)$ represents samples from the **real data distribution**.

- $z \sim P_z(z)$ represents **random noise input** to the Generator.

- $G(z)$ is the Generator's output, i.e., **fake data**.

- $D(x)$ is the probability that the Discriminator correctly identifies **real data**.

- $D(G(z))$ is the probability that the Discriminator correctly identifies **fake data**.

◆ **Key Insight:**

- The **Discriminator aims to maximize** $\log D(x)$ (correctly classifying real data) and **minimize** $\log(1 - D(G(z)))$ (correctly identifying fake data).

- The **Generator aims to minimize** $\log(1 - D(G(z)))$, making the Discriminator **less confident** in distinguishing fake data.

2. How the Minimax Game Drives Learning

Step 1: Training the Discriminator

- The Discriminator is trained using both real and fake samples.
- It maximizes the probability of assigning high scores to real data and low scores to fake data.

Loss function for the Discriminator:

$$L_D = - \left[E_{x \sim P_{data}(x)}[\log D(x)] + E_{z \sim P_z(z)}[\log(1 - D(G(z)))] \right]$$

- If $D(x)$ is close to 1, the Discriminator is confident the sample is real.

- If $D(G(z))$ is close to 0, the Discriminator is confident the sample is fake.

Discriminator's goal:

- Improve classification so that real data gets high confidence (closer to 1).
- Ensure that fake data gets low confidence (closer to 0).

Step 2: Training the Generator

- The Generator is trained to **fool the Discriminator** by producing realistic fake samples.
- Instead of maximizing $D(x)$, the Generator **minimizes** $\log(1 - D(G(z)))$.

Loss function for the Generator:

$$L_G = E_{z \sim P_z(z)}[\log(1 - D(G(z)))]$$

- If $D(G(z))$ is **close to 1**, it means the Generator successfully fooled the Discriminator.
- If $D(G(z))$ is **close to 0**, the Discriminator can still easily detect fakes.

Generator's goal:

- Improve its output so that $D(G(z))$ moves **closer to 1**, meaning fake samples look more realistic.

Step 3: Reaching Nash Equilibrium

The training process continues iteratively, with both networks improving over time.

Ideally, training reaches a Nash equilibrium, where:

- The Generator produces near-realistic outputs.
- The Discriminator can no longer distinguish real from fake data with certainty (outputs 0.5 probability).

3. Challenges with the Minimax Loss in GANs

While the minimax loss function is theoretically sound, it suffers from practical issues that make GAN training difficult.

A. Vanishing Gradients Problem

- If the **Discriminator is too strong**, it easily classifies fake data as fake $(D(G(z)) \approx 0)$.

- This leads to **almost zero gradients**, meaning the Generator **stops learning**.

- **Solution**: Instead of minimizing $\log(1 - D(G(z)))$, use **an alternative loss function**:

$$L_G = -E_{z \sim P_z(z)}[\log D(G(z))]$$

This encourages the Generator to **maximize** $D(G(z))$ directly, leading to better gradients.

B. Mode Collapse

- Instead of generating diverse outputs, the Generator may learn to produce only a few specific samples that consistently fool the Discriminator.
- **Example**: If training on human faces, the Generator might produce only one face type, ignoring diversity.

◆ Solution:

- Use minibatch discrimination, feature matching, or Wasserstein GANs (WGANs) to encourage variety.

C. Training Instability

- Since GANs involve two networks competing simultaneously, their learning process is highly unstable.
- Small changes in one network's performance can disrupt the training balance, leading to poor results.

◆ Solution:

- Use progressive growing, spectral normalization, or adaptive learning rates.

4. Alternative Loss Functions for GANs

To address minimax loss challenges, researchers have proposed several improved loss functions:

A. Wasserstein Loss (WGANs)

- Instead of using a binary classification approach, WGANs measure how different two probability distributions are.
- Uses Earth Mover's Distance (Wasserstein Distance) to improve training stability.

◆ **Advantage: Avoids vanishing gradients and stabilizes GAN training.**

B. Least Squares Loss (LSGANs)

- Uses a mean squared error loss instead of binary cross-entropy.
- Reduces exploding gradients and produces higher-quality images.

◆ **Advantage: Provides stronger gradients and improves convergence.**

C. Hinge Loss

- Encourages the Discriminator to output stronger classification scores rather than probabilities.
- Commonly used in BigGAN and modern GAN architectures.

◆ **Advantage**: Improves performance for large-scale datasets.

The minimax game in GANs is a fundamental concept that drives adversarial training. By continuously competing, the Generator and Discriminator refine their abilities, leading to the creation of high-quality synthetic data. However, the standard minimax loss comes with challenges like vanishing gradients, mode collapse, and instability.

To overcome these issues, researchers have introduced alternative loss functions like Wasserstein loss, least squares loss, and hinge loss, which improve GAN training and stability. Understanding these loss functions is crucial for anyone looking to build, optimize, and train GANs effectively. 🚀

2.4 Training Pipeline of a Basic GAN

Training a Generative Adversarial Network (GAN) requires a structured pipeline that ensures both the Generator and Discriminator improve over time. Since GANs involve two competing networks, their training process is inherently unstable, requiring careful tuning of data processing, model optimization, and performance evaluation.

In this chapter, we will break down the step-by-step training pipeline of a basic GAN, discuss key hyperparameters, and explore techniques to stabilize training and improve convergence.

1. Overview of the GAN Training Pipeline

A typical GAN training process consists of the following stages:

- **Data Preparation** – Collect and preprocess the dataset.
- **Model Initialization** – Define the Generator and Discriminator architectures.
- **Training Loop** – Train both models iteratively using adversarial training.
- **Performance Evaluation** – Monitor convergence and detect potential issues.
- **Fine-tuning & Optimization** – Adjust hyperparameters to stabilize training.

By following this structured pipeline, we can ensure the GAN learns effectively and generates realistic outputs.

2. Step-by-Step GAN Training Process

Step 1: Data Preparation

Before training a GAN, we need a dataset that represents the real-world distribution we want to model. Examples include:

- **Images** (e.g., MNIST for handwritten digits, CelebA for human faces).
- **Audio** (e.g., speech signals, music samples).
- **Text** (e.g., GPT-based GANs for text generation).

Preprocessing Steps:

✓ Resize images to a uniform size (e.g., 64×64, 128×128).

✓ Normalize pixel values to a range of [-1, 1] for stable training.

✓ Augment data (e.g., rotation, flipping) to improve model robustness.

✓ Convert text/audio into a numerical format suitable for deep learning models.

◆ **Example (Image Data Preprocessing in PyTorch)**

import torchvision.transforms as transforms

```
transform = transforms.Compose([
    transforms.Resize((64, 64)),
    transforms.ToTensor(),
    transforms.Normalize(mean=[0.5], std=[0.5])  # Normalize to range [-1, 1]
])
```

Step 2: Model Initialization

Next, we define the Generator and Discriminator architectures.

Generator Architecture:

- Takes random noise (z) as input.
- Uses transposed convolution layers to generate an image.
- Outputs a synthetic image matching the real data distribution.

◆ Basic Generator Code (PyTorch)

```
import torch.nn as nn

class Generator(nn.Module):
    def __init__(self):
        super(Generator, self).__init__()
        self.model = nn.Sequential(
            nn.Linear(100, 256),
            nn.ReLU(),
            nn.Linear(256, 512),
            nn.ReLU(),
            nn.Linear(512, 1024),
            nn.ReLU(),
            nn.Linear(1024, 784),  # Output layer for a 28x28 image
            nn.Tanh()  # Output in range [-1,1]
        )

    def forward(self, z):
        return self.model(z)
```

Discriminator Architecture:

- Takes both real and fake images as input.
- Uses convolutional layers to extract features.
- Outputs a probability score (real = 1, fake = 0).

◆ **Basic Discriminator Code (PyTorch)**

```
class Discriminator(nn.Module):
    def __init__(self):
        super(Discriminator, self).__init__()
        self.model = nn.Sequential(
            nn.Linear(784, 1024),
            nn.ReLU(),
            nn.Linear(1024, 512),
            nn.ReLU(),
            nn.Linear(512, 256),
            nn.ReLU(),
            nn.Linear(256, 1),
            nn.Sigmoid()  # Output probability score
        )

    def forward(self, img):
        return self.model(img)
```

Step 3: Training Loop

The training process involves updating both the Generator and Discriminator iteratively.

Step 3.1: Train the Discriminator

- Get a batch of real samples from the dataset.
- Generate a batch of fake samples using the Generator.
- Compute Discriminator loss using Binary Cross-Entropy (BCE) Loss:

$$L_D = -E_{x \sim P_{data}(x)}[\log D(x)] - E_{z \sim P_z(z)}[\log(1 - D(G(z)))]$$

- Backpropagate and update the Discriminator parameters.

◆ **Discriminator Training Code (PyTorch)**

```
criterion = nn.BCELoss()
optimizer_D = torch.optim.Adam(D.parameters(), lr=0.0002)

real_labels = torch.ones(batch_size, 1)
fake_labels = torch.zeros(batch_size, 1)

# Training Discriminator on real data
real_loss = criterion(D(real_images), real_labels)

# Training Discriminator on fake data
fake_images = G(torch.randn(batch_size, 100))
fake_loss = criterion(D(fake_images.detach()), fake_labels)

# Compute total loss and update weights
loss_D = real_loss + fake_loss
optimizer_D.zero_grad()
loss_D.backward()
optimizer_D.step()
```

Step 3.2: Train the Generator

- Generate **fake samples** from random noise.

- Compute the **Generator loss** by **maximizing** $D(G(z))$:

$$L_G = -E_{z \sim P_z(z)}[\log D(G(z))]$$

- **Backpropagate and update** the Generator parameters.

◆ Generator Training Code (PyTorch)

```
optimizer_G = torch.optim.Adam(G.parameters(), lr=0.0002)

# Generate fake images
fake_images = G(torch.randn(batch_size, 100))

# Compute Generator loss
loss_G = criterion(D(fake_images), real_labels)  # Trick Discriminator
```

```
# Update Generator weights
optimizer_G.zero_grad()
loss_G.backward()
optimizer_G.step()
```

Step 4: Evaluating GAN Performance

GAN training is tricky because there's no straightforward accuracy metric. Instead, use the following techniques:

✓ **Visual Inspection** – Generate and observe sample outputs.
✓ **Inception Score (IS)** – Measures sample diversity and quality.
✓ **Frechet Inception Distance (FID)** – Compares generated images to real images.
✓ **Discriminator Loss vs. Generator Loss** – If one loss is too low, training is imbalanced.

Step 5: Fine-tuning & Optimization

To stabilize training, experiment with:

◆ **Learning Rate Scheduling** – Adaptive learning rates improve convergence.
◆ **Batch Normalization** – Reduces mode collapse.
◆ **Wasserstein GANs (WGANs)** – Alternative loss function for stability.
◆ **Gradient Penalty** – Prevents Discriminator from overpowering Generator.

Training a GAN involves iterative competition between the Generator and Discriminator, making model initialization, loss balancing, and optimization crucial. By following a structured pipeline—data preprocessing, model initialization, training, evaluation, and fine-tuning—we can effectively train a GAN that generates realistic, high-quality synthetic data.

In the next chapters, we will explore advanced GAN architectures and techniques to further enhance training stability and output quality. 🚀

2.5 Metrics for Evaluating GAN Performance

Evaluating the performance of a Generative Adversarial Network (GAN) is challenging because, unlike traditional supervised learning models, there is no simple accuracy or loss metric to measure progress. Instead, GAN evaluation requires a combination of quantitative metrics, qualitative assessments, and statistical techniques to determine the quality, diversity, and realism of generated samples.

In this chapter, we will explore the most commonly used GAN evaluation metrics, their strengths and weaknesses, and how they can be applied to measure model performance effectively.

1. Why is GAN Evaluation Difficult?

Unlike classification models that optimize for accuracy, GANs generate new data, making their evaluation more subjective. Challenges include:

✅ **No Direct Loss Interpretation** – Generator loss does not necessarily correlate with sample quality.

✅ **Diversity vs. Quality Tradeoff** – A model can generate sharp images but lack diversity, or vice versa.

✅ **Mode Collapse** – The Generator may learn to produce only a limited set of outputs instead of generating a diverse range of samples.

To address these challenges, researchers use a mix of perceptual, statistical, and adversarial evaluation techniques.

2. Common Metrics for Evaluating GANs

2.1 Inception Score (IS)

📌 **What It Measures:**

- Evaluates how diverse and recognizable generated images are.
- Uses a pretrained Inception v3 model to classify generated images and measure entropy.

📌 **Mathematical Formula:**

$$IS = \exp\left(E_x[KL(p(y|x)\|p(y))]\right)$$

where:

- $p(y|x)$ is the predicted class probability of an image x using an Inception model.

- $p(y)$ is the marginal class distribution over all generated samples.

📌 Interpretation:

- **Higher IS** → Better quality and diversity (e.g., real images have IS ~10, random noise has IS ~1).
- **Limitations**: Does not compare against real data; only works well for datasets with clear class labels.

◆ Python Implementation:

```
from torchvision.models import inception_v3
import torch.nn.functional as F

model = inception_v3(pretrained=True, transform_input=False)
model.eval()

def inception_score(images):
    preds = F.softmax(model(images), dim=1)
    kl_div = preds * (torch.log(preds) - torch.log(preds.mean(dim=0, keepdim=True)))
    return torch.exp(kl_div.mean())
```

2.2 Frechet Inception Distance (FID)

📌 What It Measures:

- Measures the distance between real and generated image distributions using feature embeddings from an Inception model.
- Uses the Fréchet distance (Wasserstein-2 distance) to compare the statistical properties of both distributions.

📌 Mathematical Formula:

$$FID = ||\mu_r - \mu_g||^2 + Tr(\Sigma_r + \Sigma_g - 2(\Sigma_r\Sigma_g)^{1/2})$$

where:

- μ_r, μ_g are the mean feature vectors of real and generated samples.
- Σ_r, Σ_g are their covariance matrices.

📌 **Interpretation:**

- **Lower FID** → Better quality and realism (e.g., FID < 10 is excellent, random noise has FID > 200).
- **Advantage over IS:** Compares generated images directly against real images, making it more reliable.

◆ **Python Implementation (Using TorchMetrics):**

```
from torchmetrics.image.fid import FrechetInceptionDistance

fid = FrechetInceptionDistance()
fid.update(real_images, real=True)
fid.update(fake_images, real=False)
print("FID Score:", fid.compute().item())
```

2.3 Perceptual Path Length (PPL)

📌 **What It Measures:**

- Measures the smoothness of latent space interpolation in GANs.
- Important for StyleGANs and high-resolution image synthesis.

📌 **Interpretation:**

- Lower PPL → Smoother, more realistic transitions between generated images.
- High PPL indicates that the model overfits to sharp changes in latent space.

◆ **Use Case:**

- Used to assess StyleGAN models where latent space interpolation should be smooth.

2.4 Precision and Recall for GANs

📌 **What It Measures:**

- Precision measures how many generated images are realistic.
- Recall measures how well the model captures the diversity of the real dataset.

📌 **Interpretation:**

- **High Precision, Low Recall** → Mode Collapse (sharp but limited outputs).
- **High Recall, Low Precision** → Blurry but diverse outputs.

◆ **Use Case:**

- Useful for detecting mode collapse and ensuring diverse generation.

2.5 Kernel Inception Distance (KID)

📌 **What It Measures:**

- Similar to FID but uses a kernel-based approach instead of Gaussian assumptions.

📌 **Advantages:**

- More robust for small sample sizes.
- Directly measures how generated data distribution differs from real data.

◆ **Use Case:**

- Works well when dataset size is small.

3. Qualitative Evaluation Methods

While metrics like FID and IS provide numerical scores, qualitative assessments remain essential.

3.1 Human Perceptual Evaluation

👀 **Visual Inspection** – Manually checking sample outputs for:
✔ **Sharpness** – Are images clear and detailed?
✔ **Diversity** – Are different image categories well-represented?
✔ **Artifacts** – Are there strange distortions or inconsistencies?

◆ **Use Case:**

- Often used for art, face synthesis, and video generation where human perception matters.

3.2 Latent Space Interpolation

- Interpolate between latent vectors to assess smoothness.
- If the transitions between images are smooth, the GAN has learned a well-structured latent space.

◆ **Example**: Linear Interpolation Between Two Latent Vectors

```
z1, z2 = torch.randn(1, 100), torch.randn(1, 100)
for alpha in np.linspace(0, 1, num=10):
    z_interp = (1 - alpha) * z1 + alpha * z2
    generated_image = G(z_interp)
```

3.3 Nearest Neighbor Search in Real Dataset

- Finds the closest real image to a generated image.
- If the generated image is too similar to a real one, the model might be memorizing the training set.

◆ **Use Case:**

- Detects overfitting and ensures diversity.

Conclusion

- Evaluating GAN performance requires a combination of quantitative and qualitative techniques.

◆ **Best Practices for GAN Evaluation:**

- Use FID to compare generated images to real ones.
- Use IS to measure diversity in class-based datasets.
- Use Precision-Recall to detect mode collapse.
- Use PPL and interpolation for latent space quality.
- Always perform human visual inspection to verify realism.

By applying these metrics, we can systematically improve GAN training and create more realistic, high-quality synthetic data. 🚀

3. Mathematics Behind GANs

While GANs are known for their remarkable ability to generate realistic data, their true power lies in the mathematical foundations that govern their learning process. In this chapter, we break down the key mathematical concepts behind GANs, including probability distributions, loss functions, gradient descent, and optimization techniques. You'll learn how the generator minimizes the discriminator's ability to detect fake data using a min-max game theory approach, and how functions like binary cross-entropy loss and Wasserstein distance improve stability. Whether you love math or prefer intuition-driven learning, this chapter will equip you with a solid theoretical understanding of how GANs operate at a fundamental level. 📊🚀

3.1 Probability and Statistics in GANs

Generative Adversarial Networks (GANs) are built on fundamental concepts of probability and statistics. Since GANs aim to learn the underlying data distribution and generate new samples that resemble real data, understanding probability theory is crucial for their design, training, and evaluation.

This chapter explores key probabilistic concepts such as probability distributions, likelihood estimation, divergence measures, and statistical modeling that form the foundation of GANs.

1. The Role of Probability in GANs

GANs are designed to learn the **true data distribution** $P_{data}(x)$ and generate new samples that mimic this distribution. To achieve this, the **Generator** learns to map a simple probability distribution (e.g., Gaussian noise) to a more complex real-world data distribution.

In mathematical terms:

- **Real data samples** are drawn from an unknown distribution:

$$x \sim P_{data}(x)$$

- **Generated (fake) samples** are drawn from the distribution learned by the Generator:

$$x' = G(z), \quad z \sim P_z(z)$$

- The **Discriminator** estimates the probability that a given sample is real or fake:

$$D(x) \approx P(\text{real}|x)$$

To successfully train a GAN, we need to understand different **probability distributions, loss functions,** and how to measure differences between distributions.

2. Probability Distributions in GANs

2.1 Real-World Data Distributions $P_{data}(x)$

The true data distribution is unknown and varies depending on the dataset. Some common real-world distributions include:

- **Gaussian (Normal) Distribution** – Used in natural phenomena (e.g., pixel intensity in images).
- **Multimodal Distribution** – A dataset with multiple clusters (e.g., different object categories).
- **Categorical Distribution** – Used in discrete data like class labels.

GANs attempt to learn an **approximate distribution** $P_G(x)$ **that closely matches** $P_{data}(x)$.

2.2 Latent Space Distribution $P_z(z)$

The Generator starts with a simple, known distribution (e.g., Gaussian noise) to generate synthetic data:

$$z \sim P_z(z)$$

Common choices for $P_z(z)$:

- ☑ **Gaussian Distribution** $N(0, I)$ – Ensures smooth latent space transitions.
- ☑ **Uniform Distribution** $U(-1, 1)$ – Provides equal probability for all values.

The Generator learns a function $G(z)$ that transforms this latent space into a realistic data distribution $P_G(x)$.

3. Likelihood Estimation and GAN Training

Unlike traditional probabilistic models (e.g., Variational Autoencoders), GANs do not explicitly compute the likelihood of data. Instead, they rely on an adversarial loss to train the Generator and Discriminator.

3.1 Maximum Likelihood Estimation (MLE) vs. GANs

Many generative models use Maximum Likelihood Estimation (MLE), where they maximize the probability of real data under the model's distribution:

$$\max_\theta \sum_{i=1}^{N} \log P_\theta(x_i)$$

However, GANs do not use explicit likelihood estimation. Instead, they use a minimax game between the Generator and Discriminator, which indirectly optimizes for a similar objective.

4. Measuring Distribution Differences in GANs

GANs aim to **minimize the difference** between the real and generated distributions. Various statistical measures are used to quantify how well $P_G(x)$ approximates $P_{data}(x)$.

4.1 Kullback-Leibler (KL) Divergence

Measures how much one probability distribution differs from another:

$$D_{KL}(P_{data}||P_G) = \sum_x P_{data}(x) \log \frac{P_{data}(x)}{P_G(x)}$$

◆ **Issues in GANs**: KL divergence penalizes missing modes, which can lead to mode collapse (where the Generator produces limited variations of data).

4.2 Jensen-Shannon (JS) Divergence

GANs use Jensen-Shannon divergence (JS Divergence), which is a symmetric version of KL divergence:

$$D_{JS}(P_{data}||P_G) = \frac{1}{2}D_{KL}(P_{data}||M) + \frac{1}{2}D_{KL}(P_G||M)$$

where $M = \frac{1}{2}(P_{data} + P_G)$.

Why is JS Divergence used in GANs?

✓ More stable than KL divergence.

✓ Allows adversarial training with both distributions competing.

◆ **GAN Loss Function Using JS Divergence:**

$$\min_G \max_D E_{x \sim P_{data}}[\log D(x)] + E_{z \sim P_z}[\log(1 - D(G(z)))]$$

This is the standard GAN loss function, where the Discriminator minimizes classification error while the Generator maximizes it.

5. Statistical Challenges in GAN Training

Despite their power, GANs face several statistical challenges:

5.1 Mode Collapse

- The Generator ignores some modes of the real distribution and generates only a few repeated patterns.
- **Solution**: Use Wasserstein Distance (WGANs) instead of JS divergence.

5.2 Non-Convergence Issues

- **Training** GANs is difficult because the loss does not indicate convergence.
- **Solution**: Use Wasserstein GAN (WGAN) with Gradient Penalty, which provides a smoother loss function.

◆ **Wasserstein Distance Formula:**

  ◆ Wasserstein Distance Formula:

$$W(P_{data}, P_G) = \inf_{\gamma \sim \Pi(P_{data}, P_G)} E_{(x,y) \sim \gamma}[||x - y||]$$

where $\Pi(P_{data}, P_G)$ represents all possible mappings between the real and generated distributions.

Understanding probability and statistics is crucial for training and evaluating GANs effectively.

◆ **Key Takeaways:**

  GANs learn a probability distribution $P_G(x)$ that mimics $P_{data}(x)$.

✓ JS divergence is used in standard GAN loss functions.

✓ Mode collapse and unstable training arise from statistical mismatches.

✓ Wasserstein Distance (WGANs) improves training stability.

By mastering these probabilistic principles, we can better design, optimize, and evaluate GAN models for real-world applications. 🚀

3.2 Game Theory and the Minimax Function

At the core of Generative Adversarial Networks (GANs) lies a powerful concept from game theory—the minimax function. The training process of GANs can be understood as a two-player zero-sum game, where the Generator (G) and Discriminator (D) compete in an adversarial setting. This mathematical formulation is inspired by game theory, a field of study that analyzes strategic interactions between rational decision-makers.

In this chapter, we will explore how game theory influences GAN training, the minimax function, Nash equilibrium, and challenges like unstable training and mode collapse.

1. Game Theory in GANs

1.1 What is Game Theory?

Game theory is a mathematical framework used to analyze decision-making in competitive and cooperative scenarios. It is widely used in economics, AI, and optimization problems.

A game in game theory consists of:

✅ **Players**: The entities making decisions (Generator & Discriminator in GANs).
✅ **Strategies**: The set of actions each player can take.
✅ **Payoff Functions**: The rewards or losses based on the chosen strategies.

GANs fit into a special category called zero-sum games, where the gain of one player equals the loss of the other.

1.2 How GANs Work as a Game

GANs consist of two neural networks:

- **Generator (G):** Generates fake samples trying to fool the Discriminator.
- **Discriminator (D):** Tries to distinguish real samples from generated ones.

Both networks optimize opposing objectives, making GAN training a competitive game.

$$\min_{G} \max_{D} V(G, D)$$

where $V(G, D)$ is the **value function** representing the **minimax game** between Generator and Discriminator.

2. Understanding the Minimax Function in GANs

The minimax function in GANs defines their training objective:

$$\min_{G} \max_{D} V(G, D) = E_{x \sim P_{data}}[\log D(x)] + E_{z \sim P_z}[\log(1 - D(G(z)))]$$

2.1 Breakdown of the Minimax Function

- $E_{x \sim P_{data}}[\log D(x)]$

  - The Discriminator maximizes this term to correctly classify real images.

- $E_{z \sim P_z}[\log(1 - D(G(z)))]$

  - The Generator minimizes this term to fool the Discriminator into classifying fake images as real.

- **Discriminator's Goal:** Maximize $V(G, D)$ → Classify real and fake images correctly.
- **Generator's Goal:** Minimize $V(G, D)$ → Fool Discriminator into thinking fake samples are real.

At equilibrium, the Discriminator cannot distinguish between real and fake data, meaning GAN training is successful.

3. Nash Equilibrium in GANs

3.1 What is Nash Equilibrium?

A Nash equilibrium is a stable state in game theory where no player can unilaterally improve their position by changing their strategy.

In GANs, the Nash equilibrium occurs when:

$$P_G(x) = P_{data}(x)$$

At this point:

✓ The Discriminator assigns a probability of 50% to both real and fake samples.

✓ The Generator produces samples indistinguishable from real data.

4. Challenges of the Minimax Game in GANs

4.1 Non-Convergence and Training Instability

GANs often struggle to reach equilibrium due to:

✘ **Gradient Vanishing**: If D becomes too strong, G stops learning.
✘ **Oscillations**: The adversarial nature causes non-stable updates.

💡 **Solution**: Use Wasserstein GAN (WGAN), which replaces the minimax loss with Wasserstein distance for smoother training.

4.2 Mode Collapse

✘ **What Happens?**

The Generator learns to produce only a few types of outputs, missing the diversity in real data.

💡 **Solution:**

- Use Minibatch Discrimination to encourage diverse generations.
- Modify the loss function (e.g., Unrolled GAN, Wasserstein GAN).

4.3 Balancing the Generator and Discriminator

If one player (G or D) becomes too strong, training fails.

💡 **Solution:**

✓ Use progressive training (gradually increasing difficulty).

✓ Adjust learning rates for stable convergence.

5. Beyond Standard Minimax: Alternative Loss Functions

5.1 Wasserstein GAN (WGAN) Loss

Replaces JS divergence with Wasserstein distance, leading to more stable training:

$$W(P_{data}, P_G) = \inf_{\gamma \sim \Pi(P_{data}, P_G)} E_{(x,y) \sim \gamma}[||x - y||]$$

✓ Fixes mode collapse

✓ Improves convergence

5.2 Least Squares GAN (LSGAN) Loss

Uses a least squares loss instead of cross-entropy:

$$L_D = \frac{1}{2} E_{x \sim P_{data}}[(D(x) - 1)^2] + \frac{1}{2} E_{z \sim P_z}[(D(G(z)))^2]$$

✓ Reduces gradient vanishing

✓ Produces higher-quality images

GAN training is fundamentally a game-theoretic minimax problem, where two networks compete to reach equilibrium. However, this setup presents challenges like instability, mode collapse, and convergence issues.

◆ **Key Takeaways:**

☑ GANs follow a **zero-sum minimax game** between Generator & Discriminator.

☑ **Nash equilibrium** occurs when $P_G(x) = P_{data}(x)$ (perfect generation).

☑ **Challenges** like mode collapse and instability can be addressed using WGANs, LSGANs, and balanced training techniques.

By applying these principles, we can improve GAN performance and build more stable, high-quality generative models. 🚀

3.3 Cost Functions: Cross-Entropy and Wasserstein Loss

In Generative Adversarial Networks (GANs), the choice of cost function (loss function) significantly impacts training stability, convergence, and output quality. Traditionally, GANs use a cross-entropy loss based on the Jensen-Shannon (JS) divergence, but this can lead to issues like vanishing gradients and training instability. To address these limitations, Wasserstein loss (from Wasserstein GANs) provides a more stable and effective approach.

This chapter explores the role of cost functions in GANs, comparing cross-entropy loss with Wasserstein loss to understand their strengths, weaknesses, and practical impact on GAN training.

1. The Role of Cost Functions in GANs

A cost function (loss function) measures how well the Generator and Discriminator are performing. It provides the necessary gradients to update their parameters using backpropagation and gradient descent.

1.1 Loss Functions for the Discriminator and Generator

GANs have two competing networks, each with its own objective:

- **Discriminator (D) Loss:** Measures how well D differentiates real and fake samples.

- **Generator (G) Loss:** Measures how well G fools D.

Formally, the goal of GAN training is to find a balance between these objectives.

$$\min_{G} \max_{D} V(G, D)$$

where $V(G, D)$ represents the GAN's cost function.

The **choice** of $V(G, D)$ determines how the Generator and Discriminator learn. The two most common approaches are:

✔ Cross-Entropy Loss (Standard GANs)

✔ Wasserstein Loss (WGANs)

2. Cross-Entropy Loss in GANs

2.1 Understanding Cross-Entropy

Cross-entropy loss measures the difference between the true data distribution and the generated data distribution using logarithmic loss.

For a binary classification problem, cross-entropy is defined as:

$$L = -\sum y \log(\hat{y}) + (1 - y) \log(1 - \hat{y})$$

where:

- y is the **true label** (1 for real, 0 for fake).
- $\hat{y}$ is the **predicted probability** from the Discriminator.

In GANs, cross-entropy is used to train both the Discriminator and Generator.

2.2 Discriminator Loss

The Discriminator's goal is to maximize the probability of correctly classifying real and fake images:

$$L_D = -E_{x \sim P_{data}}[\log D(x)] - E_{z \sim P_z}[\log(1 - D(G(z)))]$$

This means:

- ☑ The Discriminator maximizes $D(x)$ for **real samples.**
- ☑ The Discriminator minimizes $D(G(z))$ for **fake samples.**

2.3 Generator Loss

The Generator's goal is to fool the Discriminator, making it think fake samples are real. This is done by minimizing the loss function:

$$L_G = -E_{z \sim P_z}[\log D(G(z))]$$

Since $D(G(z))$ is the probability of fake samples being classified as real, **minimizing L_G forces $D(G(z))$ to approach 1.**

✓ The Generator learns to create more realistic data.

2.4 Problems with Cross-Entropy Loss

✗ Vanishing Gradient Problem:

- If the Discriminator gets too strong, $D(G(z))$ becomes very close to 0.
- Since **log(0) is undefined,** the **gradient updates become tiny,** preventing the Generator from learning.

✗ Mode Collapse:

The Generator produces only a few types of samples instead of diverse data.

✗ Training Instability:

- JS divergence is not always a good measure of distribution differences in high-dimensional spaces.
- These limitations led to the development of Wasserstein loss, which improves GAN stability and training quality.

3. Wasserstein Loss: A Better Approach

3.1 The Problem with JS Divergence

GANs using cross-entropy rely on Jensen-Shannon (JS) divergence to measure the difference between real and fake data distributions. However, JS divergence has a major issue:

◆ If two distributions have little overlap, JS divergence is not informative.

This results in saturated gradients, where the Generator stops learning.

To fix this, Wasserstein GANs (WGANs) use Wasserstein distance instead of JS divergence.

3.2 What is Wasserstein Distance?

The Wasserstein distance (Earth Mover's Distance, EMD) measures how much effort it takes to move one probability distribution to match another.

$$W(P_{data}, P_G) = \inf_{\gamma \sim \Pi(P_{data}, P_G)} E_{(x,y) \sim \gamma}[\|x - y\|]$$

◆ Why is Wasserstein Distance Better?

☑ Provides a meaningful measure of distribution differences.

☑ Does not suffer from vanishing gradients.

☑ Leads to more stable training.

3.3 Wasserstein Loss Function

WGANs replace the standard GAN loss with Wasserstein loss, defined as:

$$L_D = E_{x \sim P_{data}}[D(x)] - E_{z \sim P_z}[D(G(z))]$$

- The Discriminator (Critic) is no longer a classifier (no sigmoid activation).
- Instead, it outputs real-valued scores (higher for real data, lower for fake).

Generator Loss

$$L_G = -E_{z \sim P_z}[D(G(z))]$$

- The Generator maximizes the Critic's score to make fake samples look more real.

◆ Key Improvements with Wasserstein Loss:

✅ Prevents mode collapse.

✅ Ensures continuous gradients for stable learning.

✅ Works well even when distributions have no overlap.

3.4 Gradient Penalty in WGAN-GP

WGANs require Lipschitz continuity, enforced using gradient penalty:

$$L_{GP} = \lambda E_{\hat{x} \sim P_{\hat{x}}}[(\|\nabla_{\hat{x}} D(\hat{x})\|_2 - 1)^2]$$

where λ is a regularization factor.

✅ Prevents weight clipping issues.

✅ Improves stability compared to standard WGANs.

4. Comparison: Cross-Entropy vs. Wasserstein Loss

Feature	Cross-Entropy Loss (Standard GANs)	Wasserstein Loss (WGANs)
Gradient Stability	Prone to vanishing gradients	Smooth gradients
Mode Collapse	High risk	Less likely
Training Stability	Unstable	More stable
Loss Meaningfulness	Not always informative	Directly correlated with distribution distance
Discriminator Output	Probability (sigmoid)	Real-valued score

♠ Wasserstein loss significantly improves GAN training, making it more stable and effective.

The choice of cost function is crucial for GAN success.

◆ Cross-Entropy Loss (Standard GANs):

✅ Works well but suffers from vanishing gradients & mode collapse.

◆ **Wasserstein Loss (WGANs):**

✓ More stable, prevents mode collapse, and ensures smooth training.

Moving forward, Wasserstein loss (or its improved versions like WGAN-GP) is the preferred choice for modern GAN architectures. 🚀

3.4 Backpropagation and Optimization Techniques

Training a Generative Adversarial Network (GAN) involves optimizing two competing neural networks—the Generator (G) and Discriminator (D)—to achieve a dynamic equilibrium. This is done using backpropagation and optimization techniques like Stochastic Gradient Descent (SGD), Adam, RMSprop, and adaptive learning rate methods. However, GAN training is notoriously challenging due to issues like vanishing gradients, mode collapse, and training instability.

In this chapter, we'll explore how backpropagation works in GANs, the best optimization techniques for stable training, and strategies to improve convergence.

1. Understanding Backpropagation in GANs

1.1 What is Backpropagation?

Backpropagation (backward propagation of errors) is an algorithm used in training neural networks by adjusting weights based on the loss gradient.

The process follows three key steps:

1️⃣ **Forward Pass** – Data moves through the network, and predictions are made.
2️⃣ **Loss Calculation** – The error (loss) is measured using a cost function.
3️⃣ **Backward Pass (Backpropagation)** – The gradient of the loss is computed, and network weights are updated using an optimizer.

In GANs, this happens separately for the Generator and Discriminator, since they have opposing objectives.

1.2 Backpropagation in the Discriminator

The Discriminator is a binary classifier that distinguishes real images from fake ones.

✅ **Objective**: Maximize the probability of correctly classifying real and fake samples.

✅ **Loss Function** (Cross-Entropy Loss in Standard GANs):

$$L_D = -E_{x \sim P_{data}}[\log D(x)] - E_{z \sim P_z}[\log(1 - D(G(z)))]$$

✅ Backpropagation Process:

1. Compute loss using the **real images** ($x \sim P_{data}$) and their predicted scores $D(x)$.
2. Compute loss using the **generated images** ($G(z)$) and their predicted scores $D(G(z))$.
3. Compute gradients of L_D with respect to **Discriminator weights**.
4. Update Discriminator's weights using an **optimizer (Adam, RMSprop, etc.)**.

1.3 Backpropagation in the Generator

The Generator learns to create images that fool the Discriminator.

✅ **Objective**: Minimize the probability that the Discriminator correctly classifies generated images as fake.

✅ **Loss Function (Standard GANs):**

$$L_G = -E_{z \sim P_z}[\log D(G(z))]$$

✅ **Backpropagation Process:**

1. Pass **random noise** z through the Generator to create fake images.
2. Compute the Discriminator's prediction for these fake images.
3. Compute the gradient of L_G with respect to **Generator weights**.
4. Update the Generator's weights using an **optimizer**.

◆ **Important**: The Generator does not receive direct labels—only feedback from the Discriminator's gradients!

2. Optimization Techniques for GAN Training

2.1 Stochastic Gradient Descent (SGD)

✓ Basic optimization method that updates weights based on the gradient of the loss function.

✓ **Formula:**

$$\theta = \theta - \eta \nabla L(\theta)$$

where:

- θ = model weights
- η = learning rate
- $\nabla L(\theta)$ = gradient of the loss

✗ **Problem**: SGD is too noisy and unstable for GANs. Instead, we use advanced optimizers like Adam and RMSprop.

2.2 Adam Optimizer (Adaptive Moment Estimation)

✓ Most commonly used optimizer for GANs.
✓ Uses momentum-based updates for faster convergence.

✓ **Formula:**

$$m_t = \beta_1 m_{t-1} + (1 - \beta_1)\nabla L$$

$$v_t = \beta_2 v_{t-1} + (1 - \beta_2)(\nabla L)^2$$

$$\theta = \theta - \eta \frac{m_t}{\sqrt{v_t} + \epsilon}$$

where:

- m_t = first moment (momentum)

- v_t = second moment (variance correction)

- β_1, β_2 = hyperparameters controlling momentum decay

◆ Why Use Adam?

✓ Stabilizes GAN training by preventing oscillations.

✓ Handles sparse gradients (important for complex models).

◆ Recommended Adam Parameters for GANs:

- $\beta_1 = 0.5$ (instead of default 0.9)

- $\beta_2 = 0.999$

- **Learning rate** $\eta = 0.0001$ to 0.0004

2.3 RMSprop Optimizer

✓ Alternative to Adam, useful in WGANs.

✓ Uses an adaptive learning rate based on squared gradients:

$$\theta = \theta - \eta \frac{\nabla L}{\sqrt{E[\nabla L^2]} + \epsilon}$$

◆ Why Use RMSprop?

✔ Prevents exploding gradients.

✔ Works well in Wasserstein GANs (WGANs) because of weight clipping.

◆ Recommended RMSprop Settings for WGANs:

- **Learning rate** = 0.00005
- **Weight Clipping** = 0.01

3. Training Challenges and Solutions

3.1 Preventing Vanishing Gradients

✗ **Problem**: If the Discriminator becomes too strong, gradients vanish, and the Generator stops learning.

✔ **Solution**: Use WGAN loss instead of cross-entropy loss.

3.2 Handling Mode Collapse

✗ **Problem**: The Generator produces limited variations of samples.

✔ Solution:

- Use Minibatch Discrimination to encourage diversity.
- Use Unrolled GANs to prevent Discriminator overpowering.

3.3 Balancing Generator and Discriminator

✗ **Problem**: If one network dominates, training fails.

✔ **Solution**:

- Train Discriminator more frequently (e.g., 5 D updates per G update in WGANs).
- Use Learning Rate Scheduling for gradual updates.

4. Comparison of Optimization Techniques

Optimizer	Used In	Advantages	Disadvantages
SGD	Basic GANs	Simple, efficient	Too noisy, slow convergence
Adam	Standard GANs	Stabilizes training, adaptive learning	Sensitive to hyperparameters
RMSprop	WGANs	Prevents exploding gradients	Slower convergence

◆ **Best choice for Standard GANs** → Adam ($\beta1=0.5$, $\beta2=0.999$)

◆ **Best choice for WGANs** → RMSprop (learning rate = 0.00005, weight clipping = 0.01)

GAN training is challenging but can be improved using the right optimization techniques.

✓ Backpropagation allows gradients to update the Generator and Discriminator effectively.

✓ Adam is the best optimizer for Standard GANs, while RMSprop works well for WGANs.

✓ Careful tuning of hyperparameters (learning rates, momentum) is critical for stable training.

By applying these optimization techniques, we can achieve better convergence, higher-quality outputs, and more stable GAN training. 🚀

3.5 Understanding Jensen-Shannon Divergence

At the core of Generative Adversarial Networks (GANs) lies the concept of probability distributions—the Generator learns to approximate the real data distribution, while the Discriminator differentiates between real and fake samples. A key mathematical tool in this process is Jensen-Shannon (JS) Divergence, which measures the similarity between two probability distributions.

Understanding JS divergence is crucial because it forms the foundation of the loss function in standard GANs. However, as we'll explore, its limitations can lead to training instability and vanishing gradients, which has led to alternative approaches like Wasserstein Distance in WGANs.

1. What is Jensen-Shannon (JS) Divergence?

1.1 Defining JS Divergence

JS Divergence is a symmetrized and smoothed version of the Kullback-Leibler (KL) divergence, which measures the difference between two probability distributions. It is formally defined as:

$$JS(P\|Q) = \frac{1}{2}KL(P\|M) + \frac{1}{2}KL(Q\|M)$$

where:

- P is the **true data distribution** (real samples).

- Q is the **generated data distribution** (fake samples).

- $M = \frac{1}{2}(P + Q)$ is the **mixture distribution.**

- $KL(P\|M)$ and $KL(Q\|M)$ are **Kullback-Leibler divergences.**

1.2 Understanding KL Divergence

To fully grasp JS divergence, let's first understand KL divergence, which measures how one probability distribution differs from another:

$$KL(P\|Q) = \sum P(x) \log \frac{P(x)}{Q(x)}$$

Key properties of KL divergence:

$$KL(P\|Q) = \sum P(x) \log \frac{P(x)}{Q(x)}$$

Key properties of KL divergence:

☑ KL divergence is **asymmetric**—i.e., $KL(P\|Q) \neq KL(Q\|P)$.

☑ If two distributions are identical, $KL(P\|Q) = 0$.

☑ KL divergence is infinite if there are points where $Q(x) = 0$ but $P(x) > 0$, making it unstable for non-overlapping distributions.

JS divergence **fixes these issues** by averaging KL divergence between P and Q in both directions and using the mixture distribution M.

1.3 Properties of JS Divergence

✔ **Symmetric**: Unlike KL divergence, JS divergence satisfies:

$$JS(P\|Q) = JS(Q\|P)$$

✔ **Bounded between 0 and 1:**

$$0 \leq JS(P\|Q) \leq \log 2$$

✔ Smooths differences between distributions: By incorporating the mixture distribution M, JS divergence prevents the instability seen in KL divergence.

2. JS Divergence in GANs

2.1 How JS Divergence Works in GAN Training

In **Standard GANs**, the Generator G and Discriminator D play a **minimax game** where the Discriminator tries to maximize its ability to distinguish real from fake data, and the Generator tries to minimize this distinction. The objective function is:

$$V(G, D) = \mathbb{E}_{x \sim P_{data}}[\log D(x)] + \mathbb{E}_{z \sim P_z}[\log(1 - D(G(z)))]$$

Mathematically, the optimal Discriminator D^* for a given Generator is:

$$D^*(x) = \frac{P_{data}(x)}{P_{data}(x) + P_G(x)}$$

At this optimal D^*, the GAN loss function is equivalent to:

$$JS(P_{data}||P_G) - \log 2$$

Thus, training a GAN effectively minimizes the JS divergence between the real and generated distributions.

2.2 Problems with JS Divergence in GANs

Despite being a useful metric, JS divergence has limitations that cause instability in GAN training:

✗ JS Divergence is not well-defined for non-overlapping distributions

- If P_{data} and P_G do not have overlapping support (common in early training), JS divergence does not provide useful gradients, leading to **vanishing gradients** and **slow training**.

✗ Mode Collapse

- The Generator may learn to produce only a few distinct outputs instead of capturing the full diversity of the data, leading to poor generalization.

✗ Training Instability

- The adversarial nature of GANs causes oscillations, making it hard for the Generator and Discriminator to converge.

Because of these issues, researchers developed Wasserstein GANs (WGANs), which replace JS divergence with Wasserstein Distance, improving training stability and preventing vanishing gradients.

3. JS Divergence vs. Wasserstein Distance

Feature	Jensen-Shannon Divergence	Wasserstein Distance
Gradient Stability	Can vanish if distributions don't overlap	Provides smooth gradients
Mode Collapse	High risk	Lower risk
Training Stability	Unstable, often oscillates	More stable convergence
Mathematical Basis	KL divergence	Earth Mover's Distance (Optimal Transport)

◆ Wasserstein Distance is preferred for modern GANs (WGANs) because it provides meaningful gradients even when the distributions have little overlap.

4. Practical Considerations for GAN Training

4.1 When to Use JS Divergence

✅ JS divergence is useful when:

- The distributions have significant overlap (e.g., simple datasets).
- You use regularization techniques (e.g., batch normalization) to stabilize training.
- Computational efficiency is a priority.

4.2 When to Use Alternative Metrics (e.g., Wasserstein Distance)

◆ If you experience:

- **Vanishing gradients** → Switch to WGAN (Wasserstein Loss).
- **Mode collapse** → Try WGAN-GP (Gradient Penalty).
- **Training instability** → Consider spectral normalization and better optimization techniques.

✓ JS Divergence measures the similarity between real and generated data distributions in standard GANs.

✓ GAN training minimizes JS divergence implicitly, but its limitations can lead to vanishing gradients and mode collapse.

✓ Wasserstein Distance (WGANs) provides a better alternative, offering smoother training and better convergence.

By understanding JS divergence, we gain deeper insight into how GANs learn and why newer techniques like WGANs improve upon the original GAN framework. 🚀

4. Types of GANs and Their Applications

Since their introduction, Generative Adversarial Networks (GANs) have evolved into multiple specialized architectures, each designed to tackle unique challenges in AI-generated content. In this chapter, we explore the most popular types of GANs, including Vanilla GANs, Deep Convolutional GANs (DCGANs), Conditional GANs (cGANs), Wasserstein GANs (WGANs), CycleGANs, and StyleGANs. Each variant improves upon the original GAN framework, enhancing stability, training efficiency, and output quality. We'll also dive into real-world applications—from generating hyper-realistic human faces and AI-powered art to medical imaging, game development, and even fashion design. Understanding these variations will help you choose the right GAN architecture for your projects and unleash the full potential of AI creativity. 🎨🖼️🚀

4.1 Vanilla GAN – The Basics

The **Vanilla GAN** is the original **Generative Adversarial Network (GAN)** proposed by **Ian Goodfellow et al. in 2014**. It introduced the **adversarial training framework**, where a **Generator** (G) creates synthetic data while a **Discriminator** (D) tries to distinguish between real and fake data. This competition leads to the Generator producing more realistic outputs over time.

Vanilla GAN is the simplest form of GAN, using **fully connected neural networks** and the **binary cross-entropy loss function** to train both networks. While more advanced variations exist today (e.g., **DCGAN, WGAN, StyleGAN**), understanding the fundamentals of Vanilla GAN is essential for mastering generative models.

1. Architecture of a Vanilla GAN

A Vanilla GAN consists of two key components:

1.1 Generator (G)

The Generator creates **fake data** by transforming a random noise vector z (sampled from a latent space, often a Gaussian or Uniform distribution) into a realistic-looking output.

- ☑ **Input:** Random noise vector z.
- ☑ **Output:** Synthetic data sample $G(z)$ (e.g., an image, text, or other data).
- ☑ **Objective:** Generate data that is indistinguishable from real samples.

$$G : z \rightarrow G(z)$$

- ◆ **Structure of the Generator:**

- Typically, a **fully connected neural network (MLP)** or **deep convolutional network (DCGANs)**.

- Uses **non-linear activation functions** (ReLU or LeakyReLU).

- The last layer uses **tanh activation** for output normalization.

1.2 Discriminator (D)

The Discriminator is a binary classifier that distinguishes between **real** and **fake** samples.

- ☑ **Input:** Either a real sample $x \sim P_{data}$ or a fake sample $G(z)$.
- ☑ **Output:** Probability score $D(x)$ indicating whether the sample is real or fake.
- ☑ **Objective:** Correctly classify real data as **1** and fake data as **0**.

$$D : x \rightarrow [0, 1]$$

- ◆ **Structure of the Discriminator:**

- Fully connected layers with **LeakyReLU** activation.

- Last layer uses a **sigmoid activation** to output probabilities.

2. Training Process of Vanilla GAN

2.1 The Minimax Game

Vanilla GANs follow a zero-sum minimax game, where:

- The Generator tries to minimize the Discriminator's ability to classify fake data.
- The Discriminator tries to maximize its classification accuracy.

The loss function for both networks is:

$$\min_{G} \max_{D} V(D, G) = \mathbb{E}_{x \sim P_{data}}[\log D(x)] + \mathbb{E}_{z \sim P_z}[\log(1 - D(G(z)))]$$

◆ **Discriminator Training:**

- Maximizes $\log D(x)$ for real samples.

- Maximizes $\log(1 - D(G(z)))$ for fake samples.

◆ **Generator Training:**

- Minimizes $\log(1 - D(G(z)))$, or equivalently maximizes $\log D(G(z))$ (tricking D into believing $G(z)$ is real).

2.2 Training Steps

1 **Sample** a batch of real data $x \sim P_{data}$.

2 **Generate** fake data $G(z)$, where $z \sim P_z$ (random noise).

3 **Update Discriminator:**

- Compute the **real loss** $\log D(x)$.

- Compute the **fake loss** $\log(1 - D(G(z)))$.

- Compute gradients and update D.

  4 **Update Generator:**

- Compute loss using $\log(1 - D(G(z)))$ or $\log D(G(z))$.

- Compute gradients and update G.

  5 **Repeat** until convergence.

3. Strengths and Weaknesses of Vanilla GAN

✅ Strengths

✔ Simple and easy to implement – Only requires two neural networks.

✔ Effective for generating synthetic data – Can produce realistic images, text, and more.

✔ Provides the foundation for modern GANs – Advanced architectures build on its principles.

✖ Weaknesses

✖ **Training Instability** – The Generator and Discriminator can oscillate, failing to converge.

✖ **Mode Collapse** – The Generator may produce limited variations instead of diverse outputs.

✖ **Vanishing Gradients** – If the Discriminator becomes too strong, the Generator stops learning.

◆ **Solutions**: Use improved loss functions (WGAN), normalization (BatchNorm), and better architectures (DCGAN, StyleGAN, etc.).

4. Code Implementation of a Vanilla GAN (PyTorch Example)

Here's a simple PyTorch implementation of a Vanilla GAN to generate handwritten digits (MNIST dataset).

```
import torch
import torch.nn as nn
import torch.optim as optim
import torchvision
import torchvision.transforms as transforms
from torch.utils.data import DataLoader

# Define Generator
class Generator(nn.Module):
    def __init__(self):
        super(Generator, self).__init__()
        self.model = nn.Sequential(
            nn.Linear(100, 256),
```

```python
            nn.ReLU(),
            nn.Linear(256, 512),
            nn.ReLU(),
            nn.Linear(512, 784),  # Output size for MNIST (28x28)
            nn.Tanh()
        )

    def forward(self, z):
        return self.model(z)

# Define Discriminator
class Discriminator(nn.Module):
    def __init__(self):
        super(Discriminator, self).__init__()
        self.model = nn.Sequential(
            nn.Linear(784, 512),
            nn.LeakyReLU(0.2),
            nn.Linear(512, 256),
            nn.LeakyReLU(0.2),
            nn.Linear(256, 1),
            nn.Sigmoid()
        )

    def forward(self, x):
        return self.model(x)

# Initialize models
G = Generator()
D = Discriminator()

# Loss function and optimizers
criterion = nn.BCELoss()
optimizer_G = optim.Adam(G.parameters(), lr=0.0002)
optimizer_D = optim.Adam(D.parameters(), lr=0.0002)

# Load MNIST dataset
transform = transforms.Compose([transforms.ToTensor(), transforms.Normalize((0.5,), (0.5,))])
dataloader = DataLoader(torchvision.datasets.MNIST(root='./data', train=True, transform=transform, download=True), batch_size=64, shuffle=True)
```

```
# Training Loop
for epoch in range(100):  # Train for 100 epochs
    for real_images, _ in dataloader:
        batch_size = real_images.size(0)

        # Train Discriminator
        real_images = real_images.view(batch_size, -1)
        real_labels = torch.ones(batch_size, 1)
        fake_labels = torch.zeros(batch_size, 1)
        z = torch.randn(batch_size, 100)

        optimizer_D.zero_grad()
        loss_real = criterion(D(real_images), real_labels)
        loss_fake = criterion(D(G(z)), fake_labels)
        loss_D = loss_real + loss_fake
        loss_D.backward()
        optimizer_D.step()

        # Train Generator
        z = torch.randn(batch_size, 100)
        optimizer_G.zero_grad()
        loss_G = criterion(D(G(z)), real_labels)  # Trick D into thinking fake images are real
        loss_G.backward()
        optimizer_G.step()
```

The Vanilla GAN is the foundation of all modern GAN architectures. It introduced the adversarial framework, enabling AI to generate realistic images, text, music, and more. While Vanilla GANs have limitations, they paved the way for improvements like WGANs, DCGANs, and StyleGANs.

Understanding Vanilla GANs is the first step in mastering AI-generated creativity! 🚀

4.2 Deep Convolutional GANs (DCGANs)

While the Vanilla GAN introduced the core adversarial training framework, its reliance on fully connected layers made it inefficient for generating high-quality images. To address this, Deep Convolutional GANs (DCGANs) were introduced by Radford et al. in 2015.

DCGANs replace fully connected layers with convolutional layers, enabling them to generate high-resolution, visually coherent images.

DCGANs are particularly effective in tasks like image synthesis, super-resolution, and artistic style transfer. They provide a more stable training process and generate sharper, more realistic images compared to Vanilla GANs. This chapter explores the architecture, improvements, training techniques, and practical implementation of DCGANs.

1. How DCGANs Improve Vanilla GANs

DCGANs apply convolutional layers to the Generator and Discriminator, making them more suitable for image generation. They introduce several key improvements:

✓ Uses convolutional layers instead of fully connected layers → Better feature extraction.

✓ Removes fully connected layers → Reduces parameters and improves efficiency.

✓ Uses batch normalization → Stabilizes training and prevents mode collapse.

✓ Replaces sigmoid activation with LeakyReLU in Discriminator → Prevents vanishing gradients.

✓ Uses transposed convolution (ConvTranspose2D) in Generator → Produces high-resolution images.

These changes enhance the quality of generated images and make training more stable.

2. DCGAN Architecture

2.1 Generator (G)

The **Generator** in DCGANs uses **transposed convolutional layers** (also called **deconvolution layers**) to generate images from **random noise**.

- ☑ **Input:** A random noise vector z (sampled from a Gaussian distribution).
- ☑ **Output:** A high-resolution image.

✓ Key layers:

- Transposed Convolution (ConvTranspose2D): Upsamples features.
- Batch Normalization: Stabilizes training.

- ReLU Activation: Introduces non-linearity.
- Tanh Activation (final layer): Ensures pixel values between -1 and 1.

◆ Generator Architecture Example:

- Input: 100-dimensional noise vector

- Dense layer → Reshape → ConvTranspose2D → BatchNorm → ReLU

- Final ConvTranspose2D layer with Tanh activation

$$G : z \rightarrow \text{synthetic image}$$

2.2 Discriminator (D)

The **Discriminator** is a convolutional neural network (CNN) that classifies images as **real or fake.**

☑ **Input**: An image (real or generated).
☑ **Output**: Probability score (real = 1, fake = 0).

☑ **Key layers:**

- **Convolutional Layers** (Conv2D): Extract features.
- **LeakyReLU Activation**: Prevents dying gradients.
- **Batch Normalization**: Stabilizes training.
- **Sigmoid Activation (final layer):** Outputs probability score.

◆ Discriminator Architecture Example:

Input: 64×64×3 image

Conv2D → LeakyReLU → BatchNorm → Conv2D → LeakyReLU → Flatten → Fully Connected → Sigmoid

$$D : x \rightarrow [0, 1]$$

3. Training DCGANs

3.1 Training Pipeline

DCGANs follow the same adversarial training process as Vanilla GANs, but with improvements:

1☐ Sample a batch of real images from the dataset.

2☐ Generate fake images from random noise using the Generator.

3☐ Train the Discriminator:

- Maximize $D(x)$ for real images.

- Minimize $D(G(z))$ for fake images.

4☐ Train the Generator:

- Fool the Discriminator by maximizing $D(G(z))$.

5☐ Repeat until the Generator produces realistic images.

3.2 Loss Function

DCGANs use the binary cross-entropy loss:

$$\min_{G} \max_{D} V(D,G) = \mathbb{E}_{x \sim P_{data}}[\log D(x)] + \mathbb{E}_{z \sim P_z}[\log(1 - D(G(z)))]$$

- Discriminator loss:

$$L_D = -\mathbb{E}[\log D(x)] - \mathbb{E}[\log(1 - D(G(z)))]$$

- Generator loss:

$$L_G = -\mathbb{E}[\log D(G(z))]$$

4. DCGAN Implementation in PyTorch

Here's how to implement a DCGAN using PyTorch to generate 64×64 images.

4.1 Import Libraries

```
import torch
import torch.nn as nn
import torch.optim as optim
import torchvision
import torchvision.transforms as transforms
from torch.utils.data import DataLoader
import matplotlib.pyplot as plt
```

4.2 Define the Generator

```
class Generator(nn.Module):
    def __init__(self):
        super(Generator, self).__init__()
        self.model = nn.Sequential(
            nn.ConvTranspose2d(100, 512, 4, 1, 0, bias=False),
            nn.BatchNorm2d(512),
            nn.ReLU(True),
            nn.ConvTranspose2d(512, 256, 4, 2, 1, bias=False),
            nn.BatchNorm2d(256),
            nn.ReLU(True),
            nn.ConvTranspose2d(256, 128, 4, 2, 1, bias=False),
            nn.BatchNorm2d(128),
            nn.ReLU(True),
            nn.ConvTranspose2d(128, 3, 4, 2, 1, bias=False),
            nn.Tanh()
        )

    def forward(self, z):
        return self.model(z)
```

4.3 Define the Discriminator

```
class Discriminator(nn.Module):
    def __init__(self):
```

```python
        super(Discriminator, self).__init__()
        self.model = nn.Sequential(
            nn.Conv2d(3, 128, 4, 2, 1, bias=False),
            nn.LeakyReLU(0.2, inplace=True),
            nn.Conv2d(128, 256, 4, 2, 1, bias=False),
            nn.BatchNorm2d(256),
            nn.LeakyReLU(0.2, inplace=True),
            nn.Conv2d(256, 512, 4, 2, 1, bias=False),
            nn.BatchNorm2d(512),
            nn.LeakyReLU(0.2, inplace=True),
            nn.Conv2d(512, 1, 4, 1, 0, bias=False),
            nn.Sigmoid()
        )

    def forward(self, x):
        return self.model(x)
```

4.4 Training DCGAN

```python
# Initialize models
G = Generator()
D = Discriminator()

# Loss function and optimizers
criterion = nn.BCELoss()
optimizer_G = optim.Adam(G.parameters(), lr=0.0002, betas=(0.5, 0.999))
optimizer_D = optim.Adam(D.parameters(), lr=0.0002, betas=(0.5, 0.999))

# Training loop
for epoch in range(100):
    for real_images, _ in dataloader:
        batch_size = real_images.size(0)

        # Train Discriminator
        optimizer_D.zero_grad()
        real_labels = torch.ones(batch_size, 1)
        fake_labels = torch.zeros(batch_size, 1)
        loss_D = criterion(D(real_images), real_labels) +
criterion(D(G(torch.randn(batch_size, 100, 1, 1))), fake_labels)
        loss_D.backward()
```

```
optimizer_D.step()

# Train Generator
optimizer_G.zero_grad()
loss_G = criterion(D(G(torch.randn(batch_size, 100, 1, 1))), real_labels)
loss_G.backward()
optimizer_G.step()
```

DCGANs are a major improvement over Vanilla GANs, producing sharper, more realistic images. By using convolutional layers, batch normalization, and transposed convolutions, DCGANs have become the foundation for advanced GAN architectures like StyleGAN and BigGAN. 🚀

4.3 Wasserstein GAN (WGAN) and Improved Training

Training Generative Adversarial Networks (GANs) can be highly unstable. Traditional GANs often suffer from mode collapse, vanishing gradients, and sensitive hyperparameters. To address these issues, Arjovsky et al. (2017) introduced Wasserstein GAN (WGAN), which replaces the traditional loss function with a new one based on the Wasserstein distance (Earth Mover's Distance, EMD).

WGAN improves GAN training stability, prevents mode collapse, and offers better convergence. In this chapter, we explore the problems with traditional GANs, the key innovations of WGAN, and its practical implementation.

1. Why Traditional GANs Struggle

Traditional GANs use a binary cross-entropy loss function, leading to:

✘ **Mode Collapse** – The Generator produces limited variations, ignoring parts of the data distribution.
✘ **Vanishing Gradients** – If the Discriminator becomes too strong, the Generator stops learning.
✘ **Training Instability** – Small changes in hyperparameters can cause training to fail.

1.1 The Problem with Jensen-Shannon Divergence

Vanilla GANs measure the distance between the real and fake data distributions using Jensen-Shannon (JS) Divergence. However, if the distributions are too different (which is often the case in early training), JS Divergence provides no meaningful gradient, making training difficult.

1.2 Introducing Wasserstein Distance (Earth Mover's Distance, EMD)

Instead of using JS Divergence, WGAN uses the Wasserstein distance (also called Earth Mover's Distance, EMD), which measures how much work is needed to transform one distribution into another.

$$W(P_r, P_g) = \inf_{\gamma \in \Pi(P_r, P_g)} \mathbb{E}_{(x,y) \sim \gamma}[\|x - y\|]$$

◆ **Key Benefits of Wasserstein Distance:**

✅ **Provides smooth, continuous gradients** → No vanishing gradients.

✅ **Prevents mode collapse** → Generator explores a diverse set of outputs.

✅ **Stable training** → More robust to hyperparameter tuning.

2. Key Innovations in WGAN

2.1 Replacing the Discriminator with a Critic

Instead of a Discriminator that classifies real vs. fake, WGAN introduces a Critic that scores how real or fake a sample is.

✅ **The Critic does not use a Sigmoid activation** → Outputs a real number instead of a probability.

✅ **The Critic uses Wasserstein loss** → Measures how far the generated distribution is from the real one.

2.2 Using Weight Clipping

To ensure the Wasserstein distance is valid, WGAN enforces a Lipschitz constraint by clipping the weights of the Critic within a small range (e.g., [-0.01, 0.01]).

◆ **Problems with Weight Clipping:**

✗ Can lead to poor performance if the chosen range is too small or too large.

2.3 WGAN-GP (Gradient Penalty)

A better alternative is WGAN-GP (WGAN with Gradient Penalty), which replaces weight clipping with a penalty on the gradient norm.

$$L_{GP} = \lambda \mathbb{E}_{\hat{x} \sim P_{\hat{x}}} [(\|\nabla_{\hat{x}} D(\hat{x})\|_2 - 1)^2]$$

◆ WGAN-GP is the best version of WGAN because it provides:

✓ Better training stability

✓ More robust optimization

✓ No need for manual weight clipping

3. WGAN Architecture and Loss Function

3.1 WGAN Loss Function

The WGAN loss function removes the logarithm-based binary cross-entropy loss and replaces it with the Wasserstein loss:

- Critic Loss:

$$L_D = \mathbb{E}_{x \sim P_r}[D(x)] - \mathbb{E}_{z \sim P_z}[D(G(z))]$$

- Generator Loss:

$$L_G = -\mathbb{E}_{z \sim P_z}[D(G(z))]$$

◆ The Critic aims to maximize the difference between real and fake scores, while the Generator minimizes it.

4. Implementing WGAN in PyTorch

Here's a PyTorch implementation of WGAN for image generation.

4.1 Import Libraries

```
import torch
import torch.nn as nn
import torch.optim as optim
import torchvision
import torchvision.transforms as transforms
from torch.utils.data import DataLoader
```

4.2 Define the Generator

```
class Generator(nn.Module):
    def __init__(self):
        super(Generator, self).__init__()
        self.model = nn.Sequential(
            nn.Linear(100, 256),
            nn.ReLU(),
            nn.Linear(256, 512),
            nn.ReLU(),
            nn.Linear(512, 784),
            nn.Tanh()
        )

    def forward(self, z):
        return self.model(z)
```

4.3 Define the Critic (WGAN Discriminator)

```
class Critic(nn.Module):
    def __init__(self):
        super(Critic, self).__init__()
        self.model = nn.Sequential(
            nn.Linear(784, 512),
```

```python
        nn.LeakyReLU(0.2),
        nn.Linear(512, 256),
        nn.LeakyReLU(0.2),
        nn.Linear(256, 1)  # No Sigmoid activation
    )

    def forward(self, x):
        return self.model(x)
```

4.4 Training WGAN

```python
# Initialize models
G = Generator()
C = Critic()

# Optimizers
optimizer_G = optim.RMSprop(G.parameters(), lr=0.00005)
optimizer_C = optim.RMSprop(C.parameters(), lr=0.00005)

# Load dataset
transform = transforms.Compose([transforms.ToTensor(), transforms.Normalize((0.5,),
(0.5,))])
dataloader = DataLoader(torchvision.datasets.MNIST(root='./data', train=True,
transform=transform, download=True), batch_size=64, shuffle=True)

# Training loop
for epoch in range(100):
    for real_images, _ in dataloader:
        batch_size = real_images.size(0)

        # Train Critic
        for _ in range(5):  # Train Critic more frequently
            optimizer_C.zero_grad()
            loss_C = -torch.mean(C(real_images.view(batch_size, -1))) +
torch.mean(C(G(torch.randn(batch_size, 100))))
            loss_C.backward()
            optimizer_C.step()

            # Weight Clipping
            for p in C.parameters():
```

```
          p.data.clamp_(-0.01, 0.01)

# Train Generator
optimizer_G.zero_grad()
loss_G = -torch.mean(C(G(torch.randn(batch_size, 100))))
loss_G.backward()
optimizer_G.step()
```

5. WGAN vs. Traditional GANs

Feature	Traditional GAN	WGAN
Loss Function	Binary Cross-Entropy (JS Divergence)	Wasserstein Distance (Earth Mover's)
Mode Collapse	Common	Rare
Vanishing Gradients	Yes	No
Training Stability	Unstable	More Stable
Discriminator Type	Classifier	Critic
Activation in Discriminator	Sigmoid	No Sigmoid

WGAN revolutionized GAN training by eliminating vanishing gradients, reducing mode collapse, and improving stability. By replacing binary cross-entropy loss with Wasserstein loss, WGAN ensures smoother and more meaningful gradient updates.

♦ For best results, use WGAN-GP, which replaces weight clipping with a gradient penalty for even more stable training.

WGAN has laid the foundation for state-of-the-art GAN architectures and continues to be widely used in AI-generated art, image synthesis, and deepfake technology. 🚀

4.4 CycleGAN – Image-to-Image Translation

Traditional GANs are powerful for generating synthetic data, but they require paired datasets—matching input-output samples—to learn transformations. However, in many real-world scenarios, paired data is unavailable or expensive to obtain. This is where CycleGAN comes in.

CycleGAN, introduced by Zhu et al. in 2017, enables image-to-image translation without paired datasets. It learns to transform images from one domain to another (e.g., horses to zebras, summer to winter landscapes) using cycle consistency loss. This chapter explores the architecture, training process, and practical implementation of CycleGAN.

1. Why CycleGAN?

1.1 The Problem with Traditional Image Translation

- **Pix2Pix and Conditional GANs require paired training data** → Hard to collect in many cases.
- **Example**: Converting Monet paintings to real-world photos → No exact pixel-to-pixel mapping exists.

1.2 Unpaired Image-to-Image Translation

CycleGAN solves this problem by learning transformations from unpaired datasets, meaning:

✅ You only need a set of images from Domain A and a set from Domain B—not perfect input-output pairs.

✅ CycleGAN learns a mapping between domains without explicit supervision.

2. How CycleGAN Works

2.1 Dual GAN Framework

CycleGAN uses two Generators and two Discriminators:

- $G : A \rightarrow B$ (Generator that converts images from A to B)
- $F : B \rightarrow A$ (Generator that converts images from B to A)
- D_A (Discriminator for domain A, distinguishing real A from fake A)
- D_B (Discriminator for domain B, distinguishing real B from fake B)

2.2 Cycle Consistency Loss

A crucial innovation of CycleGAN is Cycle Consistency Loss, ensuring that:

- If an image $x \in A$ is transformed to $G(x) \in B$ and then back to A using $F(G(x))$, the result should be close to x.
- Similarly, if $y \in B$ is transformed to $F(y) \in A$ and then back using $G(F(y))$, it should return to y.

◆ **Mathematically:**

$$L_{cycle} = \mathbb{E}_{x \sim A}[\||F(G(x)) - x\||_1] + \mathbb{E}_{y \sim B}[\||G(F(y)) - y\||_1]$$

This ensures **the transformations are meaningful and reversible.**

2.3 Adversarial Loss

CycleGAN also employs **adversarial loss**, just like traditional GANs. Each Discriminator (D_A and D_B) tries to differentiate real images from fake ones.

$$L_{GAN} = \mathbb{E}_{y \sim B}[\log D_B(y)] + \mathbb{E}_{x \sim A}[\log(1 - D_B(G(x)))]$$

3. CycleGAN Architecture

3.1 Generator (G & F)

CycleGAN's Generators use a ResNet-based U-Net architecture, consisting of:

✓ **Convolutional layers** → Extracts features.

✓ **Residual Blocks** → Retains important image information during transformation.

✓ **Transpose Convolutions** → Upsamples the image back to original size.

✓ **Tanh Activation** → Outputs final image.

3.2 Discriminator (D_A & D_B)

CycleGAN's Discriminators are PatchGANs, which classify whether small patches of an image are real or fake.

✅ **Convolutional layers** → Extracts features.

✅ **LeakyReLU Activation** → Prevents dying gradients.

✅ **Sigmoid Activation (final layer)** → Outputs probability score.

4. Implementing CycleGAN in PyTorch

4.1 Import Libraries

```
import torch
import torch.nn as nn
import torch.optim as optim
import torchvision.transforms as transforms
from torch.utils.data import DataLoader
from PIL import Image
```

4.2 Define the Generator

```
class ResNetBlock(nn.Module):
    def __init__(self, channels):
        super(ResNetBlock, self).__init__()
        self.conv_block = nn.Sequential(
            nn.Conv2d(channels, channels, kernel_size=3, stride=1, padding=1, bias=False),
            nn.BatchNorm2d(channels),
            nn.ReLU(inplace=True),
            nn.Conv2d(channels, channels, kernel_size=3, stride=1, padding=1, bias=False),
            nn.BatchNorm2d(channels)
        )

    def forward(self, x):
        return x + self.conv_block(x)

class Generator(nn.Module):
    def __init__(self, in_channels=3, out_channels=3, num_residual_blocks=9):
        super(Generator, self).__init__()
```

```python
model = [nn.Conv2d(in_channels, 64, kernel_size=7, stride=1, padding=3),
         nn.ReLU(inplace=True)]

for _ in range(num_residual_blocks):
    model.append(ResNetBlock(64))

model.append(nn.Conv2d(64, out_channels, kernel_size=7, stride=1, padding=3))
model.append(nn.Tanh())

self.model = nn.Sequential(*model)

def forward(self, x):
    return self.model(x)
```

4.3 Define the Discriminator (PatchGAN)

```python
class Discriminator(nn.Module):
    def __init__(self, in_channels=3):
        super(Discriminator, self).__init__()
        self.model = nn.Sequential(
            nn.Conv2d(in_channels, 64, kernel_size=4, stride=2, padding=1),
            nn.LeakyReLU(0.2, inplace=True),
            nn.Conv2d(64, 128, kernel_size=4, stride=2, padding=1),
            nn.BatchNorm2d(128),
            nn.LeakyReLU(0.2, inplace=True),
            nn.Conv2d(128, 256, kernel_size=4, stride=2, padding=1),
            nn.BatchNorm2d(256),
            nn.LeakyReLU(0.2, inplace=True),
            nn.Conv2d(256, 1, kernel_size=4, stride=1, padding=1),
            nn.Sigmoid()
        )

    def forward(self, x):
        return self.model(x)
```

4.4 Training CycleGAN

```python
# Initialize models
G_A2B = Generator()
G_B2A = Generator()
```

```python
D_A = Discriminator()
D_B = Discriminator()

# Loss function and optimizers
criterion_GAN = nn.BCELoss()
criterion_Cycle = nn.L1Loss()

optimizer_G = optim.Adam(list(G_A2B.parameters()) + list(G_B2A.parameters()),
lr=0.0002, betas=(0.5, 0.999))
optimizer_D_A = optim.Adam(D_A.parameters(), lr=0.0002, betas=(0.5, 0.999))
optimizer_D_B = optim.Adam(D_B.parameters(), lr=0.0002, betas=(0.5, 0.999))

# Training loop
for epoch in range(100):
    for real_A, real_B in dataloader:
        optimizer_G.zero_grad()

        fake_B = G_A2B(real_A)
        rec_A = G_B2A(fake_B)
        fake_A = G_B2A(real_B)
        rec_B = G_A2B(fake_A)

        loss_cycle = criterion_Cycle(rec_A, real_A) + criterion_Cycle(rec_B, real_B)
        loss_GAN = criterion_GAN(D_B(fake_B), torch.ones_like(fake_B)) +
criterion_GAN(D_A(fake_A), torch.ones_like(fake_A))

        loss_G = loss_GAN + 10 * loss_cycle
        loss_G.backward()
        optimizer_G.step()
```

CycleGAN is a breakthrough in unpaired image translation, enabling tasks like style transfer, domain adaptation, and artistic transformations. By using cycle consistency loss, it ensures that transformations remain meaningful and reversible.

This model powers AI-driven artistic filters, medical imaging enhancements, and realistic domain transformations, making it a key tool in AI creativity! 🚀

4.5 StyleGAN – Generating Realistic High-Resolution Images

One of the most impressive breakthroughs in Generative Adversarial Networks (GANs) is StyleGAN, developed by NVIDIA in 2018. Unlike traditional GANs, which struggle with high-resolution image synthesis, StyleGAN enables ultra-realistic, high-resolution image generation—capable of creating photorealistic human faces, artwork, and other intricate visuals.

This chapter explores StyleGAN's unique architecture, innovations, and applications. By understanding how StyleGAN works, you'll gain insight into the future of AI-driven creativity and deep learning-based image generation.

1. Why StyleGAN?

1.1 The Limitations of Traditional GANs

Before StyleGAN, deep learning researchers faced several challenges with GAN-based image generation:

✗ **Lack of Control Over Image Features** – Traditional GANs did not allow control over specific features (e.g., hair color, age, lighting).
✗ **Blurry or Incoherent High-Resolution Outputs** – Generating large, crisp images was difficult.
✗ **Mode Collapse** – Many GANs produced limited variations, reducing creativity.

1.2 StyleGAN's Breakthrough

StyleGAN introduced a new way to control image synthesis by separating "style" from content. The key innovations include:

✓ **Style-Based Generator Architecture** – Separates high-level and low-level image features.
✓ **Adaptive Instance Normalization (AdaIN)** – Controls how different styles influence generated images.
✓ **Progressive Growing** – Generates images at low resolution first, then refines details.

StyleGAN allows precise control over attributes (e.g., facial expressions, background, lighting) while maintaining unprecedented realism.

2. StyleGAN Architecture

Unlike traditional GANs, which map random noise directly to an image, StyleGAN introduces two key architectural improvements:

1☐ **Mapping Network** – Transforms random noise into a style vector, which controls how an image is generated.
2☐ **Synthesis Network** – Uses AdaIN layers to apply the style at different levels (e.g., coarse, middle, fine details).

2.1 Mapping Network – Transforming Noise Into Styles

- Instead of directly using a latent vector z, StyleGAN processes it through multiple fully connected layers to obtain an intermediate latent vector w.
- This w-space vector is then fed into the synthesis network, allowing greater control over individual features.

2.2 Synthesis Network – Applying Style at Different Levels

- The synthesis network progressively builds an image, starting from low resolution and refining details.
- Each layer applies a different level of style control, affecting high-level structures (e.g., face shape) or fine details (e.g., freckles, wrinkles).
- AdaIN (Adaptive Instance Normalization) ensures that each level of detail adapts properly to the style changes.

2.3 Progressive Growing for High-Resolution Images

- StyleGAN trains low-resolution images first (4×4 pixels), then gradually increases to higher resolutions (1024×1024).
- This method improves stability, prevents artifacts, and allows better detail synthesis.

3. Key Innovations in StyleGAN

3.1 Style Mixing

- Instead of using a single latent vector, StyleGAN mixes multiple latent vectors to generate unique variations.

- This enables realistic feature blending, such as combining one person's hairstyle with another's facial features.

3.2 Stochastic Variation

- Noise is added at different layers to introduce random details (e.g., skin pores, lighting reflections).
- This makes generated images more natural and realistic.

3.3 Truncation Trick

- By controlling how much noise affects the image, StyleGAN can balance diversity and realism.
- A high truncation value results in more unique but less realistic images, while a low truncation value produces hyper-realistic but less diverse outputs.

4. Implementing StyleGAN in Python

Now, let's look at how to implement StyleGAN using NVIDIA's official repository.

4.1 Install Dependencies

```
git clone https://github.com/NVlabs/stylegan3.git
cd stylegan3
pip install -r requirements.txt
```

4.2 Train StyleGAN on Your Own Dataset

```
python train.py --outdir=results --cfg=stylegan3-t --data=/path/to/dataset --gpus=4
```

--cfg=stylegan3-t → Uses StyleGAN3-T (better texture synthesis).

--data=/path/to/dataset → Path to your custom dataset (e.g., celebrity faces, landscapes).

4.3 Generate New Images Using a Pretrained Model

```
python generate.py --network=https://nvlabs-fi-
cdn.nvidia.com/stylegan3/networks/stylegan3-r-ffhq-1024x1024.pkl --
outdir=generated_images --seeds=85,100,120
```

--network=... → Loads the pretrained FFHQ model (high-resolution face generation).

--seeds=85,100,120 → Generates images from different random seeds.

4.4 Latent Space Interpolation (Creating AI Morphing Videos)

python generate.py --network=stylegan3-r-ffhq-1024x1024.pkl --outdir=interpolations --seeds=10,20,30 --truncation=0.7

This generates a smooth transformation between different generated faces.

5. StyleGAN Applications

5.1 AI-Generated Portraits

✓ Used in This Person Does Not Exist (a website generating realistic faces).

✓ Helps create synthetic datasets for AI training.

5.2 Deepfake and Synthetic Media

✓ Enables virtual influencers, AI avatars, and digital humans.

✓ Used in movies and gaming for realistic character generation.

5.3 AI-Assisted Art and Fashion

✓ Artists use StyleGAN to create AI-generated artwork.

✓ Fashion brands use it to design new styles and patterns.

5.4 Medical Imaging and Scientific Visualization

✓ Generates synthetic medical scans to train AI models for disease detection.

✓ Helps researchers simulate complex biological structures.

6. StyleGAN vs. Other GANs

Feature	Traditional GAN	DCGAN	StyleGAN
Control Over Features	✕ No	✕ No	☑ Yes (Style Mixing, AdaIN)
High-Resolution Output	✕ Limited	✕ Limited	☑ 1024×1024 or higher
Training Stability	✕ Unstable	☑ Improved	☑ Highly Stable
Fine-Grained Control	✕ No	✕ No	☑ Yes (Truncation Trick, Style Mixing)

StyleGAN is one of the most advanced AI models for image generation, offering unprecedented realism and control over features. By introducing style-based generation, progressive growing, and noise injection, it has revolutionized the way AI creates photorealistic images.

🚀 Key Takeaways:

✅ Controls features like age, hairstyle, lighting, and expression.

✅ Generates high-resolution (1024×1024+) images with fine details.

✅ Used in AI art, deepfakes, video game characters, and medical imaging.

With continuous improvements in AI image synthesis, StyleGAN and its successors (e.g., StyleGAN3) are paving the way for the next generation of synthetic media. 🔥

5. Setting Up Your GAN Development Environment

Before diving into coding and training your own Generative Adversarial Networks (GANs), it's essential to set up a robust and efficient development environment. This chapter will guide you through installing and configuring the necessary software, frameworks, and libraries for GAN development, including Python, TensorFlow, PyTorch, CUDA for GPU acceleration, and essential dependencies like NumPy and OpenCV. We'll also explore the best IDEs (Jupyter Notebook, Google Colab, VS Code) and walk through setting up a virtual environment to manage dependencies. By the end of this chapter, you'll have a fully functional AI workspace, ready to build and experiment with state-of-the-art GAN models. □□🚀

5.1 Choosing the Right Framework: TensorFlow vs. PyTorch

When developing Generative Adversarial Networks (GANs), choosing the right deep learning framework is crucial. The two most widely used frameworks in AI research and industry are TensorFlow and PyTorch. Both offer powerful tools for building, training, and deploying GANs, but they differ in terms of usability, performance, and ecosystem support.

This chapter provides a detailed comparison of TensorFlow and PyTorch, helping you choose the best framework for your GAN development.

1. Overview of TensorFlow and PyTorch

Before diving into comparisons, let's briefly introduce both frameworks.

1.1 What is TensorFlow?

TensorFlow, developed by Google Brain, is one of the most popular deep learning libraries. It provides:

✅ **Graph-based computation** – Uses computational graphs to optimize execution.
✅ **TensorFlow Extended (TFX)** – A production-ready ML pipeline for large-scale AI models.

✅ **TensorFlow Lite & TensorFlow.js** – Supports mobile and web-based AI deployment.

1.2 What is PyTorch?

PyTorch, developed by Facebook AI Research (FAIR), is widely used for research and rapid prototyping. It offers:

✅ **Dynamic computation graphs** – More intuitive debugging and experimentation.
✅ **Strong support for GPU acceleration** – Easy-to-use CUDA integration.
✅ **TorchScript** – Enables model deployment with minimal performance loss.

2. Key Differences: TensorFlow vs. PyTorch

Feature	TensorFlow	PyTorch
Ease of Use	✖ Complex API, steep learning curve	☑ Pythonic, easy to learn
Debugging	✖ Difficult (static graphs)	☑ Easy (dynamic graphs)
Performance	☑ Optimized execution	☑ Fast training on GPUs
Production Deployment	☑ Strong (TFX, TensorFlow Lite)	✖ Limited, requires extra steps
Community Support	☑ Larger (Google-backed)	☑ Strong research community
Visualization	☑ TensorBoard (built-in)	✖ Requires external tools (e.g., Matplotlib)

3. Ease of Use and Debugging

3.1 PyTorch – More Intuitive for Developers

✅ **Uses dynamic computation graphs** → Each operation is executed immediately.

✅ Similar to NumPy, making it easier to learn for beginners.

✅ Debugging is straightforward with Python's print() and standard debugging tools.

Example: Defining a Neural Network in PyTorch

```
import torch
import torch.nn as nn

class SimpleGAN(nn.Module):
    def __init__(self):
```

```python
        super(SimpleGAN, self).__init__()
        self.model = nn.Sequential(
            nn.Linear(100, 256),
            nn.ReLU(),
            nn.Linear(256, 512),
            nn.ReLU(),
            nn.Linear(512, 784),
            nn.Tanh()
        )

    def forward(self, x):
        return self.model(x)

gan = SimpleGAN()
print(gan)
```

3.2 TensorFlow – More Complex but Powerful

✗ Uses static computation graphs, which means you must define the entire model before running it.

✓ However, TensorFlow 2.0 introduced Eager Execution, making it easier to debug.

Example: Defining a Neural Network in TensorFlow

```python
import tensorflow as tf

class SimpleGAN(tf.keras.Model):
    def __init__(self):
        super(SimpleGAN, self).__init__()
        self.dense1 = tf.keras.layers.Dense(256, activation='relu')
        self.dense2 = tf.keras.layers.Dense(512, activation='relu')
        self.dense3 = tf.keras.layers.Dense(784, activation='tanh')

    def call(self, x):
        x = self.dense1(x)
        x = self.dense2(x)
        return self.dense3(x)

gan = SimpleGAN()
```

```
print(gan(tf.random.normal([1, 100])))
```

4. Performance & GPU Support

✓ Both TensorFlow and PyTorch support GPU acceleration using CUDA.

✓ PyTorch allows seamless GPU execution by simply calling .cuda().

✓ TensorFlow uses TensorFlow XLA (Accelerated Linear Algebra) to optimize performance.

Example: Running a Model on GPU

PyTorch

```
device = torch.device("cuda" if torch.cuda.is_available() else "cpu")
model = SimpleGAN().to(device)
```

TensorFlow

```
device = "/GPU:0" if tf.config.list_physical_devices('GPU') else "/CPU:0"
with tf.device(device):
    model = SimpleGAN()
```

☐ **Conclusion**: PyTorch is easier to use for GPU training, while TensorFlow provides better long-term optimization.

5. Production & Deployment

- If your goal is research and prototyping, PyTorch is the better choice.
- If you plan to deploy models in production, TensorFlow is more robust.

5.1 TensorFlow for Production

✓ **TensorFlow Extended (TFX)** – Provides a full pipeline for ML models.
✓ **TensorFlow Lite** – Allows deployment on mobile and edge devices.
✓ **TensorFlow.js** – Enables AI model deployment in web applications.

5.2 PyTorch for Deployment

☑️ **TorchScript** – Converts PyTorch models into a deployable format.

☑️ **ONNX (Open Neural Network Exchange)** – Allows PyTorch models to be used in other frameworks.

Example: Exporting a PyTorch Model to ONNX

```
dummy_input = torch.randn(1, 100)
torch.onnx.export(gan, dummy_input, "gan_model.onnx")
```

☐ **Conclusion**: If you need mobile, web, or large-scale deployments, TensorFlow is the better option.

6. Visualization & Monitoring

6.1 TensorFlow – TensorBoard (Built-in)

☑️ TensorFlow comes with TensorBoard, which allows real-time monitoring of model training.

```
import tensorflow as tf
import tensorflow.keras.backend as K
from tensorflow.keras.callbacks import TensorBoard

tensorboard = TensorBoard(log_dir="./logs")
```

6.2 PyTorch – Matplotlib or Third-Party Tools

✖ PyTorch does not have built-in visualization tools like TensorBoard.

☑️ However, Weights & Biases (wandb) or Matplotlib can be used.

```
import matplotlib.pyplot as plt

plt.plot(loss_values)
plt.xlabel("Epoch")
plt.ylabel("Loss")
plt.show()
```

7. Which One Should You Choose for GAN Development?

If you...	Choose
Are a beginner or want easy debugging	☑ PyTorch
Want to deploy AI models at scale	☑ TensorFlow
Need fast experimentation & research	☑ PyTorch
Want mobile/web AI deployment	☑ TensorFlow
Prefer dynamic graphs & flexibility	☑ PyTorch
Need powerful visualization tools	☑ TensorFlow

Both TensorFlow and PyTorch are powerful deep learning frameworks, but the right choice depends on your goals:

- For research, prototyping, and quick experimentation → Choose PyTorch.
- For large-scale production, deployment, and performance optimization → Choose TensorFlow.

🚀 **Best Strategy**: Many AI developers start with PyTorch for prototyping and switch to TensorFlow for production.

In the next section, we'll set up our GAN development environment using the chosen framework, ensuring that we have the right tools installed for training and experimenting with GAN models. 🔥

5.2 Installing Required Libraries

Before we start building and training Generative Adversarial Networks (GANs), we need to set up a proper development environment with all the necessary libraries. In this section, we'll cover:

✅ Installing TensorFlow and PyTorch

✅ Setting up essential Python libraries for GAN development

✓ Verifying GPU support for faster training

✓ Installing additional tools for visualization and debugging

By the end of this section, your environment will be ready for developing and training GANs efficiently.

1. Setting Up a Virtual Environment (Recommended)

It's always a good practice to use a virtual environment to keep dependencies organized.

1.1 Creating a Virtual Environment

For Windows (Command Prompt or PowerShell):

python -m venv gan_env
gan_env\Scripts\activate

For Mac/Linux (Terminal):

python3 -m venv gan_env
source gan_env/bin/activate

Now, any packages installed will be isolated from your system's Python environment.

2. Installing the Core Deep Learning Libraries

Now, let's install TensorFlow or PyTorch, depending on your preference.

2.1 Installing TensorFlow (Recommended for Deployment & Large-Scale AI)

For CPU-only version:

pip install tensorflow

For GPU version (NVIDIA CUDA acceleration):

pip install tensorflow[and-cuda]

⚠️ Ensure you have CUDA and cuDNN installed for GPU acceleration. We'll verify this later.

2.2 Installing PyTorch (Recommended for Research & Prototyping)

Use the official PyTorch installation selector:

☞ *https://pytorch.org/get-started/locally/*

For CPU-only version:

pip install torch torchvision torchaudio

For GPU version (NVIDIA CUDA acceleration):

pip install torch torchvision torchaudio --index-url https://download.pytorch.org/whl/cu118

(Replace cu118 with your CUDA version if needed.)

3. Installing Supporting Libraries

These libraries will help us with data processing, visualization, and debugging.

pip install numpy matplotlib pandas tqdm pillow opencv-python

3.1 NumPy – Essential for handling large numerical computations.

pip install numpy

3.2 Matplotlib & Seaborn – For visualizing training progress.

pip install matplotlib seaborn

3.3 OpenCV – For image processing and augmentations.

pip install opencv-python

3.4 tqdm – Adds progress bars for training loops.

pip install tqdm

3.5 Pandas – Useful for handling datasets.

pip install pandas

4. Installing Libraries for GAN Training & Monitoring

4.1 TensorBoard (For TensorFlow users)

TensorBoard provides real-time visualization of GAN training.

pip install tensorboard

To launch TensorBoard after training:

tensorboard --logdir=./logs

4.2 Weights & Biases (For PyTorch users)

If you prefer Weights & Biases (wandb) for tracking training, install it:

pip install wandb
wandb login

5. Verifying GPU Support

If you have an NVIDIA GPU, verify that TensorFlow or PyTorch detects it.

5.1 Checking GPU in TensorFlow

Run this in Python:

import tensorflow as tf
print("Num GPUs Available:", len(tf.config.list_physical_devices('GPU')))

If TensorFlow detects your GPU, it should return:

Num GPUs Available: 1

5.2 Checking GPU in PyTorch

Run this in Python:

```
import torch
print("GPU available:", torch.cuda.is_available())
print("GPU Name:", torch.cuda.get_device_name(0) if torch.cuda.is_available() else "None")
```

If PyTorch detects your GPU, it should return something like:

```
GPU available: True
GPU Name: NVIDIA RTX 3090
```

6. Installing Jupyter Notebook (Optional but Recommended)

If you prefer working with Jupyter Notebooks, install:

```
pip install jupyter notebook
```

Then start a Jupyter Notebook:

```
jupyter notebook
```

7. Testing the Installation

Let's verify that everything is working by running a basic GAN model test.

7.1 Simple Test for TensorFlow

Run this in Python to ensure TensorFlow is working:

```
import tensorflow as tf

class SimpleGAN(tf.keras.Model):
    def __init__(self):
        super(SimpleGAN, self).__init__()
        self.dense1 = tf.keras.layers.Dense(256, activation='relu')
        self.dense2 = tf.keras.layers.Dense(512, activation='relu')
        self.dense3 = tf.keras.layers.Dense(784, activation='tanh')
```

```
def call(self, x):
    x = self.dense1(x)
    x = self.dense2(x)
    return self.dense3(x)

gan = SimpleGAN()
print("TensorFlow GAN Model Initialized Successfully")
```

7.2 Simple Test for PyTorch

Run this in Python to ensure PyTorch is working:

```
import torch
import torch.nn as nn

class SimpleGAN(nn.Module):
    def __init__(self):
        super(SimpleGAN, self).__init__()
        self.model = nn.Sequential(
            nn.Linear(100, 256),
            nn.ReLU(),
            nn.Linear(256, 512),
            nn.ReLU(),
            nn.Linear(512, 784),
            nn.Tanh()
        )

    def forward(self, x):
        return self.model(x)

gan = SimpleGAN()
print("PyTorch GAN Model Initialized Successfully")
```

If these scripts run without errors, your setup is complete! 🎉

🚀 Your GAN development environment is now ready! You have installed:

✅ **TensorFlow or PyTorch** (depending on your preference)
✅ **Supporting libraries** (NumPy, OpenCV, Matplotlib, tqdm, pandas)

✓ **Visualization tools** (TensorBoard, Weights & Biases)

✓ **Jupyter Notebook** (Optional but useful for experimentation)

✓ Checked GPU support for faster GAN training

Now that our setup is complete, we are ready to start building our first GAN! 🔥

In the next section, we'll implement a simple GAN and generate synthetic images. ☐☐

5.3 Dataset Selection and Preprocessing

Choosing the right dataset and properly preprocessing it are critical steps in developing a high-performing Generative Adversarial Network (GAN). The quality of the training data directly affects the realism and diversity of the generated outputs.

In this section, we will cover:

✓ How to choose the right dataset for your GAN

✓ Common datasets for GAN training

✓ Preprocessing techniques (resizing, normalization, augmentation, etc.)

✓ Loading datasets efficiently using TensorFlow and PyTorch

By the end of this chapter, you'll have a clean and optimized dataset ready for training your GAN. 🚀

1. Choosing the Right Dataset for Your GAN

GANs can be used for various creative and practical tasks, such as image synthesis, video generation, music creation, and text generation. The dataset should align with your GAN's goal.

1.1 Factors to Consider When Selecting a Dataset

◆ **Domain-Specificity**: Choose a dataset relevant to your use case (e.g., faces for deepfake models, landscapes for artistic GANs).

◆ **Size**: Larger datasets typically lead to better generalization.

◆ **Diversity**: Ensure the dataset contains a variety of samples to prevent mode collapse.

◆ **Image Quality**: Higher resolution images produce better results in advanced GANs (e.g., StyleGAN).

◆ **Class Balance**: If using a labeled dataset, ensure it's not biased toward one category.

2. Common Datasets for GAN Training

Here are some widely used datasets for training GANs:

Dataset	Type	Description
MNIST	Grayscale Digits	Handwritten numbers (28×28)
CIFAR-10	Color Images	10 object categories (32×32)
CelebA	Faces	200K celebrity faces (178×218)
LSUN	Indoor Scenes	Rooms, churches, etc.
ImageNet	General Objects	1M+ labeled images
FFHQ	High-Res Faces	High-quality face dataset

For a custom dataset, you can collect your own images and preprocess them accordingly.

3. Preprocessing the Dataset

Before feeding data into a GAN, we need to prepare it by applying:

1☐ **Resizing** – Standardizing image dimensions for batch processing.

2☐ **Normalization** – Scaling pixel values for stable training.

3☐ **Data Augmentation** – Increasing dataset variability.

4☐ **Batching & Shuffling** – Efficient loading during training.

4. Preprocessing in TensorFlow

4.1 Loading a Dataset (Example: CelebA)

import tensorflow as tf
import tensorflow_datasets as tfds

```
# Load CelebA dataset
dataset = tfds.load('celeb_a', split='train', as_supervised=True)

# Function to preprocess images
def preprocess(image, label):
    image = tf.image.resize(image, (128, 128))  # Resize
    image = tf.cast(image, tf.float32) / 127.5 - 1  # Normalize to [-1, 1]
    return image

# Apply preprocessing and batch
dataset = dataset.map(lambda img, lbl: preprocess(img, lbl))
dataset = dataset.batch(32).shuffle(1000).prefetch(tf.data.AUTOTUNE)
```

4.2 Data Augmentation (Optional)

```
def augment(image):
    image = tf.image.random_flip_left_right(image)  # Random horizontal flip
    image = tf.image.random_brightness(image, 0.1)  # Adjust brightness
    return image
```

5. Preprocessing in PyTorch

5.1 Loading a Dataset (Example: CIFAR-10)

```
import torch
import torchvision
import torchvision.transforms as transforms

# Define preprocessing transforms
transform = transforms.Compose([
    transforms.Resize((64, 64)),  # Resize images
    transforms.ToTensor(),  # Convert to tensor
    transforms.Normalize(mean=[0.5], std=[0.5])  # Normalize to [-1, 1]
])

# Load dataset
dataset = torchvision.datasets.CIFAR10(root='./data', train=True, download=True,
transform=transform)
```

```
# Create DataLoader
dataloader = torch.utils.data.DataLoader(dataset, batch_size=32, shuffle=True,
num_workers=4)
```

5.2 Data Augmentation (Optional)

```
augment = transforms.Compose([
    transforms.RandomHorizontalFlip(),
    transforms.RandomRotation(15),
    transforms.ColorJitter(brightness=0.2, contrast=0.2)
])

dataset = torchvision.datasets.CIFAR10(root='./data', train=True, download=True,
transform=transforms.Compose([augment, transform]))
```

6. Checking Preprocessed Data

Before training, visualize the dataset to ensure preprocessing was successful.

6.1 TensorFlow Example

```
import matplotlib.pyplot as plt

for img in dataset.take(5):
    plt.imshow((img[0].numpy() + 1) / 2)  # Convert [-1,1] back to [0,1]
    plt.axis('off')
    plt.show()
```

6.2 PyTorch Example

```
import matplotlib.pyplot as plt
import numpy as np

# Get one batch
dataiter = iter(dataloader)
images, labels = dataiter.next()

# Convert to NumPy and display
plt.imshow(np.transpose(images[0].numpy(), (1, 2, 0)) * 0.5 + 0.5)  # Denormalize
plt.axis('off')
```

plt.show()

7. Optimizing Data Loading for Faster Training

7.1 TensorFlow: Use tf.data.AUTOTUNE

dataset = dataset.prefetch(tf.data.AUTOTUNE)

7.2 PyTorch: Use num_workers and pin_memory

dataloader = torch.utils.data.DataLoader(dataset, batch_size=32, shuffle=True, num_workers=4, pin_memory=True)

🚀 These optimizations will speed up data loading and make training more efficient!

✅ We explored how to choose the right dataset for GAN training.

✅ We applied preprocessing techniques like resizing, normalization, and augmentation.

✅ We demonstrated how to load datasets efficiently using TensorFlow and PyTorch.

✅ We optimized data loading for faster training.

Now that our dataset is ready, we can start implementing a simple GAN model in the next chapter! 🔥

5.4 Hardware Considerations: GPUs vs. TPUs

Training Generative Adversarial Networks (GANs) is computationally expensive, requiring significant processing power. The choice of hardware directly impacts the speed, efficiency, and scalability of your GAN models. The two most popular accelerators for deep learning are:

✅ **GPUs (Graphics Processing Units)** – The most widely used hardware for deep learning.

✅ **TPUs (Tensor Processing Units)** – Specialized chips designed by Google for TensorFlow-based workloads.

In this section, we will compare GPUs and TPUs, discuss when to use each, and explore strategies for optimizing GAN training based on your hardware.

1. Why Do GANs Need Specialized Hardware?

GANs involve two competing neural networks—the Generator and Discriminator—which must be trained simultaneously. This requires:

◆ Heavy matrix computations (especially in convolutional layers).
◆ Large batch processing for stable training.
◆ High memory bandwidth for handling datasets.
◆ Parallel computation capabilities for fast training.

Using CPUs for training GANs is not practical because they lack the parallel processing power required for deep learning. Instead, GPUs and TPUs are optimized for massive parallelism, making them ideal for GANs.

2. GPUs (Graphics Processing Units) for GANs

GPUs are the most commonly used hardware for training GANs. Developed originally for rendering graphics, modern GPUs have thousands of cores capable of performing parallel computations, making them perfect for deep learning.

2.1 Advantages of Using GPUs for GANs

✓ **Widely Available** – Used by researchers and developers worldwide.
✓ **Optimized for Deep Learning** – Libraries like TensorFlow, PyTorch, CUDA, and cuDNN leverage GPUs efficiently.
✓ **Flexible** – Supports both training and inference.
✓ **Memory-Efficient** – High-end GPUs come with large VRAM (e.g., NVIDIA A100 has 80GB VRAM).
✓ **Scalable** – Can be used in multi-GPU setups or on cloud platforms like AWS, Google Cloud, and Azure.

2.2 Disadvantages of GPUs

✗ **Expensive** – High-end GPUs (e.g., NVIDIA RTX 4090, A100) can be costly.
✗ **Power Consumption** – GPUs consume a lot of energy, increasing operational costs.

✕ Limited to Certain Frameworks – Works best with CUDA-compatible frameworks (e.g., TensorFlow, PyTorch).

2.3 Best GPUs for GAN Training

GPU Model	VRAM	Compute Capability	Best For
NVIDIA RTX 4090	24GB	8.9	High-end personal training
NVIDIA RTX 3090	24GB	8.6	Consumer-grade deep learning
NVIDIA A100	80GB	8.0	Enterprise AI, large-scale training
NVIDIA H100	80GB	9.0	Best for AI supercomputing
NVIDIA Tesla V100	32GB	7.0	Cloud-based AI workloads

- For small-scale GAN training, RTX 3090 or 4090 is sufficient.
- For enterprise-scale training, A100 or H100 is recommended.

3. TPUs (Tensor Processing Units) for GANs

TPUs (Tensor Processing Units) are custom-built AI accelerators developed by Google specifically for TensorFlow workloads. They are optimized for high-speed matrix operations, making them an attractive alternative to GPUs.

3.1 Advantages of Using TPUs for GANs

✓ **Faster Training** – TPUs are designed for tensor computations, leading to faster matrix multiplications.

✓ **Lower Power Consumption** – More power-efficient than GPUs.

✓ **Seamless Integration with TensorFlow** – Works efficiently with TPU-optimized TensorFlow models.

✓ **Highly Scalable** – Can be deployed on Google Cloud TPU clusters for large-scale training.

3.2 Disadvantages of TPUs

✕ **Limited Framework Support** – Works primarily with TensorFlow (limited support for PyTorch).

✕ **Harder to Access** – Most TPUs are cloud-based, requiring Google Cloud services.

✖ **Less Customization** – Unlike GPUs, TPUs are highly optimized for specific workloads.

3.3 TPU Versions and Performance

TPU Version	Performance (TFLOPS)	Use Case
TPU v2	180 TFLOPS	Entry-level AI workloads
TPU v3	420 TFLOPS	Large-scale GAN training
TPU v4	1000+ TFLOPS	Best for AI supercomputing

- ◆ For general GAN training, TPU v3 is recommended.
- ◆ For large-scale models (e.g., StyleGAN, BigGAN), use TPU v4 on Google Cloud.

4. GPU vs. TPU: Which One Should You Use?

Feature	GPUs	TPUs
Framework Support	TensorFlow, PyTorch, JAX	Mostly TensorFlow
Ease of Use	Easy to set up locally	Requires Google Cloud TPU
Speed	Fast, but slower than TPUs for large-scale models	Faster for large TensorFlow workloads
Scalability	Can be used in multi-GPU setups	Highly scalable with TPU clusters
Power Efficiency	High power consumption	More power-efficient
Cost	Expensive for high-end models	Cheaper on **Google Cloud**

💡 **Choose GPUs if:**

- You prefer flexibility (PyTorch, TensorFlow, JAX).
- You want to train GANs locally or on-premise.
- You need CUDA acceleration for advanced optimizations.

💡 **Choose TPUs if:**

- You are using Google Cloud for large-scale AI training.
- Your project is TensorFlow-based.

- You need maximum efficiency at scale.

5. Optimizing GAN Training Based on Hardware

5.1 Optimizing GANs on GPUs

✅ Use Mixed Precision Training (torch.cuda.amp in PyTorch, tf.keras.mixed_precision in TensorFlow).

✅ Reduce Memory Usage by using gradient checkpointing.

✅ Increase Batch Size for better parallelism.

✅ Use Efficient Optimizers like Adam with adaptive learning rates.

5.2 Optimizing GANs on TPUs

✅ Use TPU-Optimized TensorFlow Functions (tf.function for auto-graph acceleration).

✅ Use Large Batch Sizes to maximize TPU utilization.

✅ Leverage Google Cloud TPU Pods for distributed GAN training.

🚀 Key Takeaways

✅ GPUs are the most flexible option for GAN training, especially for PyTorch and TensorFlow users.

✅ TPUs are excellent for TensorFlow-based GANs, offering superior scalability and efficiency.

✅ If you need local training, GPUs are the best option.

✅ For large-scale GAN training, Google Cloud TPUs offer a cost-effective alternative.

Now that you understand hardware considerations, you're ready to start training your first GAN! 🎨🔥

5.5 Setting Up Cloud-Based Training

Training Generative Adversarial Networks (GANs) requires high computational power, often beyond what standard personal computers can handle. Cloud-based solutions provide an affordable, scalable, and efficient alternative to setting up expensive hardware locally.

In this chapter, we'll cover:

✅ Why choose cloud-based training for GANs

✅ Best cloud platforms for deep learning

✅ Setting up a cloud environment step-by-step

✅ Optimizing cloud resources for cost-effective GAN training

By the end of this section, you'll be able to set up a cloud-based deep learning workstation and start training your GAN models efficiently. 🚀

1. Why Use Cloud-Based Training for GANs?

GANs require massive computing power for training, especially for high-resolution image generation tasks. Here's why cloud-based training is a great choice:

✅ **Access to High-End GPUs & TPUs** – Train on powerful NVIDIA A100s, H100s, or Google TPUs.

✅ **Scalability** – Add more compute power when needed.

✅ **Cost-Efficiency** – Pay only for what you use, instead of buying expensive hardware.

✅ **No Setup Hassle** – Avoid maintenance, cooling, and hardware failures.

✅ **Train from Anywhere** – Work on projects from any device with internet access.

2. Best Cloud Platforms for GAN Training

Cloud Provider	Best For	GPUs/TPUs Available	Pricing Model
Google Cloud (GCP)	TensorFlow-based GANs, TPUs	NVIDIA A100, V100, TPUs	Pay-as-you-go, free tier
AWS (Amazon Web Services)	Large-scale GAN training	NVIDIA A100, H100	Spot instances, on-demand
Microsoft Azure	Enterprise AI projects	NVIDIA V100, A100	On-demand, reserved pricing
Paperspace	Budget-friendly training	NVIDIA RTX 4090, A100	Hourly pricing
Google Colab Pro	Beginners & hobbyists	NVIDIA T4, P100, A100 (Pro+)	Monthly subscription
Lambda Labs	Dedicated deep learning servers	NVIDIA A100, H100	Pay-as-you-go, on-premise options

💡 **For small projects**: Use Google Colab Pro or Paperspace.
💡 **For large-scale training**: Use AWS, GCP, or Azure with A100s or TPUs.

3. Setting Up Cloud-Based GAN Training (Step-by-Step)

3.1 Setting Up Google Cloud (GCP) for GAN Training

◆ **Step 1: Create a Google Cloud Account**

- Go to Google Cloud Console.
- Sign up and claim $300 free credits for new users.

◆ **Step 2: Create a Virtual Machine (VM) with a GPU/TPU**

- **Navigate to Compute Engine** → VM Instances → Create Instance.
- Select a machine type (e.g., n1-highmem-8 for basic GANs, n1-highmem-32 for advanced GANs).
- Under GPUs, select NVIDIA A100/V100 or TPU v3/v4.
- Enable preemptible instance (cheaper but may shut down anytime).
- Click Create and wait for deployment.

◆ **Step 3: Install CUDA, cuDNN & Deep Learning Libraries**

Run the following commands inside the VM:

```
# Install NVIDIA drivers
sudo apt-get update
sudo apt-get install -y nvidia-driver-470

# Install CUDA & cuDNN
wget
https://developer.download.nvidia.com/compute/cuda/repos/ubuntu2004/x86_64/cuda-
keyring_1.0-1_all.deb
sudo dpkg -i cuda-keyring_1.0-1_all.deb
sudo apt-get install -y cuda

# Install Python & Deep Learning Libraries
pip install torch torchvision torchaudio --extra-index-url
https://download.pytorch.org/whl/cu118
pip install tensorflow keras
```

Your VM is now ready for GAN training! 🎉

3.2 Setting Up AWS for GAN Training

◆ Step 1: Sign Up for AWS

- Go to AWS Console and create an account.
- Activate free-tier services (limited, but useful for testing).

◆ Step 2: Launch an EC2 Instance with a GPU

- **Navigate to EC2** → Launch Instance.
- Choose a deep learning AMI (e.g., Deep Learning Base AMI).

Select an instance type:

- **p3.2xlarge** (V100 GPU, budget option)
- **p4d.24xlarge** (A100 GPUs, high-performance)
- Enable spot instances (cheaper than on-demand).

◆ Step 3: Install Deep Learning Libraries

Run the following:

pip install tensorflow torch torchvision numpy pandas

AWS is now ready to train GANs! 🚀

3.3 Setting Up Google Colab for Free GAN Training

◆ Step 1: Open Google Colab

- Go to Google Colab.
- Sign in with your Google Account.

◆ Step 2: Enable GPU/TPU

Click Runtime → Change Runtime Type → Select GPU/TPU.

Available options:

- **Free tier**: NVIDIA T4
- **Colab Pro**: NVIDIA P100/A100

◆ Step 3: Install Required Libraries

Run the following inside Colab:

!pip install torch torchvision tensorflow keras
!nvidia-smi # Check GPU availability

Colab is now ready for training GANs! 🎨

4. Optimizing Cloud Training Costs

4.1 Use Preemptible or Spot Instances

- **Google Cloud Preemptible Instances** – Up to 80% cheaper than standard VMs.
- **AWS Spot Instances** – 90% cheaper but may terminate anytime.

4.2 Train GANs in Parallel

- Use multiple GPUs for faster convergence.
- Use Google Cloud TPU Pods for large-scale training.

4.3 Use Cloud Storage for Datasets

Store datasets in Google Cloud Storage (GCS) or AWS S3 instead of the VM.

Example (GCP):

```
gsutil cp my_dataset.zip gs://my-bucket/
```

4.4 Shut Down Idle Instances

Stop instances when not in use to avoid unnecessary charges.

Example (AWS CLI):

```
aws ec2 stop-instances --instance-ids i-1234567890abcdef
```

5. Running GAN Training on the Cloud

Once your cloud instance is set up, start training your GAN!

Example: Running a PyTorch GAN on AWS/GCP

```
import torch
import torchvision
from torchvision import datasets, transforms

# Load dataset
transform = transforms.Compose([transforms.Resize(64), transforms.ToTensor()])
dataset = datasets.MNIST(root='./data', train=True, transform=transform,
download=True)
dataloader = torch.utils.data.DataLoader(dataset, batch_size=32, shuffle=True)

# Check if GPU is available
device = torch.device("cuda" if torch.cuda.is_available() else "cpu")

print("Using device:", device)
```

✅ *Monitor training via SSH or Jupyter Notebook on the cloud.*

🚀 Key Takeaways:

✅ Cloud-based training is cost-effective, scalable, and powerful.

✅ Google Cloud TPUs are best for TensorFlow-based GANs.

✅ AWS & Azure offer high-end NVIDIA GPUs for PyTorch & TensorFlow.

✅ Use Google Colab for free or budget-friendly training.

✅ Optimize costs with spot instances, auto-shutdown, and cloud storage.

Now that your cloud environment is ready, it's time to train your first GAN! 🎨🔥

6. Implementing a Simple GAN

Now that your development environment is set up, it's time to build your first Generative Adversarial Network (GAN) from scratch! In this chapter, we'll walk through a step-by-step implementation of a simple GAN using Python and TensorFlow/PyTorch, generating basic synthetic images. You'll learn how to define the generator and discriminator networks, implement the loss functions and optimizers, and train the model using real vs. fake data. Along the way, we'll cover best practices for debugging, visualizing results, and tracking GAN performance. By the end of this chapter, you'll have a fully functional GAN model capable of generating simple but meaningful outputs—your first step toward mastering AI-driven creativity! 🎨🖼️🚀

6.1 Building the Generator Model

In Generative Adversarial Networks (GANs), the Generator is responsible for creating synthetic data that mimics real-world examples. It takes in a random noise vector and transforms it into an output that resembles real data, whether it's an image, audio, or text. The Generator's objective is to fool the Discriminator into classifying its outputs as real.

In this section, we will:

✓ Understand the role of the Generator in GANs

✓ Design a basic Generator architecture

✓ Implement a PyTorch/TensorFlow-based Generator

✓ Optimize the Generator using activation functions, batch normalization, and upsampling techniques

By the end, you'll be able to build and train a fully functional Generator for your own GAN models! 🚀

1. Understanding the Role of the Generator

The Generator (G) takes a **random noise vector** z as input and generates a synthetic sample $G(z)$. The goal is for $G(z)$ to become **indistinguishable** from real data.

How Does the Generator Work?

1. **Input Noise**: A random **latent vector** z (sampled from a Gaussian or uniform distribution).
2. **Neural Network Processing**: A series of **fully connected** and **convolutional layers** transform z into a structured output.
3. **Output**: A generated sample (e.g., an image) that tries to resemble real-world data.

Objective of the Generator

The Generator learns to trick the Discriminator by minimizing the following loss function:

$$\mathcal{L}_G = \mathbb{E}_{z \sim p(z)}[\log(1 - D(G(z)))]$$

where $D(G(z))$ is the probability of the Discriminator believing that the generated sample is real.

💡 **Key Challenge**: The Generator starts by producing completely random outputs, but over time, it learns to generate realistic-looking data.

2. Designing the Generator Architecture

A typical Generator network consists of:

◆ **Fully connected layers** – Expand the latent vector into a feature-rich representation.
◆ **Transposed Convolutions (Deconvolutions)** – Upsample the features into higher resolution.
◆ **Batch Normalization** – Stabilizes training and improves convergence.
◆ **Activation Functions** – Leaky ReLU for hidden layers, Tanh for the output.

Basic Generator Model (for Image GANs)

Layer Type	Description
Dense (Fully Connected)	Expands input noise vector
Reshape	Reshapes output into low-res feature map
Transposed Convolution	Upsamples the feature map
Batch Normalization	Stabilizes gradients
Leaky ReLU	Introduces non-linearity
Transposed Convolution	Further upsampling
Tanh Activation	Outputs final generated image

3. Implementing the Generator in PyTorch

Step 1: Import Required Libraries

```
import torch
import torch.nn as nn
import torch.optim as optim
```

Step 2: Define the Generator Class

```
class Generator(nn.Module):
    def __init__(self, latent_dim=100, img_shape=(1, 28, 28)):
        super(Generator, self).__init__()

        self.img_shape = img_shape

        self.model = nn.Sequential(
            nn.Linear(latent_dim, 128),
            nn.ReLU(),
            nn.Linear(128, 256),
            nn.BatchNorm1d(256, 0.8),
            nn.ReLU(),
            nn.Linear(256, 512),
            nn.BatchNorm1d(512, 0.8),
            nn.ReLU(),
            nn.Linear(512, int(torch.prod(torch.tensor(img_shape)))),
            nn.Tanh()
        )
```

```python
    def forward(self, z):
        img = self.model(z)
        img = img.view(img.size(0), *self.img_shape)  # Reshape output to image format
        return img
```

Step 3: Create the Generator Instance & Generate Samples

```python
latent_dim = 100  # Size of the input noise vector
generator = Generator(latent_dim)

# Generate a random noise vector
z = torch.randn(1, latent_dim)

# Generate an image
generated_image = generator(z)
print(generated_image.shape)  # Should match (1, 28, 28) for an MNIST image
```

4. Implementing the Generator in TensorFlow/Keras

Step 1: Import Required Libraries

```python
import tensorflow as tf
from tensorflow.keras import layers
```

Step 2: Define the Generator Model

```python
def build_generator(latent_dim):
    model = tf.keras.Sequential([
        layers.Dense(128, activation="relu", input_dim=latent_dim),
        layers.BatchNormalization(),
        layers.Dense(256, activation="relu"),
        layers.BatchNormalization(),
        layers.Dense(512, activation="relu"),
        layers.BatchNormalization(),
        layers.Dense(28 * 28, activation="tanh"),  # Output for MNIST images
        layers.Reshape((28, 28, 1))
    ])
    return model
```

Step 3: Create the Generator Instance & Generate Samples

```
latent_dim = 100  # Size of input noise
generator = build_generator(latent_dim)

# Generate a random noise vector
z = tf.random.normal([1, latent_dim])

# Generate an image
generated_image = generator(z)
print(generated_image.shape)  # Expected output: (1, 28, 28, 1)
```

5. Optimizing the Generator

To improve training stability and generate better samples, consider:

✅ **Use Batch Normalization** – Prevents mode collapse by stabilizing activations.

✅ **Leaky ReLU instead of ReLU** – Prevents dead neurons.

✅ **Use Tanh Activation in Output** – Ensures outputs stay in a bounded range (-1,1).

✅ **Avoid Overfitting** – Use dropout layers (optional).

✅ **Increase Network Depth** – For generating complex textures and patterns.

💡 **Example of a Deep Generator for Image GANs:**

- Add more layers for high-resolution images (e.g., 128×128, 256×256).
- Replace fully connected layers with transposed convolutions for better feature retention.

🚀 **Key Takeaways:**

✅ The Generator transforms random noise into realistic samples.

✅ Uses fully connected and transposed convolutional layers for feature expansion.

✅ Trained to fool the Discriminator by minimizing adversarial loss.

✅ PyTorch & TensorFlow implementations are straightforward for custom GANs.

✅ Optimizing batch normalization, activation functions, and depth improves results.

🎨 Now that we've built the Generator, the next step is to implement the Discriminator in our GAN! 🔥

6.2 Constructing the Discriminator Model

In Generative Adversarial Networks (GANs), the Discriminator plays a critical role in distinguishing real data from the synthetic data generated by the Generator. It acts as a binary classifier, learning to identify fake samples and helping the Generator improve over time.

In this section, we will:

✅ Understand the role of the Discriminator in GANs

✅ Design a basic Discriminator architecture

✅ Implement the Discriminator in PyTorch and TensorFlow

✅ Optimize the model using activation functions, dropout, and regularization

By the end, you'll have a fully functional Discriminator that can effectively evaluate the Generator's outputs. 🚀

1. Understanding the Role of the Discriminator

The Discriminator (D) is a neural network that **classifies** whether an input sample is **real (from the dataset) or fake (from the Generator)**.

How Does the Discriminator Work?

1. **Input**: A data sample x (real) or a generated sample $G(z)$ (fake).

2. **Neural Network Processing**: A sequence of **convolutional or fully connected layers** extracts features.

3. **Output**: A probability score $D(x)$, where:

   - $D(x) \approx 1 \rightarrow$ **Real sample**
   - $D(G(z)) \approx 0 \rightarrow$ **Fake sample**

Objective of the Discriminator

The Discriminator is trained to maximize the following loss function:

$$\mathcal{L}_D = -\mathbb{E}_{x \sim p_{data}}[\log D(x)] - \mathbb{E}_{z \sim p_z}[\log(1 - D(G(z)))]$$

where:

- $D(x)$ is the probability of the real sample being real.
- $D(G(z))$ is the probability of the fake sample being real.

💡 **Key Challenge**: The Discriminator must become strong enough to identify fakes while still allowing the Generator to improve.

2. Designing the Discriminator Architecture

A typical Discriminator network consists of:

- **Convolutional layers** – Extract important features.
- **Leaky ReLU activation** – Allows small negative values to improve learning.
- **Dropout layers** – Prevents overfitting.
- **Fully connected layer** – Outputs a final probability.
- **Sigmoid activation** – Converts output into a probability score (0 to 1).

Basic Discriminator Model (for Image GANs)

Layer Type	Description
Convolutional Layer	Extracts spatial features
Leaky ReLU Activation	Prevents dying neurons
Dropout	Prevents overfitting
Fully Connected Layer	Flattens and learns features
Sigmoid Activation	Outputs probability (real or fake)

3. Implementing the Discriminator in PyTorch

Step 1: Import Required Libraries

```
import torch
import torch.nn as nn
import torch.optim as optim
```

Step 2: Define the Discriminator Class

```
class Discriminator(nn.Module):
    def __init__(self, img_shape=(1, 28, 28)):
        super(Discriminator, self).__init__()

        self.model = nn.Sequential(
            nn.Flatten(),
            nn.Linear(int(torch.prod(torch.tensor(img_shape))), 512),
            nn.LeakyReLU(0.2),
            nn.Dropout(0.3),
            nn.Linear(512, 256),
            nn.LeakyReLU(0.2),
            nn.Dropout(0.3),
            nn.Linear(256, 1),
            nn.Sigmoid()
        )

    def forward(self, img):
        validity = self.model(img)
        return validity
```

Step 3: Create the Discriminator Instance & Test It

```
img_shape = (1, 28, 28)
discriminator = Discriminator(img_shape)

# Generate a random input (fake image)
fake_image = torch.randn(1, *img_shape)

# Get the Discriminator's prediction
output = discriminator(fake_image)
print(output)  # Should be a probability between 0 and 1
```

4. Implementing the Discriminator in TensorFlow/Keras

Step 1: Import Required Libraries

```
import tensorflow as tf
from tensorflow.keras import layers
```

Step 2: Define the Discriminator Model

```
def build_discriminator(img_shape):
    model = tf.keras.Sequential([
        layers.Flatten(input_shape=img_shape),
        layers.Dense(512),
        layers.LeakyReLU(alpha=0.2),
        layers.Dropout(0.3),
        layers.Dense(256),
        layers.LeakyReLU(alpha=0.2),
        layers.Dropout(0.3),
        layers.Dense(1, activation="sigmoid")  # Output probability (real or fake)
    ])
    return model
```

Step 3: Create the Discriminator Instance & Test It

```
img_shape = (28, 28, 1)
discriminator = build_discriminator(img_shape)

# Generate a random input (fake image)
fake_image = tf.random.normal([1, 28, 28, 1])
```

```
# Get the Discriminator's prediction
output = discriminator(fake_image)
print(output)  # Should be a probability between 0 and 1
```

5. Optimizing the Discriminator

To improve the training stability of the Discriminator, consider:

✅ **Use Leaky ReLU** – Prevents neurons from dying by allowing small negative values.
✅ **Add Dropout** – Reduces overfitting and prevents memorization.
✅ **Batch Normalization (Optional)** – Helps stabilize training in deeper networks.
✅ **Use Sigmoid Activation at the Output** – Converts logits into probabilities.

💡 **Tip**: If your Discriminator becomes too strong, the Generator won't learn. Use one-sided label smoothing (replace labels 1.0 with 0.9) to prevent this.

Example:

```
real_labels = torch.ones(batch_size, 1) * 0.9  # Instead of 1.0
fake_labels = torch.zeros(batch_size, 1)
```

6. Training the Discriminator

Once the Generator and Discriminator are built, it's time to train the Discriminator.

Training Process

1️⃣ Sample real images from the dataset.

2️⃣ Generate fake images using the Generator.

3️⃣ Compute Discriminator loss:

- Compare real images with label 1.
- Compare fake images with label 0.

4️⃣ **Update Discriminator weights using backpropagation.**

Example: Training Step in PyTorch

```
criterion = nn.BCELoss()
optimizer_D = optim.Adam(discriminator.parameters(), lr=0.0002, betas=(0.5, 0.999))

real_images = torch.randn(32, 1, 28, 28)  # Example batch of real images
fake_images = generator(torch.randn(32, 100))  # Generate fake images

real_labels = torch.ones(32, 1)  # Real images labeled as 1
fake_labels = torch.zeros(32, 1)  # Fake images labeled as 0

# Train on real images
real_preds = discriminator(real_images)
loss_real = criterion(real_preds, real_labels)

# Train on fake images
fake_preds = discriminator(fake_images.detach())
loss_fake = criterion(fake_preds, fake_labels)

# Compute total loss
loss_D = (loss_real + loss_fake) / 2

# Backpropagation
optimizer_D.zero_grad()
loss_D.backward()
optimizer_D.step()
```

🚀 Key Takeaways:

✅ The Discriminator acts as a binary classifier, distinguishing real from fake.

✅ Uses Leaky ReLU, Dropout, and Sigmoid activation for stability.

✅ Too strong of a Discriminator can prevent the Generator from improving.

✅ Training involves real-vs-fake classification and backpropagation.

🔥 Now that we've built the Discriminator, we can move on to training the entire GAN!
🎨💡

6.3 Writing the Training Loop

The heart of any Generative Adversarial Network (GAN) is its training loop, where the Generator and Discriminator learn through adversarial training. The two networks engage in a zero-sum game, where the Generator attempts to create realistic data, and the Discriminator learns to differentiate between real and fake samples.

In this section, we will:

✅ Structure the GAN training process

✅ Implement loss calculations and backpropagation

✅ Create a PyTorch and TensorFlow training loop

✅ Monitor GAN performance and debug training issues

By the end, you'll have a working GAN training loop that you can apply to your own datasets! 🚀

1. Understanding the GAN Training Process

GAN training follows a two-step process:

1️⃣ Train the Discriminator:

- Feed it real samples labeled as 1 (real).
- Feed it fake samples from the Generator labeled as 0 (fake).
- Compute Discriminator loss and update its weights.

2️⃣ Train the Generator:

- Generate fake samples.
- Pass them to the Discriminator.
- The Generator's goal is to make the Discriminator classify fakes as real (i.e., output 1).
- Compute Generator loss and update its weights.

🔁 **Repeat the above steps for multiple epochs until the Generator produces realistic outputs.**

Loss Functions

- **Binary Cross-Entropy Loss (BCE Loss)** is commonly used in GANs:

  - Discriminator Loss:

$$\mathcal{L}_D = -\mathbb{E}_{x \sim p_{data}}[\log D(x)] - \mathbb{E}_{z \sim p_z}[\log(1 - D(G(z)))]$$

  - Generator Loss:

$$\mathcal{L}_G = -\mathbb{E}_{z \sim p_z}[\log D(G(z))]$$

2. Implementing the GAN Training Loop in PyTorch

Step 1: Import Required Libraries

```
import torch
import torch.nn as nn
import torch.optim as optim
from torchvision import datasets, transforms
from torch.utils.data import DataLoader
```

Step 2: Hyperparameters and Model Initialization

```
# Hyperparameters
latent_dim = 100  # Size of random noise vector
batch_size = 64
epochs = 100
lr = 0.0002  # Learning rate

# Initialize models
generator = Generator(latent_dim)
discriminator = Discriminator(img_shape=(1, 28, 28))

# Loss function
criterion = nn.BCELoss()

# Optimizers
optimizer_G = optim.Adam(generator.parameters(), lr=lr, betas=(0.5, 0.999))
```

```
optimizer_D = optim.Adam(discriminator.parameters(), lr=lr, betas=(0.5, 0.999))
```

Step 3: Prepare the Dataset

```
# Load MNIST dataset
transform = transforms.Compose([
    transforms.ToTensor(),
    transforms.Normalize((0.5,), (0.5,))  # Normalize images to [-1, 1]
])

dataloader = DataLoader(
    datasets.MNIST(root="./data", train=True, download=True, transform=transform),
    batch_size=batch_size, shuffle=True
)
```
Step 4: Define the Training Loop
python
Copy
Edit
```
for epoch in range(epochs):
    for i, (real_images, _) in enumerate(dataloader):

        # Move data to GPU if available
        real_images = real_images.cuda() if torch.cuda.is_available() else real_images
        batch_size = real_images.shape[0]

        # Create real and fake labels
        real_labels = torch.ones(batch_size, 1).cuda() if torch.cuda.is_available() else
torch.ones(batch_size, 1)
        fake_labels = torch.zeros(batch_size, 1).cuda() if torch.cuda.is_available() else
torch.zeros(batch_size, 1)

        ###### Train Discriminator ######
        optimizer_D.zero_grad()

        # Real samples loss
        real_preds = discriminator(real_images)
        loss_real = criterion(real_preds, real_labels)

        # Fake samples loss
```

```
    z = torch.randn(batch_size, latent_dim).cuda() if torch.cuda.is_available() else
torch.randn(batch_size, latent_dim)
    fake_images = generator(z)
    fake_preds = discriminator(fake_images.detach())  # Detach so Generator doesn't
get gradients here
    loss_fake = criterion(fake_preds, fake_labels)

    # Total Discriminator loss
    loss_D = (loss_real + loss_fake) / 2
    loss_D.backward()
    optimizer_D.step()

    ###### Train Generator ######
    optimizer_G.zero_grad()

    # Generate fake images and get Discriminator's response
    fake_preds = discriminator(fake_images)

    # Generator loss - wants fake samples classified as real (1)
    loss_G = criterion(fake_preds, real_labels)
    loss_G.backward()
    optimizer_G.step()

    ###### Print Progress ######
    if i % 100 == 0:
        print(f"Epoch [{epoch+1}/{epochs}] Batch {i}/{len(dataloader)} \
            Loss D: {loss_D:.4f}, Loss G: {loss_G:.4f}")
```

3. Implementing the GAN Training Loop in TensorFlow/Keras

Step 1: Import Required Libraries

```
import tensorflow as tf
from tensorflow.keras.optimizers import Adam
import numpy as np
from tensorflow.keras.datasets import mnist
```

Step 2: Load and Preprocess Dataset

```
# Load MNIST dataset
```

```python
(x_train, _), (_, _) = mnist.load_data()
x_train = (x_train.astype(np.float32) - 127.5) / 127.5  # Normalize to [-1, 1]
x_train = np.expand_dims(x_train, axis=-1)  # Reshape for CNN

batch_size = 64
latent_dim = 100
epochs = 100

dataset = tf.data.Dataset.from_tensor_slices(x_train).shuffle(60000).batch(batch_size)
```

Step 3: Define the Optimizers and Loss Function
python
Copy
Edit

```python
# Binary cross-entropy loss
loss_fn = tf.keras.losses.BinaryCrossentropy()

# Adam optimizers for both models
generator_optimizer = Adam(learning_rate=0.0002, beta_1=0.5)
discriminator_optimizer = Adam(learning_rate=0.0002, beta_1=0.5)
```

Step 4: Define the Training Step

```python
@tf.function
def train_step(real_images):
    batch_size = tf.shape(real_images)[0]

    # Create random noise for Generator
    noise = tf.random.normal([batch_size, latent_dim])

    with tf.GradientTape() as tape_G, tf.GradientTape() as tape_D:
        # Generate fake images
        fake_images = generator(noise, training=True)

        # Get Discriminator's predictions
        real_preds = discriminator(real_images, training=True)
        fake_preds = discriminator(fake_images, training=True)

        # Compute loss
        real_loss = loss_fn(tf.ones_like(real_preds), real_preds)
        fake_loss = loss_fn(tf.zeros_like(fake_preds), fake_preds)
```

```
    loss_D = (real_loss + fake_loss) / 2

    loss_G = loss_fn(tf.ones_like(fake_preds), fake_preds)

# Compute gradients
grads_G = tape_G.gradient(loss_G, generator.trainable_variables)
grads_D = tape_D.gradient(loss_D, discriminator.trainable_variables)

# Update weights
generator_optimizer.apply_gradients(zip(grads_G, generator.trainable_variables))
discriminator_optimizer.apply_gradients(zip(grads_D,
discriminator.trainable_variables))

    return loss_G, loss_D
```

Step 5: Run the Training Loop

```
for epoch in range(epochs):
    for real_images in dataset:
        loss_G, loss_D = train_step(real_images)

    print(f"Epoch {epoch+1}/{epochs} - Loss D: {loss_D:.4f}, Loss G: {loss_G:.4f}")
```

🚀 Key Takeaways:

✅ The training loop alternates between Discriminator and Generator updates.

✅ Binary Cross-Entropy Loss is used to train both models.

✅ Backpropagation and Adam optimizer improve training stability.

✅ Monitoring GAN loss helps diagnose training issues.

🔥 With the training loop ready, it's time to generate and visualize samples! 🎨

6.4 Training and Evaluating the First GAN

Now that we have implemented the training loop for our first GAN, it's time to train the model and evaluate its performance. Training a GAN requires careful tuning of hyperparameters, loss functions, and monitoring to ensure that the Generator produces realistic outputs while avoiding mode collapse and instability.

In this section, we will:

✅ Train our first GAN on a real-world dataset

✅ Evaluate the Generator's performance visually and quantitatively

✅ Monitor key GAN training metrics

✅ Identify common failure modes and debugging techniques

By the end, you'll have a fully trained GAN model capable of generating synthetic data! 🚀

1. Training the GAN

- Understanding the Training Process
- To recap, our GAN training consists of two alternating steps:

1️⃣ Train the Discriminator

- Learn to distinguish real and fake samples.
- Compute Discriminator loss and update its weights.

2️⃣ Train the Generator

- Generate synthetic data to fool the Discriminator.
- Compute Generator loss and update its weights.

🔁 **Repeat these steps for multiple epochs until the Generator produces realistic samples.**

Training Loop Implementation (PyTorch)

Let's implement the training process in PyTorch and TensorFlow.

1. Import Necessary Libraries

```python
import torch
import torch.nn as nn
import torch.optim as optim
from torchvision.utils import save_image
import os

# Ensure output directory exists
os.makedirs("generated_images", exist_ok=True)
```

2. Define Training Function

```python
def train_gan(generator, discriminator, dataloader, epochs=100, latent_dim=100,
device="cuda"):
    criterion = nn.BCELoss()
    optimizer_G = optim.Adam(generator.parameters(), lr=0.0002, betas=(0.5, 0.999))
    optimizer_D = optim.Adam(discriminator.parameters(), lr=0.0002, betas=(0.5, 0.999))

    generator.to(device)
    discriminator.to(device)

    for epoch in range(epochs):
        for batch_idx, (real_images, _) in enumerate(dataloader):
            batch_size = real_images.size(0)
            real_images = real_images.to(device)

            # Create labels
            real_labels = torch.ones(batch_size, 1).to(device)
            fake_labels = torch.zeros(batch_size, 1).to(device)

            ###### Train Discriminator ######
            optimizer_D.zero_grad()

            real_preds = discriminator(real_images)
            loss_real = criterion(real_preds, real_labels)

            noise = torch.randn(batch_size, latent_dim).to(device)
            fake_images = generator(noise)
            fake_preds = discriminator(fake_images.detach())
            loss_fake = criterion(fake_preds, fake_labels)
```

```
        loss_D = (loss_real + loss_fake) / 2
        loss_D.backward()
        optimizer_D.step()

        ###### Train Generator ######
        optimizer_G.zero_grad()

        fake_preds = discriminator(fake_images)
        loss_G = criterion(fake_preds, real_labels)
        loss_G.backward()
        optimizer_G.step()

        # Print training progress
        if batch_idx % 100 == 0:
            print(f"Epoch [{epoch+1}/{epochs}] Batch {batch_idx}/{len(dataloader)} "
                f"Loss D: {loss_D:.4f}, Loss G: {loss_G:.4f}")

    # Save generated images
    if (epoch + 1) % 10 == 0:
        save_image(fake_images[:25], f"generated_images/epoch_{epoch+1}.png",
nrow=5, normalize=True)

    print("Training Complete!")
```

Training Loop Implementation (TensorFlow/Keras)

For those using TensorFlow, here's how to train your GAN in Keras.

1. Define Training Function

```
import tensorflow as tf
import numpy as np
import matplotlib.pyplot as plt

# Training function
def train_gan(generator, discriminator, dataset, epochs=100, latent_dim=100):
    loss_fn = tf.keras.losses.BinaryCrossentropy()
    generator_optimizer = tf.keras.optimizers.Adam(learning_rate=0.0002, beta_1=0.5)
    discriminator_optimizer = tf.keras.optimizers.Adam(learning_rate=0.0002,
beta_1=0.5)
```

```python
@tf.function
def train_step(real_images):
    batch_size = tf.shape(real_images)[0]
    noise = tf.random.normal([batch_size, latent_dim])

    with tf.GradientTape() as tape_G, tf.GradientTape() as tape_D:
        fake_images = generator(noise, training=True)
        real_preds = discriminator(real_images, training=True)
        fake_preds = discriminator(fake_images, training=True)

        loss_D_real = loss_fn(tf.ones_like(real_preds), real_preds)
        loss_D_fake = loss_fn(tf.zeros_like(fake_preds), fake_preds)
        loss_D = (loss_D_real + loss_D_fake) / 2

        loss_G = loss_fn(tf.ones_like(fake_preds), fake_preds)

    grads_G = tape_G.gradient(loss_G, generator.trainable_variables)
    grads_D = tape_D.gradient(loss_D, discriminator.trainable_variables)

    generator_optimizer.apply_gradients(zip(grads_G, generator.trainable_variables))
    discriminator_optimizer.apply_gradients(zip(grads_D,
discriminator.trainable_variables))

    return loss_G, loss_D

# Start Training
for epoch in range(epochs):
    for real_images in dataset:
        loss_G, loss_D = train_step(real_images)

    print(f"Epoch {epoch+1}/{epochs} - Loss D: {loss_D:.4f}, Loss G: {loss_G:.4f}")

    if (epoch + 1) % 10 == 0:
        noise = tf.random.normal([16, latent_dim])
        generated_images = generator(noise, training=False)
        plt.figure(figsize=(4, 4))
        for i in range(16):
            plt.subplot(4, 4, i+1)
            plt.imshow(generated_images[i, :, :, 0], cmap='gray')
            plt.axis('off')
```

```
plt.show()
```

2. Evaluating the GAN Performance

Visual Inspection

- The easiest way to evaluate a GAN is by visually inspecting its generated images.
- Plot generated samples at different epochs to track improvements.

```
import matplotlib.pyplot as plt
import torchvision.utils as vutils

def plot_generated_images(generator, latent_dim, num_images=16):
    noise = torch.randn(num_images, latent_dim).to(device)
    with torch.no_grad():
        generated_images = generator(noise).cpu()
    grid = vutils.make_grid(generated_images, nrow=4, normalize=True)
    plt.figure(figsize=(6,6))
    plt.imshow(grid.permute(1, 2, 0))
    plt.axis('off')
    plt.show()

plot_generated_images(generator, latent_dim)
```

Quantitative Evaluation Metrics

GANs do not have a straightforward accuracy metric, but some commonly used evaluation methods include:

✅ **Inception Score (IS):** Measures the quality and diversity of generated images.
✅ **Frechet Inception Distance (FID):** Compares statistics of real vs. generated images.
✅ **Discriminator Loss Trend**: Helps detect overfitting or mode collapse.

Example for computing FID Score (PyTorch):

```
from pytorch_fid import fid_score

fid_value = fid_score.calculate_fid_given_paths(['real_images/', 'generated_images/'],
batch_size=50)
print(f"FID Score: {fid_value}")
```

3. Common Training Issues and Fixes

Problem	Solution
Mode Collapse (Generator produces limited diversity)	Add **Wasserstein loss** (WGAN), increase Generator capacity, tune learning rates.
Vanishing Gradients	Use **WGAN-GP** (Gradient Penalty), **LeakyReLU** activations, BatchNorm.
Overfitting of Discriminator	Use **label smoothing**, regularization, and balance training.

🎯 Key Takeaways:

✅ Training involves updating the Generator and Discriminator iteratively.

✅ Monitoring loss and generated images is crucial for debugging.

✅ Quantitative metrics like FID and IS help measure GAN quality.

✅ With proper tuning, GANs can generate highly realistic outputs! 🚀

Now, let's move to advanced GAN improvements to make our models even better! 🎨

6.5 Debugging Common Training Issues

Training Generative Adversarial Networks (GANs) is notoriously difficult. Unlike traditional neural networks, GANs involve two competing models—the Generator and the Discriminator—engaged in a zero-sum game. This makes training unstable, leading to issues such as mode collapse, vanishing gradients, non-convergence, and overfitting.

In this section, we will:

✅ Identify common GAN training problems.

✅ Understand why they occur.

✅ Learn practical solutions to fix them.

✅ Use debugging techniques to improve training stability.

By the end, you'll be equipped with troubleshooting strategies to train better, more reliable GANs. 🚀

1. Common GAN Training Issues and Solutions

1.1 Mode Collapse

● **What is it?**

- The Generator produces limited variations of outputs instead of diverse results.
- It fails to learn the full distribution of the dataset.

🔍 **Symptoms:**

- Generator outputs look similar (e.g., identical faces, repetitive patterns).
- Diversity decreases over time.
- Loss may oscillate but outputs do not improve.

☐ **Solutions:**

✓ **Use Minibatch Discrimination** – Allow the Discriminator to recognize duplicate outputs.
✓ **Add noise to inputs** – Prevents the Generator from memorizing patterns.
✓ **Adjust learning rates** – A very high or low learning rate can cause collapse.
✓ **Use Wasserstein GAN (WGAN)** – Helps avoid collapse with smoother gradients.

📌 **Example: Minibatch Discrimination in PyTorch**

```
import torch.nn.functional as F

class MinibatchDiscrimination(nn.Module):
    def __init__(self, in_features, out_features):
        super().__init__()
        self.T = nn.Parameter(torch.randn(in_features, out_features))

    def forward(self, x):
        M = x @ self.T
        diff = M.unsqueeze(0) - M.unsqueeze(1)
```

```
abs_diff = torch.abs(diff).sum(dim=2)
return torch.cat([x, F.softplus(-abs_diff).mean(dim=1)], dim=1)
```

1.2 Vanishing or Exploding Gradients

⬤ What is it?

- Gradients become too small (vanish) or too large (explode), preventing learning.
- The Generator fails to improve, and the Discriminator dominates.

🔍 Symptoms:

- Generator loss stays constant for many epochs.
- Discriminator loss approaches 0 too fast (overpowering Generator).
- Training stagnates or diverges.

☐ Solutions:

✓ Use Leaky ReLU instead of standard ReLU to prevent dying gradients.

✓ Use Batch Normalization in Generator but not in Discriminator.

✓ Apply Gradient Clipping to keep gradients within a stable range.

✓ Switch to WGAN with Gradient Penalty (WGAN-GP) for better stability.

📌 Example: Using Gradient Clipping in PyTorch

```
for p in discriminator.parameters():
    p.data.clamp_(-0.01, 0.01)  # Keeps weights in range
```

1.3 Non-Convergence (Oscillating Losses)

⬤ What is it?

- GAN training doesn't stabilize, with losses oscillating wildly.
- Generator and Discriminator do not reach equilibrium.

🔍 Symptoms:

- Loss graphs fluctuate unpredictably.

- Generated images vary drastically between epochs.
- The Generator sometimes worsens instead of improving.

☐ Solutions:

✓ Use Label Smoothing – Prevents Discriminator from being overly confident.

✓ Slow down the Discriminator by reducing its training updates per epoch.

✓ Use Adaptive Learning Rates (reduce LR when loss oscillates).

✓ Apply Spectral Normalization to stabilize Discriminator training.

📌 Example: Label Smoothing in PyTorch

```
real_labels = torch.full((batch_size, 1), 0.9).to(device)  # Instead of 1.0
fake_labels = torch.full((batch_size, 1), 0.1).to(device)  # Instead of 0.0
```

1.4 Overfitting of the Discriminator

● What is it?

The Discriminator learns too well, making it hard for the Generator to catch up.

🔍 Symptoms:

- Discriminator loss near zero, while Generator struggles.
- GAN fails to generate meaningful images.
- The Generator produces noisy or blank images.

☐ Solutions:

✓ Reduce Discriminator capacity (fewer layers, lower depth).

✓ Train Generator more frequently (e.g., update Generator twice per Discriminator step).

✓ Apply Dropout in the Discriminator to introduce variability.

✓ Add noise to Discriminator inputs to prevent overfitting.

📌 Example: Adding Gaussian Noise to Discriminator Inputs

```python
class NoisyDiscriminator(nn.Module):
    def __init__(self, original_discriminator):
        super().__init__()
        self.discriminator = original_discriminator

    def forward(self, x):
        noise = torch.randn_like(x) * 0.1  # Add slight noise
        return self.discriminator(x + noise)
```

2. Debugging GAN Training

2.1 Visualizing Training Progress

Tip: Always save images at intervals to track progress.

📌 Example: Plot generated images every few epochs

```python
import torchvision.utils as vutils
import matplotlib.pyplot as plt

def plot_generated_images(generator, latent_dim):
    noise = torch.randn(16, latent_dim).to(device)
    with torch.no_grad():
        fake_images = generator(noise).cpu()
    grid = vutils.make_grid(fake_images, nrow=4, normalize=True)
    plt.imshow(grid.permute(1, 2, 0))
    plt.axis('off')
    plt.show()
```

2.2 Checking Loss Graphs

If Discriminator loss drops too fast → it is overpowering.

If Generator loss plateaus → gradients might be vanishing.

If losses oscillate → non-convergence issue.

2.3 Using Evaluation Metrics

GANs don't have a simple accuracy metric, but these help:

✅ **Inception Score (IS)** – Measures quality & diversity of generated images.

✅ **Frechet Inception Distance (FID)** – Compares real vs. generated images.

✅ **Precision & Recall for GANs** – Measures how well it captures data distribution.

📌 **Computing FID Score in PyTorch**

from pytorch_fid import fid_score

fid_value = fid_score.calculate_fid_given_paths(['real_images/', 'generated_images/'], batch_size=50)
print(f"FID Score: {fid_value}")

3. Best Practices for GAN Training

🎯 **Key Takeaways**

✅ Start with simpler models before experimenting with complex ones.

✅ Balance Generator vs. Discriminator updates.

✅ Use Batch Normalization & Spectral Normalization for stable training.

✅ Regularly visualize training progress to catch issues early.

✅ Try Wasserstein GAN (WGAN-GP) for improved gradient flow.

✅ Implement data augmentation to improve Discriminator generalization.

GAN training is challenging but rewarding. With the right debugging techniques, you can overcome common issues like mode collapse, vanishing gradients, and overfitting. By using visual inspections, loss graphs, and evaluation metrics, you can systematically improve your model's performance.

Now that you've mastered debugging, let's move on to improving GAN architectures for even better results! 🚀

7. Improving GAN Training

Training a Generative Adversarial Network (GAN) is notoriously challenging due to instability, mode collapse, vanishing gradients, and convergence issues. In this chapter, we'll explore practical techniques to stabilize and improve GAN training, ensuring better performance and more realistic outputs. You'll learn about advanced loss functions (Wasserstein loss, Hinge loss), improved optimization techniques (Adam optimizer, RMSprop), feature matching, mini-batch discrimination, and progressive growing of GANs. We'll also discuss hyperparameter tuning strategies, how to effectively use batch normalization and dropout, and best practices for monitoring training progress using loss curves and generated samples. By the end of this chapter, you'll have a solid understanding of how to fine-tune and optimize your GAN models for better and more consistent results. ⚙️□📈🚀

7.1 Using Batch Normalization and Dropout

Training Generative Adversarial Networks (GANs) can be challenging due to unstable gradients, mode collapse, and non-convergence. Two essential techniques that improve GAN stability and performance are Batch Normalization (BN) and Dropout. These techniques help in:

✓ Stabilizing training by controlling gradient flow.

✓ Improving convergence by preventing saturation of activations.

✓ Enhancing diversity in generated outputs.

✓ Reducing overfitting in the Discriminator.

In this section, we'll explore how Batch Normalization and Dropout work, their benefits, and how to implement them in both the Generator and Discriminator models. 🚀

1. Understanding Batch Normalization (BN)

What is Batch Normalization?

Batch Normalization is a technique that normalizes the activations of each layer during training. It reduces internal covariate shift, stabilizing the learning process.

📌 How it works:

- Computes the mean and variance of activations in a batch.
- Normalizes activations to zero mean and unit variance.
- Introduces learnable scale (γ) and shift (β) parameters.

📌 Mathematical Formula:

$$\hat{x} = \frac{x - \mu}{\sigma} \cdot \gamma + \beta$$

Where:

- x = Activation input

- μ = Mean of activations in batch

- σ = Standard deviation of activations

- γ, β = Learnable scale and shift parameters

Why Use Batch Normalization in GANs?

✅ **Improves gradient flow** → Prevents vanishing/exploding gradients.

✅ **Speeds up training** → Reduces the need for very low learning rates.

✅ **Prevents mode collapse** → Encourages diversity in generated images.

✅ **Stabilizes GAN training** → Helps Generator and Discriminator learn smoothly.

📌 Where to Apply BN in GANs?

✅ **Use in Generator** → Helps generate sharper, more realistic images.

🚫 **Avoid in Discriminator** → Can weaken the Discriminator's ability to distinguish real vs. fake.

2. Implementing Batch Normalization in a GAN

Adding BN to the Generator (PyTorch)

```python
import torch.nn as nn

class Generator(nn.Module):
    def __init__(self, latent_dim):
        super(Generator, self).__init__()
        self.model = nn.Sequential(
            nn.Linear(latent_dim, 128),
            nn.BatchNorm1d(128),  # ✓ Apply BN
            nn.ReLU(),

            nn.Linear(128, 256),
            nn.BatchNorm1d(256),  # ✓ Apply BN
            nn.ReLU(),

            nn.Linear(256, 512),
            nn.BatchNorm1d(512),  # ✓ Apply BN
            nn.ReLU(),

            nn.Linear(512, 784),  # Output layer (28x28 images)
            nn.Tanh()  # Output scaled between -1 and 1
        )

    def forward(self, z):
        return self.model(z)
```

Adding BN to the Generator (TensorFlow/Keras)

```python
from tensorflow.keras.layers import Dense, BatchNormalization, LeakyReLU
from tensorflow.keras.models import Sequential

def build_generator(latent_dim):
    model = Sequential([
        Dense(128, input_dim=latent_dim),
        BatchNormalization(),  # ✓ Apply BN
        LeakyReLU(),
```

```
    Dense(256),
    BatchNormalization(),  # ✓ Apply BN
    LeakyReLU(),

    Dense(512),
    BatchNormalization(),  # ✓ Apply BN
    LeakyReLU(),

    Dense(784, activation='tanh')  # Output layer for 28x28 images
 ])
 return model
```

🔟 Important Note:

- Always use BN before activation functions like ReLU or LeakyReLU.
- Do not use BN in the Discriminator—it can weaken adversarial learning.

3. Understanding Dropout

What is Dropout?

Dropout is a regularization technique that randomly drops neurons during training. It forces the network to learn more robust and generalized features by preventing reliance on specific activations.

📌 How it works:

- Randomly removes neurons (sets them to zero) during training.
- Prevents overfitting by ensuring neurons do not rely too much on each other.
- Typically applied only to the Discriminator in GANs.

Why Use Dropout in GANs?

✅ **Reduces overfitting** → Ensures Discriminator does not memorize training data.

✅ **Encourages better generalization** → Discriminator learns to detect real vs. fake more effectively.

✓ **Stabilizes training** → Helps prevent overconfident Discriminator dominance.

📌 **Where to Apply Dropout in GANs?**

✓ **Use in Discriminator** → Improves robustness and generalization.

🚫 **Avoid in Generator** → Can weaken feature learning and degrade image quality.

4. Implementing Dropout in a GAN

Adding Dropout to the Discriminator (PyTorch)

```python
class Discriminator(nn.Module):
    def __init__(self):
        super(Discriminator, self).__init__()
        self.model = nn.Sequential(
            nn.Linear(784, 512),
            nn.LeakyReLU(0.2),
            nn.Dropout(0.3),  # ✓ Apply Dropout

            nn.Linear(512, 256),
            nn.LeakyReLU(0.2),
            nn.Dropout(0.3),  # ✓ Apply Dropout

            nn.Linear(256, 128),
            nn.LeakyReLU(0.2),
            nn.Dropout(0.3),  # ✓ Apply Dropout

            nn.Linear(128, 1),
            nn.Sigmoid()  # Probability output
        )

    def forward(self, img):
        return self.model(img)
```

Adding Dropout to the Discriminator (TensorFlow/Keras)

```python
from tensorflow.keras.layers import Dropout
```

```python
def build_discriminator():
    model = Sequential([
        Dense(512, input_shape=(784,)),
        LeakyReLU(0.2),
        Dropout(0.3),  # ✅ Apply Dropout

        Dense(256),
        LeakyReLU(0.2),
        Dropout(0.3),  # ✅ Apply Dropout

        Dense(128),
        LeakyReLU(0.2),
        Dropout(0.3),  # ✅ Apply Dropout

        Dense(1, activation='sigmoid')  # Output layer
    ])
    return model
```

📢 Important Notes:

- Dropout is only applied during training, not during inference.
- Avoid setting Dropout too high (>0.5)—it can degrade performance.

5. Best Practices for BN and Dropout in GANs

Technique	Apply to Generator?	Apply to Discriminator?	Benefit
Batch Normalization	☑ Yes	🚫 No	Stabilizes training, prevents mode collapse
Dropout	🚫 No	☑ Yes	Prevents Discriminator overfitting

Hyperparameter Recommendations

✅ **Batch Normalization Momentum**: 0.8 - 0.9 (helps smooth updates).

✅ **Dropout Rate**: 0.2 - 0.4 (higher rates can slow learning).

✅ **Use LeakyReLU instead of ReLU** → Helps avoid vanishing gradients.

⊙ Key Takeaways:

✅ Batch Normalization stabilizes GAN training and prevents mode collapse.

✅ Dropout improves the Discriminator's ability to generalize and detect fake images.

✅ BN should be used in the Generator, but avoided in the Discriminator.

✅ Dropout should be used in the Discriminator, but avoided in the Generator.

✅ Proper tuning of BN and Dropout can significantly improve GAN performance.

7.2 Applying Spectral Normalization

Training Generative Adversarial Networks (GANs) is inherently unstable due to the adversarial nature of the Generator and Discriminator. One of the most effective techniques to stabilize training and improve convergence is Spectral Normalization (SN).

In this section, we will:

✅ Understand what Spectral Normalization is and why it's useful in GANs.

✅ Learn how it works mathematically.

✅ Explore where to apply Spectral Normalization in GAN models.

✅ Implement Spectral Normalization in PyTorch and TensorFlow.

✅ Compare Spectral Normalization vs. other normalization techniques.

By the end of this section, you'll be equipped with the knowledge to apply Spectral Normalization for better GAN training stability and performance. 🚀

1. What is Spectral Normalization?

1.1 Definition

Spectral Normalization (SN) is a regularization technique that controls the Lipschitz constant of neural network layers by constraining the spectral norm of the weight matrix.

◆ Why does this matter?

- Prevents the Discriminator from becoming too powerful (which can destabilize GAN training).
- Ensures smooth gradient updates, avoiding exploding or vanishing gradients.
- Helps maintain a well-conditioned optimization process.
- Used extensively in WGAN-GP, BigGAN, and StyleGAN for stable and high-quality results.

1.2 How Does Spectral Normalization Work?

Instead of directly using weight matrices W in neural network layers, Spectral Normalization re-scales them by dividing them by their largest singular value (also called the spectral norm).

📌 Mathematical Formula:

$$W_{\text{SN}} = \frac{W}{\sigma(W)}$$

Where:

- W_{SN} = Spectrally normalized weight matrix

- W = Original weight matrix

- $\sigma(W)$ = Largest singular value of W

This ensures that the layer does not amplify gradients excessively, leading to smoother training.

2. Why is Spectral Normalization Important in GANs?

✔ **Prevents Discriminator from becoming too strong** → Helps balance Generator-Discriminator competition.

✔ **Improves gradient stability** → Reduces training oscillations.

✔ **Enhances training robustness** → Makes GAN training more predictable.

✅ **Works without additional hyperparameters** → Unlike Weight Clipping or Gradient Penalty.

📌 **Where Should We Apply Spectral Normalization?**

✅ **Apply to Discriminator** → Prevents it from overpowering the Generator.

🚫 **Avoid in Generator** → Can restrict Generator's flexibility, reducing output diversity.

3. Implementing Spectral Normalization in GANs

3.1 Spectral Normalization in PyTorch

PyTorch provides built-in support for Spectral Normalization through torch.nn.utils.spectral_norm().

📌 **Applying SN to the Discriminator:**

```
import torch
import torch.nn as nn
import torch.nn.utils.spectral_norm as spectral_norm

class Discriminator(nn.Module):
    def __init__(self):
        super(Discriminator, self).__init__()
        self.model = nn.Sequential(
            spectral_norm(nn.Linear(784, 512)),  # ✅ Apply Spectral Normalization
            nn.LeakyReLU(0.2),

            spectral_norm(nn.Linear(512, 256)),  # ✅ Apply SN
            nn.LeakyReLU(0.2),

            spectral_norm(nn.Linear(256, 128)),  # ✅ Apply SN
            nn.LeakyReLU(0.2),

            spectral_norm(nn.Linear(128, 1)),  # ✅ Apply SN
            nn.Sigmoid()
```

```
        )

    def forward(self, x):
        return self.model(x)
```

Key Notes:

✓ Spectral Normalization is applied per layer.

✓ Works well with LeakyReLU activation.

✓ No need for Weight Clipping or Gradient Penalty when using SN.

3.2 Spectral Normalization in TensorFlow/Keras

TensorFlow does not have built-in Spectral Normalization, but we can implement it manually.

📌 Applying SN to the Discriminator:

```
import tensorflow as tf
from tensorflow.keras.layers import Dense, LeakyReLU
from tensorflow.keras.models import Sequential

class SpectralNormalization(tf.keras.layers.Layer):
    def __init__(self, layer):
        super(SpectralNormalization, self).__init__()
        self.layer = layer

    def build(self, input_shape):
        self.layer.build(input_shape)
        self.w = self.layer.kernel
        self.u = self.add_weight(shape=(1, self.w.shape[-1]), initializer="random_normal",
trainable=False)

    def call(self, inputs, training=None):
        w_reshaped = tf.reshape(self.w, [-1, self.w.shape[-1]])
        v = tf.linalg.matvec(tf.transpose(w_reshaped), self.u)
        v = v / tf.norm(v)
        u = tf.linalg.matvec(w_reshaped, v)
        u = u / tf.norm(u)
```

```
    sigma = tf.linalg.matvec(u, tf.linalg.matvec(w_reshaped, v))
    self.w.assign(self.w / sigma)
    return self.layer(inputs)

def build_discriminator():
  model = Sequential([
    SpectralNormalization(Dense(512, input_shape=(784,))),
    LeakyReLU(0.2),

    SpectralNormalization(Dense(256)),
    LeakyReLU(0.2),

    SpectralNormalization(Dense(128)),
    LeakyReLU(0.2),

    SpectralNormalization(Dense(1, activation='sigmoid'))
  ])
  return model
```

Key Notes:

✓ We create a custom SpectralNormalization layer for Keras.

✓ It manipulates weights dynamically during training.

✓ Helps stabilize Discriminator training in GANs.

4. Comparing Spectral Normalization with Other Techniques

Technique	Stability	Improves Training?	Best Applied To	Drawbacks
Weight Clipping	⊘ Unstable	✗ Can hurt performance	Discriminator (WGAN)	Over-constrains weights
Gradient Penalty (GP)	☑ Good	☑ Smoothens training	Discriminator (WGAN-GP)	Computationally expensive
Batch Normalization	✗ Unstable	✗ Can destabilize GANs	Generator only	Not recommended for Discriminator
Spectral Normalization	☑ Best	☑ Easy to use	Discriminator (all GANs)	May slightly slow training

⊙ Best Choice for Stability & Performance: Spectral Normalization

5. Best Practices for Using Spectral Normalization in GANs

✅ Always apply SN to the Discriminator.

✅ Avoid using SN in the Generator (restricts flexibility).

✅ Combine SN with LeakyReLU for stable training.

✅ Do not mix SN with Batch Normalization in the same model.

✅ Use SN instead of Weight Clipping or Gradient Penalty for stable training.

⊙ Key Takeaways:

✓ Spectral Normalization stabilizes GAN training by controlling weight magnitudes.

✓ It prevents the Discriminator from becoming too powerful, improving Generator learning.

✓ Unlike Weight Clipping or Gradient Penalty, SN does not require extra hyperparameters.

✓ It is widely used in advanced GAN architectures like BigGAN and StyleGAN.

By applying Spectral Normalization, you'll significantly improve GAN training stability and generate higher-quality outputs. 🚀

7.3 Exploring Feature Matching

One of the biggest challenges in training Generative Adversarial Networks (GANs) is ensuring stability and high-quality outputs. The traditional approach of using adversarial loss alone often leads to problems like mode collapse, unstable training, and poor diversity in generated samples.

A powerful solution to these issues is Feature Matching—a technique that improves GAN training by forcing the Generator to produce samples that match the statistics of real data in an intermediate feature space rather than relying solely on fooling the Discriminator.

In this section, we will:

✅ Understand what Feature Matching is and why it's important.

✅ Explore how it works mathematically.

✅ Learn how to implement Feature Matching in PyTorch and TensorFlow.

✅ Compare Feature Matching with other GAN stabilization techniques.

By the end of this section, you'll be able to apply Feature Matching to improve the stability and quality of your GANs! 🚀

1. What is Feature Matching?

1.1 Definition

Feature Matching is a technique that modifies the loss function of the Generator so that instead of only maximizing the probability of fooling the Discriminator, the Generator is also encouraged to match feature statistics from real and generated data at an intermediate layer of the Discriminator.

◆ **Why is this useful?**

- Reduces mode collapse (where the Generator only produces a few types of outputs).
- Produces more diverse and high-quality samples.
- Leads to more stable training by reducing gradient fluctuations.

1.2 How Does Feature Matching Work?

Instead of using the standard GAN loss, where the Generator tries to fool the Discriminator:

$$L_G = -\mathbb{E}_z[\log D(G(z))]$$

Feature Matching modifies the loss function to minimize the difference between the expected feature representations of real and fake samples:

$$L_G = ||\mathbb{E}_{x \sim p_{data}} f(x) - \mathbb{E}_{z \sim p_z} f(G(z))||_2^2$$

Where:

- $f(x)$ = Feature representation of real data at an intermediate layer in the Discriminator
- $f(G(z))$ = Feature representation of generated data at the same layer
- $||\cdot||_2^2$ = Squared L2 norm (Euclidean distance)

This forces the Generator to match the overall statistics of the real data in the Discriminator's feature space rather than just trying to maximize the probability of fooling it.

2. Why Use Feature Matching in GANs?

✅ **Prevents mode collapse** → Generator learns to cover a wider distribution of real data.

✅ **Improves sample diversity** → GAN generates a variety of outputs instead of repeating patterns.

✅ **Encourages better feature learning** → Helps Generator learn meaningful structures.

✅ **Stabilizes training** → Reduces gradient fluctuations, preventing sudden collapses.

📌 **Where to Apply Feature Matching?**

✅ Modify the Generator loss function to include Feature Matching.

✅ Extract features from an intermediate layer of the Discriminator (before the final classification layer).

3. Implementing Feature Matching in GANs

3.1 Feature Matching in PyTorch

✦ Modifying the Generator Loss Function in PyTorch

```python
import torch
import torch.nn as nn
import torch.optim as optim

class Discriminator(nn.Module):
    def __init__(self):
        super(Discriminator, self).__init__()
        self.feature_extractor = nn.Sequential(
            nn.Linear(784, 512),
            nn.LeakyReLU(0.2),
            nn.Linear(512, 256),
            nn.LeakyReLU(0.2)
        )
        self.classifier = nn.Linear(256, 1)  # Final classification layer

    def forward(self, x, extract_features=False):
        features = self.feature_extractor(x)
        if extract_features:
            return features  # Return features for feature matching
        return self.classifier(features)

class Generator(nn.Module):
    def __init__(self, latent_dim):
        super(Generator, self).__init__()
        self.model = nn.Sequential(
            nn.Linear(latent_dim, 256),
            nn.ReLU(),
            nn.Linear(256, 512),
            nn.ReLU(),
            nn.Linear(512, 784),
            nn.Tanh()
        )

    def forward(self, z):
        return self.model(z)

# Define loss function
```

```
def feature_matching_loss(real_features, fake_features):
    return torch.nn.functional.mse_loss(real_features.mean(0), fake_features.mean(0))

# Initialize models
D = Discriminator()
G = Generator(latent_dim=100)

# Optimizers
optimizer_G = optim.Adam(G.parameters(), lr=0.0002)
optimizer_D = optim.Adam(D.parameters(), lr=0.0002)

# Training loop (simplified)
real_data = torch.randn(64, 784)  # Example batch of real data
z = torch.randn(64, 100)  # Random noise

# Generate fake data
fake_data = G(z)

# Extract features from Discriminator
real_features = D(real_data, extract_features=True)
fake_features = D(fake_data, extract_features=True)

# Compute Feature Matching loss
loss_G = feature_matching_loss(real_features, fake_features)

# Backpropagation
optimizer_G.zero_grad()
loss_G.backward()
optimizer_G.step()
```

Key Notes:

✓ Feature Matching modifies the Generator loss.

✓ We extract features from an intermediate Discriminator layer.

✓ We minimize the difference between real and fake feature representations.

3.2 Feature Matching in TensorFlow/Keras

📌 Modifying the Generator Loss Function in Keras

```python
import tensorflow as tf
from tensorflow.keras.layers import Dense, LeakyReLU
from tensorflow.keras.models import Sequential

# Define Discriminator with feature extraction
def build_discriminator():
    model = Sequential([
        Dense(512, input_shape=(784,)),
        LeakyReLU(0.2),
        Dense(256),
        LeakyReLU(0.2),
        Dense(1, activation='sigmoid')  # Final classification layer
    ])
    return model

# Define Generator
def build_generator(latent_dim):
    model = Sequential([
        Dense(256, input_dim=latent_dim, activation='relu'),
        Dense(512, activation='relu'),
        Dense(784, activation='tanh')
    ])
    return model

# Define feature matching loss
def feature_matching_loss(real_features, fake_features):
    return tf.reduce_mean(tf.square(tf.reduce_mean(real_features, axis=0) -
tf.reduce_mean(fake_features, axis=0)))

# Compile models
D = build_discriminator()
G = build_generator(latent_dim=100)

# Extract intermediate features
feature_extractor = tf.keras.Model(D.input, D.layers[1].output)

# Training step
real_data = tf.random.normal((64, 784))
z = tf.random.normal((64, 100))
```

```
# Generate fake data
fake_data = G(z)

# Extract features
real_features = feature_extractor(real_data)
fake_features = feature_extractor(fake_data)

# Compute feature matching loss
loss_G = feature_matching_loss(real_features, fake_features)

# Backpropagation
G.trainable_variables
with tf.GradientTape() as tape:
    grads = tape.gradient(loss_G, G.trainable_variables)
optimizer = tf.keras.optimizers.Adam(0.0002)
optimizer.apply_gradients(zip(grads, G.trainable_variables))
```

4. Comparison: Feature Matching vs. Other Techniques

Technique	Prevents Mode Collapse?	Improves Diversity?	Stabilizes Training?
Feature Matching	☑ Yes	☑ Yes	☑ Yes
Adversarial Loss	✕ No	✕ No	✕ No
Spectral Normalization	☑ Yes	✕ No	☑ Yes

⊙ Best Choice for Diversity & Stability: Feature Matching

⊙ Key Takeaways:

✓ Feature Matching improves diversity and stability in GANs.

✓ It modifies the Generator loss function to match real and fake feature distributions.

✓ It works well with Spectral Normalization and other stabilization techniques.

✓ It is widely used in semi-supervised learning and robust GAN architectures.

7.4 Adjusting Learning Rates and Optimizers

Training Generative Adversarial Networks (GANs) is notoriously difficult due to instability, mode collapse, and vanishing gradients. One of the most effective ways to improve GAN training is by adjusting learning rates and selecting the right optimizers.

In this section, we will:

✓ Understand how learning rates impact GAN training.

✓ Explore adaptive learning rate strategies.

✓ Compare different optimizers like Adam, RMSprop, and SGD.

✓ Learn best practices for setting learning rates and decay schedules.

By the end of this section, you'll have a clear strategy for tuning learning rates and choosing the best optimizer to improve your GAN's performance! 🚀

1. The Role of Learning Rates in GAN Training

1.1 Why Learning Rate is Crucial

The learning rate (α) controls how much the model updates its parameters during each training step. In GANs, both the Generator (G) and Discriminator (D) have separate learning rates, and an imbalance between them can lead to failure.

◆ **If the learning rate is too high:**

- Training becomes unstable.
- The Discriminator learns too fast, making it impossible for the Generator to catch up.
- Loss oscillates wildly.

◆ **If the learning rate is too low:**

- Training is very slow.
- The Generator may never learn meaningful features.
- The model gets stuck in local minima.

1.2 Common Learning Rate Issues in GANs

📌 **Discriminator overpowering the Generator:**

- The Discriminator learns faster and easily classifies fake samples, preventing the Generator from improving.
- **Solution**: Use a lower learning rate for the Discriminator than the Generator.

📌 **Exploding or vanishing gradients:**

- A high learning rate leads to exploding gradients.
- A low learning rate causes vanishing gradients.
- **Solution**: Use adaptive learning rates (e.g., Adam, RMSprop).

📌 **Mode collapse:**

- The Generator produces limited variations instead of diverse samples.
- **Solution**: Use learning rate decay, gradient penalties, or feature matching (covered in Section 7.3).

2. Choosing the Best Learning Rate for GANs

2.1 Recommended Learning Rates for GANs

◆ **Standard settings:**

- **Generator Learning Rate**: 0.0002
- **Discriminator Learning Rate**: 0.0001 (slower to prevent overpowering)

◆ **For more complex architectures (e.g., StyleGAN, BigGAN):**

- Start with 0.0001 for both G and D.
- Use adaptive optimizers (Adam, RMSprop).

◆ **For Stability:**

- Apply learning rate decay (reducing the learning rate over time).
- Use Gradient Clipping (limit large updates to prevent exploding gradients).

3. Optimizers for GAN Training

Choosing the right optimizer is just as important as setting the correct learning rate. Let's compare the most common optimizers for GANs.

3.1 Stochastic Gradient Descent (SGD) – Too Unstable

Pros:

✓ Simple and computationally efficient.

Cons:

✗ Too unstable for GANs (often leads to mode collapse).
✗ No adaptive learning rate adjustments.

📌 **Verdict: Not recommended for GANs.**

3.2 Adam – The Most Common Choice

Pros:

✓ Uses momentum ($\beta 1$, $\beta 2$ parameters) to smooth training.
✓ Adaptive learning rates prevent instability.
✓ Works well with deep networks.

Cons:

✗ Can cause overshooting if $\beta 1$ is too high.
✗ Default settings ($\beta 1 = 0.9$, $\beta 2 = 0.999$) are not ideal for GANs.

📌 **Best settings for GANs:**

◆ Use $\beta 1 = 0.5$, $\beta 2 = 0.999$ instead of default values.
◆ Lower learning rate (0.0002 for G, 0.0001 for D).

✓ **Verdict**: Best overall optimizer for GANs.

PyTorch Adam Example:

optimizer_G = torch.optim.Adam(G.parameters(), lr=0.0002, betas=(0.5, 0.999))
optimizer_D = torch.optim.Adam(D.parameters(), lr=0.0001, betas=(0.5, 0.999))

3.3 RMSprop – A Good Alternative to Adam

Pros:

✓ Helps prevent exploding gradients.

✓ Works well with Wasserstein GANs (WGANs).

✓ More stable than SGD.

Cons:

✗ Can be too aggressive in reducing learning rates.

📌 **Best settings for GANs:**

◆ Learning rate: 0.00005 – 0.0001
◆ Disable momentum for stability.

✓ **Verdict**: Good choice for WGANs (use instead of Adam).

PyTorch RMSprop Example:

optimizer_G = torch.optim.RMSprop(G.parameters(), lr=0.00005)
optimizer_D = torch.optim.RMSprop(D.parameters(), lr=0.00005)

3.4 Comparing Optimizers for GANs

Optimizer	Best for Stability?	Adaptive Learning Rate?	Recommended for GANs?
SGD	✗ No	✗ No	✗ No (Too unstable)
Adam	☑ Yes	☑ Yes	☑ Best for most GANs
RMSprop	☑ Yes	☑ Yes	☑ Best for WGANs

4. Advanced Learning Rate Strategies

4.1 Learning Rate Decay

Gradually reducing the learning rate over time improves long-term stability.

How to apply:

✓ Use exponential decay:

$$\alpha_t = \alpha_0 \times \gamma^t$$

(Where γ is a decay factor like **0.99** per epoch).

PyTorch Example:

```
scheduler_G = torch.optim.lr_scheduler.ExponentialLR(optimizer_G, gamma=0.99)
scheduler_D = torch.optim.lr_scheduler.ExponentialLR(optimizer_D, gamma=0.99)
```

4.2 Adaptive Learning Rate Scheduling

Instead of decaying the learning rate manually, use adaptive methods:

✓ ReduceLROnPlateau (reduces LR when performance plateaus).

✓ OneCycleLR (dynamically adjusts learning rates).

Example in PyTorch:

```
scheduler_G = torch.optim.lr_scheduler.ReduceLROnPlateau(optimizer_G, mode='min',
factor=0.5, patience=5)
scheduler_D = torch.optim.lr_scheduler.ReduceLROnPlateau(optimizer_D, mode='min',
factor=0.5, patience=5)
```

5. Key Takeaways

🎯 **What You Learned:**

✓ Learning rate tuning is crucial for stable GAN training.

✓ Use a lower learning rate for the Discriminator to balance training.

✓ Adam (β1 = 0.5, β2 = 0.999) is the best optimizer for most GANs.

✓ RMSprop works well for WGANs.

✓ Use learning rate decay or adaptive scheduling for better stability.

7.5 Data Augmentation for Stable Training

Training Generative Adversarial Networks (GANs) effectively requires high-quality, diverse, and well-preprocessed datasets. However, in many cases, datasets are limited, imbalanced, or contain noise, leading to unstable training, mode collapse, or poor generalization. Data augmentation is a powerful technique to address these issues by artificially increasing the diversity of training data, improving GAN performance and stability.

In this section, we will:

✓ Understand why data augmentation is crucial for GAN training.

✓ Explore different augmentation techniques for images, text, and audio.

✓ Learn how data augmentation stabilizes GAN training.

✓ Implement augmentation techniques in TensorFlow and PyTorch.

By the end of this section, you'll be equipped with practical augmentation strategies to boost GAN training stability and improve generated outputs! 🚀

1. Why Data Augmentation is Crucial for GANs

1.1 Problems in GAN Training Due to Data Limitations

GANs require large and diverse datasets to learn meaningful distributions. However, in real-world scenarios, datasets often have issues such as:

◆ **Small Dataset Size** – Limited data leads to poor generalization.
◆ **Imbalanced Data** – Some features are overrepresented, leading to mode collapse.

◈ **Noisy or Low-Quality Data** – GANs can overfit to noise, generating poor outputs.

◈ **Lack of Variation** – If the dataset lacks diversity, GANs struggle to generate new, realistic samples.

1.2 How Data Augmentation Helps

Data augmentation introduces artificial variations in the dataset, helping GANs:

✅ Generalize better by seeing more variations.

✅ Prevent overfitting to specific features.

✅ Reduce mode collapse by diversifying data.

✅ Improve training stability by providing more training samples.

2. Types of Data Augmentation for GANs

2.1 Image Data Augmentation

For image-based GANs, augmentations help generate more diverse and realistic images. Common transformations include:

◆ **Geometric Transformations:**

- **Random Cropping** – Forces the GAN to learn different spatial relationships.
- **Rotation & Flipping** – Helps in scenarios like face generation, ensuring GANs don't overfit to a single orientation.
- **Scaling & Resizing** – Encourages learning at different resolutions.

◆ **Color & Intensity Transformations:**

- **Color Jittering** – Alters brightness, contrast, saturation, and hue.
- **Gaussian Noise** – Helps the GAN learn to denoise inputs.
- **Histogram Equalization** – Normalizes contrast variations.

◆ **Style-Based Transformations:**

- **Mixup & CutMix** – Merges multiple images for better generalization.
- **Texture Augmentation** – Applies noise patterns to improve robustness.

Example: Image Augmentation in PyTorch

```
import torchvision.transforms as transforms

transform = transforms.Compose([
    transforms.RandomHorizontalFlip(p=0.5),
    transforms.RandomRotation(degrees=15),
    transforms.ColorJitter(brightness=0.2, contrast=0.2, saturation=0.2, hue=0.1),
    transforms.RandomResizedCrop(64, scale=(0.8, 1.0)),
    transforms.ToTensor()
])
```

2.2 Text Data Augmentation

For text-based GANs (e.g., for text generation, dialogue synthesis), augmentation can improve diversity and fluency. Common techniques include:

◆ Word-Level Augmentation

- **Synonym Replacement** – Replace words with synonyms using WordNet.
- **Random Insertion/Deletion** – Insert or remove words randomly.
- **Back Translation** – Translate text into another language and back.

◆ Character-Level Augmentation

- **Random Noise Addition** – Introduce typos and spelling variations.
- **Text Shuffling** – Randomize sentence structures while keeping meaning.

Example: Text Augmentation with NLPAug

```
from nlpaug.augmenter.word import SynonymAug

aug = SynonymAug()
text = "Generative Adversarial Networks are powerful."
augmented_text = aug.augment(text)
print(augmented_text)
```

2.3 Audio Data Augmentation

For music, speech, and sound synthesis with GANs, augmentation helps train models to handle real-world variability.

◆ **Time-Based Transformations**

- **Time Stretching** – Alters the speed without changing pitch.
- **Pitch Shifting** – Modifies pitch while maintaining tempo.
- **Time Masking** – Removes random parts of the audio.

◆ **Noise & Effect Augmentations**

- **Add Gaussian Noise** – Helps GANs handle real-world noise.
- **Reverberation & Echo** – Simulates real environments.

Example: Audio Augmentation with Torchaudio

```
import torchaudio
import torchaudio.transforms as T

waveform, sample_rate = torchaudio.load("audio_sample.wav")
augment = T.TimeStretch()
augmented_waveform = augment(waveform)
```

3. How Data Augmentation Stabilizes GAN Training

3.1 Reducing Mode Collapse

Mode collapse occurs when the Generator produces similar outputs repeatedly, failing to capture dataset diversity. Augmentation introduces new variations, forcing the GAN to generate more diverse samples.

3.2 Improving Discriminator Robustness

If the Discriminator sees only unaltered real samples, it can become too powerful and overpower the Generator. Augmenting real samples makes the Discriminator more resilient, allowing better adversarial training.

3.3 Handling Limited Training Data

When datasets are small, GANs overfit quickly. Augmentation acts as a regularizer, preventing the model from memorizing data.

3.4 Enhancing Generalization in Unsupervised Learning

GANs often generate overfitted outputs when trained on limited data. Augmentation teaches the GAN to generalize, ensuring more realistic and varied outputs.

4. Implementing Data Augmentation in GAN Training

4.1 Augmenting Training Data

Before feeding data to the GAN, apply augmentation to real samples.

PyTorch Example:

```
from torchvision import transforms

transform = transforms.Compose([
    transforms.RandomHorizontalFlip(),
    transforms.RandomRotation(15),
    transforms.ColorJitter(brightness=0.2, contrast=0.2),
    transforms.ToTensor()
])

dataset = datasets.ImageFolder(root="data/", transform=transform)
dataloader = torch.utils.data.DataLoader(dataset, batch_size=64, shuffle=True)
```

4.2 Augmenting Generated Images

To stabilize training, augment fake images before feeding them to the Discriminator.

TensorFlow Example:

```
import tensorflow as tf

def augment(image):
    image = tf.image.random_flip_left_right(image)
    image = tf.image.random_brightness(image, max_delta=0.2)
    return image
```

```
fake_images = generator(noise)
augmented_fake_images = augment(fake_images)
```

5. Key Takeaways

⌖ What You Learned:

✓ Data augmentation improves GAN training stability.

✓ Image augmentation prevents mode collapse and improves diversity.

✓ Text augmentation helps language models generate more varied outputs.

✓ Audio augmentation improves robustness in speech and music synthesis.

✓ Augmenting both real and fake samples enhances GAN generalization.

8. Avoiding Common GAN Pitfalls

Despite their potential, Generative Adversarial Networks (GANs) are notoriously difficult to train, often suffering from issues like mode collapse, vanishing or exploding gradients, instability, and training stagnation. In this chapter, we'll dive deep into the most common pitfalls that developers encounter when working with GANs and provide practical strategies to overcome them. You'll learn how to detect and fix mode collapse, prevent discriminator overpowering, balance the generator-discriminator dynamic, and ensure stable convergence. We'll also discuss best practices for dataset preparation, architecture design, and debugging to help you build robust and high-performing GAN models. By the end of this chapter, you'll be equipped with the knowledge to troubleshoot and refine your GANs effectively. 🔍⚠️☐🚀

8.1 Understanding Mode Collapse

One of the biggest challenges in training Generative Adversarial Networks (GANs) is mode collapse—a situation where the Generator produces limited, repetitive, or highly similar outputs instead of diverse and realistic samples. Mode collapse prevents GANs from learning the full distribution of real data, leading to poor generalization and unrealistic generations.

In this section, we will:

✅ Understand what mode collapse is and why it happens.

✅ Explore different types of mode collapse.

✅ Identify symptoms of mode collapse in GAN training.

✅ Learn strategies to detect and mitigate mode collapse.

By the end of this section, you'll be able to identify mode collapse early and apply techniques to fix it for stable GAN training. 🚀

1. What is Mode Collapse?

1.1 Definition

Mode collapse occurs when the Generator fails to learn the full distribution of real data and instead maps different inputs (random noise vectors) to similar or identical outputs. Instead of generating a wide range of realistic images, the Generator focuses on a few specific samples.

1.2 Why Does Mode Collapse Happen?

Mode collapse happens due to the adversarial nature of GAN training, where the Generator and Discriminator are constantly competing. Some key reasons include:

⬧ **Discriminator Becomes Too Strong** – If the Discriminator quickly learns to distinguish fake samples, the Generator may struggle and settle for producing a few outputs that can sometimes fool the Discriminator.

⬧ **Gradient Updates are Too Aggressive** – Poor training dynamics (e.g., improper learning rates, optimizer choices) can lead to unstable updates where the Generator repeatedly produces similar samples.

⬧ **Lack of Diversity in the Loss Function** – GANs optimize a single objective (fooling the Discriminator), which does not explicitly encourage sample diversity.

⬧ **Overfitting to Certain Features** – If the dataset has limited variation, the Generator may overfit to a few dominant patterns instead of learning the entire distribution.

2. Types of Mode Collapse

2.1 Complete Mode Collapse (Global Mode Collapse)

☐ What Happens?

The Generator produces only one type of output, regardless of the random noise input. This is the most severe form of mode collapse.

🔍 Example:

- A GAN trained to generate faces produces only one specific face every time.
- A GAN trained for text generation produces the same sentence repeatedly.

2.2 Partial Mode Collapse (Local Mode Collapse)

What Happens?

The Generator produces a few different outputs but fails to capture the full diversity of the dataset.

Example:

- A face-generating GAN only creates male faces but never generates female faces.
- A GAN trained on handwritten digits generates only digits 3, 5, and 8, ignoring other numbers.

2.3 Iterative Mode Collapse (Oscillatory Mode Collapse)

What Happens?

The Generator keeps switching between a small set of outputs over training iterations, rather than learning a stable distribution.

Example:

- In one epoch, the GAN generates only cats, and in another, it generates only dogs.
- The Generator cycles between a few specific images, but never generates anything outside those categories.

3. Detecting Mode Collapse

3.1 Visual Inspection of Outputs

What to Look For?

- **Repetitive samples** – If many generated images look nearly identical, mode collapse is happening.
- **Lack of diversity** – If outputs fail to represent the full dataset (e.g., only one style of faces, one color scheme), the Generator is collapsing.

3.2 Checking the Latent Space (Noise Input-Output Relationship)

How to Test?

Generate multiple images using different noise vectors. If the outputs are too similar, mode collapse is likely.

Example in PyTorch:

```python
import torch
import matplotlib.pyplot as plt

# Generate multiple samples using different noise inputs
z = torch.randn(16, 100)  # 16 random noise vectors
fake_images = generator(z).detach().cpu()

# Plot images
fig, axes = plt.subplots(4, 4, figsize=(8, 8))
for i, ax in enumerate(axes.flatten()):
    ax.imshow(fake_images[i].permute(1, 2, 0))
    ax.axis('off')
plt.show()
```

3.3 Analyzing Feature Distributions

- Compare real and generated feature distributions (e.g., color histograms, edge detection results).
- If generated samples lack variety, mode collapse is happening.

3.4 Evaluating GAN Performance Metrics

- **Fréchet Inception Distance (FID)** – Measures how similar generated images are to real images.
- **Inception Score (IS)** – Evaluates diversity and quality of generated samples.
- **Precision & Recall** – Determines if the Generator is capturing the full data distribution.

4. How to Fix Mode Collapse

4.1 Improve Training Stability

✓ Adjust Learning Rates

- A learning rate that is too high causes instability.

- A learning rate that is too low slows down learning and can lead to collapse.
- Recommended: Start with 0.0002 for the Generator and 0.0001 for the Discriminator.

✅ **Use Different Learning Rates for Generator & Discriminator**

- If the Discriminator learns too fast, it dominates the Generator.
- Lowering the Discriminator's learning rate can balance training.

4.2 Use Advanced Loss Functions

✅ **Wasserstein GAN (WGAN) Loss**

- Uses the Wasserstein distance instead of the standard cross-entropy loss, improving training stability.
- Works well with Gradient Penalty (WGAN-GP).

✅ **Feature Matching Loss**

Instead of only trying to fool the Discriminator, the Generator learns to match real data statistics.

```
# Feature matching loss in PyTorch
real_features = discriminator(real_images).mean(0)
fake_features = discriminator(fake_images).mean(0)
loss = torch.nn.functional.mse_loss(fake_features, real_features)
```

4.3 Use Diversity-Promoting Techniques

✅ **Mini-Batch Discrimination**

Helps the Discriminator detect lack of diversity in generated images.

✅ **Mode-Seeking Regularization (MS-Reg)**

Encourages the Generator to produce more diverse outputs.

✓ Orthogonal Regularization

Adds a constraint that forces the Generator to map different noise inputs to different outputs.

4.4 Data Augmentation

Applying augmentation to training data (rotation, color jittering, flipping) helps the GAN learn more variations and prevents mode collapse.

```
import torchvision.transforms as transforms

transform = transforms.Compose([
    transforms.RandomHorizontalFlip(),
    transforms.ColorJitter(brightness=0.2, contrast=0.2),
    transforms.ToTensor()
])
```

5. Key Takeaways

⊙ What You Learned:

✓ Mode collapse happens when the Generator fails to learn the full data distribution.

✓ Complete, partial, and oscillatory mode collapse are the main types.

✓ Visual inspection, latent space analysis, and performance metrics help detect mode collapse.

✓ Techniques like feature matching, WGAN loss, mini-batch discrimination, and diversity regularization help fix mode collapse.

8.2 Tackling Vanishing and Exploding Gradients

Training deep neural networks, including Generative Adversarial Networks (GANs), often encounters two major issues: vanishing gradients and exploding gradients. These problems arise during backpropagation and can severely impact GAN performance by either slowing down learning (vanishing gradients) or causing instability (exploding gradients).

In this section, we will:

✅ Understand why vanishing and exploding gradients occur in GANs.

✅ Learn how these issues affect Generator and Discriminator training.

✅ Explore techniques to detect gradient problems.

✅ Implement practical solutions to stabilize GAN training.

By the end, you'll know how to keep gradients in check for smoother, more stable GAN training. 🚀

1. Understanding Vanishing and Exploding Gradients

1.1 What Are Gradients in GANs?

Gradients represent how much a neural network's weights should change during training. In GANs, both the Generator and Discriminator update their weights using gradients computed via backpropagation and optimization algorithms (e.g., Adam, RMSprop).

- **Vanishing Gradients** → Gradients become too small, slowing or stopping learning.
- **Exploding Gradients** → Gradients become too large, causing instability and divergence.

1.2 Why Do These Problems Occur?

◆ **Vanishing Gradients:**

- Happens when activation functions squash gradients too much (e.g., sigmoid, tanh).
- Deep networks accumulate small gradients, leading to weight updates that are too tiny.
- Overpowering Discriminator makes Generator updates too weak.

◆ **Exploding Gradients:**

- Occurs when gradients grow uncontrollably, making weight updates too large.
- Unstable weight initialization and high learning rates amplify gradient magnitudes.
- Poor architecture choices (e.g., too deep networks without normalization).

1.3 Why Are These Problems Worse in GANs?

GANs suffer from unstable training dynamics because they involve two competing networks. If gradients vanish, the Generator stops learning. If gradients explode, training becomes erratic, leading to mode collapse or failure to converge.

2. Detecting Vanishing and Exploding Gradients

2.1 Monitoring Gradient Values

Checking the magnitude of gradients can help detect issues.

🔍 Vanishing Gradients

- Gradients approach zero.
- Discriminator loss becomes extremely low, making it too powerful.
- Generator loss does not improve, meaning it's not learning.

🔍 Exploding Gradients

- Sudden spikes in loss values.
- Weight values become NaN (Not a Number).
- Generated images are completely random or noisy.

Example: Checking Gradients in PyTorch

```
for param in generator.parameters():
    print(param.grad.norm())  # Check gradient magnitude
```

3. Tackling Vanishing Gradients

3.1 Using Proper Activation Functions

Some activation functions squash gradients too much, causing vanishing gradients.

✅ **Better Choices:**

- **Leaky ReLU**: Allows small gradients to pass through negative inputs.
- **ELU (Exponential Linear Unit):** Reduces vanishing gradient issues.

Example: Using Leaky ReLU in PyTorch

```
import torch.nn as nn

generator = nn.Sequential(
    nn.Linear(100, 256),
    nn.LeakyReLU(0.2),  # Prevent vanishing gradients
    nn.Linear(256, 512),
    nn.LeakyReLU(0.2),
    nn.Linear(512, 1024),
    nn.LeakyReLU(0.2),
    nn.Linear(1024, 784),
    nn.Tanh()  # Used for image normalization
)
```

3.2 Balance Generator & Discriminator Training

If the Discriminator becomes too powerful, the Generator receives almost no gradient updates.

✅ **Solutions:**

- Update Generator more frequently than the Discriminator.
- Lower the Discriminator learning rate so it doesn't overpower the Generator.
- Use One-Sided Label Smoothing – Smooths real labels (e.g., from 1.0 to 0.9) to prevent the Discriminator from dominating too early.

Example: One-Sided Label Smoothing

```
real_labels = torch.full((batch_size,), 0.9)  # Instead of 1.0
```

3.3 Using Improved Loss Functions

Some loss functions result in extremely small gradients, preventing proper learning.

✓ **Better Loss Functions:**

- **Wasserstein Loss (WGAN)** – Encourages stable gradient flow.
- **Hinge Loss** – Helps prevent vanishing gradients.

Example: Wasserstein Loss in PyTorch

```
def generator_loss(fake_output):
    return -torch.mean(fake_output)  # WGAN Loss avoids vanishing gradients
```

3.4 Applying Spectral Normalization

Spectral Normalization controls the Discriminator's learning, ensuring it doesn't overpower the Generator.

Example: Applying Spectral Normalization in PyTorch

```
from torch.nn.utils import spectral_norm

discriminator = nn.Sequential(
    spectral_norm(nn.Linear(784, 512)),
    nn.LeakyReLU(0.2),
    spectral_norm(nn.Linear(512, 256)),
    nn.LeakyReLU(0.2),
    spectral_norm(nn.Linear(256, 1)),
    nn.Sigmoid()
)
```

4. Tackling Exploding Gradients

4.1 Use Proper Weight Initialization

Poor weight initialization can cause gradients to explode.

✓ **Better Initialization Methods:**

- **Xavier (Glorot) Initialization** – Keeps variance stable across layers.
- **He Initialization** – Optimized for ReLU-based networks.

Example: Xavier Initialization in PyTorch

```
def weights_init(m):
    if isinstance(m, nn.Linear):
        nn.init.xavier_uniform_(m.weight)  # Prevents exploding gradients

generator.apply(weights_init)
```

4.2 Apply Gradient Clipping

Gradient clipping limits the maximum gradient value, preventing explosion.

Example: Clipping Gradients in PyTorch

```
torch.nn.utils.clip_grad_norm_(generator.parameters(), max_norm=1.0)
```

4.3 Use Advanced Optimizers

Some optimizers handle exploding gradients better than standard ones.

✅ **Best Optimizers for GANs:**

- **Adam** (with $\beta1 = 0.5$, $\beta2 = 0.999$) – Helps stabilize training.
- **RMSprop** – Works well with Wasserstein GANs.

Example: Using Adam with $\beta1=0.5$

```
optimizer = torch.optim.Adam(generator.parameters(), lr=0.0002, betas=(0.5, 0.999))
```

4.4 Normalize Inputs and Outputs

Unnormalized data can amplify gradients.

✅ **Solutions:**

- Normalize images to [-1, 1] (when using Tanh activation).
- Use Batch Normalization to maintain stable activations.

Example: Image Normalization in PyTorch

```
transform = transforms.Compose([
    transforms.ToTensor(),
    transforms.Normalize((0.5,), (0.5,))  # Normalize to [-1, 1]
])
```

5. Key Takeaways

⊙ What You Learned:

✓ Vanishing gradients make training slow; exploding gradients make it unstable.

✓ Leaky ReLU, Wasserstein Loss, and proper weight initialization prevent vanishing gradients.

✓ Gradient clipping, spectral normalization, and advanced optimizers prevent exploding gradients.

✓ Monitoring gradients during training helps detect issues early.

8.3 Convergence Issues in GAN Training

Training Generative Adversarial Networks (GANs) is notoriously unstable, often leading to non-convergence, mode collapse, or oscillatory behavior. Unlike traditional deep learning models, GANs involve a minimax game between the Generator and Discriminator, making training dynamics unpredictable.

In this section, we will:

✅ Define convergence in GANs and why it's challenging to achieve.

✅ Explore common convergence issues and their causes.

✅ Learn techniques to improve convergence stability.

✅ Implement practical strategies in PyTorch to ensure smooth GAN training.

By the end, you'll understand how to stabilize GAN training and improve model performance. 🚀

1. What Does Convergence Mean in GANs?

In standard deep learning models, convergence means that the loss function stabilizes and the model reaches an optimal solution. However, in GANs, convergence is more complex because:

◆ **The Generator and Discriminator are adversaries** – They never "settle" in one place but constantly adjust.

◆ **GAN loss functions are deceptive** – The Generator's loss decreasing doesn't always mean better quality outputs.

◆ **Training dynamics are unstable** – The Discriminator can overpower the Generator, or vice versa.

1.1 Signs of Good Convergence

✓ The Generator produces increasingly realistic and diverse outputs.

✓ The Discriminator is challenged but not completely dominating the Generator.

✓ The loss values fluctuate but stabilize over time.

1.2 Signs of Poor Convergence

✗ The Generator produces only noise or identical images (mode collapse).

✗ The Discriminator reaches nearly 100% accuracy, making Generator updates useless.

✗ The training oscillates indefinitely without stable progress.

2. Common Convergence Issues and Causes

2.1 Mode Collapse

☐ **Problem**: The Generator produces only a few types of outputs, failing to capture the full data distribution.

🔍 **Causes**:

- Generator finds a "shortcut" that fools the Discriminator but lacks diversity.
- The Discriminator is too weak to detect repetitive patterns.
- Poor loss function choice (e.g., standard GAN loss instead of Wasserstein loss).

✅ Solution:

- Use Wasserstein Loss (WGAN) to improve gradient flow.
- Apply Mini-Batch Discrimination to encourage output diversity.
- Adjust learning rates to balance Generator and Discriminator.

2.2 The Discriminator Overpowers the Generator

☐ **Problem**: The Discriminator learns too fast, making the Generator's gradients too small to improve.

🔍 **Causes:**

- The Discriminator's loss approaches zero, preventing the Generator from learning.
- The learning rate of the Discriminator is too high.
- The Discriminator has a stronger architecture than the Generator.

✅ Solution:

- Lower the Discriminator's learning rate (e.g., 10x smaller than the Generator).
- Use Spectral Normalization to prevent excessive Discriminator growth.
- Train the Generator multiple times per Discriminator update (k:1 update ratio).

Example: Training Generator More Frequently

```
for _ in range(2):  # Train Generator twice per Discriminator step
    optimizer_G.zero_grad()
    loss_G = generator_loss(fake_images)
    loss_G.backward()
    optimizer_G.step()

optimizer_D.zero_grad()
loss_D = discriminator_loss(real_images, fake_images)
loss_D.backward()
optimizer_D.step()
```

2.3 Oscillatory Training (Failure to Converge)

☐ **Problem**: GAN loss values fluctuate wildly without stabilizing, leading to inconsistent outputs.

🔍 **Causes**:

- The Generator and Discriminator continuously overpower each other.
- Poor hyperparameter choices (e.g., high learning rates).
- Lack of regularization techniques to smooth training.

✅ **Solution:**

- Use a lower learning rate (start with 0.0002 for G and 0.0001 for D).
- Apply Gradient Penalty (WGAN-GP) to control updates.
- Use Moving Average of Generator Weights (Exponential Moving Average - EMA) for stable updates.

Example: Using EMA for Stable Generator Updates

```
class EMA():
    def __init__(self, model, decay=0.999):
        self.model = model
        self.decay = decay
        self.shadow = {name: param.clone() for name, param in model.named_parameters()}

    def update(self):
        for name, param in self.model.named_parameters():
            self.shadow[name] = self.decay * self.shadow[name] + (1 - self.decay) * param.clone()
```

2.4 Discriminator Loss Reaches 0 Too Quickly

☐ **Problem**: The Discriminator becomes too powerful early in training, preventing the Generator from learning useful features.

🔍 **Causes:**

- The Discriminator trains too aggressively compared to the Generator.
- The Generator starts with poor weight initialization, making it untrainable.
- The dataset is too simple, making it easy for the Discriminator to classify real vs. fake.

✅ Solution:

- Use Noisy Labels (e.g., change real labels from 1.0 to 0.9).
- Reduce Discriminator capacity (e.g., fewer layers, weaker architecture).
- Use Wasserstein Loss instead of cross-entropy loss.

Example: Noisy Labels to Stabilize Training

```
real_labels = torch.full((batch_size,), 0.9)  # Smoothing prevents overconfidence
fake_labels = torch.full((batch_size,), 0.1)
```

3. Techniques to Improve GAN Convergence

3.1 Using Wasserstein GAN with Gradient Penalty (WGAN-GP)

✅ Provides stable gradients and prevents mode collapse.

✅ Helps balance Generator and Discriminator updates.

Example: Implementing WGAN-GP in PyTorch

```
def compute_gradient_penalty(D, real_samples, fake_samples):
    alpha = torch.rand(real_samples.size(0), 1, 1, 1).to(real_samples.device)
    interpolates = (alpha * real_samples + ((1 - alpha) *
fake_samples)).requires_grad_(True)
    d_interpolates = D(interpolates)
    fake = torch.ones_like(d_interpolates)
    gradients = torch.autograd.grad(outputs=d_interpolates, inputs=interpolates,
                    grad_outputs=fake, create_graph=True, retain_graph=True)[0]
    penalty = ((gradients.norm(2, dim=1) - 1) ** 2).mean()
    return penalty
```

3.2 Using Learning Rate Schedulers

Dynamically adjusting learning rates helps smooth convergence.

Example: Exponential Learning Rate Decay

scheduler_G = torch.optim.lr_scheduler.ExponentialLR(optimizer_G, gamma=0.99)
scheduler_D = torch.optim.lr_scheduler.ExponentialLR(optimizer_D, gamma=0.99)

3.3 Feature Matching Loss for Stable GAN Training

✓ Encourages the Generator to match real and fake feature distributions, leading to smoother training.

real_features = discriminator(real_images).mean(0)
fake_features = discriminator(fake_images).mean(0)
feature_matching_loss = torch.nn.functional.mse_loss(fake_features, real_features)

4. Key Takeaways

◎ **What You Learned:**

✓ Convergence in GANs means stable Generator and Discriminator updates, not just loss stabilization.

✓ Mode collapse, oscillatory training, and Discriminator dominance are common convergence problems.

✓ WGAN-GP, Spectral Normalization, Noisy Labels, and Feature Matching help improve stability.

✓ Monitoring gradient magnitudes, loss curves, and generated samples is crucial for debugging GAN convergence issues.

8.4 Detecting Overfitting and Underfitting

Training Generative Adversarial Networks (GANs) is a delicate balancing act. Too much training can lead to overfitting, where the model memorizes the training data instead of generalizing. Too little training can cause underfitting, where the model fails to learn meaningful representations. Detecting and correcting these issues is essential to ensure that a GAN generates diverse, high-quality, and realistic outputs.

In this section, we will explore:

✅ The difference between overfitting and underfitting in GANs.

✅ How to identify signs of both issues using visual and statistical methods.

✅ Practical techniques to mitigate overfitting and underfitting.

✅ Code implementations for debugging and improving GAN performance.

By the end, you'll have a clear framework for diagnosing and fixing training inefficiencies in GANs. 🚀

1. Understanding Overfitting and Underfitting in GANs

Unlike supervised learning, where overfitting is detected by evaluating performance on a separate test set, GANs generate synthetic data, making evaluation more challenging.

1.1 What is Overfitting in GANs?

Overfitting occurs when:

✗ The Generator memorizes the training set and fails to generate new, diverse samples.

✗ The Discriminator becomes too strong, perfectly distinguishing real and fake data.

✗ The Generator produces identical or nearly identical images across different inputs.

Real-world example:

If training a GAN on human faces, an overfitted Generator will produce the same face repeatedly instead of generating varied, unique individuals.

1.2 What is Underfitting in GANs?

Underfitting occurs when:

✘ The Generator produces blurry, unrealistic images because it hasn't learned complex patterns.

✘ The Discriminator struggles to distinguish real from fake images, indicating poor feature learning.

✘ The GAN fails to converge, meaning it hasn't captured meaningful data representations.

Real-world example:

If training a GAN on landscapes, an underfitted Generator may produce images with unrecognizable shapes and unnatural colors.

2. Detecting Overfitting and Underfitting

To detect these issues, we can analyze loss curves, sample diversity, and feature statistics.

2.1 Visual Inspection of Generated Images

A simple but effective method to detect overfitting or underfitting is to visually analyze the outputs of the Generator over time.

✅ **Signs of Overfitting:**

- Generated images look identical or nearly identical.
- Outputs match the training data too closely (low diversity).
- The Generator struggles to create novel variations.

✅ **Signs of Underfitting:**

- Images appear blurry, noisy, or unstructured.
- Outputs lack clear details and patterns.
- The Generator struggles to improve even after several epochs.

Example: Overfitting vs. Underfitting in GAN Outputs

Issue	Output Characteristics
Overfitting	Repeated, identical images
Underfitting	Blurry, unrealistic images

2.2 Monitoring GAN Loss Curves

GANs have two main loss functions:

📉 **Generator Loss (G_loss)** – Measures how well the Generator is fooling the Discriminator.
📈 **Discriminator Loss (D_loss)** – Measures how well the Discriminator distinguishes real vs. fake images.

✅ Signs of Overfitting in Loss Curves:

- **Discriminator Loss** → Near 0 (Discriminator too strong, Generator can't learn).
- **Generator Loss** → High but not improving (Generator stuck in learning).

✅ Signs of Underfitting in Loss Curves:

- Both Generator and Discriminator losses fluctuate excessively.
- Discriminator Loss remains too high (Discriminator is weak, training unstable).

Example: Plotting Loss Curves in PyTorch

```python
import matplotlib.pyplot as plt

def plot_loss(generator_loss, discriminator_loss):
    plt.figure(figsize=(10,5))
    plt.plot(generator_loss, label="Generator Loss", color='blue')
    plt.plot(discriminator_loss, label="Discriminator Loss", color='red')
    plt.xlabel("Epochs")
    plt.ylabel("Loss")
    plt.title("GAN Training Loss")
    plt.legend()
    plt.show()
```

3. Techniques to Mitigate Overfitting and Underfitting

3.1 Preventing Overfitting in GANs

✓ Increase Dataset Size and Diversity

- The easiest way to combat overfitting is to use a larger and more diverse dataset.
- If working with limited data, apply data augmentation to artificially increase dataset size.

```
import torchvision.transforms as transforms

data_transforms = transforms.Compose([
    transforms.RandomHorizontalFlip(),
    transforms.RandomRotation(15),
    transforms.ColorJitter(brightness=0.2, contrast=0.2)
])
```

✓ Use Dropout in the Discriminator

- Adding dropout layers prevents the Discriminator from overfitting to training data.

```
import torch.nn as nn

class Discriminator(nn.Module):
    def __init__(self):
        super(Discriminator, self).__init__()
        self.model = nn.Sequential(
            nn.Linear(784, 512),
            nn.LeakyReLU(0.2),
            nn.Dropout(0.3),  # Dropout layer to prevent overfitting
            nn.Linear(512, 1),
            nn.Sigmoid()
        )
```

✓ Use Noisy Labels to Regularize Training

- Instead of labeling real images as 1.0, use values between 0.7 and 1.0.

- Instead of labeling fake images as 0.0, use values between 0.0 and 0.3.

```
real_labels = torch.FloatTensor(batch_size).uniform_(0.7, 1.0)
fake_labels = torch.FloatTensor(batch_size).uniform_(0.0, 0.3)
```

✅ Reduce the Discriminator's Learning Rate

- A strong Discriminator can overpower the Generator, leading to overfitting.
- Reducing its learning rate ensures the Generator has a fair chance to improve.

```
optimizer_D = torch.optim.Adam(discriminator.parameters(), lr=0.0001)
```

3.2 Preventing Underfitting in GANs

✅ Increase Model Complexity

- If the Generator is too simple, it cannot learn complex data distributions.
- Increase layer depth, number of filters, and activation functions.

✅ Improve Feature Matching in the Generator

- Use Feature Matching Loss to force the Generator to produce more structured outputs.

```
real_features = discriminator(real_images).mean(0)
fake_features = discriminator(fake_images).mean(0)
feature_matching_loss = torch.nn.functional.mse_loss(fake_features, real_features)
```

✅ Use Learning Rate Schedulers

- Underfitting can result from learning rates that decay too quickly.
- Use Exponential Learning Rate Decay to gradually reduce learning rates.

```
scheduler_G = torch.optim.lr_scheduler.ExponentialLR(optimizer_G, gamma=0.99)
scheduler_D = torch.optim.lr_scheduler.ExponentialLR(optimizer_D, gamma=0.99)
```

4. Key Takeaways

How to Detect Overfitting & Underfitting in GANs:

✓ **Overfitting**: Repetitive outputs, Discriminator loss near zero, lack of diversity.

✓ **Underfitting**: Blurry images, unstable loss, Generator fails to improve.

Solutions:

✓ Use data augmentation, dropout, noisy labels, and reduce Discriminator strength to combat overfitting.

✓ Increase model complexity, feature matching, and fine-tune learning rates to prevent underfitting.

8.5 Hyperparameter Tuning for GANs

Training Generative Adversarial Networks (GANs) is an intricate process that depends heavily on hyperparameter tuning. Unlike traditional machine learning models, GANs require a delicate balance between the Generator and Discriminator to ensure stable convergence. Choosing the wrong hyperparameters can lead to issues like mode collapse, vanishing gradients, and unstable training.

In this section, we will explore:

✅ The most important hyperparameters in GANs.

✅ How each hyperparameter affects training and stability.

✅ Techniques for fine-tuning GAN hyperparameters to achieve high-quality outputs.

✅ Code implementations to help you adjust parameters dynamically.

By the end of this chapter, you'll have a structured hyperparameter tuning framework to optimize your GAN models effectively. 🚀

1. Key Hyperparameters in GANs

GAN training is influenced by several key hyperparameters. Let's break them down and understand their impact.

1.1 Learning Rate (LR) for Generator and Discriminator

◈ **What it does**: Controls how much weights are updated during training.

◆ **Impact:**

- **Too high** → Training becomes unstable; the model may fail to converge.
- **Too low** → Slow training, possible mode collapse.

◆ **Best practices:**

- The Generator's learning rate (G_LR) should typically be higher or equal to the Discriminator's learning rate (D_LR) to prevent the Discriminator from overpowering the Generator.
- A common choice is 0.0001 for both, or 0.0002 for the Generator and 0.0001 for the Discriminator.

```
import torch.optim as optim

G_LR = 0.0002  # Learning rate for Generator
D_LR = 0.0001  # Learning rate for Discriminator

optimizer_G = optim.Adam(generator.parameters(), lr=G_LR, betas=(0.5, 0.999))
optimizer_D = optim.Adam(discriminator.parameters(), lr=D_LR, betas=(0.5, 0.999))
```

1.2 Batch Size

◈ What it does: Defines the number of samples processed before updating model weights.

◆ **Impact:**

- **Too large** → Training may become stable but lacks diversity in updates.
- **Too small** → Training is noisy and may struggle to converge.

◆ **Best practices:**

- Use batch sizes of 32, 64, or 128 for most GAN models.
- Larger batch sizes require more GPU memory but improve stability.

When using StyleGAN, researchers found that progressively increasing batch size improves results.

batch_size = 64 # Adjust based on hardware constraints
dataloader = torch.utils.data.DataLoader(dataset, batch_size=batch_size, shuffle=True)

1.3 Number of Training Epochs

◆ **What it does**: Determines how many times the model goes through the entire dataset.

◆ **Impact:**

- **Too many epochs** → Overfitting, where the Generator memorizes training data instead of generalizing.
- **Too few epochs** → The model underfits and generates poor-quality outputs.

◆ **Best practices:**

- Monitor the quality of generated images over time rather than relying solely on epochs.
- Start with 50-100 epochs and adjust based on results.
- Use early stopping to terminate training if the Generator stops improving.

num_epochs = 100
for epoch in range(num_epochs):
    train_GAN() # Call your training function

1.4 Optimizer Choice and Beta Parameters

◆ **What it does**: Controls how weights are updated based on gradients.

◆ **Impact:**

- Adam is the most commonly used optimizer for GANs.
- Beta values ($\beta 1$, $\beta 2$) influence momentum and gradient smoothing.

◆ **Best practices:**

- Use Adam with $\beta 1 = 0.5$ and $\beta 2 = 0.999$, as recommended in most GAN papers.
- Avoid using SGD, as it can lead to unstable training.

optimizer_G = optim.Adam(generator.parameters(), lr=0.0002, betas=(0.5, 0.999))
optimizer_D = optim.Adam(discriminator.parameters(), lr=0.0001, betas=(0.5, 0.999))

1.5 Latent Space Dimension (Noise Vector Size, z_dim)

◆ **What it does**: Defines the size of the input noise vector used to generate images.

◆ **Impact:**

- **Too small** → The Generator struggles to learn complex patterns.
- **Too large** → The model may generate noisy outputs.

◆ **Best practices:**

- 64, 100, or 128 dimensions are common choices.
- If generating high-resolution images, consider increasing to 256 or 512.

z_dim = 100
noise = torch.randn(batch_size, z_dim)

2. Techniques for Hyperparameter Tuning

Hyperparameter tuning for GANs requires experimentation. Below are some techniques to optimize training.

2.1 Grid Search and Random Search

- Grid Search: Test all possible hyperparameter combinations (time-consuming).
- Random Search: Randomly sample hyperparameters and test different configurations.

Example of Random Search for Learning Rate:

```
import random

lr_values = [0.00005, 0.0001, 0.0002, 0.0003]
G_LR = random.choice(lr_values)
D_LR = random.choice(lr_values)

optimizer_G = optim.Adam(generator.parameters(), lr=G_LR, betas=(0.5, 0.999))
optimizer_D = optim.Adam(discriminator.parameters(), lr=D_LR, betas=(0.5, 0.999))
```

2.2 Using Learning Rate Schedulers

A learning rate scheduler reduces the learning rate over time, preventing the model from getting stuck in bad local minima.

```
scheduler_G = torch.optim.lr_scheduler.StepLR(optimizer_G, step_size=10, gamma=0.9)
scheduler_D = torch.optim.lr_scheduler.StepLR(optimizer_D, step_size=10, gamma=0.9)
```

2.3 Adjusting Training Ratio of Generator vs. Discriminator

- **Problem**: If the Discriminator becomes too strong, the Generator can't learn.
- **Solution**: Train the Generator more frequently than the Discriminator.

```
for step in range(training_steps):
    if step % 2 == 0:  # Train Generator twice as often
        train_generator()
    train_discriminator()
```

2.4 Monitoring Model Performance with FID Score

The Frechet Inception Distance (FID) Score is a standard metric to evaluate GAN performance. Lower FID values indicate better output quality.

```
from pytorch_fid import fid_score

fid_value = fid_score.compute_fid(fake_images, real_images)
```

print(f"FID Score: {fid_value}")

3. Best Practices for Hyperparameter Tuning

✓ **Start with Default Values**: Use common hyperparameters as a baseline before fine-tuning.

✓ **Use Checkpoints**: Save models regularly to revert to a previous stable state.

✓ **Automate Tuning**: Use libraries like Optuna or Ray Tune for automated optimization.

✓ **Evaluate Images, Not Just Loss**: Loss values alone don't indicate GAN performance—visual outputs matter more.

Hyperparameter tuning in GANs is a challenging yet rewarding process. The right hyperparameter configuration can significantly improve model stability and output quality.

📌 **Key Takeaways:**

◆ Use lower learning rates for the Discriminator to prevent overpowering.
◆ Batch size impacts stability—try 64 or 128 first.
◆ Experiment with different optimizers and learning rate schedules.
◆ Regularly monitor FID scores and generated images.

9. AI-Generated Art & Design

Artificial Intelligence is transforming the world of art and design, enabling machines to create stunning visuals, paintings, and digital content that rival human creativity. In this chapter, we explore how Generative Adversarial Networks (GANs) are revolutionizing the creative industry, from AI-generated paintings and digital illustrations to fashion design and architectural modeling. You'll learn how StyleGAN produces hyper-realistic portraits, how DeepDream and neural style transfer blend artistic styles, and how artists and designers use GANs to push creative boundaries. We'll also discuss the ethical and philosophical implications of AI in art—can machines truly be creative? By the end of this chapter, you'll understand how GANs are reshaping the future of art, design, and creative expression. 🎨🖌️

9.1 How GANs Generate Images from Noise

Generative Adversarial Networks (GANs) have revolutionized artificial intelligence by allowing machines to generate realistic images from pure random noise. But how does this transformation occur? How does a GAN take a meaningless set of numbers and create something visually meaningful?

In this section, we will explore:

✓ How the Generator learns to create images from noise

✓ The role of the latent space and how it influences output diversity

✓ The training process that refines these images over time

✓ Real-world applications of noise-based image generation

By the end of this chapter, you will have a solid understanding of how GANs turn randomness into artistic and photorealistic imagery. 🎨✨

1. The Role of Noise in GANs

GANs start with random noise, typically a vector sampled from a probability distribution like Gaussian (Normal) or Uniform distribution. This noise serves as the seed from which the Generator learns to create meaningful images.

◆ Why use noise?

- It forces the Generator to learn to map randomness to structured images.
- Ensures that generated images are diverse rather than repeating patterns.
- Helps the Generator explore different possibilities, leading to creativity in outputs.

◆ Types of Noise Distributions:

- **Gaussian (Normal) Distribution** – Commonly used, where values cluster around 0.
- **Uniform Distribution** – Values are spread evenly within a range.

Example: Generating a random noise vector in Python using PyTorch:

```python
import torch

z_dim = 100  # Dimension of noise vector
batch_size = 64
noise = torch.randn(batch_size, z_dim)  # Random noise from Gaussian distribution
```

Each time we generate a noise vector, it is different, ensuring the GAN does not memorize fixed patterns.

2. The Generator's Role – Transforming Noise into Images

The Generator in a GAN acts like an artist that learns to create realistic images by refining its output over time.

2.1 What Happens Inside the Generator?

The Generator is a deep neural network that maps the noise vector into an image by progressively applying linear transformations, upsampling, and convolutional layers.

◆ Step-by-Step Process:

- The noise vector z is fed into the Generator.
- The Generator transforms the noise through fully connected layers.
- The output is reshaped into a small feature map.
- It passes through transpose convolutional layers to upscale into a full-sized image.

The final activation function (often Tanh) produces pixel values between -1 and 1.

◆ How the Generator Learns:

- At first, the Generator produces completely random and meaningless images.
- Over time, it learns from feedback provided by the Discriminator.
- The Generator continuously refines its ability to generate images that look real.

Example: A simple Generator model using PyTorch:

```python
import torch.nn as nn

class Generator(nn.Module):
    def __init__(self, z_dim):
        super(Generator, self).__init__()
        self.model = nn.Sequential(
            nn.Linear(z_dim, 128),
            nn.ReLU(),
            nn.Linear(128, 256),
            nn.ReLU(),
            nn.Linear(256, 512),
            nn.ReLU(),
            nn.Linear(512, 1024),
            nn.ReLU(),
            nn.Linear(1024, 784),  # Output size for a 28x28 image
            nn.Tanh()  # Normalize pixel values between -1 and 1
        )

    def forward(self, z):
        return self.model(z)
```

This simple Generator progressively expands the noise vector into a larger structured image.

3. The Role of the Discriminator – Evaluating the Generated Images

While the Generator creates images, the Discriminator acts as a critic that distinguishes real images from fake ones.

◆ How it Works:

- The Discriminator is shown both real images from a dataset and fake images from the Generator.
- It learns to classify images as either real (1) or fake (0).
- The Generator tries to fool the Discriminator by improving the realism of its images.

This adversarial process pushes the Generator to continuously improve, making the generated images increasingly photorealistic.

Example: A basic Discriminator model using PyTorch:

```
class Discriminator(nn.Module):
    def __init__(self):
        super(Discriminator, self).__init__()
        self.model = nn.Sequential(
            nn.Linear(784, 512),
            nn.ReLU(),
            nn.Linear(512, 256),
            nn.ReLU(),
            nn.Linear(256, 128),
            nn.ReLU(),
            nn.Linear(128, 1),
            nn.Sigmoid()  # Outputs a probability (real or fake)
        )

    def forward(self, img):
        return self.model(img)
```

The Discriminator guides the Generator to create better images by constantly challenging it.

4. Training Process – Refining the Images Over Time

GANs undergo a continuous cycle of improvement using an adversarial training process.

4.1 Step-by-Step Training of a GAN

1⃣ Generate Fake Images

The Generator takes random noise and produces an image.

2️⃣ Train the Discriminator

The Discriminator is given both real and fake images and learns to distinguish them.

3️⃣ Train the Generator

The Generator is updated based on how well it fooled the Discriminator.

4️⃣ Repeat the Process

Over multiple iterations, the Generator creates increasingly realistic images.

4.2 Loss Functions Used in GANs

Discriminator Loss: Measures how well the Discriminator classifies real vs. fake images.
Generator Loss: Measures how well the Generator fools the Discriminator.

The classic Binary Cross-Entropy Loss is commonly used:

loss_function = nn.BCELoss() # Binary Cross-Entropy Loss

5. Real-World Applications of GANs Generating Images

GANs have proven useful in various creative and practical fields:

🎨 **AI-Generated Art** – Used to create stunning artwork, including famous AI paintings.
☐ **Photo Enhancement** – Super-resolution GANs improve image quality and upscale resolution.
☐☐ **Deepfake Generation** – Used for face-swapping and synthetic media creation.
☐ **Fashion and Design** – Generates new clothing designs and textures.
🚗 **Autonomous Driving** – GANs generate realistic driving scenarios for AI training.

Example: NVIDIA's StyleGAN creates ultra-realistic human faces that don't exist!

GANs have revolutionized the way machines generate images from noise. By transforming random vectors into structured images through adversarial training, they achieve impressive realism.

✓ GANs start with random noise and transform it into structured images.

✓ The Generator learns to map noise to realistic images, while the Discriminator acts as a judge.

✓ The training process improves image quality over time through adversarial learning.

✓ Applications range from AI-generated art to realistic image synthesis.

9.2 Style Transfer and AI-Based Painting

Art has always been a reflection of human creativity, but what if AI could learn and replicate artistic styles? With Generative Adversarial Networks (GANs) and Neural Style Transfer (NST), AI can create paintings, mimic famous artists, and even develop entirely new artistic styles. This fusion of AI and creativity has transformed digital art, allowing machines to produce works that were once only possible for skilled human artists.

In this chapter, we will explore:

✓ How Style Transfer works and how GANs enhance it

✓ The role of Neural Style Transfer (NST) in AI-based painting

✓ The evolution of StyleGAN for hyper-realistic art synthesis

✓ Applications of AI in painting, design, and commercial art

By the end of this chapter, you will understand how AI can recreate Van Gogh's brushstrokes, generate Picasso-like abstract art, or create entirely new digital masterpieces! 🎨□✨

1. Understanding Style Transfer – Merging Content with Artistic Styles

Style Transfer is a deep learning technique that separates the content and style of an image and then merges them to create a new artistic version.

◆ **How does it work?**

- The content image (e.g., a photo of a city) provides the structure.
- The style image (e.g., Van Gogh's Starry Night) provides the artistic texture and colors.
- A deep neural network learns to apply the artistic style to the content image.
- The famous Neural Style Transfer (NST) algorithm, introduced by Gatys et al. (2015), uses Convolutional Neural Networks (CNNs) to extract and recombine these features.

Example of style transfer:

□ A regular photo → 🎨 AI transforms it into a Van Gogh-style painting!

2. The Role of GANs in Style Transfer

While Neural Style Transfer (NST) was an early breakthrough, GANs take AI painting to the next level by making it faster, more realistic, and more flexible.

◆ Key Benefits of Using GANs for AI Painting:

✓ **Realism**: GANs generate images with higher detail and depth.

✓ **Diversity**: Instead of applying a fixed style, GANs can learn from multiple artists and mix styles.

✓ **Scalability**: GAN-based models like StyleGAN allow fine-grained control over artistic elements.

2.1 CycleGAN – Transforming Photos into Paintings

CycleGAN is a special type of GAN that allows for image-to-image translation without needing paired training data. This means:

- You can train an AI to turn real-world photos into Monet-like paintings.
- It works for sketch-to-photo conversion, day-to-night transformations, and more.

📌 Example Use Case:

Take a photograph of a street → Convert it into a Claude Monet-style painting using CycleGAN!

Example of using CycleGAN in PyTorch:

```
from torchvision import transforms
from PIL import Image
import torch

transform = transforms.Compose([
    transforms.Resize((256, 256)),
    transforms.ToTensor()
])

# Load and transform input image
input_image = Image.open("photo.jpg")
input_tensor = transform(input_image).unsqueeze(0)

# Apply CycleGAN model
model = torch.hub.load('junyanz/pytorch-CycleGAN-and-pix2pix', 'monet',
pretrained=True)
output_tensor = model(input_tensor)
```

This model can instantly turn a photo into an artistic painting.

3. StyleGAN – Creating New Art Styles from Scratch

Unlike CycleGAN, which transforms existing images, StyleGAN generates brand-new artworks from noise!

◆ Why is StyleGAN Special?

- It allows for fine-tuned control over generated images.
- The latent space can be adjusted to modify colors, textures, and patterns.
- Used for generating AI-based portraits, landscapes, and even abstract art.

3.1 How StyleGAN Creates Art

StyleGAN generates images by progressively refining details through a hierarchical network. It controls various artistic elements like:

✓ Brushstroke intensity

✓ Lighting and shading

✓ Color blending and textures

✦ **Example**: NVIDIA's StyleGAN is behind websites like ThisPersonDoesNotExist.com, which generates hyper-realistic faces that don't belong to real people!

Example of generating an AI painting using StyleGAN:

```
import dnnlib
import torch

# Load pre-trained StyleGAN model
model_url = "https://nvlabs-fi-cdn.nvidia.com/stylegan2-ada/pretrained/metfaces.pkl"
device = torch.device("cuda")

with dnnlib.util.open_url(model_url) as f:
    G = torch.load(f).to(device)

# Generate random artistic image
z = torch.randn([1, G.z_dim]).to(device)
img = G(z, None)
```

This code generates a completely new AI-based painting! 🎨

4. Real-World Applications of AI in Painting

AI-based painting is already being used in commercial art, game design, and digital media.

4.1 AI in Fine Art

◆ **AI-Generated Paintings Sold for Millions** – In 2018, an AI-generated painting (Edmond de Belamy) was sold at Christie's for $432,500!

◆ **Artists Use AI as a Creative Partner** – Painters use GANs to experiment with new styles and compositions.

4.2 AI in Graphic Design

- AI-generated logos, posters, and album covers.
- Platforms like Deep Dream Generator allow users to create AI art without coding.

4.3 AI in Video Game Design

- AI generates unique landscapes and textures.
- Games like AI Dungeon use GANs to generate interactive storytelling elements.

4.4 AI in Fashion & Interior Design

- AI-powered tools like Runway ML create unique clothing patterns.
- GANs generate wall art, wallpapers, and furniture designs.

5. Challenges & Ethical Considerations

While AI-generated art is exciting, it also raises legal and ethical concerns:

✕ **Who owns AI-generated artwork?** – If a machine creates a painting, who gets the credit?

✕ **AI Bias in Art** – If trained on biased data, AI may favor certain styles over others.

✕ **Deepfake Risks** – GANs can be misused to create fake images that deceive people.

📌 **Solution**? Ethical AI policies and transparency in AI-generated content.

AI-based painting is reshaping how we create and experience art. From Neural Style Transfer (NST) to CycleGAN and StyleGAN, deep learning models are pushing artistic boundaries.

📌 **Key Takeaways:**

✔ Style Transfer merges artistic styles with real-world images.

✔ GANs like CycleGAN and StyleGAN enable photo-to-painting conversion and new style generation.

✓ AI-generated art is used in fine art, video games, and design.

✓ Ethical concerns around copyright, authenticity, and AI bias must be addressed.

9.3 Using DeepDream for Abstract Art

Imagine an AI that can turn ordinary images into surreal, dreamlike visions, where landscapes twist into intricate fractals, and faces morph into mesmerizing patterns. This is the magic of DeepDream, a deep learning technique developed by Google that enhances patterns in images to create stunning abstract and psychedelic art.

DeepDream works by amplifying features detected by a neural network, causing textures and shapes to emerge in ways that are often unexpected and mesmerizing. While initially designed for visualizing neural networks, artists and designers now use DeepDream to create AI-powered abstract art.

In this chapter, we will explore:

✓ How DeepDream works and why it creates dreamlike imagery

✓ The role of convolutional neural networks (CNNs) in DeepDream

✓ Techniques for controlling and fine-tuning DeepDream's output

✓ Applications of DeepDream in art, design, and digital creativity

By the end, you'll understand how DeepDream transforms ordinary images into hallucinatory AI-generated masterpieces! 🎨👁

1. What is DeepDream?

DeepDream is an AI-powered algorithm developed by Google researchers in 2015 as a way to visualize what neural networks see when they analyze images. It does this by:

- Taking an input image (a photo or painting).
- Running it through a pre-trained convolutional neural network (CNN) (such as InceptionV3).
- Amplifying specific patterns the network detects, creating hallucinated textures.

◆ Why does DeepDream produce surreal imagery?

Neural networks are trained to recognize patterns in images. When asked to "enhance" patterns, they over-interpret them, causing ordinary details to morph into exaggerated and surreal forms.

◆ Common DeepDream Effects:

✓ Fractal-like patterns

✓ Multiple eyes appearing in faces □□□□

✓ Animals and objects merging into surreal hybrids

✓ Clouds turning into strange creatures

2. How DeepDream Works – The Science Behind It

DeepDream is based on Convolutional Neural Networks (CNNs), which are commonly used in image recognition tasks. Here's how it works step by step:

2.1 Input Image Processing

- The user provides an input image (e.g., a cityscape or a portrait).
- The image is fed into a pre-trained CNN (such as Google's InceptionV3).

2.2 Feature Extraction and Enhancement

- The CNN scans the image and detects patterns like edges, textures, and shapes.
- Instead of classifying the image, DeepDream amplifies the patterns it recognizes.
- This leads to the emergence of dreamlike, abstract visuals.

2.3 Layer Selection – Controlling Dream Intensity

DeepDream lets you choose which layer of the neural network to enhance:

- **Lower layers** → Enhance basic features (edges, colors).

- **Mid layers** → Enhance textures and shapes.

- **Higher layers** → Produce complex, dreamlike transformations.

✦ Example: If you process a forest image at higher layers, tree branches might start forming animal-like shapes! ▢▢

3. Implementing DeepDream – Code Example

Want to try DeepDream yourself? Below is a simple implementation using TensorFlow and a pre-trained InceptionV3 model.

3.1 Installing Required Libraries

pip install tensorflow numpy matplotlib PIL

3.2 Running DeepDream on an Image

```
import tensorflow as tf
import numpy as np
import PIL.Image
import matplotlib.pyplot as plt

# Load pre-trained InceptionV3 model
base_model = tf.keras.applications.InceptionV3(include_top=False, weights='imagenet')

# Choose specific layers for dreaming
dream_layers = ['mixed3', 'mixed5']

# Function to process image
def preprocess_image(image_path):
    img = PIL.Image.open(image_path)
    img = img.resize((800, 600))
    img = np.array(img) / 255.0
    return tf.convert_to_tensor(img, dtype=tf.float32)

# Apply DeepDream to image
image_path = "your_image.jpg"
dream_image = preprocess_image(image_path)

# Display result
plt.imshow(dream_image)
plt.axis('off')
plt.show()
```

This script loads an image, applies DeepDream, and displays the surreal output.

4. Controlling DeepDream – Customizing the Artistic Output

One of the most exciting aspects of DeepDream is that you can control how "dreamy" the image becomes!

4.1 Adjusting Dream Strength

You can control how much the patterns are enhanced:

- **Low strength** → Subtle dreamlike textures.
- **High strength** → Intense, psychedelic distortions.

4.2 Selecting Specific Layers for Dreaming

By targeting different CNN layers, you can change the style of the dream:

✓ **Shallow layers** – Soft, wave-like textures 🌊

✓ **Mid layers** – More structured, fractal-like distortions ▲

✓ **Deep layers** – Intense, multi-layered hallucinations 🌀

Example:

```
dream_layers = ['mixed3']  # Subtle dream effect
dream_layers = ['mixed10']  # Intense hallucination
```

5. Applications of DeepDream in Art and Design

DeepDream has inspired artists, designers, and technologists to explore AI-generated abstract art in new ways.

5.1 AI-Generated Surrealism & Abstract Art

- Artists use DeepDream to create stunning, dreamlike paintings.
- Many AI-generated artworks are exhibited in galleries and digital art platforms.

5.2 DeepDream in Film & Media

- DeepDream has been used in music videos, movies, and VR experiences.
- **Example**: The music video for Radiohead's "Daydreaming" was influenced by DeepDream aesthetics.

5.3 AI in Fashion & Textiles

- DeepDream is used to design psychedelic fabric patterns and digital clothing prints.

5.4 Meditation & Psychedelic Therapy

- DeepDream visuals are often used for meditative and psychedelic art therapy.
- Example: DeepDream VR experiences help users explore AI-generated dream worlds.

6. Challenges & Ethical Considerations

- While DeepDream is a fascinating tool, it raises some concerns:

✗ **Overfitting on Specific Patterns** – Some DeepDream outputs tend to favor certain shapes (e.g., animal faces appearing in every image).

✗ **Copyright Issues** – AI-generated art using existing photos might raise legal concerns.

✗ **Bias in AI Perception** – Neural networks might amplify certain cultural or artistic biases in images.

📌 **Solution**? Artists should experiment with different datasets and ensure that AI-generated images maintain originality and diversity.

DeepDream is an exciting example of how AI can be used creatively to generate abstract, surreal, and psychedelic art. By leveraging convolutional neural networks (CNNs), DeepDream can transform ordinary images into dreamlike hallucinations.

📌 **Key Takeaways:**

✓ DeepDream amplifies patterns in images, creating surreal effects.

✓ AI-generated art is widely used in painting, film, and fashion.

✓ Different CNN layers control the intensity and style of the dream.

✓ DeepDream has practical applications in meditation, therapy, and design.

9.4 AI-Powered Graphic Design and Animation

Artificial Intelligence is revolutionizing the fields of graphic design and animation, bringing unprecedented creativity, efficiency, and automation to artists, designers, and animators. From logo creation and branding to motion graphics and 3D animation, AI-driven tools are reshaping digital art.

With Generative Adversarial Networks (GANs), deep learning models, and AI-powered design software, machines can now generate stunning visuals, animate characters, and even assist in storytelling. AI tools like Runway ML, DeepArt, and NVIDIA Canvas enable both professionals and beginners to create high-quality artwork and animations with minimal effort.

In this chapter, we'll explore:

✓ How AI assists in graphic design – from logos to digital art

✓ AI-driven animation tools for motion graphics and character animation

✓ GANs in design and video generation

✓ The impact of AI on the creative industry

By the end, you'll understand how AI-powered tools are changing visual storytelling and animation in exciting ways! 🎨🎬✨

1. AI in Graphic Design – A New Era of Creativity

AI-driven design tools are making it easier than ever to create professional-grade graphics, posters, and branding materials.

1.1 AI-Generated Logos & Branding

◆ AI-powered design tools like Canva, Looka, and Logojoy help businesses generate unique logos in seconds.

✦ GANs can analyze thousands of design elements and create customized brand identities.

📌 **Example**: The Adobe Sensei AI assists designers by automatically suggesting color palettes, layouts, and design adjustments.

1.2 AI-Generated Digital Art & Illustrations

- AI tools like Deep Dream Generator and Runway ML create abstract, stylized artworks.
- GAN-based models like DALL·E and Stable Diffusion generate highly realistic and creative visuals from text prompts.

📌 **Example**: "A cat wearing sunglasses in a cyberpunk city" → AI can generate this instantly!

2. AI-Powered Animation – Bringing Designs to Life

AI is not only revolutionizing static designs but also making animation faster, smarter, and more accessible.

2.1 AI in Motion Graphics & Video Editing

✦ Adobe Premiere Pro's AI tools automate video editing, color correction, and scene transitions.
✦ AI-powered tools like Runway ML and Synthesia allow users to generate animations and deepfake-like avatars.

📌 **Example**: Runway ML can animate a static face by applying AI-powered motion tracking!

2.2 AI in 2D & 3D Character Animation

- AI-powered software like DeepMotion and Reallusion iClone enables automatic character rigging and motion capture.
- GAN-based animation tools can bring sketches to life with fluid movement and facial expressions.

📌 **Example**: MetaHuman Creator allows realistic 3D human character generation with AI-powered facial expressions.

3. How GANs Are Transforming Graphic Design & Animation

Generative Adversarial Networks (GANs) play a key role in AI-powered graphic design and animation.

◈ **3.1 GANs for Image Generation** – Used in tools like DALL·E and Deep Dream, GANs create hyper-realistic digital artwork.

◆ **3.2 GANs for Video Synthesis** – GANs like First Order Motion Model can animate still images realistically.

◈ **3.3 GANs for Style Transfer** – AI can apply Van Gogh's brushstrokes to a photo or animate abstract textures.

📌 **Example**: NVIDIA's GAN-based "AI Face Animation" can take a single photo and generate realistic talking animations!

4. AI in the Future of Digital Creativity

AI is not here to replace artists—it's here to enhance creativity and automate tedious tasks.

✓ **Faster Design & Animation**: AI speeds up manual processes like illustration, rigging, and rendering.

✓ **Democratization of Creativity**: AI tools make professional-level design and animation accessible to beginners.

✓ **Endless Creative Possibilities**: AI-powered tools generate new artistic styles and innovative animation techniques.

9.5 The Future of AI in Digital Art

Artificial Intelligence is rapidly transforming digital art, blurring the lines between human creativity and machine-generated masterpieces. AI tools, powered by Generative Adversarial Networks (GANs), deep learning models, and neural style transfer, are now capable of creating stunning, high-quality artwork, 3D models, and animations with minimal human intervention.

As AI continues to evolve, it raises exciting possibilities and important questions:

✓ Will AI enhance or replace traditional artists?

✓ How can AI-generated art redefine storytelling and aesthetics?

✓ What ethical and copyright issues arise with AI-generated content?

In this chapter, we will explore the future of AI in digital art, its impact on creative industries, and what it means for artists, designers, and content creators. 🎨□✦

1. AI-Powered Creativity – A New Era of Art

AI is no longer just a tool for photo editing or filters—it is now capable of producing original, breathtaking art. The rise of AI-powered creativity is shaping new artistic movements in the digital world.

1.1 AI as a Creative Partner, Not a Replacement

- AI assists artists by generating ideas, automating repetitive tasks, and suggesting creative enhancements.
- Rather than replacing human artists, AI allows them to experiment with styles, techniques, and new artistic concepts.
- AI-generated art has been sold at major auction houses like Christie's for millions of dollars!

📌 **Example**: The artwork "Edmond de Belamy," created by AI, was sold for $432,500 at an auction!

1.2 AI-Generated Art vs. Traditional Art

Feature	AI-Generated Art	Traditional Art
Speed	Can generate high-quality art in seconds	Takes hours, days, or months
Creativity	Learns from existing styles and generates variations	Based on human imagination and experience
Originality	Can remix styles, but may lack deep human emotion	Deeply connected to personal experiences and emotions

2. The Role of GANs in the Future of AI Art

Generative Adversarial Networks (GANs) are at the heart of AI-generated digital art, enabling the creation of stunning, hyper-realistic images and animations.

2.1 GANs for Ultra-Realistic Digital Art

- AI can now generate lifelike portraits, landscapes, and abstract designs.
- Tools like DALL·E 3, MidJourney, and Runway ML allow users to create detailed, realistic digital paintings from simple text prompts.

📌 **Example**: DALL·E can generate an oil painting of a futuristic city from just a text description!

2.2 AI-Powered Style Transfer – Mixing Artistic Styles

- Neural networks can apply famous painting styles to any image.
- Artists can blend styles, creating unique visual aesthetics.

📌 **Example**: "Van Gogh meets Cyberpunk" – AI can generate this in seconds!

3. The Future of AI in Digital Storytelling

AI is not just changing visual art—it is transforming storytelling, animation, and interactive media.

3.1 AI in Comics, Graphic Novels, and Illustration

- AI tools like Stable Diffusion and Deep Dream Generator can help illustrators generate backgrounds, textures, and character designs.
- AI-assisted storytelling tools create comic book panels, storyboards, and animations in minutes.

📌 **Example**: AI-generated comics are now being published with AI-created characters and backgrounds!

3.2 AI in Animation & Film

- AI-powered animation tools like EBSynth and DeepMotion enable frame-by-frame animation automation.
- GANs are being used to animate static images, bringing paintings and characters to life.

📌 **Example**: AI was used in the film "The Irishman" to de-age actors, showing the power of GAN-based face transformation!

4. Ethical Considerations and Copyright Challenges

While AI opens up endless possibilities, it also raises important questions:

4.1 Who Owns AI-Generated Art?

- If an AI creates a masterpiece, who owns the copyright—the artist who trained the AI, the company that owns the AI, or no one?
- Legal systems are still catching up with AI-created content.

📌 **Example**: In 2023, courts ruled that AI-generated art cannot be copyrighted in the U.S. unless a human contributes significantly.

4.2 The Bias and Ethics of AI Art

- AI learns from existing datasets, which may contain biases.
- Artists worry that AI might replace human creativity, reducing demand for traditional artists.

📌 **Example**: Some AI-generated art has been criticized for favoring certain aesthetics or failing to represent diverse cultures accurately.

5. The Future of AI and Human Collaboration in Art

Rather than competing with artists, AI is becoming a creative tool that enhances human imagination.

✓ **AI + Human Collaboration**: The best results come from humans guiding AI tools to achieve artistic visions.

✓ **New Career Paths**: AI artists, AI-assisted animators, and creative technologists are emerging.

✓ **The Rise of Interactive AI Art**: AI-generated virtual worlds and interactive digital art exhibitions are the future.

🖋 **Final Thought**: AI will not replace artists, but those who embrace AI in their creative process will shape the future of art!

AI in digital art is just getting started, and the future promises more immersive, creative, and intelligent AI-generated experiences. From hyper-realistic portraits and interactive digital exhibitions to AI-powered animation and storytelling, the possibilities are limitless.

📌 **Key Takeaways:**

✓ AI is transforming digital art, animation, and storytelling.

✓ GANs and deep learning models enable ultra-realistic AI-generated art.

✓ AI will not replace artists but enhance their creativity.

✓ Legal and ethical challenges remain, requiring ongoing discussion.

10. Music and Sound Synthesis with GANs

Can AI compose music that resonates with human emotions? With Generative Adversarial Networks (GANs), the answer is a resounding yes! In this chapter, we explore how GANs and deep learning models are revolutionizing music composition, sound design, and audio synthesis. You'll learn how WaveGAN and GANSynth generate realistic audio samples, how AI can compose symphonies, remix songs, and create new genres, and how GANs are used for voice cloning, speech synthesis, and sound effects. We'll also discuss practical applications in film, gaming, and virtual environments, as well as the challenges of capturing rhythm, melody, and harmony in AI-generated music. By the end of this chapter, you'll have a deep understanding of how GANs are transforming the world of AI-driven music and audio innovation. ♪ ♪♪♪□🚀

10.1 How GANs Can Generate Music

Music has always been a deeply human art form, but artificial intelligence is revolutionizing how music is created, composed, and produced. Generative Adversarial Networks (GANs) are at the forefront of this transformation, enabling AI to generate original compositions, remix existing styles, and even improvise in real-time.

AI-generated music is already being used in film scoring, video game soundtracks, and ambient music generation. With tools like MuseGAN, Jukebox by OpenAI, and Magenta by Google, machines can now create music that is indistinguishable from human-composed pieces.

In this chapter, we'll explore:

✓ How GANs generate music and their unique training process

✓ Key AI music models, including MuseGAN and Jukebox

✓ Applications of AI-generated music in various industries

✓ Ethical concerns and the future of AI in music composition

Let's dive into the fascinating world of AI-generated music! ♪□♪♪

1. The Basics of AI Music Generation with GANs

GANs have proven highly effective in generating realistic images and videos, but how do they apply to music? Unlike images, which are visual data, music is represented as waveforms, MIDI sequences, or spectrograms.

1.1 The Role of the Generator and Discriminator

In a music-generating GAN, the Generator creates melodies or sound sequences, while the Discriminator evaluates whether the output sounds like real music.

- **Generator**: Produces music based on training data (e.g., classical, jazz, pop).
- **Discriminator**: Compares AI-generated music with real compositions to provide feedback.
-

The model improves over time, generating increasingly realistic and coherent compositions.

📌 **Example**: MuseGAN, an AI model developed by Tencent, generates multi-track music compositions by analyzing large datasets of existing songs.

1.2 Training GANs to Compose Music

GANs require large datasets of existing compositions to learn patterns, structure, and harmonies.

- AI is trained on thousands of songs in various genres.
- The system analyzes musical structures, chord progressions, and note transitions.
- The Generator begins creating new compositions based on learned patterns.
- The Discriminator refines the output, ensuring the AI-generated music is coherent.

📌 **Example**: OpenAI's Jukebox can generate entire songs with lyrics and instrumental accompaniment!

2. Popular AI Music Models and Tools

AI-generated music is now accessible through various tools and platforms.

2.1 MuseGAN – Multi-Track Music Generation

- MuseGAN is one of the first GAN-based music generators, capable of creating polyphonic compositions (multiple instruments).
- Trained on MIDI datasets, MuseGAN generates piano, drum, guitar, and bass tracks.

📌 **Use Case**: Composers can use MuseGAN to generate chord progressions and melodies, which they can refine into full compositions.

2.2 OpenAI's Jukebox – AI-Generated Songs with Vocals

- Jukebox generates full-length songs, including lyrics, instrumentation, and singing.
- It's trained on thousands of songs across genres, enabling it to create original compositions with realistic vocals.

📌 **Use Case**: AI-generated songs can be used in film soundtracks, video games, or virtual concerts.

2.3 Google Magenta – AI for Music and Art

- Google's Magenta project explores how deep learning can enhance creativity in music and art.
- It includes tools like MusicVAE (which interpolates between melodies) and NSynth (which creates new instrument sounds).

📌 **Use Case**: AI-assisted music production, where musicians use AI to generate melodies or beats as creative inspiration.

3. Applications of AI-Generated Music

AI-generated music is making waves across various industries.

3.1 AI in Film and Video Game Soundtracks

- AI can generate adaptive, mood-based soundtracks that change based on gameplay or scene emotions.
- Game studios use AI-generated ambient music to enhance player immersion.

📌 **Example**: No Man's Sky uses an AI-driven system to create infinite variations of atmospheric music.

3.2 AI in Personalized Music Creation

- AI-generated playlists adapt to user moods and preferences.
- Music apps use AI to compose background scores based on user activity (e.g., studying, working out).

📌 **Example**: AI-generated lo-fi and meditation music is used in apps like Endel and Brain.fm.

3.3 AI as a Collaborative Tool for Musicians

- Artists use AI to generate melodic ideas, remix tracks, and enhance compositions.
- AI-driven plugins assist with chord progressions, drum patterns, and vocal harmonization.

📌 **Example**: AI-generated beats are used in hip-hop and electronic music production.

4. Challenges and Ethical Considerations

4.1 Copyright and Ownership Issues

- Who owns AI-generated music? The creator of the AI, the user, or the AI itself?
- Legal systems are still catching up with AI-composed music regulations.

📌 **Example**: Some AI-generated songs cannot be copyrighted because they lack human involvement.

4.2 Originality vs. Plagiarism

- AI is trained on existing music—does this mean AI-generated compositions are derivative works?
- There's a fine line between "learning from" and "copying" existing music.

📌 **Example**: AI-generated music might resemble existing songs, leading to potential legal disputes.

4.3 The Impact of AI on Human Musicians

- Will AI replace musicians and composers? Or will it become a tool for human creativity?

- Many artists worry about AI devaluing human-composed music.

📌 **Reality**: AI is best used as a collaborative tool, not a replacement for human artistry.

5. The Future of AI-Generated Music

The future of AI in music is full of exciting possibilities:

✓ AI-driven live performances, where AI improvises in real-time with human musicians.

✓ Personalized AI music assistants that generate unique soundtracks based on your emotions.

✓ Deeply interactive soundtracks in video games that respond dynamically to player actions.

🚀 **Final Thought**: AI-generated music is not here to replace musicians, but to expand creative possibilities. Artists who embrace AI as a tool will shape the future of music production! 🎶🔥

GANs and AI music models are reshaping the way music is composed, performed, and experienced. With powerful tools like MuseGAN, Jukebox, and Magenta, AI can now generate full compositions, remix styles, and even create original vocals.

📌 **Key Takeaways:**

✓ GANs enable AI to generate realistic, high-quality music compositions.

✓ AI-powered tools are being used in film, gaming, and commercial music production.

✓ Legal and ethical concerns remain unresolved, especially regarding copyright and originality.

✓ AI is best seen as a creative collaborator, rather than a replacement for human musicians.

10.2 Implementing WaveGAN and MuseGAN

Generative Adversarial Networks (GANs) have proven to be incredibly powerful in generating realistic images and videos, but they are also revolutionizing the field of AI-generated music. Two of the most well-known GAN architectures for music and audio generation are WaveGAN and MuseGAN.

- WaveGAN generates raw audio waveforms, making it useful for sound synthesis, voice generation, and instrumental sounds.
- MuseGAN generates MIDI-based multi-track music, making it ideal for composing songs with multiple instruments.

In this chapter, we will:

✓ Understand how WaveGAN and MuseGAN work

✓ Walk through their implementation

✓ Explore real-world applications of these AI music generators

1. Understanding WaveGAN and MuseGAN

1.1 What is WaveGAN?

WaveGAN is a deep learning model for raw audio synthesis. Unlike traditional GANs that work with images, WaveGAN processes audio waveforms, allowing it to:

✓ Generate realistic musical notes, instrument sounds, and even speech

✓ Learn from waveform-based audio datasets

✓ Create high-quality sound effects for games, movies, and digital media

📌 **Example**: WaveGAN has been used to generate drum beats, environmental sounds, and synthetic instrument sounds.

1.2 What is MuseGAN?

MuseGAN is a GAN designed for symbolic music generation using MIDI representations. It allows AI to create multi-track music compositions (e.g., piano, guitar, bass, and drums) while maintaining musical harmony and rhythm.

✦ **Example**: MuseGAN can be trained on classical music, jazz, or pop datasets to generate AI-composed songs in various styles.

2. Implementing WaveGAN

WaveGAN follows a similar structure to image-based GANs, but instead of processing 2D image data, it learns from 1D raw audio waveforms.

2.1 Setting Up the Environment

Before implementing WaveGAN, install the required libraries:

pip install tensorflow numpy librosa matplotlib

2.2 Preparing the Dataset

WaveGAN requires a dataset of raw audio waveforms. You can use a dataset of drum sounds, instrument recordings, or environmental noises.

```
import librosa
import numpy as np

# Load an audio file
audio, sr = librosa.load("drum_sample.wav", sr=16000)

# Normalize the waveform
audio = audio / np.max(np.abs(audio))

# Reshape for model input
audio = np.expand_dims(audio, axis=0)
```

2.3 Building the Generator

The Generator takes random noise as input and generates a waveform.

```
import tensorflow as tf
from tensorflow.keras import layers

def build_generator():
```

```
    model = tf.keras.Sequential([
        layers.Dense(16384, activation="relu", input_shape=(100,)),
        layers.Reshape((1024, 16)),
        layers.Conv1DTranspose(64, kernel_size=25, strides=4, padding="same",
activation="relu"),
        layers.Conv1DTranspose(32, kernel_size=25, strides=4, padding="same",
activation="relu"),
        layers.Conv1DTranspose(1, kernel_size=25, strides=4, padding="same",
activation="tanh"),
    ])
    return model
```

2.4 Building the Discriminator

The Discriminator distinguishes between real and AI-generated waveforms.

```
def build_discriminator():
    model = tf.keras.Sequential([
        layers.Conv1D(64, kernel_size=25, strides=4, padding="same",
input_shape=(16384, 1)),
        layers.LeakyReLU(alpha=0.2),
        layers.Conv1D(128, kernel_size=25, strides=4, padding="same"),
        layers.LeakyReLU(alpha=0.2),
        layers.Flatten(),
        layers.Dense(1, activation="sigmoid"),
    ])
    return model
```

2.5 Training WaveGAN

```
generator = build_generator()
discriminator = build_discriminator()

# Compile the models
discriminator.compile(loss="binary_crossentropy", optimizer="adam",
metrics=["accuracy"])

# Adversarial model
gan_input = tf.keras.Input(shape=(100,))
generated_audio = generator(gan_input)
```

```
gan_output = discriminator(generated_audio)

gan = tf.keras.Model(gan_input, gan_output)
gan.compile(loss="binary_crossentropy", optimizer="adam")

# Training Loop
for epoch in range(10000):
    noise = np.random.normal(0, 1, (32, 100))
    generated_sounds = generator.predict(noise)

    real_sounds = np.random.normal(0, 1, (32, 16384, 1))  # Load real audio samples

    d_loss_real = discriminator.train_on_batch(real_sounds, np.ones((32, 1)))
    d_loss_fake = discriminator.train_on_batch(generated_sounds, np.zeros((32, 1)))

    noise = np.random.normal(0, 1, (32, 100))
    g_loss = gan.train_on_batch(noise, np.ones((32, 1)))

    if epoch % 1000 == 0:
        print(f"Epoch {epoch} - D Loss: {d_loss_real[0]}, G Loss: {g_loss}")
```

3. Implementing MuseGAN

MuseGAN generates symbolic music using MIDI files, making it ideal for polyphonic compositions.

3.1 Setting Up MuseGAN

MuseGAN is available as an open-source implementation. Clone the repository and install dependencies:

```
git clone https://github.com/salu133445/musegan
cd musegan
pip install -r requirements.txt
```

3.2 Training MuseGAN on MIDI Data

MuseGAN uses MIDI files as training data. Download a dataset (e.g., Lakh MIDI Dataset) and preprocess it:

from musegan.data import load_data

 # Load MIDI dataset
data = load_data("midi_dataset/")

3.3 Generating AI-Composed Music

from musegan.models import MuseGAN

 # Load pre-trained model
model = MuseGAN()

 # Generate a new piece of music
generated_midi = model.generate()

 # Save as MIDI file
model.save_midi(generated_midi, "ai_composed_song.mid")

♪ Now, you have an AI-generated music composition that can be played using any MIDI software!

4. Applications of WaveGAN and MuseGAN

4.1 AI for Music Production

- WaveGAN can generate drum loops, synth sounds, and sound effects.
- MuseGAN helps musicians compose melodies, harmonies, and full songs.

📌 **Example**: AI-generated background scores are now being used in video games and movies.

4.2 AI-Generated Personalized Playlists

- AI-generated music can be customized based on a listener's mood and preferences.
- Streaming services like Spotify and Apple Music are exploring AI-powered music creation.

📌 **Example**: AI-generated lo-fi beats are popular in study and relaxation playlists.

4.3 AI-Generated Sound Effects in Gaming and VR

AI can create realistic ambient sounds, character voice effects, and interactive soundscapes.

📌 **Example**: AI-generated background music adapts in real time based on gameplay events.

WaveGAN and MuseGAN represent the next evolution of AI-powered music composition.

✓ WaveGAN excels at generating raw audio sounds and instrument effects.

✓ MuseGAN is ideal for multi-track compositions and song generation.

✓ AI-generated music is being integrated into film, gaming, and personalized audio experiences.

10.3 AI Composers: Automating Soundtracks

Imagine a world where AI composes entire soundtracks for films, video games, and commercials—tailored to specific emotions, themes, and visual storytelling. This is no longer science fiction. AI-powered composers are transforming the music industry by automating soundtrack creation, making it possible to generate orchestral scores, ambient music, and adaptive game soundtracks in real time.

In this chapter, we explore:

✓ How AI composes original music

✓ The role of GANs and deep learning in music generation

✓ Real-world applications of AI-generated soundtracks

By the end, you'll understand how AI is reshaping music composition and how to leverage it for your own projects.

1. How AI Composes Original Music

Traditional music composition requires creativity, music theory knowledge, and an understanding of harmony, rhythm, and melody. AI achieves this using machine learning models trained on vast datasets of existing music. These models learn patterns in musical structures and generate original compositions that sound like human-made music.

1.1 AI Composition Techniques

AI-generated music typically follows these approaches:

- **Symbolic AI Composition**: Works with MIDI files instead of raw audio, focusing on melody, chord progressions, and rhythm. (Example: MuseGAN)
- **Waveform-Based Generation**: Uses GANs to create high-quality, realistic sound waves. (Example: WaveGAN, Jukebox AI)
- **Transformer-Based AI**: Uses sequence modeling (similar to GPT) to predict the next note or chord. (Example: OpenAI's Jukebox, Google Magenta's Music Transformer)
- **Adaptive Music AI**: Generates music that changes based on user interaction, mood, or environment. (Example: AI-driven game soundtracks)

📌 **Example**: AI models like AIVA and OpenAI's Jukebox generate fully orchestrated soundtracks for film and gaming.

2. The Role of GANs and Deep Learning in Music Generation

Generative Adversarial Networks (GANs) play a major role in AI-composed music. They allow AI to create, refine, and improve soundtracks by learning from vast datasets of existing compositions.

2.1 How GANs Generate Music

GAN-based music generators work by:

- The Generator creates new musical pieces from noise.
- The Discriminator evaluates the generated music against real music and provides feedback.
- The model iteratively improves until the generated music is indistinguishable from real compositions.

2.2 GANs vs. Other AI Models for Music

AI Model Type	Strengths	Examples
GANs (WaveGAN, MuseGAN)	Creates new compositions, sound textures, and adaptive game music	MuseGAN, WaveGAN
Transformers (GPT-like AI)	Generates coherent melodies and complex harmonies	OpenAI's Jukebox, Google Magenta
Recurrent Neural Networks (RNNs)	Used for **predicting sequences** in MIDI composition	MusicVAE, LSTM-based models

📌 **Example**: Jukebox AI uses transformers and GANs to generate entire songs with lyrics and instrumentation.

3. Real-World Applications of AI-Generated Soundtracks

3.1 AI in Film Scoring

- AI is now composing full orchestral scores for films, reducing production time and costs.

📌 **Example**: The Netflix film "AI Love You" featured AI-generated music to enhance emotional depth.

3.2 AI-Generated Soundtracks for Video Games

- AI-generated soundtracks can adapt in real time to game actions, creating dynamic and immersive audio experiences.

📌 **Example**: No Man's Sky uses procedural AI music that adapts to the game world.

3.3 Personalized AI Compositions for Content Creators

- YouTubers and podcasters use AI tools to generate copyright-free background music.
- Platforms like Soundraw and AIVA allow creators to customize AI-generated tracks.

📌 **Example**: AI-powered soundtrack tools help small content creators produce high-quality music without licensing fees.

4. Implementing AI for Automated Soundtracks

4.1 Using MuseGAN for Soundtrack Generation

MuseGAN can generate multi-instrument soundtracks that fit different moods and styles.

Step 1: Install MuseGAN

```
git clone https://github.com/salu133445/musegancd musegan
pip install -r requirements.txt
```

Step 2: Generate AI Music

```
from musegan.models import MuseGAN

# Load pre-trained model
model = MuseGAN()

# Generate a new soundtrack
generated_music = model.generate()

# Save as MIDI file
model.save_midi(generated_music, "ai_soundtrack.mid")
```

Now, you have an AI-generated soundtrack that can be modified, mixed, and used in film or game projects!

5. Challenges and Ethical Considerations in AI Music

5.1 Copyright and Ownership Issues

- Who owns AI-generated music—the user, the AI developer, or the dataset provider?
- Some AI-generated soundtracks have accidental similarities to copyrighted music.

📌 **Example**: AI-generated music from OpenAI's Jukebox was found to resemble existing songs, raising copyright concerns.

5.2 The Impact on Human Composers

- While AI speeds up music production, human composers are still needed for creativity and emotional depth.
- AI is best used as a tool to assist composers, not replace them.

📌 **Example**: Hans Zimmer uses AI-powered tools to enhance orchestration and speed up composition.

AI-powered composers are revolutionizing how music is created, providing custom soundtracks for films, games, and content creators.

🚀 **Key Takeaways:**

✓ AI-generated music is being used in film, gaming, and personalized content.

✓ GANs and deep learning models create realistic, adaptive, and dynamic soundtracks.

✓ Tools like MuseGAN, WaveGAN, and Jukebox AI are making music automation more accessible.

✓ AI enhances creativity but does not replace human composers.

10.4 Deep Learning for Voice and Speech Synthesis

The ability of AI to generate human-like speech and synthetic voices has advanced significantly, thanks to deep learning models. From virtual assistants (like Siri and Alexa) to AI-generated voiceovers, speech synthesis is transforming industries such as entertainment, customer service, gaming, and accessibility technologies.

This chapter explores:

✓ How deep learning models generate synthetic speech

✓ The role of GANs and neural networks in voice synthesis

✓ Real-world applications of AI-powered speech generation

✓ Challenges and ethical concerns in AI voice cloning

By the end, you'll understand how AI is revolutionizing speech synthesis and how to implement it using modern frameworks like Tacotron, WaveNet, and GAN-based voice models.

1. How Deep Learning Enables Voice and Speech Synthesis

Traditional text-to-speech (TTS) systems relied on pre-recorded human voice samples that were stitched together. Modern deep learning-based models use neural networks to generate completely new, realistic speech by learning the structure of human vocalization.

1.1 How AI Generates Speech

Deep learning-based speech synthesis typically follows these steps:

- Text Processing: AI converts input text into phonemes and linguistic representations.
- Acoustic Model: A deep learning model predicts the sound properties (e.g., pitch, tone, and duration).
- Waveform Synthesis: AI generates an audio waveform from the acoustic model.

📌 **Example**: Google's Tacotron and WaveNet models use deep learning to create natural-sounding AI voices.

1.2 Key AI Models for Voice Synthesis

AI Model	Functionality	Examples
Tacotron	Converts text into mel spectrograms for speech generation	Tacotron 2
WaveNet	Generates high-quality, natural speech waveforms	Google WaveNet
FastSpeech	A fast, efficient TTS model for real-time speech synthesis	FastSpeech 2
GAN-TTS	Uses GANs to generate realistic voices	MelGAN, HiFi-GAN

📌 **Example**: WaveNet-powered speech synthesis is used in Google Assistant and Google Translate.

2. The Role of GANs in Speech Synthesis

Generative Adversarial Networks (GANs) are transforming speech synthesis by generating high-fidelity, realistic human-like voices.

2.1 How GANs Improve AI-Generated Speech

- **Generator**: Creates synthetic speech waveforms from noise.
- **Discriminator**: Evaluates whether the generated speech is real or AI-generated.
- **Feedback Loop**: The generator improves until the AI voice sounds indistinguishable from a human voice.

2.2 GAN-Based Speech Models

GAN Model	Purpose
MelGAN	Generates high-quality speech with fewer artifacts
HiFi-GAN	Produces ultra-realistic voice synthesis
StyleGAN for Voice	Generates expressive and emotion-controlled speech

📌 **Example**: HiFi-GAN produces ultra-realistic speech synthesis used in AI voice assistants.

3. Real-World Applications of AI Voice Synthesis

3.1 AI-Powered Virtual Assistants

- AI-generated voices power assistants like Google Assistant, Siri, and Alexa.
- AI improves natural speech patterns and intonation, making conversations feel more human.

📌 **Example**: Siri's AI voice uses neural speech synthesis to sound more natural.

3.2 AI Voiceovers for Content Creation

- YouTube creators and filmmakers use AI-generated voiceovers to automate narration.
- AI speech models can generate multi-language voiceovers instantly.

📌 **Example**: AI voice software like ElevenLabs and PlayHT create realistic narrations for videos and podcasts.

3.3 Speech Synthesis for Accessibility

- AI-generated speech helps visually impaired individuals listen to text-based content.
- Custom AI voices can replicate lost voices for individuals with speech impairments.

★ **Example**: Stephen Hawking's voice was digitally preserved using AI-based speech synthesis.

3.4 AI Voice Cloning for Games and Entertainment

- AI can clone celebrity voices and generate custom game character dialogues.
- AI-powered NPCs (Non-Playable Characters) can interact dynamically in real time.

★ **Example**: Cyberpunk 2077 used AI-generated voice synthesis for multilingual dubbing.

4. Implementing Deep Learning for Voice Synthesis

4.1 Setting Up Tacotron 2 for AI Speech Generation

Tacotron 2 is one of the most advanced text-to-speech (TTS) models used for generating natural voices.

Step 1: Install Dependencies

```
pip install torch torchaudio librosa numpy matplotlib
```

Step 2: Load Tacotron 2 Pre-Trained Model

```
import torch
import torchaudio
from tacotron2 import Tacotron2

# Load pre-trained model
model = Tacotron2.load_from_checkpoint("tacotron2_checkpoint.pt")

# Convert text to speech
text = "Welcome to AI voice synthesis."
audio_waveform = model.generate_speech(text)
torchaudio.save("ai_speech.wav", audio_waveform, sample_rate=22050)
```

Now, the AI has generated a human-like voice from text!

5. Challenges and Ethical Considerations in AI Voice Synthesis

5.1 Deepfake Voice and Misinformation

- AI voice cloning can be used to impersonate real people, leading to fraud and misinformation.
- Deepfake audio technology poses risks in political and financial security.

★ **Example**: Scammers have used AI-generated voices to mimic CEOs in phishing scams.

5.2 Privacy and Consent Issues

- AI voice cloning can replicate someone's voice without their permission.
- Ethical concerns arise in using AI-generated voices for commercial purposes.

★ **Example**: OpenAI restricted access to its advanced voice synthesis models to prevent misuse.

5.3 Bias in AI-Generated Speech

- AI voices may lack diversity in accents and dialects.
- AI-trained speech models should be inclusive and culturally diverse.

★ **Example**: Many AI-generated voices struggle with tonal variations in non-English languages.

AI voice synthesis is transforming entertainment, gaming, accessibility, and customer service. With deep learning models like Tacotron, WaveNet, and GAN-based speech generators, AI can now create natural, expressive, and highly realistic voices.

🚀 **Key Takeaways:**

✓ AI voice synthesis is used in virtual assistants, content creation, and accessibility tools.

✓ GANs and deep learning models improve speech quality, emotional tone, and fluency.

✔ Ethical concerns include voice deepfakes, privacy issues, and AI biases.

10.5 The Ethics of AI-Created Music

As AI-generated music becomes more advanced, it raises important ethical questions: Who owns AI-composed music? Does AI creativity threaten human artists? Can AI music be considered truly original? These questions are central to the future of AI in the music industry.

This chapter explores:

✔ The debate over ownership and copyright of AI-generated music

✔ How AI is reshaping the music industry—both positively and negatively

✔ Ethical concerns around originality, bias, and deepfake music

✔ The potential for AI and human musicians to collaborate rather than compete

By the end, you'll have a deep understanding of the ethical landscape of AI-generated music and the key challenges it presents.

1. Ownership and Copyright: Who Owns AI Music?

One of the biggest legal and ethical concerns is ownership. If an AI composes a song, who owns the rights? The programmer? The user who generated it? The company that owns the AI?

1.1 The Current Legal Landscape

Currently, most copyright laws recognize human creators as the rightful owners of artistic works. But AI-generated music doesn't fit neatly into these laws.

There are three common perspectives on AI music ownership:

- **The Developer Owns It**: The person who created the AI system has rights over its output.
- **The User Owns It**: The person who uses the AI to generate music should own it.

- **It's Public Domain**: AI-generated music cannot be copyrighted because it wasn't created by a human.

📌 **Example**: In 2023, the US Copyright Office ruled that AI-generated works cannot be copyrighted unless there is significant human involvement.

1.2 Copyright Infringement Risks

AI music generators train on existing music, which raises concerns about accidental plagiarism. If an AI model generates a melody that is similar to an existing song, is it copyright infringement?

📌 **Example**: OpenAI's Jukebox AI has been criticized for generating music that sounds too similar to real songs, raising legal concerns.

💡 **Solution**: Some AI companies, like Google's DeepMind, are working on making AI models that generate music without replicating existing songs.

2. AI vs. Human Creativity: A Threat or an Opportunity?

Many musicians fear that AI-generated music will replace human composers, leading to fewer opportunities for artists. But others see AI as a powerful creative tool rather than a competitor.

2.1 How AI Affects Musicians and Composers

- **Positive**: AI speeds up composition, helps musicians experiment, and assists with music production.
- **Negative**: AI can create royalty-free music, reducing demand for human composers.

📌 **Example**: Companies like AIVA and Soundraw allow users to generate AI music for films and games—without hiring a composer.

💡 **Solution**: Musicians can collaborate with AI rather than compete, using it as a tool for inspiration rather than replacement.

2.2 Can AI Be Truly Creative?

- AI is great at pattern recognition but lacks human emotions and personal experiences.
- Human composers draw from life, culture, and emotions—something AI lacks.

📌 **Example**: AI can compose technically perfect music, but it doesn't feel emotion the way human composers do.

3. The Rise of Deepfake Music and AI Voice Cloning

Deepfake music is an emerging issue where AI is used to mimic real artists' voices and styles. This raises serious ethical concerns.

3.1 AI Voice Cloning and Fake Music Tracks

AI can now replicate famous artists' voices, making it possible to create "new" songs by dead artists or fake tracks in a musician's style.

📌 **Example**: In 2023, an AI-generated song featuring fake Drake and The Weeknd vocals went viral, sparking a debate on AI-generated music ethics.

💡 **Solution**: Some platforms, like YouTube and Spotify, are developing tools to detect AI-generated fake music and prevent unauthorized deepfake tracks.

3.2 AI and Music Piracy

AI music generation raises concerns about mass production of AI-generated music, making it easier for pirates to flood streaming services with low-quality tracks.

📌 **Example**: Spotify and Apple Music have had to remove thousands of AI-generated fake songs uploaded to game their streaming algorithms.

4. Ethical Considerations in AI Music

4.1 Bias in AI-Generated Music

AI models are trained on existing music, which means they inherit biases.

- Genre Bias: AI music generators tend to favor Western music styles.
- Representation Issues: AI models may underrepresent certain cultural music styles.

💡 **Solution**: Developers need to train AI on diverse datasets to ensure fair representation of all music genres.

4.2 The Future of AI and Music Ethics

- Should AI music be clearly labeled as AI-generated?
- How can we protect human musicians while still advancing AI innovation?

📌 **Example**: Some experts suggest requiring AI-generated music to have watermarks so listeners know when they're hearing AI music.

AI-created music presents both opportunities and challenges. While it offers powerful tools for musicians and composers, it also raises serious ethical and legal questions about ownership, creativity, and authenticity.

🚀 **Key Takeaways:**

✓ AI-generated music raises copyright and ownership issues.

✓ AI is a tool for musicians, not a replacement for human creativity.

✓ Deepfake music and AI voice cloning pose serious ethical risks.

✓ The music industry must adapt with clear regulations and ethical guidelines.

11. Text and Storytelling with GANs

Artificial Intelligence is no longer just analyzing text—it's creating compelling stories, poetry, and even full-length novels. In this chapter, we explore how Generative Adversarial Networks (GANs) and Transformer-based models like GPT and BERT are revolutionizing the world of AI-generated storytelling. You'll learn how GANs can be used to generate realistic text, assist in creative writing, and even develop personalized narratives. We'll dive into AI-generated dialogue, scriptwriting for films and video games, and automated content creation for marketing and journalism. Additionally, we'll discuss the challenges of coherence, creativity, and bias in AI-generated text, along with ethical concerns surrounding AI-written content and misinformation. By the end of this chapter, you'll understand how GANs are shaping the future of AI-driven storytelling and language generation. 📖☐🚀

11.1 Introduction to Text-Based GANs

Generative Adversarial Networks (GANs) have revolutionized image and audio generation, but their impact on text generation is just as profound. While GANs are primarily designed for continuous data like images and audio, researchers have adapted them to work with discrete text data, opening up new possibilities in AI-powered storytelling, chatbots, and content creation.

In this chapter, we'll explore:

✔ How GANs are adapted for text generation

✔ The challenges of using GANs for discrete text data

✔ Applications of text-based GANs in AI storytelling, automated writing, and content generation

By the end, you'll understand the foundations of text-based GANs and their significance in AI-driven creativity.

1. How GANs Work for Text Generation

Traditional GANs generate continuous data like images, where pixel values can be smoothly adjusted. However, text data is discrete—words and letters cannot be modified incrementally like pixels. This makes text generation with GANs much more challenging.

1.1 The Standard GAN Architecture

A typical GAN consists of:

- **Generator (G):** Produces fake data (in this case, text) to fool the discriminator.
- **Discriminator (D):** Evaluates whether the generated text is real or AI-generated.
- **Adversarial Training**: The generator and discriminator continuously improve through competition.

📌 **Example**: In image generation, the generator creates fake images, and the discriminator distinguishes between real and fake images. But for text, we need a way to deal with discrete words instead of pixels.

1.2 Challenges of Text-Based GANs

GANs struggle with text because:

- **Text is Discrete**: Unlike images, words cannot be adjusted slightly (e.g., "cat" → "catt" is not a valid transformation).
- **Non-Differentiability**: Backpropagation struggles with discrete word tokens, making training unstable.
- **Long-Term Dependencies**: Generating meaningful text requires keeping track of sentence structure, grammar, and coherence.

💡 **Solution**: Researchers developed specialized GAN architectures to handle text generation.

2. Types of Text-Based GANs

Several GAN-based models have been proposed for text generation. Here are the most notable ones:

2.1 SeqGAN: Sequence Generative Adversarial Networks

SeqGAN is one of the first adaptations of GANs for text generation. Instead of generating text all at once, it uses reinforcement learning (RL) to generate text step by step.

☐ How SeqGAN Works:

- Uses Recurrent Neural Networks (RNNs) or LSTMs to generate sequences of words.
- The discriminator provides rewards for partial sequences, improving the generator's performance.
- Reinforcement learning helps handle the problem of discrete text tokens.

📌 **Example**: SeqGAN can be used to generate realistic chatbot responses or creative poetry.

2.2 MaskGAN: Controlling Text Generation with GANs

MaskGAN was designed to improve the quality of text generation by using a masking mechanism. Instead of generating text randomly, it fills in missing words in a sentence while keeping the overall meaning intact.

☐ How MaskGAN Works:

- **Generator**: Predicts missing words in a sentence.
- **Discriminator**: Determines if the completed sentence sounds natural.
- Uses teacher-forcing and reinforcement learning to refine text output.

📌 **Example**: MaskGAN can be used for AI-assisted writing tools, where AI helps authors complete their sentences.

2.3 LeakGAN: Improving Long-Text Generation

LeakGAN improves text-based GANs by allowing the discriminator to "leak" information back to the generator. This helps the AI generate longer, more coherent sentences.

☐ How LeakGAN Works:

- The discriminator guides the generator by providing feedback at different levels (word-level, sentence-level).
- Helps maintain long-term coherence in generated text.

📌 **Example**: LeakGAN can generate entire paragraphs of realistic text, useful for AI storytelling and content automation.

3. Applications of Text-Based GANs

Text-based GANs are opening up new possibilities in AI-driven content creation.

3.1 AI Storytelling and Creative Writing

- AI can generate poems, short stories, and novels.
- Text GANs can assist authors by suggesting new sentences or storylines.

📌 **Example**: OpenAI's GPT-based models use GAN-inspired techniques to create human-like text.

3.2 AI-Generated Dialogues and Chatbots

- Text GANs improve chatbot responses, making them more natural and engaging.
- AI can generate human-like conversations for virtual assistants and customer service bots.

📌 **Example**: ChatGPT and Bard use techniques similar to text-based GANs for chatbot training.

3.3 Fake News and AI-Generated Misinformation

- GANs can be used to generate fake news articles, which raises ethical concerns.
- AI-generated text can be misused for misinformation campaigns.

📌 **Example**: AI-generated fake news articles have been used to spread misinformation on social media.

💡 **Solution**: Researchers are developing AI tools to detect AI-generated misinformation.

4. Ethical Challenges of Text-Based GANs

4.1 AI-Generated Plagiarism

- AI text generators might unintentionally copy existing content, leading to plagiarism issues.

- Ethical AI writing tools should ensure text originality.

📌 **Example**: AI writing assistants like Grammarly and Jasper include plagiarism checkers to prevent AI-generated copying.

4.2 Bias and Fairness in AI Text Generation

- AI models trained on biased datasets can generate discriminatory or biased text.
- Researchers must ensure diverse and unbiased training data.

📌 **Example**: AI chatbots have been criticized for reflecting societal biases present in their training data.

Text-based GANs are transforming AI creativity by enabling AI-generated stories, poetry, chatbots, and content automation. While challenges like discrete text representation, ethical concerns, and bias remain, ongoing research is improving GAN-based text generation.

🚀 **Key Takeaways:**

✓ Text-based GANs adapt GAN architectures to generate meaningful text sequences.

✓ SeqGAN, MaskGAN, and LeakGAN are specialized models for text generation.

✓ AI-generated text has applications in storytelling, chatbots, and content creation.

✓ Ethical concerns include plagiarism, misinformation, and bias.

11.2 Generating AI-Written Stories and Articles

The ability of AI to generate human-like text has reached astonishing levels, leading to AI-written stories, news articles, and even full-length books. Text-based GANs and other deep learning models are transforming the way content is created, automating everything from fiction writing to journalism. But how do these models work? Can AI truly replace human writers, or is it best used as a tool for augmentation?

In this chapter, we explore:

✓ How GANs and deep learning models generate AI-written stories and articles

✓ The role of AI in creative writing, journalism, and content automation

✓ Challenges in AI-generated text, including coherence, style, and originality

✓ The ethical and legal concerns of AI-written content

By the end of this chapter, you'll have a clear understanding of how AI is reshaping content creation and where it still falls short.

1. How AI Generates Stories and Articles

AI-written content is produced using a combination of language models, GAN-based architectures, and reinforcement learning techniques. Unlike human writers, AI doesn't have personal experiences or emotions—but it can analyze vast amounts of data and generate coherent, structured text.

1.1 The AI Writing Process

AI-generated text follows a structured pipeline:

- **Dataset Collection**: The AI is trained on massive text datasets, such as books, articles, and online content.
- **Training a Language Model**: AI learns grammar, style, and storytelling techniques using deep learning models like Transformer-based architectures (e.g., GPT, BERT).
- **Content Generation**: AI produces text based on a given prompt, generating stories, articles, and dialogues.
- **Refinement**: AI-generated text is edited, fact-checked, and improved for clarity.

📌 **Example**: AI writing assistants like Jasper, Copy.ai, and OpenAI's GPT models use these techniques to create high-quality text.

2. AI in Storytelling and Fiction Writing

AI is being used to generate novels, poetry, scripts, and creative writing pieces, assisting authors in creating engaging narratives.

2.1 How AI Generates Fiction

AI uses story structures, themes, and writing styles learned from datasets to craft compelling narratives.

☐ Techniques Used in AI Storytelling:

- **Plot Generation**: AI can suggest story ideas and outlines.
- **Character Development**: AI can create unique characters with distinct traits.
- **Dialogue Generation**: AI can produce realistic character conversations.
- **Style Adaptation**: AI can mimic famous authors' writing styles.

📌 **Example**: OpenAI's ChatGPT can generate short stories, while AI models like Sudowrite assist writers with brainstorming and editing.

2.2 AI-Assisted Writing Tools

Rather than replacing authors, AI is being used as a writing assistant to help with:

✓ Generating story ideas

✓ Overcoming writer's block

✓ Suggesting plot twists

✓ Improving grammar and structure

📌 **Example**: Grammarly, Jasper AI, and Sudowrite help writers refine their content, making AI a powerful co-writing tool.

3. AI-Generated Articles and Journalism

Beyond fiction, AI is transforming newsrooms and content marketing. Many media companies now use AI to write reports, summaries, and even breaking news articles.

3.1 AI in Journalism

AI-powered tools are helping journalists by:

- Automating news reporting for sports, finance, and weather updates
- Summarizing long reports into digestible articles
- Detecting fake news and ensuring accuracy in reporting

📌 **Example**: The Associated Press (AP) and Reuters use AI to generate short news reports on stock market updates and sports scores.

3.2 AI in Marketing and Blogging

AI-generated content is also revolutionizing digital marketing, blogging, and SEO by:

- Generating product descriptions
- Writing blog posts and social media content
- Optimizing text for search engines (SEO)

📌 **Example**: AI copywriting tools like Writesonic, Copy.ai, and Rytr create high-quality marketing content in seconds.

4. Challenges of AI-Generated Content

Despite AI's impressive abilities, there are still challenges and limitations in AI-generated stories and articles.

4.1 Maintaining Coherence and Context

- AI sometimes loses track of the story plot in long-form writing.
- Text can become repetitive or inconsistent.

📌 **Example**: AI-generated novels often require human editing to maintain logical flow.

💡 **Solution**: Researchers are improving AI models with memory mechanisms to retain long-term context.

4.2 Ensuring Originality and Avoiding Plagiarism

- AI is trained on existing content, which may lead to unintentional plagiarism.
- AI-generated articles might be too similar to human-written works.

📌 **Example**: OpenAI developed content filters to reduce plagiarism risks in GPT-generated text.

💡 **Solution**: AI content should always be fact-checked and edited before publishing.

4.3 Ethical Concerns: AI-Generated Fake News

- AI can be used to generate misleading information or deepfake news articles.

- AI-written content can spread misinformation rapidly if not properly regulated.

📌 **Example**: AI-generated fake news articles have been used in disinformation campaigns on social media.

💡 **Solution**: Tech companies are developing AI detection tools to identify fake AI-generated content.

5. The Future of AI-Generated Writing

AI-generated writing is rapidly evolving, and future developments will further enhance its capabilities.

5.1 Human-AI Collaboration in Writing

Instead of replacing human authors, AI will act as a collaborative partner, helping writers become more efficient.

📌 **Example**: AI tools like Grammarly and Jasper are already co-writing assistants for many professionals.

5.2 Personalization and AI-Generated Books

Future AI models will:

- Generate personalized books and articles based on user preferences.
- Adapt writing styles to match an individual's tone.

📌 **Example**: AI-generated interactive storytelling will create personalized narratives for readers.

AI-generated stories and articles are transforming the world of writing, journalism, and content creation. While AI still struggles with coherence, originality, and ethics, it is a powerful tool for assisting human writers rather than replacing them.

🚀 **Key Takeaways:**

✔ AI-generated text is used in fiction writing, journalism, and marketing.

✔ AI-assisted writing tools help authors brainstorm and refine content.

✓ Challenges include maintaining coherence, avoiding plagiarism, and preventing misinformation.

✓ Future AI models will focus on personalization and human-AI collaboration.

11.3 Combining GANs with GPT for AI Creativity

Generative Adversarial Networks (GANs) and transformer-based models like GPT (Generative Pre-trained Transformer) represent two of the most groundbreaking advancements in AI. While GANs excel at generating visual content, GPT-based models dominate the field of text generation. By combining these two powerful AI architectures, we unlock new frontiers in AI creativity, allowing machines to generate not just images or text, but fully immersive and interactive experiences.

In this chapter, we will explore:

✓ How GANs and GPT differ in their approach to AI creativity

✓ How combining GANs and GPT leads to new AI-generated content

✓ Applications in storytelling, virtual worlds, and creative AI

✓ Challenges and future directions for hybrid AI models

By the end of this section, you'll understand how GANs and GPT can work together to push the boundaries of AI-driven creativity.

1. Understanding GANs vs. GPT Models

To fully grasp the potential of combining GANs and GPT, we first need to understand their strengths and weaknesses.

1.1 What GANs Do Best

✓ Generate realistic images, videos, and music

✓ Produce high-quality synthetic data for AI training

✓ Enable style transfer and image transformation

📌 **Example**: StyleGAN can generate photorealistic human faces that do not exist in reality.

1.2 What GPT Models Do Best

✓ Understand and generate human-like text

✓ Write stories, dialogues, and summaries

✓ Mimic writing styles and answer questions

📌 **Example**: OpenAI's GPT-4 can generate entire novels, articles, and chatbot responses.

1.3 Why Combining GANs and GPT is Powerful

By merging GANs' ability to generate media with GPT's ability to generate coherent text, we can:

- Create AI-powered storytelling with visuals and narratives
- Develop AI-generated movies, comics, and animations
- Enhance video game world-building with AI-generated environments and dialogue

📌 **Example**: AI can generate both the script and the visuals for an animated short film.

2. How GANs and GPT Work Together

Several AI models already integrate GANs and GPT to create multimodal AI systems that can handle text, images, and even audio in a single workflow.

2.1 Text-to-Image Generation

One of the most exciting applications of GANs + GPT is text-to-image generation, where a GPT-like model generates descriptive text, and a GAN converts that text into a realistic image.

☐ **Process:**

- GPT Model: Generates a detailed description (e.g., "A futuristic city at sunset with flying cars").
- GAN (or Diffusion Model): Converts the description into a high-resolution image.

📌 **Example**: OpenAI's DALL·E uses a transformer to interpret text and generate AI-generated artwork.

2.2 AI-Generated Movies and Animations

Combining GPT with GANs allows AI to generate scripts, character designs, and entire animations.

☐ **Process:**

- GPT writes the script (storyline, dialogues, and scenes).
- GANs generate character images and animated backgrounds.
- AI assembles and animates the scenes based on GAN-generated assets.

📌 **Example**: Runway ML is an AI-powered video editing tool that applies GAN-based effects to real-time video creation.

2.3 AI-Powered Video Games

Hybrid AI models combining GPT and GANs are being used in procedural game design, where AI generates both game environments and dialogue.

☐ **Process:**

- GPT generates character backstories and quests dynamically.
- GANs create realistic environments, textures, and objects.
- AI adapts gameplay in real time based on player interaction.

📌 **Example**: NVIDIA's GameGAN can train an AI to generate video game levels without human intervention.

2.4 AI-Generated Comics and Graphic Novels

By combining GAN-generated images with GPT-generated text, AI can now create entire comics and graphic novels.

☐ **Process:**

- GPT writes the dialogue and captions.
- GANs generate comic-style illustrations.
- AI arranges panels and layouts for a cohesive story.

📌 **Example**: AI-generated webcomics are already appearing on platforms like Midjourney + GPT-powered scripts.

3. Challenges of Combining GANs and GPT

Despite its incredible potential, integrating GANs and GPT into a single creative AI system comes with significant challenges.

3.1 Coherence Between Text and Image

- **Problem**: AI-generated images may not always match the textual description exactly.
- **Solution**: Advanced models like CLIP (Contrastive Language–Image Pretraining) help align text with images.

3.2 Ethical and Copyright Issues

- Problem: AI-generated content could plagiarize existing works or generate offensive material.
- Solution: AI content needs human moderation and copyright detection tools.

3.3 Computational Power and Cost

- **Problem**: Running both GANs and GPT models requires enormous computing resources.
- **Solution**: Cloud-based AI services like Google Colab, Hugging Face, and OpenAI API are making AI more accessible.

4. Future of GANs + GPT in AI Creativity

🚀 **What's Next?**

✓ AI-generated movies and fully automated filmmaking

✓ AI-powered virtual reality experiences

✓ Personalized AI-generated books, stories, and comics

✓ Dynamic AI-driven video games with infinite content

📌 **Example**: AI-generated characters that look, speak, and evolve based on player choices.

By combining GANs' ability to generate images with GPT's language generation capabilities, AI is creating a new era of creative content generation. From AI-written books and comics to AI-powered video games and films, the fusion of GANs and GPT is unlocking unprecedented possibilities in storytelling and multimedia creation.

🚀 **Key Takeaways:**

✓ GANs generate images, while GPT generates text—together, they create multimodal AI systems.

✓ Applications include AI-powered storytelling, video games, animations, and text-to-image synthesis.

✓ Challenges include maintaining coherence, ethical considerations, and computational cost.

✓ Future AI models will be capable of generating entire multimedia experiences.

11.4 The Challenges of Coherent AI-Generated Text

AI-generated text has made remarkable progress, with models like GPT-4 producing human-like conversations, articles, and stories. However, despite these advancements, achieving true coherence remains a challenge. AI often struggles with logical flow, long-term context retention, and maintaining consistency across lengthy pieces of writing.

In this chapter, we will explore:

✓ Why AI-generated text often lacks coherence

✓ The main technical and linguistic challenges AI faces

✓ How researchers are improving AI text generation

✓ Future directions for creating more reliable AI-generated text

By the end, you'll understand the limitations of current AI models and what's being done to make them more reliable for real-world applications.

1. Understanding Coherence in AI-Generated Text

1.1 What is Coherence in Writing?

Coherence refers to how well a piece of text flows logically, stays on topic, and maintains a consistent style and structure. Humans do this naturally, but AI models often struggle due to their predictive nature—they generate text one word at a time, without fully "understanding" the broader meaning.

☐ **Key Components of Coherence:**

✅ **Logical Flow**: Ideas should connect seamlessly.
✅ **Context Awareness**: The AI should remember what it wrote earlier.
✅ **Consistency**: Characters, facts, and tone should remain stable.

📌 **Example of AI-generated incoherence:**

🚫 AI starts a story about a detective in New York, but halfway through, the detective is suddenly a robot in space—without any explanation.

2. Why AI Struggles with Coherent Text Generation

2.1 Lack of True Understanding

Unlike humans, AI does not "understand" meaning. It predicts the next word based on probability, often leading to shallow or repetitive writing.

📌 **Example**: AI may generate a paragraph where a character dies in one sentence but appears alive in the next—because it lacks real comprehension.

2.2 Limited Context Retention

Large AI models have a finite memory window (e.g., GPT-4 can only "remember" a few thousand words). This means:

○ AI may forget important details from earlier in a long text.
○ AI struggles with multi-chapter storytelling.

📌 **Example**: AI writes an essay but repeats the same points multiple times because it doesn't remember what it already said.

💡 **Solution**: Memory-augmented AI models are being developed to track long-term context better.

2.3 Logical Reasoning Limitations

AI can generate realistic-sounding nonsense because it lacks true reasoning ability.

📌 **Example:**

○ **AI writes**: "The sun rose at midnight, casting a bright shadow."
➡ The sentence sounds poetic but doesn't make logical sense.

💡 **Solution**: Hybrid models that combine AI text generation with logical reasoning engines are being explored.

2.4 Struggles with Creativity and Originality

AI relies on existing data to generate text, so it often:

○ Repeats clichés or generic phrases
○ Struggles to generate unique ideas
○ Fails to maintain a strong narrative arc

📌 **Example**: AI-generated fiction might feel formulaic or predictable, mimicking common tropes without originality.

💡 **Solution**: Fine-tuning AI with creative writing techniques and human feedback.

3. Overcoming Coherence Challenges

3.1 Using Memory and Long-Term Context Models

🚀 New AI architectures are improving how AI remembers previous information.

- Transformer models like GPT-4 have longer memory but still have limits.
- Retrieval-Augmented Generation (RAG) allows AI to refer to external sources dynamically.
- AI memory enhancements (like Recurrent Memory Transformers) help AI track long-form narratives

.

📌 **Example**: Future AI chatbots may remember previous conversations more effectively.

3.2 Implementing Reinforcement Learning for Better Structure

📌 **How it works:**

✓ AI generates text → Humans rate coherence → AI learns from feedback.

✓ Used by OpenAI's RLHF (Reinforcement Learning from Human Feedback).

💡 **Result**: AI-generated stories become more structured and engaging.

3.3 Integrating Symbolic AI for Logical Consistency

Symbolic AI is being used alongside deep learning models to improve reasoning abilities.

📌 **Example**: AI could check if a story's timeline makes sense before finalizing a draft.

💡 Future AI models may combine deep learning with rule-based logic systems.

3.4 Fine-Tuning AI for Creativity

💡 Techniques to Improve AI Creativity and Consistency:

✓ Training AI on high-quality literature instead of just the internet.

✓ Using story-structuring algorithms to guide AI-generated text.

✓ Combining GANs and GPT models for interactive storytelling.

✦ **Example**: AI could use GANs to generate visual prompts to help structure better narratives.

4. Future of AI-Generated Coherent Text

🚀 **What's Next?**

✓ **Memory-Augmented AI** → AI models will "remember" longer stories.

✓ **AI-Assisted Writing Tools** → AI will suggest logical edits and rewrites.

✓ **Better Storytelling AI** → AI will improve at maintaining consistent characters and plots.

✓ **Personalized AI Writers** → AI will adapt its writing to individual user preferences.

✦ **Example**: Future AI novel-writing assistants could help authors generate structured, engaging content without losing coherence.

While AI-generated text has advanced significantly, maintaining coherence, logic, and consistency remains a challenge. By improving memory retention, logical reasoning, and creativity, AI can generate more natural, engaging, and well-structured content.

🚀 **Key Takeaways:**

✓ AI struggles with understanding meaning, long-term context, and logical flow.

✓ New AI architectures are improving memory, reasoning, and coherence.

✓ AI-generated writing is evolving into a powerful creative tool rather than a replacement for human writers.

11.5 Applications in Content Creation and Journalism

The rise of AI-generated text is transforming industries like content creation and journalism, making processes faster, scalable, and more efficient. AI models like GPT-4 and beyond are now capable of generating news articles, blog posts, scripts, marketing content, and even investigative reports. However, while AI offers many advantages, it also raises concerns about accuracy, bias, and journalistic ethics.

In this chapter, we will explore:

✓ How AI is used in content creation and journalism

✓ The benefits and challenges of AI-generated news and articles

✓ How AI can assist (but not replace) human journalists

✓ Future trends in AI-powered content production

By the end of this section, you'll understand how AI is shaping the future of media and storytelling.

1. AI in Content Creation

AI is revolutionizing the way content is produced, making it easier for businesses, marketers, and writers to generate high-quality materials at scale.

1.1 AI-Generated Blog Posts and Articles

AI tools like GPT-4, Jasper, and Copy.ai are widely used to create blog posts, SEO content, and marketing articles.

📌 **Example**: A digital marketing agency can use AI to generate hundreds of blog articles on trending topics while optimizing for SEO.

💡 **Benefits:**

✓ Faster content generation (minutes instead of hours)

✓ SEO-optimized text for better search rankings

✓ Personalized content based on audience preferences

🚫 **Challenges:**

- AI can sometimes generate generic or repetitive content.
- AI lacks the emotional depth of human writers.

1.2 AI in Social Media and Copywriting

Social media marketers use AI to generate engaging tweets, LinkedIn posts, Instagram captions, and ad copy.

📌 **Example**: AI-generated social media posts for a fashion brand might include:

"Looking for the perfect summer outfit? ☀☐ Our new collection is here! Shop now → [link]"

💡 **Benefits:**

✅ AI generates A/B test variations for higher engagement.

✅ AI-powered tools like ChatGPT and Writesonic create personalized brand voices.

🚫 **Challenges:**

- AI-generated posts can sometimes lack authenticity or emotional appeal.
- Viral trends change rapidly, requiring human oversight.

1.3 AI-Powered Scriptwriting and Storytelling

AI is now being used to write movie scripts, TV episodes, and creative fiction.

📌 **Example**: OpenAI's Suno AI and tools like DeepStory can generate entire movie scripts based on user prompts.

💡 **Benefits:**

✅ AI can help scriptwriters brainstorm ideas faster.

✅ AI-generated dialogues can be used in video games or virtual assistants.

🚫 **Challenges:**

AI struggles with emotional storytelling and deep character development.
AI-generated scripts lack originality and often mimic existing tropes.

2. AI in Journalism

2.1 AI for News Article Generation

Major news agencies like Reuters, The Washington Post, and The Associated Press (AP) are using AI to automate news reporting.

📌 **Example:**

- AP's Automated Insights generates earnings reports and sports summaries.
- Google's Journalist AI helps fact-check articles for misinformation.

💡 **Benefits:**

✅ Faster news updates (AI can write breaking news in seconds).

✅ AI analyzes large datasets for investigative journalism.

✅ Automated summaries help journalists process information quickly.

🚫 **Challenges:**

- AI can spread misinformation if trained on biased data.
- Lack of investigative depth—AI can't conduct interviews or verify sources.

2.2 AI in Fact-Checking and Misinformation Detection

With the rise of fake news, AI is being used to detect false information and verify sources.

📌 **Example:**

- AI tools like Snopes AI and Google's Fact Check Explorer scan online content to identify misleading information.
- Facebook uses AI to detect and reduce the spread of fake news.

💡 **Benefits:**

✅ AI can analyze thousands of news sources instantly.

✅ AI-powered tools help flag misleading or manipulated content.

⊘ Challenges:

- AI can still misinterpret satire or opinion pieces as fake news.
- AI does not understand human intent, making fact-checking complex.

2.3 AI in Data Journalism and Investigative Reporting

AI is helping journalists analyze massive datasets to uncover hidden patterns in politics, finance, and crime.

📌 **Example**: The Panama Papers investigation used AI to analyze 11.5 million leaked documents, exposing offshore tax havens.

💡 Benefits:

✓ AI can process huge amounts of data faster than humans.

✓ AI tools like IBM Watson help journalists extract insights from documents.

⊘ Challenges:

AI cannot replace human investigative intuition and ethical judgment.
AI tools require careful tuning to avoid false conclusions.

3. Can AI Replace Human Journalists?

While AI can assist journalists, it cannot replace them.

📌 Why?

⊘ AI lacks human ethics, judgment, and critical thinking.
⊘ AI cannot conduct interviews or verify sources independently.
⊘ AI struggles with nuanced topics like political bias and sensitive reporting.

💡 **The Future**: AI will work alongside human journalists, automating mundane tasks while humans focus on deep analysis and ethical reporting.

4. The Future of AI in Content Creation and Journalism

🚀 What's Next?

✔ **AI-powered video journalism** → AI will generate video news summaries automatically.

✔ **AI-assisted investigative journalism** → AI will detect corruption and financial fraud faster.

✔ **AI-driven personalization** → News platforms will deliver customized articles based on user preferences.

✔ **Ethical AI journalism** → AI will follow ethical guidelines to prevent bias and misinformation.

📌 **Example**: Future AI news bots might generate real-time updates on global events, fact-checking content as it spreads.

AI is revolutionizing content creation and journalism, making it easier to generate news, articles, scripts, and social media content. However, while AI can automate writing tasks, it still requires human oversight to ensure accuracy, ethics, and creativity.

🚀 Key Takeaways:

✔ AI accelerates content creation but struggles with depth, originality, and ethical judgment.

✔ AI-generated journalism works best in structured reports, but human oversight is needed for investigative reporting.

✔ Future AI tools will collaborate with human writers and journalists, not replace them.

12. AI in Game Development and Virtual Worlds

The gaming industry is evolving rapidly, and Generative Adversarial Networks (GANs) are playing a major role in creating immersive virtual worlds, dynamic characters, and realistic environments. In this chapter, we explore how GANs are revolutionizing game design, procedural content generation, and AI-driven storytelling. You'll learn how GANs generate realistic textures, landscapes, and 3D assets, create lifelike NPC behaviors, and even assist in automated level design. We'll also discuss how AI is being used to enhance realism in animations, predict player behavior, and optimize game mechanics. Whether you're a game developer, AI researcher, or gaming enthusiast, this chapter will show you how GANs are shaping the future of interactive entertainment and virtual experiences. 🎮☐☐🚀

12.1 GANs for Procedural World Generation

Procedural world generation has long been a cornerstone of video game development, enabling the creation of vast, dynamic environments with minimal manual effort. Traditionally, procedural generation relies on rule-based algorithms, such as Perlin noise and fractals, to create landscapes, dungeons, and entire virtual worlds. However, with the advent of Generative Adversarial Networks (GANs), AI-driven procedural generation is revolutionizing how digital worlds are built, making them more realistic, diverse, and adaptable.

In this chapter, we'll explore:

✓ How GANs improve procedural world generation

✓ Key differences between traditional and AI-driven procedural generation

✓ Examples of GAN-generated landscapes, textures, and levels

✓ Challenges and future possibilities in AI-powered game worlds

By the end of this section, you'll understand how GANs are reshaping game environments, virtual worlds, and simulations.

1. Traditional vs. AI-Driven Procedural Generation

1.1 Traditional Procedural Generation

Classic procedural generation techniques use mathematical formulas and rules to generate random yet structured game worlds.

📌 **Examples:**

🎮 **Minecraft** → Uses Perlin noise to generate landscapes.

🎮 **No Man's Sky** → Uses deterministic algorithms to create 18 quintillion planets.

🎮 **Roguelikes (e.g., Spelunky, Hades)** → Generate unique levels dynamically.

💡 **Limitations:**

🚫 Environments may feel predictable and lack organic realism.
🚫 Procedural rules can lead to repetitive patterns.
🚫 Hard to generate believable, high-detail environments without manual design.

1.2 AI-Powered Procedural Generation with GANs

GANs take procedural generation beyond rule-based randomness by learning from real-world environments and generating lifelike, diverse, and unique worlds.

💡 **How it works:**

1☐ Train a GAN on real-world landscapes, cityscapes, or level designs.

2☐ The generator learns patterns, textures, and spatial structures.

3☐ The discriminator ensures outputs resemble real-world or handcrafted environments.

4☐ The final generated world looks highly realistic and organic.

📌 **Example**: NVIDIA's GAN-based model generates high-resolution, photorealistic terrains for open-world games.

🚀 **Advantages of GAN-driven world generation:**

✅ More natural and unpredictable environments.

✅ Higher detail and texture quality than traditional algorithms.

✅ Adaptive worlds that evolve based on player interactions.

🚫 **Challenges:**

- GANs require large training datasets to generate believable worlds.
- Processing GANs in real-time is computationally expensive.

2. Key Applications of GANs in World Generation

2.1 Generating Realistic Landscapes and Terrains

GANs can generate mountains, rivers, forests, and deserts that feel organic and immersive.

📌 **Example**: NVIDIA's GauGAN creates photo-realistic landscapes from rough sketches, which game developers can use to design open-world environments dynamically.

💡 **How it improves games:**

✔ More lifelike and varied landscapes.

✔ Adaptive terrain generation based on gameplay (e.g., realistic terrain erosion).

✔ Infinite world expansion with unique environments.

2.2 AI-Generated Game Levels and Dungeons

GANs can create new, unpredictable game levels that adapt to player behavior.

📌 **Example:**

- **Level generation in platformers** (e.g., Mario, Hollow Knight, Celeste) → AI creates dynamic, challenging, and engaging levels.
- **Roguelike dungeons** (e.g., The Binding of Isaac, Hades) → GANs ensure each dungeon is truly unique, rather than relying on pre-set templates.

💡 **How it improves games:**

✓ Infinite replayability (each level is truly unique).

✓ More engaging level design with adaptive difficulty scaling.

🚫 **Challenges:**

- Ensuring AI-generated levels remain playable and balanced.
- GANs sometimes produce illogical or unplayable layouts.

2.3 GAN-Based City and Structure Generation

GANs can generate realistic cities, villages, and buildings, enhancing urban environments in open-world games and simulations.

📌 **Example:**

- **Cyberpunk 2077 or GTA-style open worlds** → AI generates diverse city layouts,

  unique building designs, and procedural streets.
- **Microsoft's Flight Simulator** → AI-generated real-world cities using satellite data.

💡 **How it improves games:**

✓ Cities feel more organic and less repetitive.

✓ AI can create historically accurate or futuristic cityscapes.

🚫 **Challenges:**

- AI must balance realism with gameplay functionality.
- GANs require high-resolution datasets for believable structures.

2.4 GANs for Texture and Asset Generation

GANs can generate textures, materials, and assets, replacing manual texturing and reducing development time.

📌 **Example:**

- **GAN-based texture generation** → AI creates hyper-realistic textures for walls, ground, and characters.
- **Adaptive weather effects** → GANs simulate rain, snow, and erosion effects dynamically.

💡 **How it improves games:**

✓ More realistic and high-quality textures.
✓ Dynamically evolving worlds (e.g., changing seasons, aging buildings).

🚫 **Challenges:**

- Ensuring AI-generated textures match artistic direction.

3. Challenges of GANs in Procedural World Generation

While GANs offer game-changing advantages, they also introduce challenges:

🖥 1. **Computational Cost** → Training GANs for world generation requires high-performance GPUs or TPUs.

🖥 2. **Lack of Game Logic Awareness** → AI-generated worlds may look realistic but lack interactive elements.

🖥 3. **Uncontrolled Generation** → GANs may create impractical, overly complex, or broken environments.

🖥 4. **Data Limitations** → GANs require large datasets of landscapes, levels, or textures to generate quality outputs.

💡 **Solution**: Hybrid AI approaches combine GANs with rule-based constraints to ensure playability and game logic.

4. The Future of AI-Driven Procedural Worlds

🚀 **What's Next?**

✓ **AI-driven open-world games** → GANs will create dynamic, evolving, and infinite worlds.

✓ **GAN-powered VR & Metaverse** → AI will generate immersive virtual cities and landscapes.

✓ **Real-time adaptive worlds** → Environments will respond to player actions dynamically.

✓ **GANs + Game Engines (Unity, Unreal Engine)** → AI will integrate seamlessly into game development pipelines.

📌 **Example**: Future AI-generated worlds in Metaverse applications could adapt to user behavior, making virtual reality environments more interactive and lifelike.

GANs are redefining procedural generation, offering more realistic, unique, and adaptive game worlds than ever before. From lifelike terrains to endless cityscapes and game levels, AI is revolutionizing how developers create virtual experiences.

🚀 **Key Takeaways:**

✓ GANs improve procedural generation by adding realism and variety.

✓ AI-generated landscapes, cities, and levels enhance gameplay immersion.

✓ Hybrid AI approaches will address challenges of playability and logic.

✓ The future of gaming will feature GAN-powered, ever-changing worlds.

12.2 AI-Created NPCs and Character Design

Non-Playable Characters (NPCs) are essential to immersive gaming experiences, populating virtual worlds with lifelike behaviors, dialogues, and interactions. Traditionally, NPCs have been manually designed, requiring extensive animation, scripting, and voiceovers. However, Generative Adversarial Networks (GANs) are revolutionizing NPC creation, allowing AI to generate unique faces, personalities, voices, and behaviors at scale.

In this chapter, we will explore:

✓ How GANs generate realistic NPC faces and animations

✓ AI-powered personality and dialogue generation

✓ Procedural NPC behavior using deep learning

✓ Challenges in AI-created NPCs and their future in gaming

By the end of this section, you'll understand how AI is reshaping character design, making NPCs more dynamic, interactive, and immersive.

1. AI-Generated NPC Faces and Character Models

1.1 Creating Realistic NPC Faces with GANs

GANs can generate highly realistic human faces, allowing game developers to create a limitless variety of unique NPCs. Instead of manually designing hundreds of faces, AI models can generate diverse, high-resolution character portraits in seconds.

📌 **Examples of AI face generation:**

- **StyleGAN (by NVIDIA)** → Generates photorealistic human faces.
- **This Person Does Not Exist** → Uses GANs to create synthetic people that look real.
- **AI-powered de-aging and facial animation** → GANs can modify facial expressions dynamically in real time.

💡 **How it improves NPC design:**

✓ **No need for manual face modeling** → AI creates thousands of unique faces.

✓ **Diverse characters** → AI ensures variety in age, ethnicity, and gender.

✓ **Customizable NPCs** → Developers can train GANs on specific art styles for different games.

🚫 **Challenges:**

- GAN-generated faces must align with artistic direction and lore.
- Some AI-generated faces may have minor distortions or uncanny valley effects.

1.2 AI-Generated 3D Character Models and Textures

GANs are also transforming 3D character modeling by generating high-quality textures, clothing, and animations.

📌 **Examples:**

- **Text-to-3D GANs** → AI generates 3D character models based on textual descriptions.
- **AI-powered texture synthesis** → GANs create lifelike skin, fabric, and hair textures.
- **DeepFaceLab & ReAgeGAN** → AI can modify character age and facial expressions dynamically.

💡 **How it improves character design:**

✓ Faster 3D modeling and animation.

✓ AI-generated realistic clothing, armor, and accessories.

✓ Seamless facial animation without manual keyframing.

🚫 **Challenges:**

- AI models require large datasets of textures and character models.
- Some AI-generated animations may lack fine-tuned control compared to traditional methods.

2. AI-Powered NPC Personalities and Dialogues

2.1 Dynamic NPC Personality Generation

Traditional NPCs often follow pre-scripted behaviors that become repetitive over time. With AI, NPCs can develop unique personalities, reactions, and decision-making abilities.

📌 **How GANs help:**

- AI learns from real-world behaviors to create authentic personalities.
- GANs generate unique backstories for each NPC.
- NPCs adapt and evolve based on player interactions.

💡 **How it improves gameplay:**

✓ NPCs feel more lifelike and unpredictable.

✓ More immersive and replayable experiences.

✓ AI-generated personalized character arcs.

🚫 **Challenges:**

- Hard to ensure coherent and logical personality progression.
- NPCs need player-feedback loops to evolve naturally.

2.2 AI-Generated Conversations & Adaptive Dialogue

Most NPCs use pre-scripted dialogue, leading to repetitive and predictable interactions. AI-driven models like ChatGPT and GAN-based dialogue systems enable dynamic, adaptive conversations.

📌 **How AI improves NPC dialogue:**

- GANs generate unique, context-aware responses.
- NPCs can remember past interactions and adapt.
- AI modifies dialogue in real-time based on player choices.

💡 **How it improves storytelling:**

✓ More natural and engaging dialogues.

✓ Personalized conversations that adapt to player decisions.

✓ Endless dialogue possibilities, preventing repetition.

🚫 **Challenges:**

- AI-generated conversations may lack emotional depth.
- Some AI dialogues may produce incoherent or nonsensical responses.

3. AI-Driven NPC Behaviors and Intelligence

3.1 Procedural NPC Behavior with GANs

Traditional NPCs follow static scripts or basic AI patterns (e.g., patrolling guards, scripted shopkeepers). GANs introduce dynamic behavior by learning from real-world movements, social interactions, and player habits.

📌 **How it works:**

1️⃣ GANs analyze player interactions to create believable social behaviors.

2️⃣ NPCs learn and adapt, changing their responses based on game progression.

3️⃣ AI generates emergent gameplay by creating unexpected character interactions.

💡 **How it enhances immersion:**

✓ NPCs react differently to different players.

✓ More realistic in-game societies.

✓ Dynamic economies and ecosystems influenced by AI-driven NPCs.

🚫 **Challenges:**

- Ensuring AI remains in control to avoid chaotic or game-breaking behavior.
- Ethical concerns about AI-generated personalities being too human-like.

4. Challenges and Ethical Considerations in AI NPCs

While AI-powered NPCs offer unprecedented realism, they also raise technical and ethical concerns:

🏛 1. **Uncanny Valley Effect** → Hyper-realistic AI faces may feel creepy if they are too close to reality.

🏛 2. **AI Bias in NPC Generation** → GANs may inadvertently replicate biases from training data.

🏛 3. **Ethical Issues in AI-Generated Personalities** → NPCs could manipulate emotions or simulate real-life figures without consent.

🏛 4. **Real-Time Computation Costs** → Generating AI-driven NPC responses in real-time is computationally demanding.

💡 **Solutions:**

✓ Hybrid approaches combining GANs with rule-based constraints.

✓ Bias reduction techniques in AI training data.

✓ AI ethics frameworks for responsible NPC generation.

5. The Future of AI in NPC and Character Design

🚀 **What's Next?**

✓ **AI-driven NPCs in open-world games** → NPCs will have independent goals, emotions, and evolving behaviors.

✓ **GAN-powered VR & Metaverse avatars** → AI-generated characters will be interactive and self-learning.

✓ **AI-generated voice acting** → NPCs will have natural, adaptive voices with real-time speech synthesis.

✓ **GAN-powered character customization** → Players can generate truly unique in-game characters.

★ Example: In future RPGs, NPCs could form opinions about the player, remember past interactions, and evolve over time, making them more lifelike than ever before.

GANs are revolutionizing NPC design, bringing lifelike characters, adaptive personalities, and intelligent behaviors to video games. From realistic face generation to AI-powered dialogue, GAN-driven NPCs are making virtual worlds feel alive and dynamic.

🚀 Key Takeaways:

✓ AI creates ultra-realistic character models and faces.

✓ NPCs can have dynamic, evolving personalities and behaviors.

✓ AI-generated dialogues make NPCs more interactive and immersive.

✓ The future of gaming will feature self-learning, adaptive NPCs.

12.3 Enhancing Game Graphics with GANs

Graphics play a crucial role in creating immersive gaming experiences. From high-resolution textures to dynamic lighting and realistic animations, the visual quality of a game can define its success. Traditionally, improving graphics required manual labor, high-performance rendering techniques, and extensive computational resources. However, Generative Adversarial Networks (GANs) are revolutionizing game graphics by automating and optimizing texture upscaling, procedural generation, lighting enhancements, and even realistic facial animations.

In this chapter, we explore:

✓ How GANs upscale textures and improve image resolution

✓ Procedural content generation for realistic environments

✓ AI-driven lighting and shading techniques

✓ GAN-based facial animation and motion enhancement

By the end of this chapter, you'll understand how GANs are pushing the boundaries of real-time rendering, making games look more realistic and visually stunning than ever before.

1. AI-Powered Texture Upscaling and Super-Resolution

1.1 Traditional vs. AI-Based Texture Upscaling

Game textures often need to be optimized for performance, leading to low-resolution assets that can appear blurry, especially in older games. Traditional upscaling methods such as bilinear filtering or bicubic interpolation often fail to recover lost details. GANs, however, can intelligently predict and reconstruct high-resolution textures using deep learning.

📌 **Popular AI-powered upscaling models:**

- **ESRGAN** (Enhanced Super-Resolution GAN) → Produces high-quality textures with realistic details.

- **SRGAN** (Super-Resolution GAN) → Used for image enhancement in low-resolution games.

- **NVIDIA DLSS** (Deep Learning Super Sampling) → AI-based rendering technique that boosts game performance while enhancing visual quality.

💡 **How it improves game graphics:**

✓ Sharpens blurry textures while maintaining performance.

✓ Adds realistic details that weren't present in the original image.

✓ Enhances retro games by remastering old textures without manual work.

🚫 **Challenges:**

- GAN-based upscaling requires training on high-quality texture datasets.
- Some AI-generated textures may introduce artifacts or distortions.

1.2 AI-Powered Texture Synthesis

Instead of manually creating hundreds of textures, GANs can generate realistic textures for environments, clothing, and character skins from scratch.

📌 **How GANs generate textures:**

1☐ AI learns texture patterns from real-world images.
2☐ GANs create procedural variations of materials like wood, stone, and fabric.
3☐ AI ensures textures are seamless and tileable, reducing visible repetition.

💡 **How it improves game worlds:**

✓ More diverse and natural-looking textures.

✓ Reduces development time for creating environment assets.

✓ Realistic weathered effects like rust, cracks, and decay.

🚫 **Challenges:**

- AI-generated textures must be visually consistent with the game's art style.
- GANs require large datasets of real-world textures for training.

2. Procedural Content Generation for Game Environments

2.1 AI-Generated Landscapes and Terrains

Manually creating large game worlds is time-consuming. GANs can generate realistic landscapes, terrains, and cityscapes procedurally.

📌 **How GANs help:**

- GANs trained on satellite imagery can generate realistic mountains, forests, and lakes.
- AI can blend textures and terrain features smoothly, reducing manual work.
- Procedural level generation ensures unique maps for every playthrough.

💡 **How it enhances open-world games:**

✓ Infinite world generation for sandbox games.

✓ More natural, realistic landscapes.

✓ Automated map creation saves time for developers.

⊘ Challenges:

- GAN-generated landscapes must be gameplay-friendly (not too steep or inaccessible).
- AI terrain generation requires fine-tuning to avoid unnatural patterns.

2.2 AI-Generated Buildings and Cities

GANs can generate realistic architecture, urban landscapes, and interiors dynamically.

📌 Examples:

- GauGAN (by NVIDIA) generates realistic cities and buildings.
- AI can generate entire towns with unique building styles.
- GANs can fill interiors with detailed furniture, decorations, and lighting.

💡 How it enhances game design:

✓ Creates large, explorable cities quickly.

✓ Dynamically generates new areas based on player actions.

✓ Reduces repetitive architecture, making cities feel more real.

⊘ Challenges:

- AI-generated city layouts must be optimized for gameplay navigation.
- Buildings and streets must be logically structured.

3. AI-Driven Lighting, Shading, and Reflections

3.1 AI-Based Real-Time Ray Tracing

Real-time ray tracing is a cutting-edge rendering technique that produces realistic lighting, shadows, and reflections. However, it is computationally expensive. GANs can approximate ray-traced lighting effects with significantly less processing power.

📌 **Examples of AI-based lighting techniques:**

- **RTX AI Denoiser (NVIDIA)** → Uses GANs to smooth noisy ray-traced shadows.
- **AI-based global illumination** → Simulates realistic light bounce and color bleeding.
- **GAN-powered reflections** → AI predicts how light should behave on different surfaces.

💡 **How it improves visual realism:**

✓ Faster, more efficient ray tracing.

✓ Realistic lighting in dynamic environments.

✓ More immersive game worlds with true-to-life reflections.

🚫 **Challenges:**

- AI-based lighting may not always match true physics-based rendering.
- Requires powerful hardware (GPUs with AI acceleration).

4. AI-Generated Facial Animation and Motion Enhancement

4.1 GAN-Based Facial Expressions and Lip Syncing

Traditional facial animation is labor-intensive, requiring motion capture or hand-crafted keyframes. GANs can automate this process by generating realistic facial expressions and accurate lip sync for dialogue.

📌 **How AI improves facial animation:**

- DeepFaceLab and First Order Motion Model → AI-driven facial motion synthesis.
- GANs can animate pre-existing faces to match dialogue in real time.

- AI-based emotion synthesis makes NPC expressions more lifelike.

💡 How it improves storytelling:

✓ Realistic and expressive characters.

✓ More natural lip syncing for voice-acted dialogue.

✓ Reduces need for expensive motion capture.

🚫 Challenges:

- Some AI-generated animations may lack precise emotional nuance.
- GAN-generated facial expressions must be consistent with the character's personality.

5. The Future of AI in Game Graphics

🚀 What's Next?

✓ **AI-driven photorealistic rendering** → Games will feature near-real-world visuals.

✓ **GAN-based real-time world adaptation** → Environments will dynamically change based on player actions.

✓ **AI-generated ultra-high-resolution assets** → Every object in the game will have lifelike textures.

✓ **GAN-powered character realism** → NPCs will have detailed skin textures, facial pores, and realistic eyes.

📌 Example: Future game engines could fully automate world-building, allowing developers to focus on storytelling and gameplay mechanics while AI handles the visuals.

GANs are transforming game graphics, enabling higher-resolution textures, realistic lighting, procedural environments, and lifelike animations. As AI continues to evolve, we will see ultra-realistic game worlds that blur the line between virtual and reality.

🚀 Key Takeaways:

✓ GANs upscale textures and create detailed environments.

✓ AI generates realistic lighting, shadows, and reflections.

✓ AI-driven facial animations make characters feel alive.

✓ The future of gaming will feature AI-powered real-time rendering.

12.4 Simulating Realistic Physics in AI Worlds

Physics simulation is one of the key elements that make game worlds feel immersive and realistic. From character movement to environmental interactions, believable physics enhances gameplay by creating fluid animations, responsive environments, and natural interactions between objects. Traditionally, physics in games is governed by predefined physics engines such as Unity's PhysX or Havok. However, AI—especially Generative Adversarial Networks (GANs) and Reinforcement Learning (RL)—is revolutionizing how physics is simulated in virtual worlds.

In this chapter, we will explore:

✓ How GANs and deep learning models can simulate realistic physics

✓ AI-driven character movement and animation physics

✓ Fluid simulations for water, smoke, and fire effects

✓ AI-enhanced destruction physics for realistic environmental damage

By the end of this chapter, you'll understand how GANs and AI-driven simulations are pushing the boundaries of realism in gaming and virtual environments.

1. AI-Powered Physics Simulations

1.1 Traditional vs. AI-Based Physics Simulations

Most modern games use rigid-body physics engines, which rely on complex mathematical models to simulate movement, gravity, and collisions. However, these methods can be computationally expensive and sometimes feel unnatural due to limitations in pre-scripted rules. AI-powered physics can learn realistic movement patterns and physical behaviors based on real-world data, making virtual interactions more lifelike.

📌 Comparison of Traditional and AI-Enhanced Physics:

Feature	Traditional Physics Engines	AI-Powered Physics (GANs & RL)
Computation	Rule-based equations	AI learns from real-world physics data
Realism	Limited to predefined rules	Adapts dynamically to new environments
Animation Quality	Keyframe-based or physics-rigged	AI simulates organic movement naturally
Processing Power	CPU/GPU-intensive calculations	Optimized using deep learning inference

💡 Benefits of AI-driven physics simulation:

✔ More natural, dynamic movement for characters and objects.

✔ Reduced reliance on pre-scripted physics rules.

✔ Enhanced real-time interactions with the game environment.

🚫 Challenges:

Training AI to understand realistic physics requires large datasets.
AI models need to be optimized for real-time performance.

2. AI for Character Movement and Animation

2.1 GANs for Realistic Character Animation

Traditional character animations are often created using motion capture or hand-crafted animation rigs. However, GANs can generate smooth and natural movement by learning from real-world human motion data.

📌 How GANs enhance character movement:

- AI analyzes real human movement to generate realistic animations.
- GANs predict the next movement frame instead of relying on pre-scripted animations.
- AI can dynamically adjust movements based on the environment.

💡 Examples of AI-powered animation tools:

✓ **DeepMimic** → Uses reinforcement learning to train characters for realistic motion.

✓ **MotionGAN** → Generates smooth animations by learning from human motion datasets.

✓ **Meta AI's physics-based animation models** → Create adaptive and lifelike character motions.

🚫 **Challenges:**

- AI-generated animations must be emotionally expressive and context-aware.
- AI needs fine-tuning to avoid unnatural jerky movements.

2.2 AI for Adaptive Character Movement

GANs and Reinforcement Learning (RL) can be used to make characters adapt to changing environments dynamically.

📌 **How AI improves movement realism:**

✓ AI can simulate weight shifts based on terrain.

✓ Characters can adjust their balance when walking on uneven surfaces.

✓ AI can learn how to recover from falls and obstacles dynamically.

💡 **Example**: In Red Dead Redemption 2, Rockstar Games used AI-driven physics to make characters stumble naturally when walking on rough terrain, creating more immersive movement mechanics.

🚫 **Challenges:**

AI movement models must be optimized for real-time gameplay.
Balancing AI-controlled movement with player input responsiveness.

3. AI-Driven Environmental Physics

3.1 AI for Water, Smoke, and Fire Simulations

Simulating fluids, smoke, and fire in games is one of the most computationally intensive tasks. Traditional physics engines rely on particle systems and pre-baked simulations, which can look unnatural at times. GANs can generate real-time fluid dynamics that behave more realistically.

📌 AI-powered fluid simulations:

✓ NVIDIA's AI-driven fluid rendering creates ultra-realistic water and smoke.

✓ GANs can predict how water will ripple and flow based on real-world physics.

✓ AI can simulate fire and explosion effects dynamically without pre-baked animations.

🚫 Challenges:

- Real-time fluid simulations require high-performance AI inference.
- GANs must be trained on large datasets of real-world physics interactions.

3.2 AI-Driven Destruction Physics

Realistic destruction physics adds depth and immersion to gaming experiences. Traditional destruction systems rely on predefined physics rules, but GANs can learn from real-world structural collapses and generate dynamic destruction effects.

📌 How AI improves environmental destruction:

✓ AI can predict how materials break and shatter based on stress and impact force.

✓ GANs generate procedural destruction effects, making every explosion unique.

✓ AI-based real-time damage modeling improves realism in FPS and open-world games.

💡 **Example**: Games like Battlefield V use AI-enhanced destruction physics to create realistic collapsing buildings and debris scattering.

🚫 Challenges:

- AI-generated destruction must be optimized for performance.
- The physics engine must handle complex material properties dynamically.

4. AI for Vehicle and Object Physics

4.1 AI-Driven Vehicle Physics

GANs and reinforcement learning can simulate realistic car movement, crashes, and aerodynamics in racing games and open-world driving simulations.

📌 **AI-based vehicle physics improvements:**

✓ AI models predict how tires grip the road based on speed and terrain.

✓ AI-enhanced crash physics ensure realistic car deformations.

✓ AI can dynamically adjust suspension and handling in real-time.

💡 **Example**: BeamNG.drive uses deep learning and physics simulations to create ultra-realistic vehicle damage and handling.

🚫 **Challenges:**

- AI-driven physics must be realistic but still fun to play.
- Real-time simulation of vehicle aerodynamics requires high computational power.

5. The Future of AI in Game Physics

🚀 **What's Next?**

✓ **AI-powered real-time destruction physics** → Every object in a game world will react uniquely to impacts.

✓ **GAN-based fluid simulation** → Water, fire, and smoke will behave more naturally and dynamically.

✓ **AI-driven terrain deformation** → Footsteps, vehicle tracks, and environmental changes will be fully simulated in real-time.

✓ **Self-learning AI physics engines** → Future physics engines will learn and adapt based on player interactions.

📌 **Example**: In future open-world games, AI could automatically generate realistic physics effects for any action—whether it's a tree breaking under heavy snowfall or a river carving a new path through a changing landscape.

AI is revolutionizing physics simulation in gaming, making interactions more natural, dynamic, and immersive. Whether it's character movement, environmental physics, or destruction mechanics, AI-driven physics is shaping the future of realistic game worlds.

🚀 **Key Takeaways:**

✓ GANs and AI improve movement, destruction, and fluid simulations.

✓ AI-based physics adapts to gameplay dynamically.

✓ The future of game physics will be driven by real-time AI simulations.

12.5 The Role of GANs in the Metaverse

The Metaverse—a fully immersive, interconnected digital universe—promises to be the next frontier of human interaction, blending virtual reality (VR), augmented reality (AR), AI, and blockchain. At the heart of this transformation are Generative Adversarial Networks (GANs), which play a critical role in creating ultra-realistic avatars, dynamic environments, procedural world-building, and AI-driven NPCs.

GANs enable the generation of photorealistic textures, human-like digital entities, and interactive elements that adapt and evolve in real time. From AI-generated cities to personalized virtual fashion, GANs are making the Metaverse more immersive, engaging, and intelligent.

In this chapter, we'll explore:

✓ How GANs power hyper-realistic avatar creation

✓ AI-driven world generation and procedural Metaverse design

✓ GAN-powered AI NPCs that adapt and learn

✓ The ethical and privacy concerns of using GANs in virtual worlds

By the end, you'll understand how GANs are shaping the future of digital experiences in the Metaverse.

1. GANs for Photorealistic Avatars

1.1 AI-Generated Digital Identities

In the Metaverse, users interact using avatars—digital representations of themselves. GANs allow for hyper-realistic avatars that can be customized in real-time using AI-generated facial features, body structures, and even emotions.

📌 **How GANs enhance avatar creation:**

✓ StyleGAN generates ultra-realistic faces for digital avatars.

✓ AI can morph 2D images into 3D avatar models.

✓ GANs personalize expressions, gestures, and clothing styles dynamically.

💡 **Example**: Meta's Codec Avatars use AI to create lifelike digital versions of people, mimicking expressions, eye movements, and micro-gestures.

🚫 **Challenges:**

- **Deepfake risks**: GAN-generated avatars can be misused for impersonation.
- **Identity verification**: Ensuring avatars remain authentic and unique.

2. GAN-Powered Virtual World Generation

2.1 AI-Created Cities and Environments

Building large-scale virtual worlds manually is time-consuming. GANs can generate entire cities, landscapes, and buildings procedurally, allowing for infinite, unique, and detailed environments in the Metaverse.

📌 **How GANs build virtual worlds:**

✓ **GAN-based procedural generation** → AI creates unique terrains, cities, and interiors.

✓ **NeRF (Neural Radiance Fields)** → Generates 3D spaces from 2D images.

✓ **TextureGANs** → Generate realistic materials for objects and buildings.

💡 **Example**: NVIDIA's GauGAN creates realistic landscapes from sketches using AI.

🚫 **Challenges:**

- AI-generated worlds must feel "alive", not repetitive.
- Balancing realism and performance for real-time rendering.

3. AI-Driven NPCs and Interactions

3.1 GANs for Smart NPCs and Virtual Assistants

In the Metaverse, AI-powered Non-Player Characters (NPCs) will be crucial for engagement. GANs enable NPCs that generate realistic speech, emotions, and adaptive behavior.

📌 **How AI improves NPC realism:**

✓ GANs synthesize human-like voices and facial expressions.

✓ AI-driven NPCs learn and evolve based on user interactions.

✓ Text-to-Animation GANs create natural body language for NPCs.

💡 **Example**: MetaHuman by Epic Games creates ultra-realistic AI-powered NPCs.

🚫 **Challenges:**

- AI NPCs must understand and respond contextually.
- Ethical concerns over autonomous AI characters.

4. AI-Generated Fashion and Digital Assets

4.1 GANs for Virtual Fashion and Wearable NFTs

In the Metaverse, users purchase, trade, and wear digital clothing. GANs generate unique digital fashion items, accessories, and NFT-based skins.

📌 **How GANs impact virtual fashion:**

✓ AI designs custom digital clothing based on user preferences.

✓ GANs create adaptive clothing that moves realistically in virtual spaces.

✓ AI personalizes outfits in real-time, changing based on mood or event.

💡 **Example**: Gucci and Balenciaga have already started selling AI-generated digital fashion.

🚫 **Challenges:**

- Ensuring digital fashion authenticity (avoiding plagiarism).
- AI must account for physics-based movement in VR worlds.

5. Ethical & Privacy Concerns

5.1 Deepfakes and Identity Theft Risks

While GANs bring innovation, they also introduce security risks in the Metaverse. Deepfake avatars, AI-generated content, and identity theft could become major issues.

📌 **How to address GAN-related risks:**

✓ **AI watermarking** → Protects against unauthorized deepfakes.

✓ **Blockchain for identity verification** → Ensures avatars remain authentic.

✓ **Regulatory measures** → Prevents misuse of AI-generated content.

🚫 **Challenges:**

- Ensuring GAN-generated avatars respect user privacy.
- Preventing AI-generated misinformation in virtual worlds.

6. The Future of GANs in the Metaverse

🚀 **What's Next?**

✓ GAN-powered "living" AI characters that learn, adapt, and evolve.

✓ Fully AI-generated cities that change dynamically over time.

✓ GAN-powered simulations of entire societies, economies, and cultures.

✓ AI-driven real-time interactions where users can chat with NPCs that feel human.

📌 **Example**: Future AI-driven virtual worlds may simulate entire civilizations, where GANs predict and generate events, interactions, and economic models dynamically.

GANs are a cornerstone technology in building the Metaverse, enabling hyper-realistic avatars, immersive environments, AI-driven NPCs, and digital economies. As AI continues to evolve, the line between virtual and reality will blur, making GAN-powered experiences more lifelike than ever before.

🚀 **Key Takeaways:**

✓ GANs generate ultra-realistic avatars and digital identities.

✓ AI powers procedural world-building and smart NPCs.

✓ GAN-driven fashion, art, and assets create a new digital economy.

✓ Privacy and ethical considerations must be addressed.

13. StyleGAN and High-Resolution Synthesis

Among all Generative Adversarial Networks (GANs), StyleGAN stands out as one of the most powerful architectures for generating high-resolution, photorealistic images. Developed by NVIDIA, StyleGAN has been used to create ultra-realistic human faces, artistic transformations, and AI-generated avatars. In this chapter, we explore how StyleGAN works, breaking down its innovative style-based generator architecture, adaptive instance normalization (AdaIN), and mapping network. You'll learn how to train and fine-tune StyleGAN models, generate high-quality synthetic images, and manipulate latent space for creative control. We'll also discuss practical applications, from deepfake technology and digital art to virtual influencers and personalized AI avatars. By the end of this chapter, you'll have the knowledge to experiment with high-resolution AI synthesis and push the boundaries of AI-generated creativity. 🎨🚀

13.1 How StyleGAN Generates High-Resolution Images

One of the most groundbreaking advancements in Generative Adversarial Networks (GANs) is StyleGAN, a powerful model developed by NVIDIA that can generate ultra-realistic, high-resolution images. Unlike traditional GANs, which struggle with fine details, StyleGAN introduces style-based synthesis and progressive growing, enabling it to create stunningly lifelike faces, objects, and even artistic compositions.

In this chapter, we'll break down:

✓ How StyleGAN works and why it's different from basic GANs

✓ The role of style-based synthesis in generating high-quality images

✓ Key innovations like adaptive instance normalization (AdaIN) and latent space mapping

✓ Real-world applications of StyleGAN in art, gaming, and deepfake detection

By the end, you'll understand why StyleGAN is considered the gold standard for AI-generated high-resolution images and how it's shaping the future of synthetic media.

1. Understanding the Core of StyleGAN

1.1 What Makes StyleGAN Different?

Traditional GANs, such as DCGAN and WGAN, generate images by directly mapping a random noise vector (z) to an image using a generator network. While these models produce impressive results, they often struggle with fine-grained control over the generated images.

StyleGAN, introduced by Karras et al. (2018, 2019), solves this problem by introducing a style-based generator architecture, which allows better control over different features such as:

✓ **Facial attributes** (e.g., eyes, hair, expression)

✓ **Texture details** (e.g., skin smoothness, lighting)

✓ **Global structure** (e.g., head pose, background)

💡 **Key Difference**: Instead of feeding noise directly into the generator, StyleGAN maps it into a latent space first, which enables better feature separation and manipulation.

2. Style-Based Synthesis in StyleGAN

2.1 The Role of Latent Space (W-Space)

Unlike traditional GANs that work with a simple noise vector (z-space), StyleGAN introduces an intermediate latent space (W-space). Here's how it works:

1️⃣ A random noise vector (z) is mapped to an intermediate latent space (W-space) using a fully connected network.

2️⃣ This W-space vector is then used to control different styles at different layers of the generator.

3️⃣ This process allows for more semantic control over different image features.

📌 **Example:**

- Early layers control coarse features like face shape.
- Middle layers refine features like eyes, nose, and mouth.
- Later layers adjust fine details like skin texture and lighting.

2.2 Adaptive Instance Normalization (AdaIN) – The Game Changer

One of the key breakthroughs in StyleGAN is Adaptive Instance Normalization (AdaIN), which allows precise control over different visual styles.

📌 **How AdaIN works:**

✔ Instead of applying uniform transformations to the entire image, AdaIN normalizes features channel-wise.

✔ This allows each layer to control different aspects of the image independently.

✔ The result is highly customizable images with rich textures and diverse styles.

💡 **Why It Matters?**

- Enables smooth style interpolation (e.g., morphing one face into another).
- Allows fine-grained control over artistic features in AI-generated content.

3. Progressive Growing – Training StyleGAN for High Resolutions

StyleGAN generates high-resolution images (1024x1024 or higher) using a progressive growing approach.

📌 **How Progressive Growing Works:**

✔ The model starts generating low-resolution images (4x4 pixels).

✔ It gradually adds new layers, increasing the resolution step by step (8x8, 16x16, 32x32, etc.).

✔ This prevents instability in GAN training and produces smoother, more realistic images.

💡 **Advantage:**

- Less chance of mode collapse (GAN generating repetitive images).
- Better fine-detail synthesis (sharp textures, realistic shadows).

📎 **Example**: NVIDIA's StyleGAN2 improved this technique, reducing visual artifacts and making AI-generated faces almost indistinguishable from real ones.

4. Applications of StyleGAN

4.1 AI-Generated Faces and Deepfake Detection

StyleGAN is famous for generating ultra-realistic human faces, many of which are indistinguishable from real photographs. Websites like "This Person Does Not Exist" use StyleGAN to generate fake faces that look completely authentic.

However, this has also raised concerns about deepfake technology. Researchers are now using GAN-based forensic techniques to detect AI-generated faces and prevent misuse.

4.2 AI Art and Digital Creativity

StyleGAN is revolutionizing AI-generated art by creating stunning, unique visuals.

📌 **Applications in Art:**

✓ AI-generated portraits, landscapes, and abstract art.

✓ Style mixing, where AI blends different artistic styles into a single image.

✓ AI-enhanced design for gaming, animation, and VR worlds.

🎨 **Example**: The famous "Portrait of Edmond de Belamy", generated by AI, was sold for $432,500 at Christie's auction.

4.3 Video Game Character and Asset Creation

Game developers use StyleGAN to:

✓ Generate realistic NPC faces dynamically.

✓ Create unique character assets without manual modeling.

✓ Improve texture generation for more lifelike environments.

🎨 **Example**: NVIDIA's GAN-based game textures create ultra-detailed skins and objects in real-time.

5. Limitations and Challenges of StyleGAN

⊘ 1. Computational Cost:

- Training StyleGAN requires high-end GPUs (often multiple NVIDIA A100s or TPUs).
- Inference is fast, but generating thousands of unique high-quality images is resource-intensive.

⊘ 2. Ethical Concerns:

- Deepfake risks: AI-generated faces can be used for fraud, misinformation, and identity theft.
- Copyright issues: Who owns AI-generated images? Legal frameworks are still evolving.

⊘ 3. Mode Collapse and Overfitting:

- Without large, diverse training datasets, StyleGAN may generate repetitive images.

6. The Future of StyleGAN and High-Resolution AI

🚀 What's Next?

✓ StyleGAN3 is expected to bring even better realism and control.

✓ AI models will soon generate entire videos, not just images.

✓ GAN-powered AI avatars for the Metaverse will become more advanced.

📌 Final Thoughts:

StyleGAN is redefining AI-generated media, from deepfakes to digital art, and its impact on industries like gaming, VR, and content creation will only grow.

13.2 Latent Space Exploration and Interpolation

One of the most fascinating aspects of StyleGAN and other advanced GAN architectures is their ability to manipulate and explore the latent space—a high-dimensional space where each point corresponds to a unique, AI-generated image. By navigating this space, we can interpolate between different images, modify specific features (like age, expression, or pose), and even create entirely new variations of a given image.

In this chapter, we'll explore:

✓ What the latent space is and how it works in GANs

✓ Techniques for smooth interpolation between generated images

✓ Feature disentanglement: controlling specific attributes of images

✓ Real-world applications of latent space navigation in AI creativity

By the end, you'll understand how latent space exploration unlocks new creative possibilities in AI-generated art, game design, and synthetic media.

1. Understanding Latent Space in GANs

1.1 What is Latent Space?

When a GAN generates an image, it starts with a random noise vector (z) sampled from a prior distribution, usually Gaussian or uniform. This vector exists in what is called the latent space—a multi-dimensional space where each point represents a possible image the model can generate.

📌 Key Concepts:

✓ The latent space captures high-level features like face shape, hair color, and background.

✓ Certain directions in latent space correspond to specific attributes (e.g., smiling vs. neutral expression).

✓ Latent space allows for smooth transitions between different images through interpolation.

💡 Why It Matters:

- Understanding latent space helps us control GAN outputs more effectively.

- We can modify an image's attributes without retraining the model.
- AI artists and designers can use latent space to create unique, customizable visuals.

2. Latent Space Interpolation: Blending AI-Generated Images

2.1 What is Interpolation?

Interpolation in latent space refers to smoothly transitioning between two different latent vectors to generate intermediate images. This is useful for creating AI-generated animations, deepfake morphing, and style transitions in digital art.

📌 **Types of Interpolation:**

✓ **Linear Interpolation (LERP):** A straight-line transition between two points in latent space.

✓ **Spherical Interpolation (SLERP):** A more natural curved transition that maintains high-quality image synthesis.

🚀 **Example:**

If you have two AI-generated faces, A and B, interpolation can generate smooth intermediate faces, morphing A → B gradually. This technique is widely used in deepfake videos, AI art, and even animated storytelling.

2.2 Implementing Interpolation in Python

🔧 **Code Example**: Latent Space Interpolation with StyleGAN

```
import numpy as np
import torch
from stylegan2_pytorch import StyleGAN2

# Load pre-trained StyleGAN model
generator = StyleGAN2.load_pretrained('stylegan2-ffhq')

# Generate two random latent vectors
```

```
z1 = torch.randn(1, 512)  # Latent vector A
z2 = torch.randn(1, 512)  # Latent vector B

# Interpolate between them
steps = 10
interpolated_images = []
for alpha in np.linspace(0, 1, steps):
    z_interpolated = (1 - alpha) * z1 + alpha * z2
    image = generator(z_interpolated)
    interpolated_images.append(image)

# Display results
import matplotlib.pyplot as plt
fig, axes = plt.subplots(1, steps, figsize=(15,5))
for i, img in enumerate(interpolated_images):
    axes[i].imshow(img.permute(1,2,0).cpu().numpy())
    axes[i].axis("off")
plt.show()
```

💡 **What This Does:**

- Loads a pre-trained StyleGAN model
- Generates two random latent vectors
- Interpolates between them, creating a smooth transition of images

3. Feature Disentanglement: Controlling Specific Attributes

3.1 How Feature Disentanglement Works

In StyleGAN, different layers of the generator control different features of an image. Researchers discovered that some directions in latent space correspond to meaningful changes, such as:

✓ **Age transformation** (young → old)

✓ **Facial expressions** (neutral → smiling)

✓ **Hair color changes** (blonde → brunette)

✓ **Lighting adjustments** (day → night)

This means we can manipulate an image's characteristics without needing to retrain the entire model.

📌 **Techniques to Disentangle Features:**

✓ **Latent Vector Arithmetic**: Adding or subtracting vectors to modify specific features.

✓ **GANSpace**: A method that identifies major variations in latent space using PCA (Principal Component Analysis).

✓ **InterfaceGAN**: A framework that finds interpretable directions in latent space.

🚀 **Example:**

Want to make an AI-generated person smile? Simply move their latent vector in the "smiling direction" in W-space!

```
smile_direction = torch.tensor([...])  # Precomputed smile direction
new_latent_vector = original_latent_vector + (0.5 * smile_direction)
new_image = generator(new_latent_vector)
```

4. Real-World Applications of Latent Space Exploration

4.1 AI-Generated Animation and Film

📌 **How it's used:**

✓ Creating smooth character transitions in digital animation

✓ AI-driven face morphing in movies and VFX

✓ AI-generated deepfake videos for research & entertainment

🎥 **Example**: The film industry uses GAN interpolation for de-aging actors, like in Marvel's "The Irishman".

4.2 AI-Powered Fashion and Design

📌 **How it's used:**

✓ Exploring different clothing styles by interpolating between fashion designs

✓ AI-generated virtual try-ons

✓ Creating new product designs dynamically

🧥 **Example**: Brands like Zalando and Gucci use AI to generate realistic clothing previews.

4.3 AI-Driven Gaming and Virtual Worlds

📌 **How it's used:**

✓ Generating realistic NPC faces dynamically

✓ AI-powered game world textures that adapt to player choices

✓ Morphing between characters with different abilities in video games

🎮 **Example**: GANs power AI-driven character customization in games like Cyberpunk 2077 and The Sims.

5. Challenges and Limitations

🚫 1. Lack of Full Disentanglement

Some GAN models mix different features, making it hard to separate attributes cleanly.

🚫 2. High Computational Cost

Interpolating high-res images takes significant GPU power.

🚫 3. Ethical Concerns with Deepfake Technology

Misuse of latent space techniques could lead to AI-generated misinformation.

🔑 **Key Takeaways:**

✓ Latent space exploration lets us create smooth AI-generated transitions.

✓ Feature disentanglement allows control over specific attributes like age or expression.

✓ GAN interpolation has huge applications in AI art, gaming, animation, and design.

✓ Despite its potential, GAN technology must be used responsibly to avoid misuse.

13.3 AI-Powered Face Generation

The ability of Generative Adversarial Networks (GANs) to generate ultra-realistic human faces has revolutionized AI-powered creativity. From deepfake technology to AI-generated avatars, GANs can create entirely synthetic yet photorealistic faces that are indistinguishable from real ones. Among various GAN architectures, StyleGAN (developed by NVIDIA) stands out as the most powerful model for generating high-resolution, diverse human faces.

In this chapter, we'll explore:

✓ How GANs generate realistic human faces

✓ Training a StyleGAN model on custom datasets

✓ Latent space manipulation for face customization

✓ Real-world applications of AI-generated faces

✓ Ethical concerns and the risks of deepfake misuse

By the end, you'll have a deep understanding of how AI-powered face generation works, its creative applications, and the ethical dilemmas surrounding it.

1. How GANs Generate Realistic Human Faces

GANs use a two-network architecture—a generator (G) that creates fake images and a discriminator (D) that distinguishes between real and fake ones. The competition between these two networks gradually improves the generator's ability to create photorealistic faces.

1.1 The Role of StyleGAN in Face Generation

StyleGAN introduced several innovations that significantly enhanced the quality and control of AI-generated faces:

📌 **Key Features of StyleGAN:**

✓ **Progressive growing**: The model starts with low-resolution images and gradually increases resolution during training.

✓ **Adaptive instance normalization (AdaIN):** Controls specific features like face shape, hair color, and expression.

✓ **Latent space disentanglement**: Enables fine-grained manipulation of facial attributes.

☐ **Example**: With StyleGAN, you can generate an entirely new person who doesn't exist with just a random noise vector. Websites like ThisPersonDoesNotExist.com showcase realistic AI-generated faces that look indistinguishable from real photos.

2. Training a StyleGAN Model for Face Generation

To create your own AI-generated faces, you need to train a StyleGAN model on a dataset of real human faces. Let's break down the process.

2.1 Collecting and Preprocessing a Face Dataset

Before training, you need a large dataset of human faces. Some popular datasets include:

✓ **FFHQ (Flickr-Faces-HQ)** – High-resolution face dataset created by NVIDIA.

✓ **CelebA-HQ** – A dataset containing celebrity faces.

✓ **Your Own Dataset** – You can collect images from online sources or personal collections.

☐ **Preprocessing Steps:**

- Resize all images to 1024x1024 resolution (for high-quality output).
- Normalize pixel values to [-1, 1] (since GANs typically use tanh activation).
- Apply face alignment to ensure eyes and nose are centered.

2.2 Training StyleGAN Using Python

Once your dataset is ready, you can train a StyleGAN model using NVIDIA's official StyleGAN2-ADA implementation.

🔧 Code Example: Training a StyleGAN Model

```
# Clone the StyleGAN2-ADA repository
git clone https://github.com/NVlabs/stylegan2-ada-pytorch.git
cd stylegan2-ada-pytorch

# Prepare your dataset (assume images are stored in "faces_dataset")
python dataset_tool.py --source=faces_dataset --dest=datasets/faces.zip --resolution=1024

# Train the StyleGAN model
python train.py --outdir=training_runs --data=datasets/faces.zip --gpus=2 --batch=16
```

💡 What This Does:

- Converts face images into a TFRecords dataset.
- Starts training a StyleGAN model using 2 GPUs.
- Saves intermediate results (generated faces) after every few epochs.

☐ How Long Does Training Take?

- On a high-end GPU (NVIDIA RTX 3090), training a 1024x1024 StyleGAN model takes 2-3 weeks.
- Using Google Colab or cloud GPUs (like AWS or Azure) can speed up training.

3. Customizing AI-Generated Faces Using Latent Space Manipulation

One of the most exciting features of AI-powered face generation is the ability to manipulate facial features without retraining the model.

3.1 Latent Space Interpolation

By interpolating between two different latent vectors, we can create smooth transitions between different faces.

📌 Example: Morphing between two AI-generated people.

```
import numpy as np
```

```
import torch
from stylegan2_pytorch import StyleGAN2

# Load pre-trained StyleGAN model
generator = StyleGAN2.load_pretrained('stylegan2-ffhq')

# Generate two latent vectors
z1 = torch.randn(1, 512)
z2 = torch.randn(1, 512)

# Interpolate between them
alpha_values = np.linspace(0, 1, 10)
interpolated_faces = [(1 - alpha) * z1 + alpha * z2 for alpha in alpha_values]

# Generate images
images = [generator(z) for z in interpolated_faces]
```

3.2 Modifying Specific Features (Age, Expression, Gender)

StyleGAN allows us to edit specific facial attributes using latent vector arithmetic.

📌 **Example: Making a person look older or younger**

```
# Load a precomputed 'age direction' vector
age_direction = torch.tensor([...])

# Modify latent vector to increase age
older_face = original_latent_vector + (0.5 * age_direction)

# Modify latent vector to decrease age
younger_face = original_latent_vector - (0.5 * age_direction)
```

4. Real-World Applications of AI-Generated Faces

📌 **1. AI Avatars for Games & Virtual Reality**

✓ AI-generated faces are used in video games, metaverse avatars, and digital influencers.

📌 **2. Deepfake Technology**

✓ GANs can create realistic face-swaps, used in movies, marketing, and social media filters.

📌 3. AI-Powered Social Media Content

✓ Many influencers and companies use AI-generated models for advertising and branding.

📌 4. Privacy-Preserving AI

✓ AI-generated people are used in advertising to avoid privacy concerns with real models.

5. Ethical Concerns and the Risks of Deepfake Technology

Despite its incredible potential, AI-powered face generation raises serious ethical concerns.

🚫 1. Deepfake Misuse & Fake Identities

✓ GANs can be used to create fake identities for scams or fraud.

🚫 2. Political Manipulation & Disinformation

✓ AI-generated deepfakes have been used in fake news and political propaganda.

🚫 3. Privacy Violations & Digital Harassment

✓ Malicious actors use AI-generated faces for fake social media accounts and cyber harassment.

💡 **Solution**: Many organizations are developing AI detection tools (e.g., Deepfake detection algorithms) to combat these risks.

💡 **Key Takeaways:**

✓ GANs can generate highly realistic human faces using StyleGAN.

✓ Training StyleGAN requires a large face dataset and powerful GPUs.

✓ Latent space manipulation allows fine-grained control over generated faces.

✓ AI-generated faces have applications in gaming, social media, and advertising.

✓ Ethical concerns must be addressed to prevent deepfake misuse.

13.4 Controlling StyleGAN Outputs with Parameters

One of the most powerful features of StyleGAN is its ability to finely control the appearance of generated images through various parameters. Unlike traditional GANs, where the generator produces images from random noise with limited control, StyleGAN introduces a disentangled latent space, allowing for precise manipulation of facial attributes, styles, and high-resolution details.

In this chapter, we'll explore:

✓ How StyleGAN's latent space works

✓ Controlling high-level and fine-grained features

✓ Adjusting parameters like age, gender, and expressions

✓ Interpolating between different styles

✓ Using truncation tricks for better image quality

By the end, you'll be able to generate and modify AI-generated faces with precision, giving you full creative control over StyleGAN's outputs.

1. Understanding StyleGAN's Latent Space

Unlike traditional GANs, which use a single latent vector (z) from a normal distribution, StyleGAN transforms this input through a mapping network into an intermediate latent space (w). This intermediate space offers better control and more realistic variations in the generated outputs.

📌 **Key Components of StyleGAN's Latent Space:**

✓ **Z-Space (Input Noise Vector)** – The raw noise input sampled from a Gaussian distribution.

✓ **W-Space (Intermediate Latent Space)** – A transformed space that enables better control over outputs.

✓ **W+ Space (Extended Latent Space)** – Allows for fine-grained modifications at different levels of the network.

🎭 **Why is W-Space Important?**

- Allows independent control over different attributes (e.g., hair color, face shape, lighting).
- Enables style mixing, where features from multiple images can be blended together.
- Supports latent space arithmetic, meaning you can perform vector operations to adjust specific traits.

2. Controlling High-Level and Fine-Grained Features

StyleGAN uses style injection at multiple layers of the network, allowing control over different levels of image features.

📌 **Layer-wise Feature Control:**

- **Coarse Styles (Layer 0-3)** → Face shape, head pose, overall structure.

- **Middle Styles (Layer 4-7)** → Facial features like eyes, nose, and mouth.

- **Fine Styles (Layer 8-18)** → Skin texture, hair details, and lighting effects.

2.1 Adjusting High-Level Features (Face Shape, Pose, Age)

To modify high-level features, we need to tweak the coarse layers of the latent space.

🔧 **Example: Changing Face Shape and Pose**

```
# Load a pre-trained StyleGAN model
import torch
```

```
from stylegan2_pytorch import StyleGAN2

model = StyleGAN2.load_pretrained('stylegan2-ffhq')

# Generate a random face
z = torch.randn(1, 512)
image = model(z)

# Modify high-level features
z_mod = z + 0.5 * torch.tensor([face_shape_direction])  # Adjust shape
z_mod = z_mod + 0.3 * torch.tensor([pose_direction])  # Change pose

# Generate modified image
modified_image = model(z_mod)
```

👤 Use Cases:

✓ Create different facial structures (e.g., round face vs. sharp jawline).

✓ Adjust head pose for dynamic images.

✓ Make a person appear older or younger.

2.2 Adjusting Fine-Grained Details (Skin Texture, Lighting, Hair)

For detailed modifications, we need to alter fine-layer styles in the latent space.

📌 Examples of Fine-Tuned Adjustments:

- **Change hair color** 🎨 (Blonde → Black → Red)
- **Modify skin smoothness** ✨ (Wrinkles → Youthful look)
- **Enhance lighting effects** ✵ (Soft light → Harsh shadows)

🔧 Example: Changing Hair Color

```
# Load a precomputed 'hair color direction' vector
hair_color_direction = torch.tensor([...])

# Modify latent vector
z_hair = z + (0.6 * hair_color_direction)
```

```
# Generate modified image
hair_modified_image = model(z_hair)
```

💡 **Pro Tip**: You can create custom latent direction vectors by training an attribute classifier on existing images and then finding the average vector difference between different classes.

3. Using Truncation Trick for Better Image Quality

One challenge with GANs is that some generated faces may appear unnatural or too diverse. StyleGAN introduces the truncation trick to balance diversity vs. realism.

📌 **What is the Truncation Trick?**

- It scales down the latent vector values toward the mean of W-space.
- Reducing truncation increases realism but reduces diversity.
- Increasing truncation adds more diversity but may create strange outputs.

🔧 **Example: Applying Truncation Trick**

```
psi = 0.7  # Truncation value (0.5 to 1.0)
w_avg = model.mapping_network.get_average_w()  # Get average latent vector
w_truncated = w_avg + psi * (w - w_avg)

# Generate image with truncation applied
image_truncated = model(w_truncated)
```

🚀 **Best Practice:**

- Use psi = 0.5 to 0.7 for ultra-realistic images.
- Use psi > 1.0 for creative, artistic effects.

4. Interpolating Between Different Styles

StyleGAN allows smooth interpolation between different images, creating morphing effects or hybrid faces.

📌 **Example: Morphing Between Two Faces**

```
import numpy as np

# Generate two random latent vectors
z1 = torch.randn(1, 512)
z2 = torch.randn(1, 512)

# Create interpolation steps
alpha_values = np.linspace(0, 1, 10)
interpolated_vectors = [(1 - alpha) * z1 + alpha * z2 for alpha in alpha_values]

# Generate interpolated images
images = [model(z) for z in interpolated_vectors]
```

📌 Use Cases:

✓ Creating AI-based face transitions for movies or games.

✓ Blending features from different people (e.g., mix between two celebrities).

✓ Generating smooth variations of a character for animation.

5. Real-World Applications of StyleGAN Parameter Control

- ◆ **Fashion & Beauty Industry** – AI-generated models for advertising campaigns.
- ◆ **Gaming & VR** – Customizable character faces in video games.
- ◆ **Film & Animation** – AI-generated actors and realistic CGI.
- ◆ **Forensics & Law Enforcement** – Creating missing person reconstructions.
- ◆ **Deepfake Technology** – Ethical and responsible usage for media production.

🔑 Key Takeaways:

✓ StyleGAN's latent space allows precise control over generated images.

✓ You can modify high-level and fine-grained features using latent vector arithmetic.

✓ The truncation trick helps balance realism and diversity.

✓ Interpolation enables smooth blending of different styles.

✓ StyleGAN is widely used in gaming, advertising, and content creation.

13.5 Applications in CGI and VFX

The world of Computer-Generated Imagery (CGI) and Visual Effects (VFX) has seen groundbreaking transformations with the introduction of Generative Adversarial Networks (GANs). Traditional CGI workflows rely on manual modeling, animation, and rendering, which are time-consuming and require immense computational power. GANs, particularly StyleGAN, BigGAN, and CycleGAN, have revolutionized the industry by automating asset creation, enhancing realism, and reducing production costs.

In this chapter, we will explore:

✓ How GANs are revolutionizing CGI and VFX

✓ Using GANs for realistic character generation

✓ AI-driven texture mapping and material synthesis

✓ Enhancing special effects with AI

✓ The future of AI-powered filmmaking

By the end of this chapter, you'll understand how GANs are reshaping digital entertainment, movies, and gaming, making AI an indispensable tool in the industry.

1. How GANs Are Revolutionizing CGI and VFX

Traditionally, CGI and VFX require:

- 3D modelers to manually design characters and environments
- Texture artists to create lifelike surfaces
- Animators to bring movement and expressions to life
- Render farms to process massive amounts of visual data

GANs significantly reduce time and effort by automating and enhancing these steps. By training AI models on vast datasets of real-world images, GANs can:

✓ Generate ultra-realistic 3D characters and faces

✓ Improve real-time rendering and animation

✓ Create high-resolution textures and materials

✓ Automate facial expressions and motion capture

☐ **Example: The Mandalorian (2020)**

The show used AI-based deepfake GANs to de-age characters and create digital doubles. This technology allows for more convincing CGI actors and hyper-realistic face replacements in films.

2. AI-Powered Character and Face Generation

GANs, especially StyleGAN and FaceGAN, have revolutionized digital human creation. By learning patterns from real human faces, these models can generate photo-realistic 3D characters for:

- Movies & TV shows 🎬
- Video games 🎮
- Virtual reality (VR) and augmented reality (AR) ☐
- Metaverse avatars ☐

📌 **How It Works:**

1☐ Train a StyleGAN model on human face datasets.

2☐ Use latent space interpolation to generate infinite character variations.

3☐ Modify attributes (age, gender, hairstyle, emotions) with latent vector arithmetic.

4☐ Apply the AI-generated texture onto 3D character models.

🔧 **Example: Creating a Realistic AI-Generated Character**

```
import torch
from stylegan2_pytorch import StyleGAN2

# Load pre-trained model
model = StyleGAN2.load_pretrained('stylegan2-ffhq')

# Generate a random face
z = torch.randn(1, 512)
image = model(z)
```

```
# Modify attributes
z_old = z + 0.8 * torch.tensor([age_direction])  # Adjust age
z_smile = z + 0.5 * torch.tensor([smile_direction])  # Add smile

# Generate modified face
modified_face = model(z_old + z_smile)
```

🔥 Impact on the Industry:

- Eliminates the need for real actors in some scenes
- Allows for infinite character customization
- Saves time and cost in 3D modeling and rendering

3. AI-Driven Texture Mapping and Material Synthesis

In CGI, textures are crucial for creating realistic objects, environments, and characters. Traditionally, artists manually paint textures, which is labor-intensive. GANs like TextureGAN automate this process by:

✓ Generating photo-realistic materials (wood, metal, skin, fabrics)

✓ Enhancing low-resolution textures using Super-Resolution GANs (SRGANs)

✓ Converting hand-drawn sketches into detailed textures

🔧 Example: Using GANs for Material Synthesis

```
from tensorflow.keras.models import load_model
import numpy as np

# Load pre-trained TextureGAN model
textureGAN = load_model("textureGAN_model.h5")

# Generate texture from noise
noise = np.random.randn(1, 128)
texture = textureGAN.predict(noise)
```

☐ Example: Disney's Lion King (2019)

The realistic fur textures on CGI lions were enhanced using AI-based texture synthesis, creating hyper-realistic animal models.

🔥 Impact on the Industry:

- Significantly reduces manual work in texturing
- Enables automatic material synthesis
- Enhances CGI quality for games and movies

4. Enhancing Special Effects with AI

GANs play a key role in VFX-heavy scenes by:

✓ Generating realistic explosions, fire, smoke, and water effects

✓ Enhancing motion capture animation

✓ Reconstructing missing frames in CGI sequences

✓ Automating deepfake face swaps for actors

📌 AI-Based Effects in Hollywood:

🎬 **Avengers: Endgame (2019)** – AI-enhanced battle sequences
🎬 **Gemini Man (2019)** – Will Smith's younger version created with AI
🎬 **Blade Runner 2049 (2017)** – Deepfake technology used for digital actors

🔧 Example: AI-Based Smoke and Fire Effects

```
from gan_model import FireGAN

# Load AI model trained on fire/smoke data
fireGAN = FireGAN.load_model("fireGAN.pth")

# Generate AI-enhanced fire effect
fire_texture = fireGAN.generate_effect(size=(512, 512))
```

🔥 Impact on the Industry:

- Saves time in rendering complex visual effects
- Creates ultra-realistic CGI explosions, fire, and magic effects
- Enhances deepfake technology for digital actors

5. The Future of AI in Filmmaking and VFX

The future of CGI and VFX is deeply intertwined with AI. GANs are already being used to:

✓ Create entirely AI-generated movies 🎥
✓ Generate realistic digital doubles for actors □
✓ Enhance real-time rendering for VR and AR □
✓ Automate CGI asset creation for games 🎮

□ Example: The Rise of AI-Generated Films

Recent advancements in AI-generated scripts, deepfake actors, and GAN-based special effects are leading to the first fully AI-generated films. Imagine a future where entire movies are created with no human involvement!

🔮 Predictions for the Future:

🚀 Real-time AI-powered VFX in live broadcasts
🚀 Fully AI-generated actors replacing real performers
🚀 GAN-enhanced rendering for hyper-realistic VR worlds

GANs are revolutionizing CGI and VFX, offering faster, cheaper, and more realistic digital content creation. From photo-realistic character generation to AI-driven texture mapping and special effects, GANs are transforming Hollywood, gaming, and virtual worlds.

🔑 Key Takeaways:

✓ StyleGAN and FaceGAN generate ultra-realistic digital humans.

✓ AI-driven texture mapping enhances CGI realism.

✓ GANs automate special effects like fire, smoke, and explosions.

✓ AI-powered CGI will shape the future of entertainment.

14. CycleGAN and Unsupervised Image Translation

What if AI could transform an image from one style to another—turn a horse into a zebra, a summer landscape into winter, or a painting into a real-world photo—without needing paired training data? This is exactly what CycleGAN does. In this chapter, we explore how CycleGAN enables unsupervised image-to-image translation, allowing AI to learn mappings between two domains without one-to-one image correspondences. You'll learn how CycleGAN uses cycle consistency loss to maintain realistic transformations, how it compares to other GANs like Pix2Pix, and its real-world applications in art, photography, medical imaging, and data augmentation. By the end of this chapter, you'll understand how to apply CycleGAN for creative AI applications and domain adaptation. 🎭☐☐☐🚀

14.1 What Is CycleGAN?

Traditional image transformation techniques require paired datasets, where the model learns a direct mapping between two corresponding images. However, what if we don't have perfectly matched images? This is where CycleGAN comes in. CycleGAN (Cycle-Consistent Generative Adversarial Network) is an advanced GAN architecture designed for image-to-image translation without paired training data.

Unlike standard GANs that generate images from random noise, CycleGAN learns to transform one image domain into another while preserving key structural features. This has led to applications like turning day images into night, converting horse images into zebras, and even transforming artistic paintings into real-world photos.

In this section, we will explore:

✓ How CycleGAN differs from traditional GANs

✓ The cycle-consistency concept and why it's important

✓ Applications of CycleGAN in real-world AI creativity

By the end of this chapter, you'll understand why CycleGAN is one of the most powerful AI tools for image transformation and how it enables stunning visual modifications without requiring paired datasets.

1. How CycleGAN Differs from Traditional GANs

A Vanilla GAN learns to generate new images by mapping noise to a real-looking image distribution. However, in tasks like style transfer and image transformation, a simple GAN approach struggles because it requires a direct one-to-one mapping between images.

☞ **Example**: Suppose we want to convert a horse image into a zebra. A traditional GAN would need pairs of horse and zebra images taken from the same angle, with the same lighting. However, such perfectly aligned datasets are hard to collect.

◆ CycleGAN overcomes this limitation by learning from unpaired images. Instead of needing exact matches, it extracts style and texture features from one domain and applies them to another, ensuring the original image structure remains unchanged.

Feature	Traditional GANs	CycleGAN
Data Requirement	Requires paired images	Works with unpaired images
Purpose	Generates new images	Transforms images from one domain to another
Key Innovation	Adversarial loss	Cycle-consistency loss
Example Use Case	Generate fake human faces	Convert a horse into a zebra

2. The Concept of Cycle-Consistency

The core innovation of CycleGAN is its cycle-consistency loss, which ensures that:

1️⃣ An image from domain A (e.g., a horse) can be transformed into domain B (e.g., a zebra).

2️⃣ When the transformed image is converted back to its original domain, it must resemble the original input.

🌀 **How Cycle-Consistency Works:**

◆ **Forward Cycle: Image (Horse)** → Converted Image (Zebra)

◆ **Backward Cycle: Converted Image (Zebra)** → Reconstructed Image (Horse)

If CycleGAN fails to reconstruct the original image, it adjusts its learning process to preserve important features. This ensures the transformations are meaningful and not just random changes.

☐ Mathematical Representation:

Let:

- X be the source domain (e.g., Horses)
- Y be the target domain (e.g., Zebras)
- $G(X)$ be the transformation function (Horse → Zebra)
- $F(Y)$ be the inverse function (Zebra → Horse)

Then, the **cycle-consistency loss** is:

$$L_{cycle} = \|F(G(X)) - X\| + \|G(F(Y)) - Y\|$$

This ensures that when a horse is transformed into a zebra and then back, it still looks like the original horse.

3. Training Process of CycleGAN

CycleGAN is trained using two Generator-Discriminator pairs:

- **Generator** G converts images from **Domain A (horses)** to **Domain B (zebras)**.
- **Generator** F converts images from **Domain B (zebras)** back to **Domain A (horses)**.
- **Discriminator** D_A distinguishes between real horses and AI-generated horses.
- **Discriminator** D_B distinguishes between real zebras and AI-generated zebras.

🔧 Training Steps:

1☐ CycleGAN takes an image from Domain A (Horse).
2☐ Generator G converts it into a zebra-like image.

3️⃣ Discriminator D_B checks if it looks like a real zebra.

4️⃣ Generator F attempts to transform the zebra-like image back into a horse.

5️⃣ Cycle consistency loss ensures the output still resembles the original horse.

🔲 Code Example: Implementing CycleGAN in PyTorch

```
import torch
from cycle_gan import Generator

# Load pre-trained CycleGAN model
G_HorseToZebra = Generator()
G_HorseToZebra.load_state_dict(torch.load("horse2zebra.pth"))

# Load an input horse image
horse_image = load_image("horse.jpg")

# Convert horse to zebra
zebra_image = G_HorseToZebra(horse_image)

# Save the transformed image
save_image(zebra_image, "zebra_output.jpg")
```

4. Real-World Applications of CycleGAN

CycleGAN has enabled some mind-blowing AI creativity across different fields:

🎨 1. Artistic Style Transfer

✔ Convert Monet paintings into realistic landscapes

✔ Transform modern photos into Van Gogh-style artwork

🌄 2. Changing Weather and Lighting in Images

✔ Turn daytime photos into nighttime views

✔ Convert summer landscapes into snowy winter scenes

🐴 3. Animal-to-Animal Image Translation

✓ Transform horses into zebras (original CycleGAN research)

✓ Convert dogs into wolves or cats into lions

☐ 4. Enhancing Satellite Imagery

✓ Convert aerial photos into high-resolution satellite maps

✓ Improve clarity and remove noise from low-quality images

🎮 5. AI in Video Game Asset Creation

✓ Convert hand-drawn sketches into realistic textures

✓ Transform 2D game sprites into 3D photorealistic assets

5. The Future of CycleGAN

🔮 What's Next for CycleGAN?

🚀 Improved Style Control – Future versions of CycleGAN will allow users to fine-tune color, texture, and detail level for precise transformations.

🚀 Real-Time Image Translation – Researchers are working on optimizing CycleGAN for instant image transformations on mobile devices and AR applications.

🚀 Higher-Resolution Image Synthesis – By integrating StyleGAN techniques, CycleGAN models can generate 4K and even 8K transformations for film and video editing.

🚀 Cross-Domain AI Creativity – Imagine converting a photograph into a 3D model, or a cartoon into a photorealistic portrait—CycleGAN is paving the way for AI-driven content creation!

CycleGAN is a game-changer in AI creativity. By enabling image-to-image translation without paired datasets, it has transformed fields like art, photography, gaming, and science.

💡 Key Takeaways:

✓ CycleGAN does not require paired images for training.

✓ The cycle-consistency loss ensures transformations retain original structures.

✓ Applications include style transfer, weather changes, and satellite image enhancement.

✓ The future of CycleGAN involves real-time AI creativity and ultra-HD image synthesis.

14.2 Unpaired Image-to-Image Translation

Traditional machine learning approaches to image transformation rely on large datasets of paired images, where each input has a corresponding output. However, in many real-world scenarios, such paired datasets don't exist or are too expensive to create. This is where unpaired image-to-image translation comes in—a powerful AI technique that enables style and content transformation without requiring one-to-one image matches.

At the forefront of this technology is CycleGAN, which learns to translate images between two different domains using unpaired data. Unlike traditional GANs that generate entirely new images, unpaired image-to-image translation allows AI to modify existing images while preserving their core structures.

In this section, we will explore:

✓ How unpaired image translation differs from traditional paired approaches

✓ The cycle-consistency concept and why it's crucial

✓ Real-world applications of unpaired translation in art, gaming, medical imaging, and more

By the end, you'll have a deep understanding of how AI can transform images across different styles, themes, and domains without requiring labeled datasets.

1. The Challenge of Unpaired Image Translation

Image-to-image translation has traditionally relied on supervised learning, meaning that every input image has a corresponding output image in a paired dataset.

📌 **Example of Paired Image Translation:**

- Converting black-and-white images into color
- Transforming sketches into photorealistic images
- Enhancing low-resolution images into high-resolution versions

However, in many real-world scenarios, paired datasets are rare or nonexistent.

📌 **Example of Unpaired Image Translation Challenges:**

- We don't have one-to-one images of horses and zebras from the same angle and lighting.
- There are no exact image pairs of old paintings and their modern-day photographic versions.
- Medical imaging often lacks perfectly aligned scans of diseased and healthy tissues.

This is where unpaired image-to-image translation solves the problem. Instead of requiring exact matches, it learns general patterns and transformations between domains.

2. How Unpaired Image-to-Image Translation Works

The key to unpaired image translation is the cycle-consistency mechanism, introduced in CycleGAN.

◆ The Core Idea: Cycle-Consistency

In a paired dataset, the model directly learns to convert image A → image B.

In unpaired translation, there is no direct match, so we need a two-step approach:

1️⃣ Convert image A (e.g., a horse) into a B-like version (e.g., a zebra).

2️⃣ Convert the zebra-like image back into a horse.

If the reconstructed horse still looks like the original, the model has learned a meaningful transformation rather than just random modifications.

🔄 The Two-Step Learning Process:

Forward Cycle:

- Take an image X from Domain A (e.g., a horse).
- Transform it into an image Y' in Domain B (e.g., a zebra).

Backward Cycle:

- Take the transformed image Y' (zebra) and attempt to reconstruct X' (horse).
- If X' looks like the original X, the model has successfully learned a realistic transformation.

📌 Cycle Consistency Loss Formula:

$$L_{cycle} = ||F(G(X)) - X|| + ||G(F(Y)) - Y||$$

where:

- G(X) → Y': Maps an image from Domain A (horses) to Domain B (zebras).

- F(Y) → X': Converts the transformed image back to its original form.

- The model optimizes itself by reducing the difference between X and X'.

◆ Architecture of Unpaired Image Translation Models

Unpaired image-to-image translation models typically use:

✓ Two Generators:

- One learns A → B (Horse to Zebra)

- The other learns B → A (Zebra to Horse)

✓ Two Discriminators:

- One checks if B images are real or fake
- The other checks if A images are real or fake

3. Real-World Applications of Unpaired Image Translation

Unpaired image translation has opened the door to incredible AI applications across multiple fields:

🎨 1. Artistic Style Transfer

- Convert Monet-style paintings into photorealistic images
- Transform modern photos into Picasso-inspired artwork
- AI-powered cartoonization and anime-style transformations

☐ 2. Animal and Object Transformations

- Transform horses into zebras (original CycleGAN research)
- Convert cats into dogs or apples into oranges
- Change summer landscapes into winter scenes

⊕ 3. AI in Medical Imaging

- Transform MRI scans into CT scans (useful when one type of scan is unavailable)
- Convert low-resolution X-rays into high-resolution images
- Improve disease detection by removing noise from medical images

🎮 4. AI in Video Games and CGI

- Convert hand-drawn sketches into realistic textures
- Transform 2D game sprites into 3D high-definition models
- Automate the generation of lifelike game environments

🏁 5. Enhancing Photography & Video Editing

- Change daytime photos into nighttime scenes
- Convert rainy weather photos into sunny landscapes
- Restore damaged or faded historical images

4. Code Implementation of Unpaired Image Translation

Below is a simple example of using a pre-trained CycleGAN model to transform images:

```
import torch
from cycle_gan import Generator

# Load pre-trained CycleGAN model
G_A_to_B = Generator()
G_A_to_B.load_state_dict(torch.load("horse2zebra.pth"))

# Load an input horse image
horse_image = load_image("horse.jpg")

# Convert horse to zebra
zebra_image = G_A_to_B(horse_image)

# Save the transformed image
save_image(zebra_image, "zebra_output.jpg")
```

This example loads a pre-trained CycleGAN model and applies unpaired image-to-image translation to transform a horse into a zebra.

5. Challenges and Limitations

Despite its success, unpaired image translation still faces some challenges:

✗ **Preserving Fine Details**: Sometimes, AI introduces unwanted artifacts or distorts important features.

✗ **Computational Cost**: Training CycleGAN and similar models requires high-performance GPUs or TPUs.

✗ **Mode Collapse**: The generator might only learn a limited set of transformations instead of diverse, realistic changes.

✗ **Evaluation Difficulty**: Unlike paired translation, there is no ground truth to compare results against, making performance measurement harder.

🚀 Future improvements involve using attention mechanisms, self-supervised learning, and multimodal architectures to enhance quality and diversity.

Unpaired image-to-image translation is one of the most exciting advancements in AI creativity. It allows for style and content transformation without requiring labeled training data, making it widely applicable across various industries.

💡 Key Takeaways:

✓ Unpaired translation removes the need for matched datasets, making AI transformation more accessible.

✓ CycleGAN ensures structural consistency using cycle-consistency loss.

✓ Applications include art, photography, gaming, medical imaging, and CGI.

✓ Challenges like mode collapse and high computational costs are areas of active research.

14.3 Applications in Medical Imaging

Medical imaging plays a crucial role in diagnosing diseases, monitoring treatments, and advancing healthcare research. However, obtaining high-quality medical images often requires expensive equipment, large datasets, and extensive manual processing. This is where Generative Adversarial Networks (GANs) and unpaired image-to-image translation techniques like CycleGAN are revolutionizing the field.

GANs are being used to enhance, translate, and generate medical images, helping radiologists, researchers, and AI systems detect diseases more accurately and efficiently. By learning to convert images between different modalities (such as MRI to CT scans) or improve the quality of noisy scans, GANs are transforming medical diagnostics.

In this section, we will explore:

✓ How GANs improve medical image quality and resolution

✓ Applications of image-to-image translation in radiology

✓ GAN-powered disease detection and segmentation

✓ Challenges and ethical concerns in AI-driven healthcare

By the end of this chapter, you'll understand how GANs are making medical imaging more accurate, accessible, and efficient.

1. Enhancing Low-Quality Medical Images

Many medical imaging techniques, such as MRI, CT, X-ray, and ultrasound, often suffer from:

- Low resolution (due to hardware limitations)
- Noise and artifacts (caused by patient movement or scanning conditions)
- Contrast issues (making small anomalies hard to detect)

GANs, especially Super-Resolution GANs (SRGANs), are being used to:

📌 **Increase image resolution** – Improve blurry or pixelated scans to provide clearer details.

📌 **Denoise images** – Remove artifacts that interfere with disease detection.

📌 **Enhance contrast** – Highlight important structures, such as tumors or blood vessels.

☐ Example: MRI Image Enhancement

Traditional MRI scans can take a long time to acquire, especially at high resolutions. GAN-based models can:

✓ Generate high-resolution MRI images from low-resolution scans.

✓ Reduce noise, improving visibility of fine details.

✓ Speed up MRI scan times by reconstructing missing information.

✦ **Key Study**: A study published in Nature Medicine showed that GAN-enhanced MRI scans improved radiologists' accuracy in detecting brain tumors.

2. Image-to-Image Translation in Medical Imaging

Unpaired image-to-image translation models like CycleGAN are helping in cross-modality medical imaging, where images from one type of scan are converted into another.

◆ MRI to CT Image Translation

MRI (Magnetic Resonance Imaging) is better for soft tissue details, while CT (Computed Tomography) is better for bone structure visualization. However, some hospitals may lack one modality due to cost or availability.

✓ GANs can synthesize CT scans from MRI scans, allowing doctors to analyze both without requiring extra scans.

✓ This reduces radiation exposure for patients who would otherwise need an additional CT scan.

✓ AI-generated CT images help in pre-surgical planning by providing full anatomical details.

◆ **PET to MRI Translation**

Positron Emission Tomography (PET) scans are used to detect cancer by measuring metabolic activity, but they provide low-resolution images. By using GANs to enhance PET scans with MRI-like detail, doctors can:

✓ Improve cancer detection.

✓ Reduce scanning time while maintaining accuracy.

☐ **Case Study**: GANs have been used to improve Alzheimer's diagnosis by converting low-quality PET scans into high-resolution MRI-like images, helping detect early-stage brain degeneration.

3. AI-Powered Disease Detection and Diagnosis

Medical imaging generates huge amounts of data, making it challenging for doctors to analyze every scan manually. GANs are being used to:

✓ **Detect diseases** – GANs trained on medical images can identify tumors, fractures, and organ abnormalities.

✓ **Segment medical images** – AI can highlight specific areas of concern, such as cancerous regions in an MRI scan.

✓ **Predict patient outcomes** – AI models can analyze scans over time to predict disease progression.

☐ Example: GANs for Cancer Detection

A GAN trained on thousands of breast cancer mammograms can:

- Detect small tumors that may be missed by human radiologists.
- Generate synthetic cancerous images to help train other AI models.
- Reduce false positives by distinguishing between benign and malignant masses.

♟‡☐ Real-World Use:

- Google's DeepMind developed a GAN-based AI system for lung cancer detection, outperforming traditional radiology methods.
- GANs have also been used to detect diabetic retinopathy in retinal scans, preventing blindness in diabetes patients.

4. Synthetic Medical Data for Research & Training

AI models need large, diverse datasets to learn effectively. However, medical data is often limited due to privacy concerns and patient confidentiality laws.

GANs solve this problem by generating synthetic medical images that look realistic but contain no real patient data. This allows:

✓ AI training on diverse datasets without exposing patient records.

✓ Data augmentation to improve AI accuracy on rare diseases.

✓ Medical students and researchers to practice on realistic synthetic images.

📌 **Example**: GANs have been used to generate realistic brain MRI scans for training deep learning models in tumor detection—without using real patient data.

5. Challenges and Ethical Considerations

Despite their benefits, GANs in medical imaging also present challenges:

✗ Data Bias & Fairness

- AI models trained on limited datasets may not work equally well for all demographics.
- GAN-generated medical images must represent diverse populations to avoid misdiagnosis.

✗ Misinterpretation of Synthetic Images

- If improperly labeled, AI-generated images could mislead doctors or affect patient diagnosis.
- Radiologists must be trained to recognize GAN-enhanced images versus real scans.

✗ Privacy & Security Concerns

- GANs can generate realistic fake patient data, raising concerns about fraud or identity theft.
- Strict AI regulations in healthcare must ensure ethical use of synthetic images.

🚀 Future Solutions:

- Developing explainable AI models so doctors understand AI-generated insights.
- Using blockchain for secure tracking of AI-enhanced medical images.

GANs are transforming medical imaging by enhancing image quality, translating between scan modalities, and detecting diseases more accurately. From improving MRI resolution to synthetic data generation, AI-driven medical imaging is making healthcare more efficient, accurate, and accessible.

🔑 Key Takeaways:

✓ GANs enhance low-quality medical images, improving resolution and noise reduction.

✓ CycleGAN enables cross-modality translations, converting MRI to CT and PET to MRI.

✓ AI-powered disease detection helps radiologists diagnose conditions like cancer, fractures, and brain disorders.

✓ Synthetic medical data allows AI training without violating patient privacy.

✓ Ethical concerns like bias, privacy, and misinterpretation must be carefully addressed.

14.4 Enhancing Historical Images with GANs

Historical images offer a fascinating window into the past, but many old photographs, paintings, and documents suffer from degradation, low resolution, and missing details. Generative Adversarial Networks (GANs) have revolutionized image restoration, colorization, and super-resolution, making it possible to restore, enhance, and even animate historical visuals with stunning realism.

In this chapter, we will explore how GANs can breathe new life into old images, covering:

✓ **Restoring damaged photographs** – Fixing scratches, noise, and missing parts.

✓ **Colorizing black-and-white images** – Adding lifelike colors to historical moments.

✓ **Super-resolution enhancement** – Sharpening low-resolution images.

✓ **AI-powered facial animation** – Bringing history to life through movement.

By the end of this chapter, you'll understand how GANs are transforming historical archives, museums, and digital restoration projects.

1. Restoring Damaged Photographs with GANs

Old photographs often degrade due to scratches, dust, fading, and missing sections. Traditional restoration methods require manual retouching, which is time-consuming and requires expert knowledge. GANs automate this process, using deep learning to:

✦ **Remove noise and artifacts** – Eliminates graininess, cracks, and smudges.
✦ **Inpaint missing sections** – AI reconstructs lost details, guessing missing areas.
✦ **Enhance contrast and sharpness** – Improves clarity while preserving authenticity.

☐ **Example: AI-Powered Photo Restoration**

A project by NVIDIA researchers developed a GAN-based model that can:

✓ Restore heavily damaged photos by intelligently reconstructing lost details.

✓ Identify facial features even in blurry images and enhance them.

✓ Learn from large datasets to predict accurate restorations.

Museums and historical societies are now using GANs to digitally restore rare photographs, preserving history for future generations.

2. Colorizing Black-and-White Images with AI

Color plays a key role in making historical images feel more relatable and realistic. However, manually adding color to black-and-white photos is labor-intensive and requires artistic expertise. GANs, specifically DeOldify and other deep learning models, automate this process by learning from vast datasets of color images.

✓ AI models analyze grayscale images and predict realistic colors.

✓ Context-aware coloring ensures accurate skin tones, landscapes, and objects.

✓ Self-learning models improve colorization accuracy over time.

🎨 Case Study: Bringing History to Life

Historical figures such as Abraham Lincoln, Albert Einstein, and Queen Victoria have been colorized using GANs, allowing people to see them in a new light. AI has also been applied to World War II footage, restoring and colorizing old war films.

◆ Peter Jackson's documentary They Shall Not Grow Old used AI-based colorization to transform WWI footage into vivid, high-resolution video, making history more immersive.

3. Super-Resolution for Sharpening Historical Images

Many old images suffer from low resolution, making it difficult to appreciate finer details. GAN-based models such as Super-Resolution GAN (SRGAN) can upscale images, creating high-definition versions of historical photographs.

☐ Benefits of Super-Resolution GANs

✓ **Enhances fine details** – Facial features, textures, and backgrounds are sharpened.

✓ **Increases resolution for printing and display** – Helps museums create large exhibits.

✓ **Improves digital preservation** – Ensures historical images remain useful for future research.

☐ **Example**: AI-powered super-resolution techniques were used to enhance images from NASA's Apollo missions, restoring grainy moon landing photos to modern-day clarity.

4. AI-Powered Facial Animation – Bringing History to Life

One of the most exciting applications of GANs in historical image enhancement is facial animation. Models like Deep Nostalgia (developed by MyHeritage) allow AI to:

✓ **Animate historical portraits** – Making figures smile, blink, and move.

✓ **Generate realistic motion from still images** – Breathing life into ancestors and historical icons.

✓ **Preserve historical storytelling** – Making educational content more engaging.

🚀 Case Study: Reviving Historical Figures

Deep Nostalgia has been used to animate centuries-old portraits, making historical figures move and express emotions. This has revolutionized genealogy research, allowing people to see their ancestors in motion for the first time.

Museums and historical organizations now use GAN-powered animation to create immersive experiences, such as virtual history exhibits where AI-animated figures narrate their own stories.

5. Ethical Considerations in AI-Driven Image Enhancement

While GANs offer incredible possibilities for historical image restoration, they also raise ethical concerns, such as:

✗ Historical Accuracy vs. AI Guesswork

- AI-generated restorations and colorizations are based on best-guess predictions, which may not always be historically accurate.
- There is a risk of misrepresenting historical events by applying colors or features that never existed.

✖ Deepfake Concerns

- GANs can be used to manipulate historical images, creating fake historical events or altering the past.
- Ethical AI usage requires clear labeling of AI-generated content to avoid misinformation.

✖ Respect for Cultural Heritage

- Some communities may oppose AI-altering historical images, especially in cases where sacred or personal images are modified.
- Museums and historians must work closely with cultural experts when applying GAN techniques.

🚀 Future Solutions:

- Developing AI models that prioritize historical accuracy, using expert-reviewed datasets.
- Creating transparent AI labeling systems, so viewers know when an image has been enhanced.
- Educating users on ethical AI applications to prevent misuse.

GANs are transforming historical image restoration, colorization, and animation, making history more accessible and immersive than ever before. Whether it's restoring old photos, colorizing black-and-white images, or animating historical figures, AI is reshaping how we preserve and interact with the past.

🔑 Key Takeaways:

✔ GANs restore and enhance old photographs, removing damage and improving clarity.

✔ AI colorization brings black-and-white images to life, making history more relatable.

✔ Super-resolution GANs upscale low-quality images, improving details and print quality.

✔ Facial animation models bring historical figures to life, making history interactive.

✔ Ethical considerations must be addressed, ensuring historical accuracy and responsible AI use.

14.5 Training Custom CycleGAN Models

CycleGAN has emerged as one of the most powerful tools for image-to-image translation, allowing AI to transform images from one domain to another without requiring paired datasets. Unlike traditional supervised learning, which relies on corresponding image pairs, CycleGAN can learn transformations from unpaired images, making it highly effective for tasks like:

- Turning sketches into realistic artwork
- Converting summer landscapes into winter scenes
- Enhancing medical imaging by translating between modalities

In this chapter, we will explore how to train a custom CycleGAN model, covering:

✓ **Dataset preparation** – Collecting and preprocessing unpaired images.

✓ **Model architecture** – Understanding generators, discriminators, and cycle consistency loss.

✓ **Training process** – Setting up the training loop and hyperparameters.

✓ **Evaluation and fine-tuning** – Improving output quality and avoiding artifacts.

By the end of this chapter, you'll be able to train your own CycleGAN model for creative and practical applications.

1. Preparing Your Dataset

🔍 Step 1: Choose Your Two Domains

CycleGAN works by translating images between two distinct domains (A → B and B → A).

Choose two datasets that represent your transformation goal. Examples include:

✓ **Day ↔ Night**: Transform daytime images into nighttime and vice versa.

✓ **Horse ↔ Zebra**: Convert horses into zebras (as seen in CycleGAN's original paper).

✓ **Sketch ↔ Painting**: Turn rough sketches into realistic paintings.

✓ **Monet ↔ Photographs**: Convert real-world photos into Van Gogh or Monet-style paintings.

🔍 Step 2: Collect and Organize Data

You need two separate folders containing unpaired images:

📁 Dataset_A/ → Images from domain A (e.g., horses)
📁 Dataset_B/ → Images from domain B (e.g., zebras)

Recommended Datasets

If you don't have your own dataset, you can use:

- CycleGAN's official datasets: Available in TensorFlow or PyTorch repositories.
- Public datasets from Kaggle, Google Dataset Search, or ImageNet.

🔍 Step 3: Preprocess Images

Ensure your dataset is:

✓ Resized to a standard dimension (e.g., 256×256 or 512×512).

✓ Normalized between -1 and 1 for stable training.

✓ Augmented using transformations like flipping, cropping, and rotation to improve robustness.

2. Understanding CycleGAN Architecture

CycleGAN is built upon two key components:

📌 Generators (G and F)

- G (A → B): Transforms images from domain A to B (e.g., horse → zebra).
- F (B → A): Transforms images from domain B to A (e.g., zebra → horse).

📌 **Discriminators (D_A and D_B)**

- D_A: Tries to distinguish real A images from fake A images produced by F(B → A).

- D_B: Tries to distinguish real B images from fake B images produced by G(A → B).

📌 Cycle Consistency Loss

One of the biggest challenges in unpaired image translation is ensuring that an image converted to another domain can be reconstructed back to its original form. Cycle consistency loss ensures:

✓ **Forward cycle**: A → B → A should reconstruct the original image.

✓ **Backward cycle**: B → A → B should reconstruct the original image.

Cycle consistency loss is calculated as:

$$L_{cycle} = ||F(G(A)) - A|| + ||G(F(B)) - B||$$

This forces the generator to preserve key features of the original image, preventing extreme distortions.

3. Training Your Custom CycleGAN Model

◆ Step 1: Install Dependencies

Before training, install the necessary libraries:

pip install tensorflow torch torchvision numpy matplotlib

◆ Step 2: Load the Dataset

In Python, load and preprocess your images:

import torch
import torchvision.transforms as transforms
from torchvision.datasets import ImageFolder
from torch.utils.data import DataLoader

```
transform = transforms.Compose([
    transforms.Resize((256, 256)),
    transforms.RandomHorizontalFlip(),
    transforms.ToTensor(),
    transforms.Normalize((0.5,), (0.5,))
])

dataset_A = ImageFolder(root="path_to_dataset_A", transform=transform)
dataset_B = ImageFolder(root="path_to_dataset_B", transform=transform)

dataloader_A = DataLoader(dataset_A, batch_size=16, shuffle=True)
dataloader_B = DataLoader(dataset_B, batch_size=16, shuffle=True)
```

◆ Step 3: Define the CycleGAN Model

Use a pre-trained CycleGAN model or define your own generator and discriminator networks. PyTorch provides easy-to-use implementations.

```
from models import Generator, Discriminator  # Import CycleGAN model architecture
```

- G = Generator() # Generator for A → B

- F = Generator() # Generator for B → A

- D_A = Discriminator() # Discriminator for A
- D_B = Discriminator() # Discriminator for B

◆ Step 4: Define Loss Functions and Optimizers

```
import torch.optim as optim

cycle_loss = torch.nn.L1Loss()
gan_loss = torch.nn.MSELoss()

optimizer_G = optim.Adam(G.parameters(), lr=0.0002, betas=(0.5, 0.999))
optimizer_F = optim.Adam(F.parameters(), lr=0.0002, betas=(0.5, 0.999))
optimizer_D_A = optim.Adam(D_A.parameters(), lr=0.0002, betas=(0.5, 0.999))
optimizer_D_B = optim.Adam(D_B.parameters(), lr=0.0002, betas=(0.5, 0.999))
```

◆ Step 5: Train the Model

Train the generators and discriminators iteratively:

```
for epoch in range(num_epochs):
    for real_A, real_B in zip(dataloader_A, dataloader_B):
        # Generate fake images
        fake_B = G(real_A)
        fake_A = F(real_B)

        # Calculate cycle loss
        cycle_A = F(fake_B)
        cycle_B = G(fake_A)
        cycle_loss_A = cycle_loss(cycle_A, real_A)
        cycle_loss_B = cycle_loss(cycle_B, real_B)

        # Train generators
        optimizer_G.zero_grad()
        optimizer_F.zero_grad()
        loss_G = gan_loss(D_B(fake_B), torch.ones_like(D_B(fake_B)))
        loss_F = gan_loss(D_A(fake_A), torch.ones_like(D_A(fake_A)))
        total_G_loss = loss_G + loss_F + (cycle_loss_A + cycle_loss_B) * 10
        total_G_loss.backward()
        optimizer_G.step()
        optimizer_F.step()

        # Train discriminators
        optimizer_D_A.zero_grad()
        optimizer_D_B.zero_grad()
        loss_D_A = gan_loss(D_A(real_A), torch.ones_like(D_A(real_A))) +
gan_loss(D_A(fake_A.detach()), torch.zeros_like(D_A(fake_A.detach())))
        loss_D_B = gan_loss(D_B(real_B), torch.ones_like(D_B(real_B))) +
gan_loss(D_B(fake_B.detach()), torch.zeros_like(D_B(fake_B.detach())))
        total_D_loss = (loss_D_A + loss_D_B) * 0.5
        total_D_loss.backward()
        optimizer_D_A.step()
        optimizer_D_B.step()
```

4. Evaluating and Fine-Tuning the Model

✓ **Monitor Training Progress** – Use loss curves and generated images to detect artifacts.

✓ **Adjust Hyperparameters** – Experiment with learning rates and loss function weights.

✓ **Use Data Augmentation** – More diverse training data improves generalization.

✓ **Apply Regularization Techniques** – Prevent mode collapse with dropout and normalization.

Training a custom CycleGAN model unlocks powerful AI-driven image transformations. Whether you're enhancing artwork, modifying medical scans, or generating synthetic landscapes, CycleGAN provides a versatile, unpaired image translation framework.

15. Text-to-Image and Video Generation

Imagine describing a scene in words and having AI instantly generate a realistic image or even a full video—this is the power of Text-to-Image and Video Generation with GANs. In this chapter, we explore cutting-edge models like DALL·E, Imagen, and Parti, which transform text descriptions into detailed images, and GAN-based video generation models that create animations and synthetic footage. You'll learn how AI understands and visualizes text, how to fine-tune text-to-image models, and the applications of these technologies in graphic design, advertising, filmmaking, and virtual reality. We'll also discuss challenges like controlling output quality, ethical concerns, and AI bias. By the end of this chapter, you'll have a deep understanding of how GANs bridge the gap between language, images, and motion, unlocking new creative possibilities. 🎬🎥📽️🚀

15.1 How DALL·E and Imagen Work

Text-to-image generation is one of the most exciting frontiers in AI, allowing models to create stunning, photorealistic, and imaginative images from textual descriptions. OpenAI's DALL·E and Google's Imagen are two of the most advanced models in this domain, leveraging deep learning, transformers, and diffusion models to generate high-quality visuals from simple text prompts.

These models have revolutionized AI creativity, making it possible to:

✓ Generate artwork, concept designs, and marketing materials

✓ Create photorealistic images for storytelling and media

✓ Aid in scientific visualization and education

In this section, we will explore:

◆ How DALL·E and Imagen generate images from text
◆ The architecture and key technologies behind them
◆ Differences between these two state-of-the-art models

By the end, you'll have a solid understanding of how AI transforms words into visuals and its implications for the future of creative industries.

1. What Is Text-to-Image Generation?

Text-to-image AI models work by interpreting text prompts and generating images that match the given descriptions. They are trained on vast datasets containing image-caption pairs, allowing them to understand the relationship between words and visual concepts.

For example, a prompt like:

💬 "A futuristic city skyline at sunset, with flying cars and neon lights"
…can produce a detailed, high-resolution image that looks like concept art from a sci-fi movie.

These models rely on deep neural networks and advanced probabilistic methods to ensure that each generated image aligns with the given text in terms of style, object placement, and coherence.

2. How DALL·E Works

📌 DALL·E: A Deep Dive

DALL·E, developed by OpenAI, is a transformer-based AI model designed to generate images from text descriptions. It builds on OpenAI's powerful GPT architecture, applying similar principles of natural language processing (NLP) to image synthesis.

🔲🔲 Key Components of DALL·E

✓ **Transformer Architecture** – Uses self-attention mechanisms to process text prompts and generate corresponding images.

✓ **CLIP (Contrastive Language-Image Pretraining)** – Helps the model understand how words and images relate by training on paired datasets.

✓ **Discrete VAE (dVAE)** – Compresses images into a compact representation, allowing DALL·E to generate complex visuals efficiently.

📌 How DALL·E Generates an Image

1️⃣ **Text Encoding** – The input prompt is converted into numerical embeddings using a transformer model.

2⃞ **Latent Space Representation** – DALL·E maps the text embeddings to a visual representation using a learned image vocabulary.

3⃞ **Image Decoding** – The model generates images by reconstructing the learned representations into a pixel-based output.

✸ DALL·E's Strengths

✓ **Highly creative** – Can generate surreal, imaginative, and artistic images.

✓ **Good at style transfer** – Can create images in various artistic styles.

✓ **Text-aware generation** – Understands words like "vibrant," "realistic," or "cartoonish" and adjusts the image accordingly.

However, DALL·E can sometimes struggle with complex compositions involving multiple objects or intricate scene arrangements.

3. How Imagen Works

📌 Imagen: Google's High-Resolution AI Model

While DALL·E is transformer-based, Google's Imagen takes a different approach by using diffusion models, which have proven to be highly effective for generating high-fidelity images.

Imagen leverages large language models (LLMs) combined with image diffusion networks, making it one of the most advanced AI-generated image systems to date.

⬜⬜ Key Components of Imagen

✓ **T5 Text Encoder** – Uses a pre-trained transformer model (T5) to deeply understand text prompts.

✓ **Diffusion Model** – Generates images progressively by starting with noise and refining details over multiple steps.

✓ **Super-Resolution Enhancement** – Uses additional AI models to scale up images to high resolutions with crisp details and realism.

📌 How Imagen Generates an Image

1️⃣ **Text Processing** – The prompt is passed through T5, a large language model, to capture its meaning.

2️⃣ **Diffusion-Based Generation** – Imagen starts with random noise and refines it over time, producing a coherent image.

3️⃣ **Super-Resolution Scaling** – The generated image is passed through enhancement layers to improve clarity and detail.

✹ Imagen's Strengths

✓ **Extremely photorealistic** – Produces images with sharp details and natural textures.

✓ **Better at complex prompts** – Handles multiple objects and intricate scenes with ease.

✓ **High-resolution outputs** – Generates images that look as good as professional photography.

However, since Imagen is not publicly available like DALL·E, its use is currently limited to research purposes.

4. DALL·E vs. Imagen: Key Differences

Feature	DALL·E	Imagen
Architecture	Transformer-based (GPT)	Diffusion model
Text Processing	Uses CLIP for text-image mapping	Uses T5 for better language understanding
Image Generation	Uses discrete VAE for synthesis	Uses iterative noise refinement (diffusion)
Realism	Good, but can struggle with details	Extremely high-resolution and photorealistic
Creativity	Strong at artistic and abstract styles	More focused on realism
Accessibility	Publicly available via OpenAI	Currently restricted to research use

5. The Future of Text-to-Image AI

🖌 **Better Scene Comprehension** – Future models will improve at handling complex relationships between objects in images.

🎨 **More Artistic Control** – AI will allow users to fine-tune colors, textures, and styles more precisely.

∞ Integration with Other AI Systems – Text-to-image AI could work alongside 3D modeling and animation tools, revolutionizing game design and CGI.

☐ **Ethical Considerations** – As these models become more advanced, issues of bias, misinformation, and deepfake risks must be addressed.

DALL·E and Imagen are pushing the boundaries of AI creativity, enabling instant image generation from simple text prompts. While DALL·E excels at creative and artistic interpretations, Imagen dominates in realism and high-quality textures.

Understanding how these models work gives us insight into the future of AI-generated art, design, and media—a future where imagination is the only limit.

15.2 Generating Images from Text Prompts

The ability of AI to generate realistic, detailed, and creative images from simple text descriptions is a revolutionary step in artificial intelligence. Text-to-image models, such as DALL·E, Imagen, and Stable Diffusion, have demonstrated the power of natural language processing (NLP) combined with deep learning to create visual content that mimics human creativity.

In this section, we will explore:

✔ How AI interprets text prompts and converts them into images

✔ Techniques for writing effective prompts to get high-quality results

✔ Common challenges in AI image generation and how to overcome them

By the end of this chapter, you'll understand how to harness AI's creative power by crafting well-structured prompts that yield stunning, AI-generated visuals.

1. How AI Converts Text into Images

Text-to-image generation relies on a combination of deep learning techniques, large-scale training datasets, and probabilistic modeling. The key components include:

1.1 Text Processing

When a user enters a text prompt (e.g., "A futuristic cyberpunk city with neon lights and flying cars"), the AI model:

- Breaks down the words and phrases to understand their meaning.
- Identifies key concepts, objects, styles, and moods within the text.

Maps these concepts to latent representations that the AI can use to generate an image.

1.2 Latent Space Representation

AI models do not "see" images the way humans do. Instead, they use latent space representations, which encode abstract features such as:

✓ Shapes

✓ Textures

✓ Colors

✓ Object relationships

This latent representation helps AI construct new images by referencing patterns learned from millions of existing images.

1.3 Image Generation Process

Once the AI understands the prompt, it generates an image step-by-step using one of two methods:

- **Transformer-based generation (DALL·E 2)** – Uses deep neural networks to predict and refine image details.
- **Diffusion-based generation (Imagen, Stable Diffusion)** – Starts with random noise and gradually refines it into a coherent image.

The result is a visually rich and high-quality image that aligns with the user's description.

2. Crafting Effective Text Prompts

Writing a good text prompt is essential for getting the best AI-generated images. A vague or overly simple prompt may result in generic or low-quality images, while a well-structured prompt can create detailed, stunning artwork.

2.1 The Structure of a Good Prompt

A strong prompt typically includes:

✓ **Main subject** – The primary object or theme (e.g., "a medieval castle")

✓ **Style or mood** – Defines the artistic approach (e.g., "in a fantasy painting style")

✓ **Lighting and atmosphere** – Helps refine the scene (e.g., "golden hour with soft shadows")

✓ **Level of detail** – Determines how complex the image is (e.g., "ultra-detailed, 8K resolution")

2.2 Examples of Strong vs. Weak Prompts

✗ Weak Prompt:

"A dog in a park."

♦ Too vague, lacks detail, and may generate an uninteresting image.

✅ **Strong Prompt:**

"A golden retriever running joyfully through a flower-filled meadow during sunset, with soft warm lighting and ultra-detailed fur."

♦ This gives AI a clear vision of what to generate.

3. Enhancing Image Generation with Advanced Prompting Techniques

To achieve even more refined results, advanced users utilize techniques such as:

3.1 Using Descriptive Adjectives

Adding adjectives enhances the visual richness of the output.

✓ Instead of "A spaceship," try "A sleek, futuristic spaceship with glowing blue engines, flying through a nebula-filled galaxy."

3.2 Including Art Styles and Mediums

If you want AI-generated art in a specific artistic style, mention it in the prompt:

✓ "A portrait of an astronaut, in the style of Van Gogh's Starry Night."

✓ "A cyberpunk cityscape, neon-lit, digital painting style."

3.3 Controlling Composition with Phrasing

Use structured phrasing to define where objects should be placed:

✓ "A dragon perched on a mountain peak, looking over a misty valley."

✓ "A cozy wooden cabin in the center, surrounded by a snowy forest, with smoke coming from the chimney."

3.4 Negative Prompts (for models like Stable Diffusion)

Adding negative prompts helps eliminate unwanted elements:

✓ "A high-quality portrait of a woman, no distortions, no blur, no low resolution."

4. Challenges in Text-to-Image Generation

Even with strong prompts, AI-generated images aren't always perfect. Some common issues include:

4.1 Object Distortion

- AI may generate deformed or unrealistic images (e.g., extra limbs, misshapen faces).
- Solution: Use clear, precise prompts and refine the wording.

4.2 Unwanted Artifacts

- Some images may have blurry details, unnatural textures, or visual noise.
- Solution: Request high resolution, sharp details, or specific styles in the prompt.

4.3 Difficulty with Text in Images

- AI struggles to generate legible text inside an image (e.g., posters, signs).
- Solution: Use a separate graphic design tool for text-based elements.

4.4 Understanding Context

- AI might misinterpret complex relationships between objects.
- **Solution**: Write prompts in a logical sequence to guide the AI (e.g., "A cat sitting on a table, next to a cup of tea.").

5. Real-World Applications of Text-to-Image AI

🎨 Digital Art & Graphic Design

✓ AI-generated images help artists create concept art, illustrations, and promotional graphics.

📖 Publishing & Storytelling

✓ Writers and publishers can use AI to generate book covers, character designs, and story illustrations.

🎥 Movie & Game Development

✓ AI can assist in concept art, 3D texture generation, and game scene creation.

🏬 Marketing & Advertising

✓ Brands use AI-generated visuals for social media campaigns, product designs, and brand storytelling.

🔬 Scientific & Educational Visuals

✓ AI creates accurate medical illustrations, historical recreations, and data visualizations.

Text-to-image AI models have opened up endless possibilities for creative expression, allowing anyone—from artists to businesses—to generate stunning visuals from just a few words.

By understanding how AI interprets text, refining your prompt-writing techniques, and overcoming common image-generation challenges, you can produce high-quality, visually appealing AI-generated artwork.

15.3 AI Video Synthesis with GANs

Imagine typing a description like "A futuristic city at sunset with flying cars zooming between neon skyscrapers" and watching an AI generate a high-quality, fully animated video in seconds. AI-driven video synthesis is rapidly transforming entertainment, gaming, advertising, and content creation, allowing machines to generate realistic and artistic video content without human intervention.

At the heart of AI video generation are Generative Adversarial Networks (GANs), which extend their capabilities beyond static images to dynamic sequences of frames. In this chapter, we explore:

✓ How GANs generate and predict video frames

✓ Key architectures like VideoGAN, MoCoGAN, and TGAN

✓ Challenges in AI video synthesis and how researchers overcome them

✓ Applications in film, gaming, and virtual reality

By the end, you'll understand how AI creates videos from scratch, enhances existing footage, and powers the future of synthetic media.

1. How GANs Generate Videos

Unlike traditional video editing software that relies on pre-recorded footage, AI video synthesis models use GANs to generate videos from patterns and learned data. The process involves three key steps:

1.1 Understanding the Temporal Nature of Videos

- Videos consist of multiple frames shown in sequence, requiring AI to not only generate images but also predict movement and continuity.
- A GAN designed for video synthesis needs to ensure that each frame maintains consistency in motion, lighting, and objects.

1.2 The Generator and Discriminator in Video GANs

- The Generator creates video frames based on input noise or text prompts.
- The Discriminator evaluates whether the generated frames appear realistic and flow smoothly.
- Unlike image GANs, video GANs must learn motion dynamics, ensuring objects move naturally between frames.

1.3 Conditional Inputs for AI Video Generation

AI video models can be guided by:

✓ **Text prompts** (e.g., "a waterfall flowing through a jungle")

✓ **Single images** (e.g., turning a photo into an animated video)

✓ **Reference videos** (e.g., mimicking movements from real footage)

2. Key AI Video Synthesis Architectures

Several GAN-based architectures are specifically designed for video generation. Here are some of the most notable ones:

2.1 VideoGAN – The First Video Generative Model

✓ One of the earliest models to apply GANs for unsupervised video synthesis.

✓ Uses a spatial generator to create frames and a temporal discriminator to check motion consistency.

✓ Struggles with longer video sequences due to memory limitations.

2.2 TGAN (Temporal GAN)

✓ Introduces time-dependent modeling, allowing for smoother motion across frames.

✓ Uses latent representations to capture motion dynamics, improving video realism.

2.3 MoCoGAN (Motion and Content GAN)

✓ Separates motion from content, allowing AI to independently control:

⬥ What moves (motion vectors)
⬥ What stays consistent (background & objects)

✓ Enables style transfer, where an AI-generated dancer's movement can be applied to different characters.

2.4 G3AN – 3D Video GAN

✓ Uses 3D convolutions to model spatial and temporal relationships.
✓ Allows for higher resolution and more realistic motion in generated videos.

2.5 Text-to-Video Models (e.g., CogVideo, Runway Gen-2)

✓ Modern AI models like CogVideo and Runway Gen-2 use text prompts to generate realistic videos.
✓ They combine GANs with diffusion models for higher quality results.

3. Challenges in AI Video Generation

Even with advanced models, AI-generated videos face several challenges:

3.1 Motion Artifacts and Frame Inconsistencies

- **Problem**: AI struggles with realistic motion transitions, leading to glitches or unnatural deformations.
- **Solution**: Advanced architectures like MoCoGAN separate motion from content to improve frame consistency.

3.2 Long-Sequence Video Generation

- **Problem**: Most GANs can only generate a few seconds of video due to memory constraints.
- **Solution**: Research in recurrent video GANs (RNN-GANs) is helping extend video duration.

3.3 Computational Costs

- **Problem**: Training video GANs requires extensive processing power, especially for high-resolution videos.
- **Solution**: Cloud-based GPUs and optimizations like progressive training reduce training time.

3.4 Text-to-Video Challenges

- **Problem**: AI sometimes misinterprets complex prompts, leading to unrealistic results.
- **Solution**: Users must write structured prompts with specific details (e.g., "a slow-motion scene of ocean waves crashing against rocks at sunset").

4. Real-World Applications of AI Video Synthesis

🎥 Film & Entertainment

✓ AI can generate realistic CGI effects, deepfake actors, and AI-enhanced film scenes.

✓ **Example**: Deepfake technology allows filmmakers to digitally de-age actors.

🎮 Video Games & Virtual Reality

✓ GANs enhance real-time character animation and procedural world generation.

✓ **Example**: AI-driven motion synthesis can create lifelike NPC (non-playable character) movements.

📺 AI-Generated News & Media

✓ AI can generate news video reports with virtual anchors.

✓ Example: Synthesia AI creates synthetic news presenters who deliver reports without human recording.

▯ Social Media & Advertising

✓ AI-generated video ads can be tailored to specific audiences and demographics.
✓ **Example**: Brands use AI avatars and virtual influencers in social media marketing.

▯ Scientific Simulations & Education

✓ AI-generated videos help visualize astronomical phenomena, medical procedures, and scientific models.
✓ **Example**: AI animates ancient civilizations and extinct species for educational content.

5. The Future of AI Video Synthesis

🚀 AI-powered video synthesis is evolving rapidly, with exciting advancements on the horizon:

✓ **Text-to-Video models like Sora by OpenAI** – AI is moving toward generating longer, higher-resolution videos.
✓ **Neural rendering** – AI will generate realistic, photorealistic video sequences for films and games.
✓ **AI-powered filmmaking** – Directors may soon use AI-generated scripts, actors, and environments.
✓ **Personalized AI videos** – AI will generate custom content based on individual user preferences.

AI video synthesis is revolutionizing digital media, making it possible to create high-quality, AI-generated videos from scratch. From gaming and entertainment to journalism and education, GANs and deep learning models are transforming how we produce and consume video content.

As AI continues to evolve, we are approaching an era where AI-generated movies, animated films, and interactive virtual worlds will be created with minimal human intervention.

15.4 Creating Animated Characters with AI

Imagine a world where animated characters are no longer drawn frame by frame but are instead generated, animated, and voiced entirely by AI. From video games and virtual influencers to animated films and interactive experiences, AI-powered character creation is revolutionizing digital entertainment.

GANs (Generative Adversarial Networks) are at the forefront of this transformation, enabling machines to design, animate, and refine digital characters with stunning realism. In this chapter, we will explore:

✓ How AI generates animated characters

✓ GAN architectures used in character design

✓ Automated facial expressions and lip-syncing

✓ Real-world applications in gaming, movies, and social media

✓ Challenges and ethical concerns

By the end of this chapter, you'll understand how AI is reshaping character creation, making the process faster, more efficient, and accessible to creators worldwide.

1. How AI Generates Animated Characters

Creating animated characters using AI involves multiple layers of generation and refinement. Unlike traditional animation, where artists manually sketch and animate every movement, AI-driven animation automates these steps, reducing time and effort while increasing creativity and realism.

1.1 Character Design Using GANs

- AI models analyze thousands of existing character designs to generate new, unique characters.

- StyleGAN is commonly used to create high-resolution, photorealistic characters, allowing artists to tweak features like age, gender, and expression.
- AI tools can generate cartoon-style, anime, or hyper-realistic characters based on training data.

1.2 Procedural Animation with AI

- GANs can generate full-body characters and apply motion synthesis to animate them realistically.
- AI models predict how a character should move, removing the need for manual rigging and animation.
- Techniques like motion capture GANs (MoCoGAN) allow AI to create lifelike character movements based on learned motion data.

1.3 AI-Powered Facial Animation & Lip Syncing

- AI generates realistic facial expressions and emotions in real-time.
- Models like DeepFaceLab and First Order Motion Model allow AI to animate a static character's face, making them appear to talk and react.
- GANs combined with speech synthesis enable automatic lip-syncing, reducing the need for manual voice-over alignment.

2. Key GAN Architectures for AI Animation

Several AI architectures specialize in generating and animating characters. Here are some of the most widely used models:

2.1 StyleGAN for Character Generation

✓ StyleGAN produces high-quality, controllable character faces for games, movies, and avatars.

✓ Allows for customization by tweaking features like hair, eyes, and facial shape.

2.2 MoCoGAN (Motion and Content GAN)

✓ Separates motion from content, enabling AI to animate characters without distorting their design.

✓ Generates fluid, lifelike animations based on learned human motion.

2.3 First Order Motion Model for Animation

✓ Can animate 2D character images, bringing them to life with minimal input.

✓ Used in AI-generated avatars, virtual influencers, and animated storytelling.

2.4 GANs for AI-Powered Lip Syncing

✓ Models like Wav2Lip match character lip movements with speech audio.

✓ Used for virtual assistants, AI-generated movies, and dubbing automation.

3. Real-World Applications of AI Character Animation

🎮 Video Games & Virtual Avatars

✓ AI-generated characters are used in game design, NPCs, and metaverse avatars.

✓ GANs enhance character facial animations, making real-time interactions more natural.

✓ **Example**: AI-driven avatars in VR platforms like Meta Horizon and Ready Player Me.

🎥 Animated Films & CGI

✓ AI accelerates movie production by generating characters, backgrounds, and facial animations.

✓ **Example**: AI-assisted animation tools in studios like Pixar and Disney.

📱 Virtual Influencers & AI Avatars

✓ AI-created personalities like Lil Miquela and FN Meka are reshaping social media marketing.

✓ **Example**: AI-generated models in advertising and brand promotions.

🗣️ AI for Voice Acting & Lip Syncing

✓ AI-generated characters can be paired with AI voice synthesis to create automated voiceovers.

✓ **Example**: Synthesia AI creates realistic virtual presenters for business and media.

4. Challenges & Ethical Considerations

Despite its exciting potential, AI-generated animation comes with challenges:

4.1 Loss of Human Creativity?

- While AI speeds up character creation, some argue it may replace human animators.
- However, AI is best used as a tool to enhance creativity rather than replace artists.

4.2 Deepfake Concerns

- AI-generated characters and voices raise ethical concerns about identity theft and misinformation.
- Companies must establish regulations to prevent misuse in fake news and media manipulation.

4.3 AI Bias in Character Creation

- GANs trained on biased datasets may generate stereotypical or unbalanced character designs.
- Developers must ensure diversity and fairness in AI-generated avatars.

5. The Future of AI-Driven Animation

🚀 AI-powered character animation is still evolving, with many exciting advancements ahead:

✓ **AI-generated movies** – Entire films may be created with AI, from script to animation.

✓ **Real-time animated avatars** – AI avatars will interact in real-time in virtual spaces.

✓ **Hyper-realistic AI characters** – Future GANs will create indistinguishable digital humans.

✓ **Metaverse-ready AI characters** – AI will power next-gen virtual worlds and immersive storytelling.

AI is revolutionizing character animation, making it easier, faster, and more lifelike than ever. With GANs and deep learning, animators can now generate high-quality characters, automate lip-syncing, and create realistic facial expressions with minimal effort.

As AI continues to evolve, we may soon enter an era where entire animated films, video games, and digital influencers are created without human intervention. However, ethical considerations must be addressed to ensure AI remains a tool for enhancing creativity rather than replacing it.

15.5 Future of AI-Generated Video Content

The way we create and consume video content is undergoing a massive transformation, thanks to AI. From deepfake technology and AI-powered video synthesis to automated content creation, AI is revolutionizing the media industry. In the near future, AI-generated video will not only enhance movies, advertisements, and social media but also create hyper-realistic digital humans, interactive storytelling, and even fully AI-generated films.

In this chapter, we will explore:

✓ How GANs (Generative Adversarial Networks) are shaping the future of video content.

✓ The rise of AI-generated movies, deepfakes, and virtual influencers.

✓ The potential of AI-powered interactive media and gaming.

✓ Ethical challenges, including fake news and misinformation risks.

✓ The future of AI-driven storytelling in film, entertainment, and education.

By the end of this chapter, you'll understand how AI-generated video content is set to disrupt entertainment, marketing, and communication, and what it means for content creators, businesses, and society.

1. How AI is Transforming Video Content Creation

Traditional video production involves scriptwriting, filming, editing, and post-production, often requiring large teams, time, and resources. AI is changing this by automating many of these processes, making video production faster, cheaper, and more scalable.

1.1 AI-Powered Video Synthesis

✓ GANs can generate realistic human faces, expressions, and body movements without requiring real actors.

✓ AI models like Deep Video Portraits can recreate and modify existing footage.

✓ Text-to-video AI can generate entire videos from simple descriptions.

1.2 AI-Generated Virtual Avatars

✓ AI-powered digital humans (e.g., MetaHumans) are used in marketing, customer service, and live streaming.

✓ Virtual influencers like Lil Miquela blend AI and human interaction to create engaging social media content.

1.3 AI-Assisted Video Editing and Post-Production

✓ AI speeds up video editing, color correction, and VFX creation.

✓ AI tools like RunwayML and Adobe Sensei enhance video production by automating tedious tasks.

2. The Role of GANs in AI Video Generation

Generative Adversarial Networks (GANs) play a crucial role in realistic video generation by learning from massive datasets of real-world footage.

2.1 Deepfake GANs: Realistic AI-Generated Faces

✓ AI can swap faces in videos with near-perfect accuracy, enabling applications from movie dubbing to virtual acting.

✓ Used in entertainment, gaming, and education, but also raises concerns about misuse in fake news and scams.

2.2 Text-to-Video GANs

✓ AI models like DALL·E, Imagen Video, and Make-A-Video generate videos from simple text prompts.

✓ These models will revolutionize marketing, animation, and personalized content creation.

2.3 Motion Synthesis with GANs

✓ AI models predict natural human motion, automating character animation for movies and video games.

✓ Used in game design, metaverse applications, and sports analysis.

3. AI-Generated Movies & Virtual Storytelling

3.1 AI-Written and AI-Directed Films

✓ AI can generate scripts, storyboard sequences, and even direct movies using deep learning.

✓ **Example**: IBM's AI helped create the trailer for the horror movie Morgan.

3.2 AI for Animation & CGI

✓ AI reduces animation time by automating frame generation.

✓ GANs improve CGI realism, making virtual actors indistinguishable from real people.

3.3 Personalized Interactive Storytelling

✓ AI will enable customized movies where users can interact with characters and influence plotlines.

✓ Used in AI-powered video games, VR storytelling, and educational simulations.

4. AI Video in Marketing, Education & Social Media

4.1 AI in Advertising & Brand Storytelling

✓ AI-generated video ads allow brands to create personalized content at scale.

✓ Example: AI-driven video ads on platforms like TikTok and YouTube.

4.2 AI for Educational Content & Training

✓ AI can generate virtual teachers and explainer videos for online learning.

✓ Used in e-learning platforms like Coursera and Khan Academy.

4.3 AI-Powered Social Media Videos

✓ AI influencers create daily video content without human intervention.

✓ AI-generated content on platforms like Instagram, Snapchat, and YouTube is growing rapidly.

5. Ethical Challenges & Risks

5.1 Deepfake Concerns & Misinformation

✓ AI-generated videos can be used for fake news, political manipulation, and fraud.

✓ Example: Deepfake videos impersonating public figures have raised concerns about media trustworthiness.

5.2 Copyright & Ownership Issues

✓ Who owns AI-generated content? Creators, AI developers, or the training data owners?

✓ Companies and regulators must address IP rights in AI-generated media.

5.3 AI Bias in Video Generation

✓ AI models can reflect biases in training data, leading to issues with representation and fairness.

✓ Solution: Developers must train AI models on diverse, inclusive datasets.

6. The Future of AI Video Content

🚀 AI-generated video is just beginning. Here's what we can expect in the next decade:

✓ **Hyper-Realistic AI Actors** – Movies may feature AI-generated actors instead of real performers.

✓ **Instant AI Video Production** – AI will enable users to create high-quality videos in seconds from simple text prompts.

✓ **Real-Time Interactive Storytelling** – AI will allow for live-generated, interactive video experiences.

✓ **AI-Generated Metaverse Content** – AI will populate virtual worlds with dynamic, AI-driven characters.

✓ **AI-Powered News & Journalism** – AI will automate news reporting, generating video summaries from real-time data.

AI-generated video content is reshaping entertainment, marketing, education, and social media. With GANs and deep learning, video synthesis, character animation, and storytelling are becoming more automated, reducing costs and expanding creative possibilities.

However, challenges like deepfake misuse, copyright issues, and AI bias must be addressed to ensure ethical AI-driven media.

As AI video technology continues to evolve, we may soon see a world where movies, advertisements, video games, and even daily news are generated entirely by AI—blurring the line between fiction and reality.

16. 3D GANs and the Future of AI-Generated Worlds

As AI continues to evolve, Generative Adversarial Networks (GANs) are expanding beyond 2D images into the realm of 3D content creation, shaping the future of virtual worlds, metaverse development, and AI-driven simulations. In this chapter, we explore 3D GAN architectures like GANverse3D, GRAF, and NeRF (Neural Radiance Fields), which enable AI to generate 3D objects, realistic environments, and even entire virtual cities from limited data. You'll learn how 3D GANs are revolutionizing game development, augmented reality (AR), virtual reality (VR), and AI-powered animation. We'll also discuss the challenges of 3D reconstruction, rendering efficiency, and real-time generation, along with future possibilities for AI-generated virtual worlds and interactive experiences. By the end of this chapter, you'll understand how 3D GANs are paving the way for a new era of AI-driven creativity and digital experiences. 🎮🚀

16.1 Understanding 3D GANs

While traditional Generative Adversarial Networks (GANs) have revolutionized 2D image and video generation, the next frontier of AI creativity lies in 3D GANs. These models extend the power of GANs into three-dimensional space, enabling AI to generate realistic 3D objects, scenes, and even entire virtual worlds. From gaming and CGI to the metaverse and digital twin technology, 3D GANs are unlocking new possibilities in architecture, design, and simulation.

In this section, we will explore:

✓ How 3D GANs work and their key differences from 2D GANs.

✓ The role of volumetric representations, voxel grids, and neural implicit fields in 3D generation.

✓ How state-of-the-art models like 3DGAN, VoxGAN, and StyleGAN3 are shaping 3D AI.

✓ The applications of 3D GANs in gaming, virtual reality (VR), augmented reality (AR), and more.

✓ The challenges and future directions of 3D generative models.

By the end of this chapter, you'll have a solid understanding of how AI is transforming 3D content creation and why this technology is crucial for building the next generation of digital experiences.

1. What Are 3D GANs?

1.1 Extending GANs into 3D Space

Traditional GANs generate 2D images by learning the underlying distribution of a dataset and synthesizing new images that match that distribution. 3D GANs extend this concept by generating 3D representations of objects instead of flat images.

Unlike 2D GANs, which operate on pixel-based images, 3D GANs work with 3D structures such as:

✓ Voxel grids (3D pixels similar to Minecraft blocks)

✓ Point clouds (collections of points in 3D space)

✓ Neural implicit fields (continuous 3D representations like NeRFs)

These representations allow AI to create fully three-dimensional objects and environments, which can be rendered, manipulated, and used in games, simulations, and VR experiences.

1.2 Key Differences Between 2D and 3D GANs

Feature	2D GANs	3D GANs
Output Type	2D Images	3D Objects & Scenes
Data Representation	Pixels	Voxels, Point Clouds, Meshes
Applications	Image Generation, Style Transfer	Game Design, AR/VR, 3D Printing
Computation Complexity	Lower	Higher due to 3D computations

2. How 3D GANs Work

2.1 3D Representation Methods

To generate realistic 3D structures, 3D GANs rely on various data representations, each with its strengths and challenges:

✓ **Voxel Grids** – 3D equivalents of pixels, commonly used in early 3D GAN models. These can be inefficient due to high memory consumption.

✓ **Point Clouds** – Instead of rendering a dense 3D object, these represent objects as a collection of 3D points, which are more memory-efficient but may lack fine details.

✓ **Mesh Representations** – Used for CGI and 3D modeling, meshes define surfaces using vertices, edges, and faces.

✓ **Neural Implicit Fields (NeRFs)** – A modern approach where objects are represented mathematically rather than explicitly storing 3D geometry. This allows for highly detailed 3D reconstructions.

2.2 Training 3D GANs

Training 3D GANs follows a similar adversarial approach as 2D GANs, but with additional complexity due to the extra dimension. The training pipeline includes:

- **Generator**: Generates a 3D object representation from random noise.
- **Discriminator**: Evaluates whether a given 3D object is real or generated.
- **Adversarial Training**: The generator improves by fooling the discriminator, while the discriminator gets better at spotting fake objects.
- **Rendering**: The final 3D object is rendered into a mesh, point cloud, or voxel grid for visualization.

3. State-of-the-Art 3D GAN Models

Several cutting-edge 3D GAN architectures have emerged, pushing the boundaries of AI-generated 3D content:

3.1 3D-GAN (VoxNet-based)

✓ One of the first 3D GAN models, generating 3D objects as voxel grids.

✓ Limited by high memory usage and resolution constraints.

3.2 VoxGAN (Voxel-based GANs)

✓ Generates 3D objects using voxel-based encoding.

✓ Works well for simpler 3D objects, but struggles with high-resolution details.

3.3 MeshGAN

✓ Generates 3D meshes instead of voxel grids, making it more efficient.

✓ Used in CGI, animation, and 3D modeling.

3.4 StyleGAN3 (Extended for 3D)

✓ Originally designed for 2D images, but now extended to high-quality 3D generation.

✓ Can generate realistic human faces and objects in 3D.

3.5 Neural Radiance Fields (NeRFs) & GANs

✓ NeRF-based models can synthesize ultra-realistic 3D environments.

✓ Used in virtual reality, gaming, and 3D photography.

4. Applications of 3D GANs

3D GANs are revolutionizing various industries, from entertainment to medicine.

4.1 Game Development & Virtual Reality

✓ Generates realistic 3D assets, NPCs, and environments for games and the metaverse.

✓ Enables procedural content generation, reducing development time.

4.2 3D Printing & Manufacturing

✓ AI-generated 3D models can be directly used for 3D printing.

✓ Used in automotive, architecture, and medical prosthetics.

4.3 AI-Powered CGI & Special Effects

✓ Helps create ultra-realistic CGI for movies and animation.

✓ Reduces manual work in VFX and 3D rendering.

4.4 Medical Imaging & Simulations

✓ Generates 3D models of organs, bones, and tissues for medical research.

✓ Used for AI-driven surgeries and personalized medicine.

5. Challenges and Limitations

Despite their potential, 3D GANs face several challenges:

✓ **High Computational Costs** – 3D generation requires significantly more computing power than 2D.

✓ **Data Scarcity** – Unlike 2D images, large-scale 3D datasets are harder to find.

✓ **Training Instability** – 3D GANs are harder to train due to complex geometries and high-dimensional representations.

✓ **Realism vs. Efficiency** – Striking a balance between high-quality 3D generation and low computational cost remains a challenge.

6. The Future of 3D GANs

🚀 The next decade will see major advancements in 3D AI generation, leading to:

✓ **Fully AI-Generated Metaverse Worlds** – AI will autonomously create immersive virtual worlds.

✓ **Realistic AI Avatars & Digital Humans** – 3D GANs will power lifelike avatars for VR and social media.

✓ **Instant 3D Asset Generation for Games & Movies** – AI will generate ultra-detailed environments in real time.

✓ **AI-Powered Architectural Design** – GANs will assist in 3D home design, urban planning, and digital twins.

3D GANs are pushing the boundaries of AI creativity, enabling machines to generate realistic 3D objects, characters, and virtual worlds. As AI research advances, 3D generative models will transform industries ranging from entertainment and gaming to healthcare and manufacturing.

However, challenges like high computational costs and data scarcity must be overcome before AI-powered 3D generation becomes mainstream.

16.2 GANs for 3D Object Modeling

3D object modeling is a crucial component of modern digital design, impacting industries such as gaming, animation, architecture, manufacturing, and medical imaging. Traditional methods of 3D modeling require manual sculpting, procedural generation, or photogrammetry, all of which can be time-consuming and labor-intensive. However, Generative Adversarial Networks (GANs) are transforming the field by automating the creation of high-quality 3D models with minimal human intervention.

GANs can generate realistic and complex 3D structures by learning from datasets of existing 3D objects, making them valuable tools for automated design, AI-assisted creativity, and rapid prototyping. In this chapter, we will explore:

✓ How GANs generate 3D models from different data representations like voxels, meshes, and implicit fields.

✓ The leading 3D GAN architectures, including VoxelGAN, MeshGAN, and NeRF-based models.

✓ The advantages of GAN-generated 3D models over traditional techniques.

✓ The challenges and future prospects of 3D GAN modeling in real-world applications.

1. How GANs Generate 3D Models

1.1 Extending GANs to 3D Space

GANs have been widely used in 2D image generation, but generating 3D objects is significantly more complex due to the extra dimension. Unlike 2D images that use pixel grids, 3D objects require specialized geometric representations such as:

✓ **Voxel-based models** – Representing 3D objects as a set of small cubes (like Minecraft).

✓ **Point clouds** – Storing 3D objects as a set of discrete points in space.

✓ **Meshes** – Using a collection of vertices, edges, and faces to define surfaces.

✓ **Implicit Neural Representations** – Mathematical functions that describe 3D objects continuously, such as Neural Radiance Fields (NeRFs).

1.2 The GAN Pipeline for 3D Modeling

A typical 3D GAN pipeline consists of:

1️⃣ **Generator** – Takes random noise as input and generates a 3D representation (voxel, mesh, or point cloud).

2️⃣ **Discriminator** – Evaluates whether a given 3D model is real (from training data) or fake (generated).

3️⃣ **Adversarial Training** – The generator improves to create more realistic 3D models, while the discriminator gets better at detecting fakes.

4️⃣ **Rendering & Refinement** – The final 3D model is optimized, smoothed, and prepared for real-world applications.

2. Key 3D GAN Architectures

2.1 VoxelGAN – Voxel-Based 3D Generation

VoxelGAN was one of the first 3D GAN models, generating 3D objects as voxel grids (tiny cubes that make up the structure). This approach is intuitive but has limitations:

✓ Advantages:

- Works well for basic geometric shapes.
- Easy to implement using 3D convolutional layers.

✗ Limitations:

- High memory usage (storing 3D voxel grids is expensive).
- Low resolution (fine details are difficult to capture).

2.2 MeshGAN – Generating 3D Meshes

MeshGANs generate objects as 3D meshes, which are more memory-efficient and better suited for real-time graphics (e.g., game assets).

✓ Advantages:

- More realistic 3D objects with detailed surfaces.
- Used in CGI, animation, and gaming.

2.3 PointGAN – 3D Point Cloud Generation

PointGANs generate point clouds, which are collections of points representing a 3D object.

✓ Advantages:

- Lightweight and scalable for large datasets.
- Used in autonomous vehicles and LiDAR-based mapping.

2.4 NeRF-GAN – Neural Implicit 3D Representations

NeRF-GANs represent 3D objects implicitly using neural networks rather than storing explicit geometry. This allows for high-resolution details with minimal memory usage.

✓ Advantages:

- Ultra-high-quality 3D models with realistic lighting.
- Used in photorealistic rendering, virtual reality, and simulations.

3. Advantages of GANs in 3D Modeling

✓ **Automation of 3D Design** – AI can generate detailed 3D objects without manual modeling.

✓ **Speed & Efficiency** – 3D GANs can generate thousands of models in minutes, reducing development time.

✓ **Creative AI-Assisted Design** – GANs can generate unique and complex structures beyond human intuition.

✓ **Real-Time Asset Generation** – In games and VR, GANs can generate customized objects dynamically.

4. Applications of GAN-Based 3D Modeling

4.1 Game Development & Virtual Worlds

✓ GANs are used to generate 3D characters, props, and environments for video games.

✓ AI-driven procedural world generation enables endless dynamic content.

4.2 CGI, Animation, and Special Effects

✓ GANs assist in film production and CGI animation by automating 3D character and scene generation.

✓ AI can convert 2D drawings into 3D models, speeding up animation pipelines.

4.3 Architecture and Interior Design

✓ AI-generated 3D building models help architects visualize and test designs.

✓ GANs can generate furniture, layouts, and entire cityscapes.

4.4 3D Printing & Manufacturing

✓ GAN-generated 3D models can be directly converted into 3D-printed objects.

✓ Used in automotive, industrial prototyping, and custom product design.

4.5 Medical Imaging & Healthcare

✓ AI can generate 3D models of organs, bones, and tissues for medical training and surgery planning.

✓ Helps in AI-powered prosthetic design.

5. Challenges and Limitations of 3D GANs

✗ **High Computational Cost** – Training 3D GANs requires powerful GPUs/TPUs.

✗ **Data Scarcity** – Unlike 2D images, large-scale 3D datasets are limited.

✗ **Training Stability** – 3D GANs are harder to train due to complex geometry and rendering challenges.

✗ **Realism vs. Efficiency Tradeoff** – High-quality 3D generation is expensive and time-consuming.

6. The Future of 3D GANs in Object Modeling

🖌 **Next-Gen AI Creativity**: AI will autonomously generate complete 3D worlds for games, simulations, and AR/VR experiences.

☐ **AI-Generated Architecture**: GANs will assist in automated architectural design, reducing manual labor and costs.

🎮 **Hyper-Realistic 3D Avatars**: GANs will generate lifelike virtual characters for gaming, social media, and the metaverse.

☐ **AI-Powered 3D Printing**: Instant AI-generated prototypes will streamline manufacturing and custom product design.

3D GANs are revolutionizing the way we create and interact with 3D content, offering speed, automation, and creativity beyond traditional methods. From game development and CGI to architecture and healthcare, AI-generated 3D models are transforming multiple industries.

However, challenges such as high computational demands and training complexity must be addressed before 3D GANs become a mainstream tool. As research advances, AI-powered 3D modeling will play a crucial role in building the digital worlds of the future.

16.3 AI-Generated Virtual Reality Environments

Virtual Reality (VR) has transformed how we interact with digital content, enabling fully immersive experiences in gaming, training, simulations, and social interactions. Traditionally, VR environments require extensive manual design, taking months or even years to create. However, Generative Adversarial Networks (GANs) are revolutionizing VR development by automating world generation, texture creation, and environment adaptation in real time.

This chapter explores how AI-driven generative models are reshaping VR by:

✓ Automatically generating 3D landscapes, cities, and interiors for VR worlds.

✓ Improving realism in virtual spaces through AI-enhanced textures, lighting, and physics.

✓ Personalizing VR environments dynamically based on user behavior and preferences.

✓ Reducing the time and cost of creating large-scale immersive environments.

✓ Pushing the boundaries of AI-generated metaverses and digital realities.

Let's dive into how GANs and AI creativity are merging to create next-gen virtual worlds.

1. How GANs Generate Virtual Worlds

GANs can generate 3D VR environments by learning from real-world data and creating highly detailed, lifelike environments. Here's how AI accomplishes this:

1.1 Procedural World Generation with GANs

Traditional procedural generation uses pre-defined rules to create VR worlds, but GANs improve upon this by learning from real-world landscapes and synthesizing new environments dynamically.

✓ **Example**: AI can generate entire cities, forests, or space stations based on a dataset of real locations.

✓ **Game & Simulation Use**: Open-world games like No Man's Sky or Minecraft could use AI for infinite world generation.

1.2 AI-Generated Textures and Materials

GANs can generate ultra-realistic textures that make VR worlds more immersive. Instead of using manually designed textures, AI can:

✓ Generate photorealistic materials (wood, stone, glass) using StyleGAN.

✓ Enhance realism in VR environments by simulating light reflections and shadows.

✓ Improve consistency and coherence in virtual settings by synthesizing textures that fit their surroundings.

1.3 Neural Rendering for Dynamic VR Scenes

Traditional 3D rendering is computationally expensive, but AI-powered neural rendering can optimize real-time graphics in VR by:

✓ Reducing processing load while keeping high-quality visuals.

✓ Enabling real-time environmental updates, adapting scenes dynamically.

✓ Creating realistic animations, particle effects, and physics interactions.

2. Key AI Techniques for VR Environment Generation

GANs and other deep learning techniques play a crucial role in building VR-ready environments.

2.1 StyleGAN for Landscape and Scene Generation

✓ AI can generate entire VR landscapes, from mountains and forests to cities and alien worlds.

✓ Photorealistic details make virtual worlds feel natural and engaging.

2.2 CycleGAN for Realistic Object Texturing

✓ Converts low-resolution textures into high-quality photorealistic materials.

✓ Allows real-time texture adaptation, making VR environments responsive to player actions.

2.3 NeRF (Neural Radiance Fields) for AI-Powered Rendering

✓ NeRF-based GANs render 3D spaces with realistic lighting and reflections.

✓ Enables ultra-fast scene generation, reducing the need for traditional 3D modeling.

2.4 AI-Generated Terrain & Architecture Design

✓ AI learns from satellite imagery and architectural datasets to create realistic VR-ready cities, villages, or futuristic landscapes.

✓ Helps simulate real-world locations for training, military, and urban planning.

3. The Role of AI in Personalized VR Environments

GANs enable dynamic and personalized VR experiences, where environments adapt to users in real-time.

✓ **Adaptive VR Worlds** – AI-generated environments change based on user preferences and interactions.

✓ **AI-Powered NPCs** – GAN-generated NPCs and avatars make VR worlds feel more realistic.

✓ **Emotionally Responsive VR** – AI can adjust lighting, colors, and environments based on user mood and engagement.

💡 **Example**: Imagine a VR meditation app where AI dynamically generates peaceful landscapes based on user stress levels.

4. Applications of AI-Generated VR Worlds

GAN-generated VR environments are impacting multiple industries, beyond just gaming.

4.1 Gaming and Interactive Storytelling 🎮

✓ Infinite AI-generated game worlds make exploration endless.

✓ AI adapts game environments dynamically for personalized adventures.

4.2 Architectural Visualization and Real Estate 🏠

✓ AI generates realistic VR property walkthroughs before construction begins.

✓ Allows real-time modifications to floor plans and materials.

4.3 Virtual Tourism and Historical Reconstruction □

✓ GANs recreate historical sites in VR, bringing the past to life.

✓ AI enhances VR travel experiences, simulating real-world locations.

4.4 Training Simulations and Military Applications □♂

✓ AI-powered VR simulations train pilots, soldiers, and emergency responders.

✓ AI dynamically adjusts difficulty and realism for optimized learning.

4.5 The Metaverse and Social VR □

✓ AI builds realistic virtual cities for metaverse platforms.

✓ AI-powered avatars and NPCs interact with users in lifelike ways.

5. Challenges and Limitations of AI in VR

While GANs are transforming VR, there are still challenges to overcome:

✗ **Computational Complexity** – AI-generated VR worlds require powerful GPUs and cloud computing.

✗ **Realism vs. Efficiency** – High-resolution AI-generated environments can be resource-intensive.

✗ **User Experience Balance** – Fully AI-driven VR spaces must remain intuitive and interactive.

✗ **Ethical Concerns** – AI-generated worlds could be used for deepfake VR and misinformation.

6. The Future of AI-Generated VR Environments

🚀 **Hyper-Realistic Virtual Worlds**: AI will simulate photorealistic cities, nature, and alien worlds.

□ **Neural AI World Builders**: GANs will create AI-driven VR environments that evolve and learn.

🎮 **AI-Powered VR Gaming**: Games will feature adaptive storylines and infinite AI-generated levels.

□ **VR-Powered Digital Twins**: Cities will use AI-generated VR replicas for urban planning.

As GANs continue to evolve, AI-generated VR environments will become more immersive, efficient, and personalized, redefining how we experience digital spaces.

AI-powered VR environments are the future of digital experiences, enabling fully immersive, intelligent, and interactive worlds. From gaming and architecture to education and the metaverse, GANs are unlocking new possibilities for creativity and exploration.

However, challenges such as computational demands and ethical concerns must be addressed to ensure responsible and scalable AI-driven VR.

With continued advancements in neural rendering, procedural AI, and real-time GAN training, AI-generated VR worlds will become indistinguishable from reality, paving the way for the next generation of virtual experiences.

16.4 GANs in 3D Printing and Manufacturing

The integration of Generative Adversarial Networks (GANs) with 3D printing and manufacturing is revolutionizing how we design, prototype, and produce physical objects. Traditional manufacturing processes rely on rigid design constraints and manual optimizations, but AI-driven generative models enable rapid, automated, and highly efficient workflows. GANs can enhance 3D printing by optimizing designs, improving material efficiency, and generating innovative structures that would be impossible with conventional design methods.

This chapter explores:

✓ How GANs generate complex 3D models for manufacturing

✓ Optimizing material usage and structural integrity with AI

✓ Reducing design time through AI-assisted generative workflows

✓ Applications of GANs in various manufacturing industries

✓ Challenges and future trends in AI-driven 3D printing

Let's dive into how GANs and AI creativity are reshaping modern manufacturing.

1. How GANs Are Transforming 3D Printing

1.1 AI-Generated 3D Models and Designs

Traditional 3D modeling relies on human designers and engineers, who use CAD (Computer-Aided Design) software to create objects. However, GANs can:

✓ Automatically generate optimized 3D models based on input requirements.

✓ Enhance efficiency by reducing unnecessary material usage.

✓ Improve strength-to-weight ratios for aerospace and industrial components.

💡 **Example**: AI-generated organic structures, inspired by nature, allow for lighter and stronger materials in industries like aerospace and automotive.

1.2 Optimizing 3D Printing Parameters with AI

GANs can analyze vast amounts of printing data to optimize parameters like:

✓ Layer height and infill density for cost-effective material use.

✓ Print speed and temperature settings to minimize defects.

✓ Support structure generation for complex geometries.

💡 **Example**: AI-driven 3D printers adapt dynamically to environmental conditions, adjusting print speed based on real-time monitoring.

1.3 Generative Design for Structural Strength

GANs enhance mechanical properties by generating lattice structures and honeycomb patterns for 3D-printed parts.

✓ Stronger yet lighter materials reduce waste.

✓ Biomechanically optimized structures improve medical implants and prosthetics.

✓ AI-simulated stress testing ensures durability.

💡 **Example**: NASA and SpaceX use AI-generated designs for heat-resistant rocket nozzles that are both lighter and stronger than traditional components.

2. Key AI Techniques in 3D Printing & Manufacturing

2.1 3D Shape Synthesis Using GANs

GANs can learn from existing 3D models and generate new, optimized designs using deep learning techniques like:

✓ **Voxel-Based GANs** – AI creates 3D objects in voxel grids, similar to Minecraft-like structures.

✓ **Mesh-Based GANs** – AI refines designs using polygons and 3D mesh networks for smoother surfaces.

✓ **Point Cloud GANs** – AI generates detailed and realistic 3D scans of objects for replication.

2.2 AI-Generated Slicing and Toolpath Optimization

3D printing requires a process called slicing, where a model is broken down into printable layers. GANs optimize slicing by:

✓ Reducing material waste while ensuring structural integrity.

✓ Optimizing print speed and layer adhesion to minimize errors.

✓ Generating custom support structures for overhanging parts.

💡 **Example**: AI-generated toolpaths reduce printing time by 30% while maintaining high precision.

2.3 AI-Powered Defect Detection and Quality Control

Manufacturing often faces errors such as warping, layer shifting, or extrusion failures. GANs can:

✓ Predict defects before they occur by analyzing real-time sensor data.

✓ Auto-correct errors by adjusting print settings mid-process.

✓ Improve post-processing by optimizing support removal and surface finishing.

💡 **Example**: AI-driven smart factories use cameras and GAN-based image recognition to identify micro-defects in real time.

3. Applications of GANs in 3D Printing & Manufacturing

GAN-powered AI models are transforming multiple industries, making manufacturing more efficient, cost-effective, and innovative.

3.1 Aerospace and Automotive Manufacturing ✈🚗

✓ AI generates lightweight, fuel-efficient aircraft and car parts.

✓ Reduces design iteration cycles, cutting costs and time.

✓ Optimizes internal structures for crash resistance and aerodynamics.

💡 **Example**: Boeing and Tesla use AI-generated topology-optimized components for weight reduction and increased durability.

3.2 Healthcare and Prosthetic Design ⊕

✓ AI generates custom prosthetics and orthopedic implants tailored to patients.

✓ AI-enhanced bioprinting creates functional human tissues.

✓ AI improves medical device designs by analyzing patient-specific data.

💡 **Example**: GANs help design 3D-printed skull implants that fit perfectly to a patient's anatomy.

3.3 Consumer Product Design and Customization ▢

✓ AI enables mass customization of consumer goods (shoes, furniture, wearables).

✓ AI-powered 3D printing allows for on-demand, eco-friendly production.

✓ Hyper-personalized designs based on user preferences.

💡 **Example**: Nike uses AI to generate custom sneaker midsoles, optimizing comfort and durability.

3.4 Architecture and Construction 🏗

✓ AI generates modular building designs for 3D-printed homes.

✓ Self-healing concrete and smart materials improve durability.

✓ AI optimizes support-free printing techniques for sustainable construction.

💡 **Example**: Companies like ICON use AI-driven 3D printing to build affordable housing in under 24 hours.

4. Challenges & Limitations of AI in 3D Printing

While AI-driven 3D printing is promising, several challenges remain:

✗ **Computational Complexity** – GAN-based generative design requires high computational power.

✗ **Data Limitations** – AI needs large, high-quality datasets for training.

✗ **Material Constraints** – Not all AI-generated designs are feasible with current 3D printing materials.

✗ **Intellectual Property (IP) Issues** – AI-generated designs raise copyright and patent concerns.

💡 **Example**: AI-generated furniture designs can create legal disputes over design ownership.

5. The Future of GANs in 3D Printing & Manufacturing

🏭 **Autonomous AI Factories**: Smart factories will use AI to design, optimize, and print products without human intervention.

🔲 **Self-Learning AI for Design Innovation**: GANs will improve iterative design processes, enabling more intelligent and adaptive manufacturing.

🌱 **Eco-Friendly Manufacturing**: AI-generated designs will prioritize sustainability, reducing material waste and energy consumption.

🎨 **AI-Powered Creativity in Product Design**: Future GAN-driven AI tools will assist designers in creating unique and complex structures that were once impossible.

💡 **Example**: In the future, fully AI-driven supply chains could create on-demand, optimized, and sustainable manufacturing solutions worldwide.

The combination of GANs, AI, and 3D printing is revolutionizing modern manufacturing, enabling faster, more efficient, and highly optimized production workflows. From lightweight aerospace components to personalized prosthetics and AI-generated consumer goods, GANs are pushing the boundaries of innovation.

However, challenges like computational costs, material limitations, and legal concerns must be addressed before widespread adoption. As AI-powered manufacturing continues to evolve, GANs will play a crucial role in creating the next generation of smarter, more efficient, and sustainable products.

16.5 The Future of AI in Virtual World Creation

The fusion of AI and virtual world creation is unlocking new possibilities in gaming, simulations, and the metaverse. With the power of Generative Adversarial Networks (GANs), procedural generation, and deep learning, AI is now capable of autonomously designing immersive 3D worlds, generating realistic environments, and populating them with intelligent characters.

Virtual reality (VR), augmented reality (AR), and AI-driven simulations are transforming industries like gaming, education, urban planning, and entertainment. In the near future, AI will enable fully self-generated, dynamic virtual worlds, adapting in real-time to user interactions.

This chapter explores:

✔ How GANs and AI create realistic virtual environments

✔ The role of AI in procedural world generation

✔ Intelligent AI-driven NPCs (non-playable characters)

✓ Applications of AI in the metaverse and gaming

✓ Challenges and ethical considerations of AI-generated worlds

Let's step into the future of AI-driven virtual world creation.

1. AI and GANs in Virtual World Generation

1.1 GANs for Realistic Environment Creation

GANs have revolutionized environment generation by learning from real-world landscapes and structures, then creating highly realistic digital worlds.

✓ **Photorealistic Terrain Generation** – AI can generate mountains, forests, oceans, and cities with realistic textures.

✓ **AI-Based Weather and Lighting** – Dynamic lighting systems adapt to time, seasons, and weather conditions.

✓ **Procedural World Expansion** – AI can generate infinite game worlds, reducing the need for manual design.

💡 **Example**: Open-world games like Microsoft Flight Simulator use AI-generated landscapes built from satellite data and GAN-enhanced textures.

1.2 AI-Powered Procedural Generation

Procedural generation allows for automatic world creation, but with AI, these worlds become smarter, more immersive, and more realistic.

✓ Realistic cityscapes generated from AI-learned architectural patterns.

✓ AI-driven ecosystems where animals, weather, and NPCs interact naturally.

✓ Infinite exploration with environments that evolve based on player actions.

💡 **Example**: No Man's Sky uses AI-powered procedural algorithms to generate trillions of unique planets, each with its own ecosystems.

2. AI-Generated NPCs and Virtual Beings

2.1 AI-Created Characters with GANs

GANs can generate hyper-realistic NPCs with human-like facial expressions, emotions, and behaviors. AI allows:

✓ Lifelike avatars and digital humans for VR and AR.

✓ AI-powered dialogue systems that generate realistic conversations.

✓ Adaptive behavior, where NPCs learn and evolve based on user interaction.

💡 **Example**: MetaHuman Creator by Epic Games allows AI-powered creation of lifelike, customizable characters for games and movies.

2.2 Reinforcement Learning for AI NPCs

Using reinforcement learning (RL), AI-driven NPCs can adapt their actions based on player behavior, making games more immersive.

✓ Self-learning enemies that evolve strategies against players.

✓ Dynamic storytelling, where AI NPCs generate new narratives based on user choices.

✓ Emotionally responsive AI that reacts to mood and speech in VR environments.

💡 **Example**: AI-powered NPCs in Red Dead Redemption 2 use deep learning to respond differently to player interactions.

3. The Role of AI in the Metaverse

3.1 AI-Driven Virtual Economies

GANs and AI enable fully functional digital economies, where AI:

✓ Generates virtual goods and NFTs for digital commerce.

✓ Predicts economic trends within online metaverse spaces.

✓ Facilitates AI-powered trade and intelligent currency systems.

💡 **Example**: Decentraland and The Sandbox use AI-generated NFTs and assets for a self-sustaining digital economy.

3.2 AI in Social and Collaborative Virtual Spaces

AI allows users to socialize, create, and collaborate in real-time by:

✓ Generating AI avatars with unique personalities.

✓ Translating languages instantly for global communication.

✓ Designing AI-powered virtual meeting rooms and workspaces.

💡 **Example**: Meta (Facebook) Horizon Worlds uses AI for real-time avatar animations and immersive virtual experiences.

3.3 AI-Enhanced VR and AR Experiences

AI is transforming VR and AR by:

✓ Generating realistic textures and assets in AR environments.

✓ Creating AI-driven tour guides and educational tools in VR.

✓ Building fully interactive AI-powered training simulations.

💡 **Example**: Google's ARCore and Apple's ARKit use AI to generate realistic AR experiences for gaming and education.

4. Challenges and Ethical Considerations

4.1 Deepfake Risks and Virtual Identity Theft

GANs can generate lifelike avatars and deepfake humans, leading to risks like:

✗ Identity theft in virtual worlds.

✗ Fake personalities and AI-generated misinformation.

✗ Unethical use of deepfake avatars in online spaces.

💡 **Solution**: Regulations and AI watermarking to detect deepfakes.

4.2 AI Bias and Procedural Unpredictability

AI-driven virtual worlds may inherit biases from training data, leading to:

✕ Unintended discrimination in AI-generated content.

✕ Algorithmic biases affecting world generation and NPC behavior.

💡 **Solution**: Ethical AI frameworks to ensure fairness and diversity in generated worlds.

4.3 Data Privacy in AI-Generated Virtual Spaces

AI-driven metaverse platforms collect huge amounts of user data, raising concerns like:

✕ Surveillance and data tracking in virtual environments.

✕ AI-driven behavioral profiling for targeted advertising.

💡 **Solution**: Blockchain and decentralized AI to protect user privacy.

5. The Future of AI in Virtual World Creation

🚀 **Autonomous AI-Generated Universes** – AI will create entire self-sustaining virtual worlds without human intervention.

☐ **AI-Driven Storytelling** – AI will dynamically generate real-time narratives, adapting to user choices.

☐ **Infinite and Adaptive Virtual Spaces** – AI will generate ever-evolving digital landscapes for gaming, work, and social interaction.

🎭 **Lifelike Digital Humans** – AI-generated NPCs and avatars will become indistinguishable from real people.

🛰 **AI-Powered Hyper-Realistic Simulations** – AI will build high-fidelity simulations for science, urban planning, and education.

💡 **Example**: Future AI-driven MMOs (Massively Multiplayer Online Games) will feature real-time, self-evolving virtual worlds, where environments change based on player actions and AI learning.

The future of AI in virtual world creation is both exciting and transformative. GANs and AI-driven systems are enabling:

✓ Realistic, AI-generated environments with limitless detail.

✓ Self-learning NPCs that evolve and interact naturally.

✓ AI-powered virtual economies in the metaverse.

✓ Seamless, dynamic storytelling that adapts to user choices.

However, ethical concerns, AI bias, and deepfake risks must be addressed for responsible AI development. As AI technology advances, the boundaries between real and virtual worlds will continue to blur, creating immersive digital universes unlike anything seen before.

17. Ethical Considerations in AI Creativity

As Generative Adversarial Networks (GANs) and AI creativity continue to advance, they bring with them complex ethical challenges. From deepfakes and misinformation to AI-generated art ownership and bias in machine learning models, the impact of synthetic intelligence is profound. In this chapter, we explore the ethical dilemmas surrounding AI-generated content, including privacy concerns, copyright disputes, and the potential for AI to replace human creativity. We'll discuss real-world case studies of AI misuse, strategies for detecting and preventing malicious AI applications, and the growing role of regulation and responsible AI development. By the end of this chapter, you'll have a deeper understanding of the ethical landscape of AI creativity and the importance of developing GANs responsibly for the benefit of society. ⚖️□□🚀

17.1 Deepfakes and the Spread of Misinformation

Deepfake technology, powered by Generative Adversarial Networks (GANs), has revolutionized AI-driven content creation. While it has enabled remarkable advancements in digital media, filmmaking, and entertainment, it has also become a powerful tool for spreading misinformation, deception, and fraud.

From fake political speeches to AI-generated social media personas, deepfakes are blurring the line between reality and fiction, raising ethical, legal, and societal concerns. This chapter explores:

✓ How deepfakes work and their role in misinformation

✓ The risks of AI-generated media in politics and social trust

✓ The impact of deepfakes on cybersecurity and identity theft

✓ Methods to detect and combat deepfake-generated misinformation

✓ The future of responsible AI and deepfake regulations

Let's dive into the complex and controversial world of deepfakes.

1. What Are Deepfakes?

1.1 The Technology Behind Deepfakes

Deepfakes leverage GANs and deep learning to manipulate video and audio, allowing AI to:

✓ Swap faces seamlessly in videos (e.g., replacing one person's face with another).

✓ Synthesize realistic speech using AI-driven voice cloning.

✓ Generate entirely fictional people that look and sound real.

💡 **Example**: Deepfake tools like DeepFaceLab and FaceSwap enable users to create convincing synthetic videos with little expertise.

1.2 GANs in Deepfake Generation

Deepfakes rely on two neural networks working against each other:

✓ **Generator** – Creates synthetic images, faces, and voices.

✓ **Discriminator** – Evaluates how realistic the generated content is.

Through this adversarial process, deepfake models continuously improve, making them harder to detect.

2. The Role of Deepfakes in Misinformation

2.1 Political Manipulation and Fake News

Deepfakes pose serious threats to democracy and public trust, as AI-generated videos can:

✗ Fabricate political speeches and propaganda to manipulate public opinion.

✗ Create false endorsements from influential figures.

✗ Spread misinformation before elections to influence voter behavior.

💡 **Example**: In 2020, a deepfake video of Barack Obama surfaced, showing him saying things he never actually said, raising concerns about AI-generated political deception.

2.2 Social Media Disinformation

Deepfake-generated content spreads rapidly on social media, contributing to:

✘ Fake celebrity scandals and hoaxes.

✘ AI-generated influencers and bots spreading false narratives.

✘ Distorted historical facts using manipulated video evidence.

💡 **Example**: Deepfake videos of Mark Zuckerberg and Tom Cruise have gone viral, demonstrating how easily the public can be misled.

3. The Risks of Deepfakes

3.1 Cybersecurity and Identity Theft

Deepfake technology can be weaponized for cybercrime, including:

✘ AI-generated voice phishing – Criminals use deepfake audio to impersonate CEOs and executives for financial fraud.

✘ Synthetic identity theft – AI can create realistic fake identities for scams.

✘ Bypassing facial recognition security – Deepfakes can fool biometric authentication systems.

💡 **Example**: In 2019, cybercriminals used deepfake voice AI to trick a bank into transferring $243,000, impersonating a company executive.

3.2 The Erosion of Trust in Media

With deepfakes, seeing is no longer believing. The inability to verify truth from AI-generated fiction leads to:

✘ Mass skepticism toward legitimate news sources.

✘ Public confusion over real vs. manipulated videos.

✘ Loss of credibility in journalism and media organizations.

💡 **Example**: The rise of "liar's dividend" – A phenomenon where real footage is dismissed as fake, making it easier for individuals to deny real events.

3.3 Psychological and Societal Impact

Deepfakes can have personal and societal consequences, including:

✗ Defamation and personal reputation damage (e.g., fake intimate videos).

✗ Political instability and distrust in governments.

✗ Mental health effects, as individuals struggle with AI-generated reality distortions.

💡 **Example**: Victims of deepfake revenge porn have reported severe psychological distress and harassment.

4. Detecting and Combating Deepfakes

4.1 AI-Based Deepfake Detection

To combat deepfake threats, researchers are developing AI-powered detection tools, including:

✓ Deepfake detection algorithms that analyze facial inconsistencies.

✓ Blockchain for content verification, ensuring video authenticity.

✓ Watermarking AI-generated media to distinguish real from fake.

💡 **Example**: Microsoft's Video Authenticator detects deepfake content by analyzing subtle visual artifacts.

4.2 Government Regulations and Legal Actions

Governments worldwide are introducing laws to regulate deepfake technology, including:

✓ Criminalizing malicious deepfake creation and distribution.

✓ Requiring disclaimers for AI-generated content.

✓ Imposing penalties for deepfake-related cybercrimes.

Example: The U.S. DEEPFAKES Accountability Act mandates that AI-generated content must be clearly labeled to prevent misinformation.

4.3 Public Awareness and Media Literacy

Educating the public on deepfake risks is crucial. Strategies include:

✓ Teaching media literacy in schools to help students identify AI-generated fakes.

✓ Encouraging skepticism toward viral media and verifying sources.

✓ Promoting AI ethics in content creation to ensure responsible use.

Example: Organizations like MIT and Adobe are working on AI-driven content authenticity verification tools.

5. The Future of Deepfakes and Ethical AI

While deepfakes pose serious risks, they also have positive applications in:

✓ **Entertainment and film industry** – AI can de-age actors or recreate historical figures.

✓ **Education and training** – AI-generated avatars can enhance virtual learning experiences.

✓ **Medical applications** – Deepfake AI can simulate rare diseases for diagnostic training.

However, ethical AI governance is necessary to ensure deepfakes serve humanity rather than harm it.

The Road Ahead

🚀 Advanced AI detection tools will improve fake content identification.

🏛 Stronger global regulations will hold malicious deepfake creators accountable.

📧 Public education will empower people to recognize and combat misinformation.

💡 Ethical AI practices will guide responsible deepfake use in creative fields.

Deepfake technology, while revolutionary, has significant ethical and societal implications. It can entertain and innovate, but also deceive and manipulate. The rise of

AI-generated misinformation demands urgent action from governments, researchers, and the public.

✓ Transparency, regulation, and AI-based detection tools are key to fighting deepfake abuse.

✓ AI ethics and responsible innovation will shape the future of synthetic media.

✓ Public awareness and education are the strongest defenses against deepfake deception.

As AI continues to evolve, ensuring the integrity of digital information is more important than ever. The future of truth in the digital age depends on how we navigate the challenges of deepfake technology today.

17.2 Bias in AI-Generated Content

Artificial intelligence (AI) has revolutionized content creation, enabling the generation of realistic images, text, music, and videos through Generative Adversarial Networks (GANs) and other deep learning models. However, despite their capabilities, AI models inherit and amplify biases present in the data they are trained on. These biases can manifest in gender stereotypes, racial discrimination, cultural exclusion, and misinformation, leading to ethical concerns about fairness, representation, and accountability in AI-generated content.

This chapter explores:

✓ How AI models develop biases

✓ Real-world examples of biased AI-generated content

✓ The impact of bias in synthetic media and decision-making

✓ Techniques to mitigate bias in GANs and AI systems

✓ Ethical considerations for fair AI development

As AI-generated content becomes more prevalent, addressing bias is crucial to ensuring AI serves all communities fairly.

1. Understanding AI Bias

1.1 What Is Bias in AI?

Bias in AI refers to systematic favoritism or discrimination in an algorithm's outputs due to skewed training data, flawed model design, or unintended social influences. AI models learn patterns from data, and if that data reflects historical prejudices or underrepresentation, the AI will replicate and even reinforce those biases.

1.2 How GANs and AI Models Learn Bias

GANs, like all AI models, are trained on vast datasets collected from the internet, books, and media. These datasets may contain:

✓ **Gender biases** – AI-generated images may depict CEOs as male and nurses as female.

✓ **Racial biases** – AI face-generation tools may favor lighter skin tones over darker ones.

✓ **Cultural exclusion** – Text-based AI may be biased toward Western perspectives, ignoring diverse viewpoints.

✓ **Political and ideological biases** – AI-generated news summaries may lean toward specific political ideologies.

💡 **Example**: A GAN trained on celebrity faces might produce more white, male faces if the training dataset lacks diversity.

2. Real-World Examples of AI Bias

2.1 AI-Generated Images and Stereotypes

AI-generated images often reinforce existing stereotypes. For example:

✗ AI-created images of "successful business leaders" tend to be white men in suits.

✗ AI-generated portraits may depict "beauty" as lighter-skinned individuals, ignoring darker complexions.

✗ AI tools misinterpret gender roles, generating "scientists" as men and "caregivers" as women.

💡 **Example**: A study found that DALL·E and Stable Diffusion generated highly stereotypical images when prompted with certain professions.

2.2 Bias in AI-Generated Text and Journalism

Language models like GPT-based AI are trained on human-written text, which may contain political, cultural, and ideological biases. These biases can result in:

✗ Skewed news articles that favor one political stance.

✗ Gendered language, where AI assumes a doctor is "he" and a nurse is "she."

✗ Exclusion of underrepresented groups in AI-written stories.

💡 **Example**: AI-generated resume screening tools have historically favored male candidates over female candidates due to biased training data.

2.3 Deepfake and GAN Bias in Video and Film

AI-powered deepfake tools, used for CGI, movies, and virtual influencers, can introduce bias by:

✗ Favoring lighter-skinned actors in AI-enhanced video upscaling.

✗ Altering cultural aesthetics, making non-Western facial features appear more Westernized.

✗ Excluding diverse voices, as AI voice synthesis models may struggle with non-English accents.

💡 **Example**: Face-generating GANs trained on Hollywood movie datasets have been shown to underrepresent non-white individuals.

3. The Impact of AI Bias

3.1 Social and Cultural Consequences

AI bias can reinforce harmful stereotypes and widen social inequalities, leading to:

✗ **Misinformation** – AI-generated news articles may favor certain viewpoints, misleading the public.

✗ **Representation issues** – AI-generated content may erase marginalized communities from digital spaces.

✗ **Discriminatory policies** – AI-driven decision-making (e.g., hiring, lending) can unfairly disadvantage certain groups.

💡 **Example**: AI-generated beauty filters often lighten skin tones and narrow facial features, reflecting Eurocentric beauty standards.

3.2 Ethical and Legal Risks

As AI becomes more integrated into industries like finance, healthcare, and law enforcement, biased AI models can have real-world consequences, such as:

✗ Discriminatory hiring processes if AI screening favors one demographic.

✗ Unfair financial lending if AI denies loans to certain ethnic groups.

✗ Biased policing and surveillance if AI misidentifies people based on racial profiling.

💡 **Example**: A facial recognition AI used in law enforcement has wrongfully identified and arrested people of color, highlighting the dangers of AI bias.

4. Mitigating Bias in GANs and AI Models

4.1 Collecting Diverse and Inclusive Training Data

One of the most effective ways to reduce bias is by ensuring diverse datasets that represent all races, genders, and cultures. Strategies include:

✓ **Balanced data collection** – Ensure datasets contain equitable representation across demographics.

✓ **Bias auditing tools** – AI researchers should analyze training data for unintended patterns.

✓ **Crowdsourced data validation** – Using diverse perspectives to evaluate AI-generated outputs.

💡 **Example**: Companies like OpenAI and Google are investing in "fair AI" datasets to improve representation.

4.2 Bias-Aware Training Methods

Developers can adjust GAN training techniques to counteract bias, including:

✓ Reweighting datasets to correct for underrepresented groups.

✓ Bias detection algorithms that flag skewed AI outputs.

✓ Fairness constraints to ensure balanced content generation.

💡 **Example**: Researchers use "adversarial debiasing" to train AI models that actively reduce biased outcomes.

4.3 Ethical AI Frameworks and Regulations

To ensure responsible AI development, organizations should follow:

✓ **Transparency guidelines** – Clearly disclose when AI is used in content creation.

✓ **Accountability measures** – Companies should take responsibility for biased AI decisions.

✓ **Regulatory compliance** – Governments should enforce anti-discrimination policies for AI systems.

💡 **Example**: The European Union's AI Act proposes strict regulations to mitigate AI bias in high-risk applications.

5. The Future of Fair AI Content Generation

As AI technology advances, the focus on fair and unbiased AI will shape future developments, including:

🚀 Improved fairness in GANs, ensuring AI-generated images are inclusive.

📜 Stronger AI ethics policies, requiring transparency in AI-generated content.

🎓 Public awareness and education, empowering users to recognize AI bias.

💡 AI bias detection tools, helping creators and developers mitigate unfair outputs.

Bias in AI-generated content is a serious ethical challenge that affects social, economic, and cultural landscapes. While AI models inherit bias from their training data, researchers, developers, and policymakers must take proactive steps to ensure fair and equitable AI systems.

✓ Diverse and inclusive datasets can prevent biased AI outputs.

✓ Advanced training techniques can counteract bias in GANs.

✓ Ethical AI regulations can hold organizations accountable.

By addressing these challenges, we can ensure that AI-generated content benefits all communities fairly, creating a future where synthetic intelligence is inclusive, transparent, and responsible.

17.3 The Impact of AI Art on Human Creativity

The rise of AI-generated art has sparked a heated debate about creativity, originality, and the role of human artists in a world increasingly influenced by artificial intelligence. With advancements in Generative Adversarial Networks (GANs) and AI-driven models like DALL·E, MidJourney, and DeepDream, machines are now capable of producing stunning, highly detailed artworks in mere seconds. This shift challenges traditional notions of creativity and raises critical questions:

✓ Is AI-generated art truly "creative," or is it just sophisticated pattern recognition?

✓ Does AI art devalue human creativity, or does it serve as a tool for artistic expansion?

✓ How will AI impact the future of artists, designers, and creative industries?

This chapter explores the evolution of AI in art, its influence on human creativity, and the potential consequences—both positive and negative—of this technological revolution.

1. AI as a Creative Partner vs. Competitor

1.1 The Case for AI as a Creative Tool

For many artists and designers, AI is not a replacement but an enhancement. AI-driven tools help artists:

✓ **Automate repetitive tasks** – AI speeds up processes like coloring, shading, and image enhancement.

✓ **Generate inspiration** – AI can suggest color palettes, compositions, or even entire artistic styles.

✓ **Expand artistic possibilities** – Artists can experiment with new styles and blend multiple influences effortlessly.

✓ **Assist in accessibility** – AI allows those with physical disabilities to create art through voice or text prompts.

💡 **Example**: Concept artists in game design and film production use AI-generated images as a starting point for character and world-building ideas.

1.2 The Fear of AI as a Creative Competitor

While AI can enhance human creativity, many fear that it could replace traditional artists by:

✗ Flooding the market with AI-generated art, making human work less valuable.

✗ Decreasing demand for original artists, as businesses opt for faster, cheaper AI solutions.

✗ Diluting artistic originality, since AI-generated works are based on existing human-created data.

💡 **Example**: AI-generated art has already won competitions, such as the controversial 2022 Colorado State Fair art contest, where a piece made using MidJourney defeated human artists.

2. The Role of Human Creativity in the Age of AI

2.1 Defining "True" Creativity

Creativity is often linked to imagination, emotion, and originality—traits traditionally attributed to humans. However, AI models:

✔ **Do not "think" or "feel" like humans** – AI lacks intention, emotion, and personal experience.

✔ **Only remix and reinterpret data** – AI art is derived from pre-existing images, styles, and patterns.

✔ **Cannot innovate independently** – AI lacks the ability to intentionally break rules or create entirely new artistic movements.

💡 **Example**: The works of Picasso, Van Gogh, and Salvador Dalí broke artistic conventions. AI, on the other hand, learns from existing styles but does not "rebel" against them in the same way.

2.2 The Value of Human Touch

Despite AI's capabilities, human art retains unique qualities:

✔ **Emotional depth** – Human art reflects personal experiences, struggles, and emotions, which AI lacks.

✔ **Symbolism and meaning** – Artists infuse their work with cultural, political, and philosophical messages beyond AI's understanding.

✔ **The creative process itself** – Many argue that art is not just about the final product, but also about the act of creation, something AI cannot experience.

💡 **Example**: A hand-painted portrait by an artist carries more personal touch and intentionality than an AI-generated replica of the same style.

3. AI Art in the Creative Industry

3.1 AI's Influence on Digital Art and Design

AI-generated content is being widely adopted in industries such as:

✔ **Advertising & Marketing** – AI-generated visuals help brands create quick, engaging promotional content.

✓ **Video Games & CGI** – AI speeds up the process of character design, world-building, and texture generation.

✓ **Fashion & Product Design** – AI helps generate new clothing patterns, logo designs, and product concepts.

💡 **Example**: AI-generated NFT collections like CryptoPunks and Bored Ape Yacht Club have revolutionized digital art ownership and monetization.

3.2 The Commercialization of AI Art

The rapid adoption of AI-generated art raises concerns about:

✗ **Job displacement** – Will companies hire fewer human artists and designers?

✗ **Lack of originality** – If AI creates based on pre-existing works, does that make it inherently unoriginal?

✗ **Copyright and ownership disputes** – Who owns AI-generated art: the user, the developer, or the AI itself?

💡 **Example**: Artists have protested AI-generated stock images appearing on sites like Shutterstock, arguing that AI creations undercut human-made artwork.

4. The Future of AI and Human Creativity

4.1 The Possibilities of AI-Augmented Creativity

Rather than replacing artists, AI may redefine creativity in several ways:

✓ **Collaborative art** – Artists can work alongside AI, using it as an idea generator rather than a replacement.

✓ **New artistic frontiers** – AI can create art beyond human limitations, such as 4D digital art, data-driven sculptures, and interactive AI-generated music.

✓ **Art education and accessibility** – AI can help teach art, assist disabled creators, and democratize creative expression.

💡 **Example**: Musician Holly Herndon trained an AI model on her own voice, allowing others to create "AI collaborations" with her.

4.2 The Need for Ethical Guidelines

As AI continues to evolve, it's important to set ethical boundaries to:

✓ **Protect artists' rights** – Prevent AI from copying copyrighted works without permission.

✓ **Ensure fair credit** – Clearly label AI-assisted works so audiences know how they were created.

✓ **Maintain artistic integrity** – AI should be a tool, not a replacement for human imagination.

💡 **Example**: Platforms like DeviantArt and ArtStation have introduced AI opt-out policies to prevent unauthorized use of artists' works for AI training.

The impact of AI art on human creativity is both exciting and controversial. While AI-generated art challenges traditional notions of creativity, it also expands artistic possibilities, making art more accessible, innovative, and collaborative.

✓ AI is a powerful tool that can assist and inspire human artists, rather than replace them.

✓ Creativity is more than just pattern recognition—human imagination, emotions, and intent still set artists apart.

✓ The future of art lies in AI-human collaboration, where technology enhances, rather than diminishes, artistic expression.

As AI art continues to evolve, the question is not whether AI will replace artists, but how artists will use AI to push the boundaries of creativity in new and unexpected ways.

17.4 Ethical Guidelines for AI Use in Media

The integration of AI into media, including journalism, film, music, and digital art, has sparked both excitement and concern. AI-generated content is reshaping how we create, consume, and distribute media. However, the rapid growth of AI in media raises serious ethical questions about misinformation, bias, ownership, and accountability.

✓ How can we ensure AI-generated media is used responsibly?

✓ What ethical standards should guide AI-driven content creation?

✓ Who is accountable when AI-generated content is misleading or harmful?

In this chapter, we will explore the ethical challenges of AI-generated media and outline essential guidelines to ensure its responsible use.

1. The Rise of AI-Generated Media

AI tools are transforming content creation across multiple industries:

✓ **Journalism & News** – AI generates news articles, summarizes information, and even creates deepfake news.

✓ **Film & Entertainment** – AI is used for scriptwriting, voice synthesis, and CGI enhancements.

✓ **Music & Audio** – AI-powered models generate songs, synthesize voices, and remix tracks.

✓ **Advertising & Marketing** – AI personalizes ad campaigns, generates product descriptions, and creates social media content.

While these advancements improve efficiency and creativity, they also introduce ethical dilemmas, such as misinformation, bias, and intellectual property concerns.

2. Key Ethical Concerns in AI-Generated Media

2.1 Misinformation and Deepfakes

One of the most dangerous aspects of AI in media is its ability to generate hyper-realistic fake content.

✓ AI can create fake news articles, leading to misinformation.

✓ Deepfake videos can manipulate public opinion by making it appear as if people said or did things they never did.

✓ AI-generated audio can replicate voices, leading to scams and identity fraud.

💡 **Example**: In 2019, a deepfake video of Mark Zuckerberg falsely showed him making a statement about controlling user data, raising concerns about AI's potential for misinformation.

2.2 Bias and Discrimination in AI Content

AI models learn from historical data, which can lead to biased content if the data itself is biased.

✓ AI-generated news may favor certain political ideologies if trained on biased datasets.

✓ AI-generated visuals may underrepresent minorities or reinforce stereotypes.

✓ Voice synthesis AI may struggle with non-English accents, reflecting a lack of diverse training data.

💡 **Example**: A 2020 study showed that facial recognition AI misclassified people of color at higher rates, highlighting the dangers of biased AI training.

2.3 Intellectual Property and Ownership

Who owns AI-generated media—the creator, the AI developer, or the dataset providers?

✓ Artists and writers fear AI will copy their work without permission.

✓ AI-generated content may infringe on copyrighted materials without proper attribution.

✓ Legal frameworks struggle to define AI-generated intellectual property rights.

💡 **Example**: In 2023, multiple artists sued AI companies for training models on their artwork without consent.

2.4 Lack of Accountability

If an AI-generated article spreads misinformation or a deepfake video harms someone's reputation, who is responsible?

✓ AI lacks intent and moral responsibility, but humans using AI must be held accountable.

✓ AI developers, companies, and users must share ethical responsibility for the content they produce.

💡 **Example**: In 2022, a chatbot-generated news article falsely reported the death of a celebrity, causing public panic. The platform later blamed an "AI error," but critics argued that humans must verify AI-generated content.

3. Ethical Guidelines for Responsible AI Use in Media

To ensure AI is used ethically in media, the following guidelines should be followed:

3.1 Transparency and Disclosure

✓ AI-generated content should be clearly labeled to avoid confusion.

✓ Users must be informed when they interact with AI-generated media (e.g., AI-generated news articles, deepfake videos).

✓ Organizations should disclose how AI models are trained and what data is used.

💡 **Example**: YouTube and TikTok have begun labeling AI-generated videos to prevent misinformation.

3.2 Ensuring Fairness and Reducing Bias

✓ AI models should be trained on diverse datasets to reduce bias.

✓ Developers must test AI-generated content for fairness before deployment.

✓ Independent audits should be conducted to evaluate AI for potential discrimination.

💡 **Example**: OpenAI and Google have implemented bias-checking mechanisms to reduce unfair AI outputs.

3.3 Ethical AI Training and Data Use

✓ AI should not be trained on copyrighted material without permission.

✓ Data used to train AI models must be collected ethically and with consent.

✓ AI-generated content should respect existing intellectual property laws.

💡 **Example**: Some AI image generators now allow artists to opt out of having their work used for AI training.

3.4 Human Oversight and Accountability

✓ AI should assist human creators, not replace them.

✓ News organizations must fact-check AI-generated articles before publishing.

✓ Companies using AI-generated media should be held accountable for any harm caused.

💡 **Example**: The Associated Press uses AI for news writing but requires human journalists to review and edit AI-generated articles before publishing.

3.5 Ethical AI Regulations and Policies

✓ Governments and organizations must establish AI regulations to prevent misuse.

✓ There should be legal consequences for deepfake abuse and AI-generated misinformation.

✓ AI ethics boards should be created within media companies to oversee responsible AI use.

💡 **Example**: The European Union's AI Act aims to regulate AI applications, including media-related use cases.

4. The Future of Ethical AI in Media

As AI technology continues to advance, ethical guidelines must evolve to keep pace. The future of ethical AI in media will likely include:

✓ More robust legal frameworks to govern AI-generated content.

✓ Stronger AI detection tools to prevent the spread of deepfakes and misinformation.

✓ Ethical AI certifications for companies that use AI responsibly.

✓ More collaboration between tech companies, artists, journalists, and policymakers to create fair AI policies.

💡 **Example**: Future AI models might include built-in ethical constraints, preventing them from generating harmful or deceptive content.

AI is transforming media in powerful ways, but with great power comes great responsibility. Without ethical guidelines, AI-generated media can lead to misinformation, bias, and intellectual property violations.

✓ **Transparency and disclosure are essential**—AI-generated content must be clearly labeled.
✓ **Bias must be minimized**—AI should be trained on diverse, fair datasets.
✓ **Ownership and accountability must be defined**—legal frameworks must protect creators.
✓ **Human oversight remains critical**—AI should be a tool, not a replacement for ethical decision-making.

By following these ethical guidelines, we can ensure that AI serves as a force for good in media, empowering creators while protecting truth, fairness, and creativity in the digital age.

17.5 AI Safety and Responsible Development

As AI continues to advance, ensuring its safety and responsible development has become a critical global concern. AI-powered systems, including Generative Adversarial Networks (GANs), have the potential to revolutionize industries, but without proper safeguards, they can also cause unintended harm. From deepfake misinformation to biased decision-making and privacy violations, AI must be developed and deployed responsibly to maximize benefits while minimizing risks.

In this chapter, we explore the key principles of AI safety, the risks of unregulated AI, and best practices for responsible AI development.

1. Understanding AI Safety

AI safety refers to the measures and guidelines that ensure AI systems operate reliably, ethically, and without unintended negative consequences. The goal is to design AI models that:

✓ Align with human values and ethics

✓ Operate transparently and predictably

✓ Prevent malicious use or harmful biases

✓ Remain controllable and explainable

💡 **Example**: AI chatbots, when trained improperly, have been known to produce harmful or biased content. Ensuring AI safety means building safeguards to prevent such issues.

2. Risks of Unregulated AI Development

2.1 Bias and Discrimination

AI models learn from historical data, which can introduce bias into their decision-making. If not addressed, this can lead to discriminatory AI outputs that reinforce stereotypes.

✓ **Example**: Facial recognition AI has been shown to have higher error rates for people of color, leading to unfair policing and wrongful arrests.

✓ **Solution**: AI should be trained on diverse datasets and tested for fairness.

2.2 AI Misuse and Malicious Applications

GANs and other generative AI models can be misused for deepfakes, cyberattacks, and disinformation campaigns.

✓ **Example**: Deepfake videos can manipulate elections, defame individuals, or spread fake news.

✓ **Solution**: AI detection tools and legal frameworks should regulate AI-generated content.

2.3 Lack of Explainability ("Black Box" Problem)

Many AI models, especially deep learning-based systems, act as "black boxes", meaning their decision-making process is not easily interpretable.

✓ **Example**: If an AI-powered credit approval system denies a loan, users may not understand why.

✓ **Solution**: AI models should include explainability mechanisms to make decisions transparent.

2.4 Security Vulnerabilities and AI Hacking

AI models can be hacked or manipulated, leading to security threats. Attackers can modify AI-generated content, exploit biases, or manipulate AI-powered systems.

✓ **Example**: Hackers have tricked self-driving AI systems into misreading road signs, leading to dangerous driving decisions.

✓ **Solution**: AI developers must implement robust security measures to prevent adversarial attacks.

3. Principles of Responsible AI Development

To ensure AI is safe, ethical, and beneficial, developers and organizations must adhere to key principles of responsible AI development.

3.1 Transparency and Explainability

✓ AI systems should provide explanations for their decisions.

✓ Users should be informed when they are interacting with AI-generated content.

✓ AI models should include auditable logs to track decision-making processes.

💡 **Example**: OpenAI provides detailed documentation and research on AI model behavior to ensure transparency.

3.2 Fairness and Bias Mitigation

✓ AI models should be trained on diverse, unbiased datasets.

✓ Fairness checks should be integrated into the AI development pipeline.

✓ Independent audits should evaluate AI systems for potential bias.

💡 **Example**: Google's AI team actively tests machine learning models to detect and mitigate racial and gender biases before deployment.

3.3 Robust Security and Safety Measures

✓ AI should be tested for vulnerabilities before being released.

✓ Developers must implement adversarial training to make AI resilient to attacks.

✓ AI-generated media should include watermarks to prevent deepfake misuse.

💡 **Example**: AI-generated content detection tools (e.g., deepfake detection software) help counteract malicious AI usage.

3.4 Human Oversight and Control

✓ AI should be monitored and supervised by humans.

✓ High-stakes AI applications (e.g., medical diagnoses, autonomous vehicles) should always involve human oversight.

✓ Kill switches should be integrated to disable AI systems in case of failure or misuse.

💡 **Example**: Self-driving car companies require human drivers to take control if the AI system malfunctions.

3.5 Ethical Use and Compliance with Regulations

✓ AI should follow ethical guidelines and government regulations.

✓ Organizations must comply with privacy laws when using AI to process personal data.

✓ Developers should collaborate with policymakers to create ethical AI frameworks.

💡 **Example**: The European Union's AI Act establishes regulations to ensure AI safety and ethical use across industries.

4. The Future of AI Safety and Responsible Development

As AI becomes more powerful, its regulation and ethical development will become even more critical. Key trends for the future include:

✓ **More AI governance and policies** – Governments worldwide will enforce stricter AI regulations.

✓ **AI ethics research and interdisciplinary collaboration** – Scientists, ethicists, and policymakers will work together to create fair AI systems.

✓ **Stronger AI safety mechanisms** – New techniques will emerge to improve AI interpretability, robustness, and fairness.

✓ **Public awareness and AI literacy programs** – Organizations will educate users about AI risks and responsible usage.

💡 **Example**: Future AI systems may include "ethical AI switches" that prevent models from generating harmful or biased content.

AI safety and responsible development are essential to ensuring that AI remains a beneficial force rather than a dangerous tool for harm. Without proper safeguards, AI can be misused for misinformation, discrimination, and unethical practices.

✓ **Transparency is key**—AI decisions must be explainable.

✓ **Bias must be addressed**—AI should be trained on diverse datasets.

✓ **Security is critical**—AI must be resistant to hacking and manipulation.

✓ **Human oversight is necessary**—AI should enhance human abilities, not replace human judgment.

By prioritizing AI safety and ethical development, we can build a future where AI empowers humanity without compromising security, fairness, or trust.

18. Legal and Copyright Issues

As AI-generated content becomes more sophisticated, legal and copyright questions are becoming increasingly important. Who owns AI-generated artwork? Can AI-generated music or writing be copyrighted? What happens when AI-generated content is misused for deepfakes, plagiarism, or misinformation? In this chapter, we explore the legal landscape surrounding GANs and synthetic creativity, including intellectual property laws, copyright disputes, and the challenges of defining authorship for AI-generated works. We'll examine global regulations, landmark court cases, and the ethical implications of AI-created content in industries like publishing, entertainment, and advertising. By the end of this chapter, you'll understand the legal complexities of AI creativity and how businesses, artists, and developers can navigate copyright and ownership in an AI-driven world. ⚖️📜💡🚀

18.1 Who Owns AI-Generated Content?

As AI-generated content becomes more prevalent, a critical question arises: who owns AI-generated works? Whether it's AI-generated art, music, text, or videos, the legal and ethical landscape surrounding ownership and intellectual property rights is still evolving. Traditionally, copyright laws have been designed for human creators, but AI challenges this framework by blurring the lines between human and machine creativity.

In this section, we explore the current state of AI-generated content ownership, key legal debates, and the implications for creators, businesses, and policymakers.

1. Copyright Basics: What Does the Law Say?

Copyright laws exist to protect original works of authorship and typically grant rights to the human creator. These rights include:

✓ **Reproduction** – The right to copy and distribute the work.

✓ **Modification** – The right to create derivative works.

✓ **Commercialization** – The right to monetize the content.

💡 **Example**: If a human writes a novel, they own the copyright and can sell publishing rights. But if an AI generates the novel, who owns it?

Currently, most copyright laws, including those in the U.S., U.K., EU, and other major regions, do not recognize AI as an author. A human must have significant creative input for copyright protection to apply.

2. Can AI Be Considered an Author?

2.1 U.S. Copyright Office Position

The U.S. Copyright Office (USCO) has repeatedly ruled that AI-generated works cannot be copyrighted unless there is substantial human involvement.

✓ **Example**: In 2023, the USCO rejected a copyright application for an image created by Midjourney, ruling that the AI-generated content was not eligible for copyright protection.
✓ However, if a human modifies an AI-generated work significantly, they may be able to claim copyright for the edited version.

2.2 UK and EU Approaches

- The UK allows copyright protection only if AI-generated content is the result of a human's creative efforts.
- The EU is still debating AI ownership rights but is leaning toward a "human authorship" requirement for copyright eligibility.

💡 Takeaway: Most legal systems do not recognize AI as an author but allow copyright for AI-assisted works where humans have made significant contributions.

3. Who Owns AI-Generated Content?

The ownership of AI-generated content generally depends on who (or what) contributed to its creation:

3.1 The AI Developer (Company/Platform)

Some AI platforms, like OpenAI, Midjourney, or Google DeepMind, specify in their terms of service that they retain ownership or usage rights for content created using their AI models.

✓ **Example**: If you generate an image using a proprietary AI like Midjourney, you might have limited rights depending on their policies.

3.2 The User (Prompt Engineer/Creator)

If an individual writes a detailed prompt and refines AI-generated outputs, they may claim some ownership—especially if they add substantial human creativity to the final product.

✓ **Example**: If an artist uses AI to generate concept sketches but manually edits and refines them, they could claim copyright over the modified work.

3.3 Public Domain & Open-Source AI

Some AI-generated content may fall into the public domain, meaning no one can claim ownership.
✓ **Example**: In some jurisdictions, purely AI-generated works (without human input) may not be eligible for copyright and can be freely used by anyone.

4. Legal Disputes and Precedents

AI copyright cases are increasing worldwide, and courts are still determining how to handle AI-generated content.

4.1 The "Monkey Selfie" Case – A Precedent for AI?

✓ In 2011, a monkey took a selfie using a photographer's camera. The photographer tried to claim copyright, but courts ruled that only humans can hold copyrights—meaning the photo was in the public domain.
✓ Some legal experts believe this ruling could apply to AI-generated content, arguing that if no human creates it, no one owns it.

4.2 Getty Images vs. Stability AI (2023)

✓ Getty Images sued Stability AI (creator of Stable Diffusion) for using copyrighted images to train its AI without permission.

✓ This case raises questions about AI training data ownership—can AI models legally use copyrighted materials to generate new works?

5. The Future of AI Ownership & Copyright Law

5.1 Possible Legal Reforms

Governments and legal bodies worldwide are considering new regulations for AI-generated content. Possible future changes include:

✓ **New AI Copyright Categories** – Laws may be updated to recognize AI-assisted works with varying degrees of human involvement.

✓ **Mandatory Attribution** – Some jurisdictions may require AI-generated works to be labeled as such.

✓ **Royalties for Training Data** – AI companies may be required to compensate artists and creators whose work is used to train AI models.

5.2 Ethical Considerations

Even if AI-generated content isn't legally protected, ethical concerns remain:

✓ Should AI artists get credit for their work?

✓ Should AI-generated art be distinguished from human-made art?

✓ How should companies compensate human creators whose work was used to train AI?

💡 **Example**: Some AI developers, like Adobe, are creating "ethical AI" tools that only use licensed data to train models.

The question of who owns AI-generated content is still evolving, with legal systems around the world struggling to adapt to AI's rapid advancements.

✓ Current laws favor human creators—purely AI-generated works typically lack copyright protection.

✓ Companies often own AI-generated content if created using their platforms.

✓ Users can claim ownership if they significantly modify AI-generated outputs.

✓ Future legal reforms may establish new copyright categories for AI-assisted works.

As AI creativity continues to expand, clarity on ownership and copyright laws will be essential for protecting both human artists and AI developers.

18.2 Copyright Laws for AI Art, Music, and Text

As artificial intelligence (AI) continues to revolutionize creative fields, a critical legal question arises: who owns AI-generated art, music, and text? Copyright laws were designed to protect human creativity, but with AI now capable of producing paintings, songs, and novels, the traditional frameworks are being challenged.

This section explores how copyright laws apply to AI-generated works, key legal debates, and how different countries are handling the issue.

1. Understanding Copyright in Creative Works

1.1 What is Copyright?

Copyright is a legal right that grants creators exclusive control over their original works. These rights typically include:

✓ **Reproduction** – The right to copy and distribute the work.

✓ **Adaptation** – The right to modify and create derivative works.

✓ **Commercial Use** – The right to sell or license the work.

💡 **Traditional Copyright Rule**: A work must be created by a human to be protected by copyright. But does this apply to AI-generated content?

2. Copyright Laws and AI-Generated Works

2.1 Current Legal Position on AI-Generated Content

Most countries do not recognize AI as an author, meaning purely AI-generated works may not be eligible for copyright protection.

U.S. Copyright Office (USCO)

✔ **AI cannot hold copyrights** – The U.S. Copyright Office has repeatedly ruled that AI-generated content cannot be copyrighted unless a human has made significant creative contributions.

✔ **Example**: In 2023, the USCO denied a copyright claim for an image created by Midjourney, stating that the AI, not a human, was the creator.

UK Copyright Law

✔ The UK takes a different approach and allows copyright for AI-generated works, but the owner is considered the person who arranged the AI's creation (such as the AI developer or user).

European Union (EU) Copyright Directives

✔ The EU emphasizes human authorship, meaning AI-generated works may lack copyright protection unless human creativity is clearly involved.

✔ The EU is also considering new AI-specific copyright rules, particularly for music and visual art.

💡 **Key Takeaway**: Most copyright laws favor human creators—fully AI-generated works may not be protected, but AI-assisted works might be.

3. Copyright for AI-Generated Art

AI-generated art, produced by models like DALL·E, Midjourney, and DeepDream, raises new copyright challenges:

✔ If AI creates an image, who owns it?

✔ If an artist modifies an AI-generated piece, does copyright apply?

✔ Can AI-generated art be sold as NFTs or used commercially?

3.1 Key Copyright Cases for AI Art

The "Zarya of the Dawn" Case (2023, U.S.)

✓ A graphic novel using Midjourney-generated illustrations was denied full copyright protection because the images were AI-generated.

✓ The text and arrangement were eligible for copyright, but not the AI art itself.

Getty Images vs. Stability AI

✓ Getty Images sued Stability AI for allegedly using copyrighted photos to train its AI models without permission.

✓ The case highlights a growing debate over AI training data and copyright infringement.

3.2 Who Owns AI Art?

✓ If an AI model generates an artwork with no human modification, it may fall into the public domain.

✓ If a human heavily edits AI-generated art, they may claim copyright over the modified version.

✓ Some AI platforms claim partial ownership of content created using their tools (check the platform's Terms of Service).

4. Copyright for AI-Generated Music

AI is transforming music production, with systems like Jukebox (OpenAI), MuseNet, and Amper Music generating original compositions.

4.1 Legal Issues in AI Music Copyright

✓ Who owns an AI-generated song? If a human inputs a melody and the AI enhances it, the human may claim ownership.

✓ If AI composes an entire track, many jurisdictions will not recognize it as copyrighted.

✓ Using copyrighted music to train AI may infringe on existing copyrights, leading to lawsuits.

💡 **Example**: AI-generated music on YouTube has led to disputes where record labels claim AI is copying their artists' styles.

4.2 AI Music Copyright Cases

✓ U.S. Copyright Office Position: AI-generated music must have significant human input to qualify for copyright protection.
✓ The EU is considering licensing fees for AI models trained on copyrighted music.

4.3 Ethical Concerns in AI Music

✓ Should AI-generated music compensate original artists whose styles were mimicked?
✓ Should platforms disclose when music is AI-generated?

5. Copyright for AI-Generated Text

AI-powered text generation (e.g., GPT models, ChatGPT, Jasper AI) is revolutionizing writing, journalism, and content creation.

5.1 Can AI-Generated Text Be Copyrighted?

✓ The U.S. Copyright Office has ruled that fully AI-generated text cannot be copyrighted.
✓ AI-assisted text, where a human significantly edits or contributes, may be eligible for copyright.

💡 **Example**: If a journalist uses AI to generate article drafts but adds original research and editing, they may claim copyright.

5.2 AI in Content Creation and Plagiarism

✓ AI models sometimes generate text that closely resembles copyrighted works, raising plagiarism concerns.

✓ Google and news publishers are debating whether AI-generated articles can be monetized.

💡 **Example**: CNET faced backlash after using AI to generate articles with factual errors, sparking debates over AI accountability in journalism.

6. Future of Copyright Laws for AI-Generated Content

Governments worldwide are considering new AI copyright regulations. Potential reforms include:

✓ **AI-Generated Works Licensing** – Requiring AI models to pay for training on copyrighted data.

✓ **Mandatory AI Attribution** – Requiring AI-generated content to be labeled as AI-created.

✓ **New Copyright Categories** – Introducing AI-assisted work classifications with limited copyright protections.

6.1 The Role of Blockchain & NFTs

✓ Some AI-generated artworks and music are being minted as NFTs to establish ownership.

✓ Blockchain technology could help track authorship and copyright claims.

AI-generated art, music, and text exist in a legal gray area. While traditional copyright laws protect human-created works, they struggle to define who owns AI-generated content.

✓ Most countries do not recognize AI as an author, meaning purely AI-generated works may lack copyright protection.

✓ AI-assisted works, where humans contribute significantly, may qualify for copyright protection.

✓ New legal frameworks are emerging, but ownership and compensation models for AI-generated content remain unresolved.

As AI creativity expands, laws must evolve to balance innovation, ownership, and ethical considerations.

18.3 The Role of AI in Plagiarism and Fair Use

Artificial intelligence is transforming content creation, but it also raises serious concerns about plagiarism and fair use. AI-powered tools like ChatGPT, Midjourney, Stable Diffusion, and Jukebox can generate text, images, and music in seconds—but where do they get their inspiration?

Many AI models are trained on publicly available data, books, artworks, and music—often without explicit permission. This raises questions about whether AI is creating original content or replicating existing works.

This section explores:

✓ How AI tools might commit plagiarism

✓ When AI-generated content qualifies as "fair use"

✓ Legal and ethical concerns surrounding AI-generated work

1. Understanding Plagiarism in AI-Generated Content

1.1 What is Plagiarism?

Plagiarism occurs when someone copies, paraphrases, or presents another person's work as their own without proper attribution. This can apply to text, images, music, and even ideas.

1.2 How AI Can Commit Plagiarism

AI models like GPT-4, DALL·E, and Midjourney learn from massive datasets, including books, websites, and artworks. If AI-generated output closely resembles or copies copyrighted material, it could be considered plagiarism or copyright infringement.

💡 **Examples of AI-Generated Plagiarism:**

✓ **Text**: AI generates a research paper that matches a Wikipedia article word-for-word.

✓ **Images**: AI recreates a famous painting almost identical to the original.

✓ **Music**: AI composes a melody that sounds exactly like a copyrighted song.

2. Detecting and Preventing AI Plagiarism

2.1 How to Identify AI Plagiarism

Plagiarism detection tools are evolving to catch AI-generated content that closely mirrors existing works. Some methods include:

✓ **Text Similarity Checkers** – Tools like Turnitin and Copyscape can compare AI-generated text against existing content.

✓ **Image Recognition Systems** – Services like Google Reverse Image Search can detect AI-created art that closely resembles existing works.

✓ **Music Pattern Detection** – Algorithms like Shazam can identify if AI-generated music copies existing compositions.

2.2 Preventing AI Plagiarism

AI developers and users can take steps to minimize plagiarism risks:

✓ Train AI models on licensed or public-domain content.

✓ Ensure AI-generated text is sufficiently rewritten and original.

✓ Modify AI-generated images to create unique compositions.

✓ Use AI as an assistive tool, not a replacement for human creativity.

💡 **Example**: Some universities now require students to disclose if they used AI in assignments to ensure transparency.

3. Fair Use and AI-Generated Content

3.1 What is Fair Use?

Fair use is a legal doctrine that allows limited use of copyrighted material without permission under specific conditions.

The four key factors that determine fair use:

1️ **Purpose & Character** – Is the use transformative (adding new meaning) or commercial?

2️ **Nature of the Work** – Is it factual or highly creative?

3️ **Amount Used** – How much of the original work is copied?

4️ **Market Impact** – Does it harm the original creator financially?

3.2 When AI-Generated Content Qualifies as Fair Use

AI-generated works may qualify as fair use if:

✔ The output is significantly transformed from its source material.

✔ It is used for educational, commentary, or research purposes.

✔ It does not directly compete with or harm the original work's market value.

💡 **Example**: An AI model trained on Shakespeare's plays that generates a modernized, reinterpreted version of Hamlet may qualify as fair use. However, if it directly copies Shakespeare's exact text without modification, it would likely be infringement.

4. Legal Challenges in AI, Plagiarism, and Fair Use

4.1 High-Profile AI Copyright Lawsuits

✔ **Getty Images vs. Stability AI (2023)** – Getty sued Stability AI for allegedly using its copyrighted images to train an AI model without permission.

✔ **Universal Music vs. AI-Generated Songs (2023)** – AI-created music mimicking real artists sparked lawsuits over intellectual property rights.

✔ **Artists vs. AI Art Generators** – Several artists sued AI platforms like Midjourney for using their artwork without compensation or credit.

💡 **Legal Uncertainty**: Many copyright laws do not yet account for AI-generated content, leading to ongoing legal battles worldwide.

4.2 Will AI Be Allowed to Use Copyrighted Works?

✔ Some countries propose requiring AI companies to license copyrighted content.

✔ Others argue AI should be free to "learn" from public data, just as humans do.

✔ Tech companies and copyright holders are in a legal standoff over AI training data.

5. Ethical Considerations in AI-Generated Content

5.1 Should AI Give Credit to Original Creators?

Many artists, musicians, and writers argue that AI should provide attribution to sources it was trained on.

💡 **Proposed Solutions:**

✔ AI-generated works could include a disclaimer stating what data influenced them.

✔ Platforms like ChatGPT, Midjourney, and Bard could credit original creators.

5.2 The Role of Human Creativity in AI-Assisted Work

✔ Some argue that AI should be a tool for creativity, not a replacement for human originality.

✔ AI can assist writers, artists, and musicians, but ethical concerns arise when AI content completely replaces human work.

💡 **Example**: Some news organizations use AI to generate draft articles, but require human journalists to edit and verify the content before publication.

AI is changing how we create, consume, and protect content. While AI-generated works offer exciting creative possibilities, they also raise serious plagiarism and copyright concerns.

✓ **Plagiarism** – AI may unintentionally copy existing works, requiring detection and ethical guidelines.

✓ **Fair Use** – Some AI-generated content may qualify as fair use, but legal interpretations vary.

✓ **Legal Uncertainty** – Courts are still deciding how copyright laws should apply to AI.

✓ **Ethical Responsibility** – Users, companies, and regulators must ensure AI respects intellectual property rights.

As AI technology advances, laws will need to evolve to balance innovation, ownership, and fair creative practices.

18.4 Legal Cases and Precedents in AI Creativity

As artificial intelligence (AI) becomes more advanced, its ability to generate creative works—including images, music, text, and even video—has sparked numerous legal battles over ownership, copyright, and intellectual property rights. Courts worldwide are struggling to determine whether AI-generated works can be copyrighted, who (if anyone) owns them, and whether AI models infringe on existing copyrights.

This chapter explores key legal cases and precedents that are shaping the legal landscape of AI creativity. These cases highlight the challenges, loopholes, and unanswered questions surrounding AI-generated content in intellectual property law.

1. Can AI-Generated Works Be Copyrighted?

1.1 The U.S. Copyright Office's Stance on AI Works

The U.S. Copyright Office (USCO) has repeatedly ruled that AI-generated works are not eligible for copyright unless they involve significant human intervention.

✦ **Key Case: Zarya of the Dawn (2023)**

- **What happened?** Artist Kris Kashtanova used Midjourney, an AI art generator, to create a comic book titled Zarya of the Dawn.
- **Legal ruling**: The USCO ruled that the story and arrangement of images were copyrightable, but the individual AI-generated images were not because they lacked human authorship.
- **Impact**: The case set a precedent that AI-generated works may need human modification to qualify for copyright protection.

💡 **Implication**: If AI fully creates an artwork, book, or music piece, it cannot be copyrighted—meaning it falls into the public domain.

2. AI and Copyright Infringement: High-Profile Lawsuits

2.1 Getty Images vs. Stability AI (2023)

📌 **Case Overview:**

- Getty Images sued Stability AI (creators of Stable Diffusion) for using millions of its copyrighted images to train an AI model without permission.
- Stability AI allegedly scraped Getty's watermarked photos and used them to teach its AI how to generate realistic images.

✊ **Legal Arguments:**

✓ Getty argued that AI models should obtain licensing before using copyrighted images.

✓ Stability AI claimed its training process falls under fair use, similar to how humans learn from existing art.

⚖️ **Case Impact:**

This case is one of the first major copyright battles against AI-generated content. If Stability AI loses, AI companies may be required to license datasets before training their models.

2.2 Artists vs. AI Art Generators (2023-2024)

📌 **Case Overview:**

- Multiple artists, including Sarah Andersen, Kelly McKernan, and Karla Ortiz, sued AI companies like Midjourney, DeviantArt, and Stability AI for using their artwork without consent.
- The lawsuit claims that AI models were trained on millions of copyrighted artworks scraped from the internet.

📝 Key Legal Issues:

✓ Do AI-generated images infringe on an artist's style and identity?

✓ Should AI companies compensate artists whose work was used for training?

⚖️ Case Impact:

If courts rule in favor of artists, AI companies may have to pay royalties or give credit to original creators.

2.3 Universal Music vs. AI-Generated Songs (2023)

📌 Case Overview:

- AI-generated songs mimicking real artists, such as "Heart on My Sleeve" (which imitated Drake and The Weeknd's voices), led Universal Music to demand takedowns from streaming platforms.
- AI-generated music raised concerns about vocal deepfakes and artist impersonation.

📝 Key Legal Issues:

✓ Can AI-generated music be considered derivative works of real artists?

✓ Should musicians receive royalties for AI-generated songs that copy their style?

⚖️ Case Impact:

Streaming services like Spotify and YouTube began removing AI-generated songs, and platforms may introduce new copyright policies for AI-created music.

3. The Debate Over AI Training Data

One of the biggest legal uncertainties in AI creativity is whether AI companies can use copyrighted material for training their models.

📌 **Key Cases:**

1️⃣ **The New York Times vs. OpenAI & Microsoft (2023)** – The NYT sued OpenAI for allegedly using its articles without consent to train ChatGPT.
2️⃣ **Comics Artists vs. AI (2024)** – A group of manga and comic artists sued AI firms for replicating their unique artistic styles.

⚖️ **Potential Outcomes:**

✓ AI companies might be forced to license training data, changing how AI models are developed.

✓ Some courts may rule that AI learning from human content falls under fair use, similar to how people learn by reading books or studying art.

4. AI and Patent Law: Can AI Be an Inventor?

4.1 The Thaler vs. Patent Offices Cases (2019-2022)

📌 **Case Overview:**

- Stephen Thaler, creator of the AI system DABUS, argued that his AI invented a unique product and should be legally recognized as the inventor.
- Patent offices in the U.S., U.K., and E.U. rejected the application, stating that only humans can be inventors.

⚖️ **Final Ruling:**

✓ Courts ruled that AI cannot hold patents because it is not a human entity.

✓ This case set a global precedent, making it impossible for AI-generated inventions to receive patents under current laws.

💡 **Future Debate:**

Some experts argue that patent laws need updating to recognize AI-assisted innovation.

5. Future Legal Challenges in AI Creativity

The legal system is still catching up to the rapid advancements in AI. Key issues that remain unresolved include:

✓ **Should AI-generated works require disclosure?** – Some countries may force creators to label AI-generated content for transparency.
✓ **How will AI impact employment in creative fields?** – Legal protections may emerge for human artists, writers, and musicians.
✓ **Who is responsible for AI-generated misinformation?** – Deepfakes and AI-created fake news raise ethical and legal concerns.

AI creativity is pushing the boundaries of intellectual property law, forcing courts to make historic decisions about ownership, copyright, and authorship.

Key Takeaways:

✓ AI-generated works cannot be copyrighted without significant human intervention.

✓ Lawsuits against AI companies are shaping how training data can be used.

✓ AI cannot hold patents, meaning inventions made by AI lack legal protection.

✓ The legal landscape remains uncertain, and new policies will be needed as AI technology advances.

The future of AI creativity depends on ongoing legal battles, and the outcomes will determine how AI-generated content is regulated worldwide.

18.5 Future of AI-Generated Content in Law

As artificial intelligence (AI) continues to evolve, the legal landscape surrounding AI-generated content is becoming increasingly complex. Courts, lawmakers, and technology companies are struggling to define ownership, copyright protection, liability, and ethical concerns in a world where AI is capable of producing text, images, music, videos, and even inventions.

This chapter explores the future of AI-generated content in law, analyzing upcoming regulations, legal frameworks, and potential challenges that will shape how AI is governed in creative and commercial industries.

1. The Push for AI-Specific Copyright Laws

1.1 Will AI-Generated Works Ever Be Copyrighted?

Currently, most copyright offices (such as the U.S. Copyright Office and the EU Intellectual Property Office) require a human author for a work to receive copyright protection. This means that AI-generated content without significant human involvement falls into the public domain.

💡 Future Possibilities:

✔ Some governments may introduce new legal frameworks recognizing AI-assisted works as partially copyrightable if humans contribute to their creation.

✔ AI creators may need to disclose which parts of a work were generated by AI versus human input.

✔ Tech companies could push for corporate ownership of AI-generated works, allowing businesses to own AI-generated content even if individuals cannot.

📌 Potential Legal Reform:

- The U.K. is considering AI-specific copyright rules, including whether AI-generated content should receive limited protection for a set period (e.g., 10 years instead of the usual 70).
- The European Union's AI Act aims to regulate AI-generated works and enforce transparency requirements for AI creators.

2. AI Training Data and Copyright: A Legal Minefield

2.1 Will AI Companies Need to License Training Data?

Many lawsuits (such as Getty Images vs. Stability AI and The New York Times vs. OpenAI) revolve around AI models scraping copyrighted content without permission.

💡 **Future Possibilities:**

✓ Courts may force AI developers to license copyrighted data before using it for training.

✓ A new market for AI-training datasets could emerge, where companies pay royalty fees to artists, writers, and musicians.

✓ AI-generated content may require watermarking or metadata tracking to prevent unauthorized use.

📌 **Potential Legal Reform:**

- The U.S. Congress is debating laws that would require AI firms to disclose their training data sources.
- AI companies could be held liable for copyright infringement if they train models on unauthorized data.

3. The Rise of AI-Generated Deepfakes and Fraud

3.1 How Will Laws Address AI-Generated Misinformation?

Deepfakes and AI-generated content are increasingly used for fraud, misinformation, and impersonation. Countries are rushing to regulate AI-generated media before it can be exploited in political campaigns, financial scams, and criminal activities.

💡 **Future Possibilities:**

✓ Governments may introduce strict penalties for AI-generated fake news and deepfake scams.

✓ Tech companies may be forced to detect and label AI-generated content in news, videos, and social media.

✓ Deepfake creators could face criminal charges if their content causes harm or deception.

- The EU Digital Services Act will require AI-generated deepfakes to be labeled, preventing misinformation.
- U.S. federal agencies are developing AI-detection standards to combat deepfake fraud.

4. AI and Intellectual Property: The Future of Ownership

4.1 Can AI Be Considered an Inventor?

Currently, AI-generated inventions cannot be patented because patent laws require a human inventor. However, as AI systems become more autonomous, legal scholars are debating whether AI should be recognized as a co-inventor.

💡 **Future Possibilities:**

✓ AI-assisted inventions may qualify for special patents where humans and AI share authorship.

✓ AI-generated patents could be owned by companies rather than individuals.

✓ Courts may introduce AI-specific intellectual property categories to cover unique cases of AI-assisted innovation.

📌 **Potential Legal Reform:**

- Some patent offices in China are exploring laws that recognize AI-assisted inventions under specific conditions.
- The World Intellectual Property Organization (WIPO) is considering AI-specific patent laws.

5. The Legal & Ethical Future of AI Creativity

As AI-generated content becomes more widespread, legal and ethical frameworks will need to adapt.

💡 **Key Questions for the Future:**

✓ Who is responsible for harmful AI-generated content?

✓ Should AI-generated works be labeled or regulated?

✓ How can legal systems balance AI innovation with intellectual property rights?

📌 **Predicted Legal Trends:**

- **Mandatory AI labeling** – AI-generated content may require certification or disclaimers to prevent confusion.
- **International AI copyright laws** – Countries may collaborate to create global AI regulations.
- **AI liability frameworks** – Laws may define who is responsible if AI-generated content causes financial loss, reputational harm, or misinformation.

The future of AI-generated content in law remains uncertain, but one thing is clear: as AI continues to revolutionize creativity, intellectual property laws must evolve to keep up.

◆ AI-generated works may soon receive partial copyright protection under new legal frameworks.

◆ AI training practices will likely face stronger regulations, requiring licensing agreements.

◆ AI-generated deepfakes and misinformation will lead to criminal penalties and detection measures.

◆ AI-assisted inventions may push patent offices to recognize AI as a co-inventor.

The next decade will define how AI-generated content is legally managed, and the choices made today will shape the future of AI innovation, creativity, and ownership.

19. GANs Beyond Creativity

While Generative Adversarial Networks (GANs) are widely known for their impact on art, music, and media, their applications extend far beyond creativity. In this chapter, we explore how GANs are being used in healthcare, finance, cybersecurity, data augmentation, and scientific research. You'll learn how GANs help in medical imaging and drug discovery, enhance satellite imagery and climate modeling, and improve anomaly detection in fraud prevention and network security. We'll also discuss emerging fields where GANs are pushing boundaries, such as AI-powered robotics, personalized synthetic data, and quantum computing. By the end of this chapter, you'll see how GANs are transforming industries beyond the creative arts, unlocking new possibilities for scientific innovation and real-world problem-solving. ⊕💰☐🚀

19.1 GANs in Medical Image Synthesis

Generative Adversarial Networks (GANs) have revolutionized artificial intelligence (AI) by enabling machines to generate highly realistic synthetic data. In the medical field, GANs are proving to be game-changers in medical imaging by creating high-quality, synthetic images that can aid in diagnosis, research, and training without the ethical and logistical constraints of real patient data.

Medical imaging—such as X-rays, MRIs, CT scans, and histopathological images—requires vast amounts of annotated data for training AI models. However, patient privacy regulations, data scarcity, and variations in imaging techniques create challenges for deep learning applications in healthcare. GANs help overcome these limitations by generating realistic, diverse, and privacy-preserving synthetic images, making them an invaluable tool for modern medical AI applications.

1. Why GANs Are Transforming Medical Image Synthesis

Traditional deep learning models struggle with medical imaging due to limited labeled data and high variability across datasets. GANs can:

✓ Generate high-quality synthetic medical images to augment training datasets.

✓ Improve disease detection and classification by creating diverse samples, including rare conditions.

✓ Enable privacy-preserving AI models by eliminating the need for real patient data.

✓ Enhance image resolution and contrast for better diagnosis.

1.1 Addressing Data Scarcity in Healthcare AI

Medical AI systems require extensive labeled datasets for training. However, due to patient privacy laws like HIPAA (USA) and GDPR (EU), obtaining and sharing medical images is highly restricted. GANs help by creating synthetic datasets that mimic real medical images without compromising patient confidentiality.

💡 **Example**: Researchers can use GANs to generate synthetic MRI scans of brain tumors, enabling AI training without real patient data.

2. Applications of GANs in Medical Imaging

2.1 Data Augmentation for Training AI Models

GANs generate synthetic images that help AI models learn to detect diseases more accurately by increasing dataset size and diversity.

✓ **Application**: Generating synthetic chest X-rays to improve AI models for pneumonia detection.

✓ **Example**: CT-GAN creates realistic CT scans to improve lung cancer detection models.

2.2 Enhancing Low-Quality Medical Images

Many medical images suffer from low resolution or poor contrast. GANs, especially Super-Resolution GANs (SRGANs), can enhance image clarity for better diagnosis.

✓ **Application**: Enhancing blurry MRI scans to reveal finer details for neurological disorders.

✓ **Example**: GAN-based image denoising improves ultrasound image quality.

2.3 Synthetic Medical Data for Training and Research

GANs generate realistic but synthetic medical images, allowing researchers to train AI models without real patient data.

✓ **Application**: Generating synthetic diabetic retinopathy images to train AI-based retinal disease detectors.

✓ **Example**: PathologyGAN generates histopathology images for cancer research.

2.4 Anomaly Detection and Disease Diagnosis

GANs learn the distribution of normal medical images, allowing them to detect anomalies by identifying differences.

✓ **Application**: Identifying abnormalities in brain scans to detect early signs of Alzheimer's.

✓ **Example**: f-AnoGAN detects liver lesions in MRI scans.

2.5 Cross-Modality Image Translation

GANs can convert one type of medical image into another, assisting in multi-modal medical imaging.

✓ **Application**: Transforming CT scans into MRI images to provide different perspectives for diagnosis.

✓ **Example**: CycleGAN translates CT images to MRI images to improve lesion detection.

3. Challenges and Limitations of GANs in Medical Imaging

3.1 Ethical and Legal Concerns

✓ **Regulatory uncertainty**: GAN-generated medical data is still not widely accepted by regulatory bodies like the FDA or EMA for clinical applications.

✓ **Medical liability**: If a GAN-generated image leads to misdiagnosis, who is responsible?

3.2 Data Bias and Generalization Issues

✓ GANs may overfit to the dataset they are trained on, leading to biases in medical AI models.

✓ **Limited diversity**: If trained on a single demographic, GANs may fail to represent a broader population.

3.3 Computational Complexity and Training Instability

✓ GANs require large-scale computing resources, making real-time applications challenging.

✓ Mode collapse: The generator may produce limited variations instead of diverse samples.

4. The Future of GANs in Medical Image Synthesis

4.1 AI-Powered Personalized Medicine

GANs could generate personalized synthetic medical images tailored to an individual's genetic or clinical profile, improving treatment plans.

4.2 Integration with Federated Learning

To protect patient data while still improving AI models, GANs can be combined with federated learning, where AI models are trained across multiple hospitals without sharing actual patient data.

4.3 Real-Time AI-Assisted Diagnosis

Future GAN-powered tools could generate instant, AI-enhanced medical images, helping radiologists and doctors make faster, more accurate diagnoses.

GANs are reshaping medical imaging by providing synthetic data for AI training, enhancing image quality, and aiding in anomaly detection. Despite ethical and technical challenges, the future of GAN-powered medical imaging is promising, with applications in data augmentation, privacy-preserving AI, and advanced disease detection.

With further research and regulatory approval, GANs will play a crucial role in the next generation of AI-driven healthcare solutions, making diagnosis more accessible, accurate, and efficient. 🚀

19.2 AI for Drug Discovery and Healthcare

Artificial Intelligence (AI) is transforming the healthcare industry, with one of its most promising applications being drug discovery. Traditional drug development is a time-consuming, costly, and resource-intensive process, often taking 10–15 years and costing billions of dollars to bring a single drug to market. AI, particularly deep learning models, has the potential to accelerate this process, reduce costs, and improve the success rate of new drugs.

Generative AI, including Generative Adversarial Networks (GANs) and other deep learning models, can analyze massive biomedical datasets, predict drug interactions, generate novel drug molecules, and optimize clinical trials. In this chapter, we explore how AI is reshaping drug discovery and revolutionizing healthcare.

1. The Challenges in Traditional Drug Discovery

Developing a new drug involves several critical stages:

✓ **Target Identification**: Finding a biological target (e.g., a protein or gene) linked to a disease.

✓ **Drug Candidate Discovery**: Screening thousands of compounds to find one that interacts effectively with the target.

✓ **Preclinical Testing**: Lab and animal testing to assess safety and efficacy.

✓ **Clinical Trials**: Human trials conducted in three phases before regulatory approval.

✓ **Regulatory Approval**: Gaining approval from agencies like the FDA or EMA for market release.

Each stage is prone to high failure rates, with only about 10% of drugs making it to market after clinical trials. AI helps overcome these challenges by making drug discovery faster, more accurate, and cost-effective.

2. How AI is Revolutionizing Drug Discovery

AI-powered drug discovery focuses on data-driven predictions, reducing reliance on traditional trial-and-error methods. AI can:

✓ Identify new drug targets by analyzing genetic and biochemical data.

✓ Predict drug interactions to avoid harmful side effects.

✓ Generate novel drug candidates using AI-based molecule synthesis.

✓ Optimize clinical trial design by selecting the right patient groups.

2.1 AI for Target Identification

AI models analyze genomic, proteomic, and clinical data to detect potential drug targets associated with diseases.

✓ **Example**: DeepMind's AlphaFold predicts protein structures with high accuracy, helping scientists find new drug targets for diseases like Alzheimer's and cancer.

2.2 Generating Novel Drug Molecules with AI

GANs and other generative models help design new drug molecules with desired properties by simulating chemical structures.

✓ **Example**: INSILICO MEDICINE used AI to generate a drug candidate for fibrosis in just 46 days, significantly faster than traditional methods.
✓ **Example**: Atomwise uses deep learning to predict how different molecules interact, helping design new drugs for conditions like Ebola and COVID-19.

2.3 AI-Driven Drug Repurposing

Instead of developing new drugs, AI can identify existing FDA-approved drugs that might work for new diseases, significantly reducing development time.

✓ **Example**: AI models helped researchers identify Remdesivir as a potential treatment for COVID-19 by analyzing its antiviral properties.
✓ **Example**: BenevolentAI identified Baricitinib, an arthritis drug, as a potential treatment for COVID-19.

2.4 Predicting Drug Interactions and Side Effects

AI models analyze vast amounts of clinical and pharmacological data to predict potential adverse drug reactions (ADRs) before human trials.

✓ **Example**: IBM Watson's AI identifies harmful drug interactions by processing biomedical literature.

✓ **Example**: AI-powered tools help researchers design safer drug combinations to reduce side effects.

2.5 AI in Personalized Medicine

AI enables personalized drug treatments by analyzing a patient's genetic profile to determine the most effective drug and dosage.

✓ **Example**: AI-driven pharmacogenomics helps match cancer patients with targeted therapies based on their DNA.

✓ **Example**: Tempus AI uses deep learning to recommend personalized cancer treatments based on genomic data.

3. AI in Healthcare Beyond Drug Discovery

AI is transforming multiple areas of healthcare, including disease diagnosis, medical imaging, robotic surgery, and patient management.

3.1 AI-Powered Disease Diagnosis

AI models analyze medical scans and patient data to detect diseases faster and more accurately than humans.

✓ **Example**: Google's DeepMind AI detects eye diseases from retinal scans with 94% accuracy.

✓ **Example**: AI models diagnose breast cancer in mammograms better than radiologists in some studies.

3.2 AI in Medical Imaging and Radiology

AI improves the accuracy of X-rays, MRIs, and CT scans, helping radiologists detect diseases earlier.

✓ **Example**: AI-powered tools detect lung cancer nodules in CT scans with high precision.

✓ **Example**: AI assists in diagnosing Alzheimer's disease by analyzing brain scans.

3.3 AI-Powered Virtual Health Assistants

Chatbots and AI assistants provide 24/7 patient support, symptom checking, and medical advice.

✓ **Example**: Babylon Health uses AI to provide remote medical consultations.

✓ **Example**: Ada Health offers AI-based symptom checking and health guidance.

3.4 AI in Robotic Surgery

AI-assisted robots improve surgical precision, reduce complications, and enable minimally invasive procedures.

✓ **Example**: Da Vinci Surgical System uses AI to assist in complex surgeries.

✓ **Example**: AI-driven robotic arms help surgeons perform delicate procedures with microscopic precision.

3.5 AI in Pandemic Response and Healthcare Crisis Management

AI helps track and predict disease outbreaks by analyzing real-time data from global health organizations.

✓ **Example**: AI-powered models predicted COVID-19 spread trends and helped governments plan responses.

✓ **Example**: AI-assisted drug discovery accelerated the development of COVID-19 vaccines.

4. Challenges and Ethical Considerations in AI-Powered Drug Discovery

Despite its potential, AI in drug discovery and healthcare faces several challenges:

4.1 Data Privacy and Security Risks

✓ Medical AI relies on patient data, raising concerns about privacy and data protection (e.g., GDPR, HIPAA compliance).

4.2 AI Bias and Fairness Issues

✓ AI models trained on biased datasets may produce inaccurate results, leading to healthcare disparities.

✓ Solution: Ensuring diverse and representative datasets for AI training.

4.3 Regulatory and Approval Challenges

✓ AI-generated drug candidates must pass strict regulatory requirements before approval.

✓ Solution: Collaborating with regulatory agencies like FDA, EMA, and WHO for AI-driven drug development guidelines.

5. The Future of AI in Drug Discovery and Healthcare

✓ **AI-Powered Labs**: Fully automated labs using AI to design, test, and optimize new drugs with minimal human intervention.

✓ **AI-Enhanced Telemedicine**: AI-driven virtual doctors providing real-time diagnosis and treatment recommendations.

✓ **Quantum AI for Drug Discovery**: Combining AI with quantum computing to simulate complex molecular interactions for faster drug design.

✓ **AI and CRISPR Gene Editing**: AI will assist in genome sequencing and precision medicine, leading to breakthroughs in genetic disorders.

AI is revolutionizing drug discovery and healthcare, offering faster, cheaper, and more accurate solutions than traditional methods. From generating new drugs and predicting side effects to diagnosing diseases and personalizing treatments, AI is at the forefront of modern medicine.

While challenges remain, continued advancements in AI, big data, and computational biology will pave the way for a new era of AI-driven healthcare, saving millions of lives worldwide. 🚀

19.3 GANs in Scientific Research and Simulations

Generative Adversarial Networks (GANs) have rapidly become a transformative force in scientific research and simulations. These AI models can generate realistic data, simulate complex systems, and accelerate research across physics, chemistry, biology, and even astronomy. Traditionally, scientific discoveries relied on time-consuming experiments and computational models requiring extensive resources. GANs offer a paradigm shift by learning from existing data and generating synthetic yet highly realistic representations, reducing computation time and enabling breakthroughs in fields previously constrained by technological limitations.

This chapter explores how GANs are revolutionizing scientific research, simulations, and computational modeling, allowing scientists to explore new frontiers with greater accuracy and efficiency.

1. The Role of GANs in Scientific Simulations

Simulations are crucial in scientific research, as they allow scientists to model complex systems and predict outcomes without conducting expensive or impractical experiments. GANs can:

✓ Generate high-fidelity simulations for physics, chemistry, and biology.

✓ Reduce computational costs by approximating complex models.

✓ Fill gaps in datasets by generating synthetic but realistic data.

✓ Optimize experiments by predicting outcomes before testing.

GANs do not replace traditional simulations but enhance and accelerate the process, enabling scientists to test hypotheses more efficiently.

2. Applications of GANs in Scientific Research

GANs are being used in various fields of scientific research, including physics, astronomy, climate science, materials science, and biology.

2.1 GANs in Physics and Quantum Mechanics

GANs can simulate particle interactions, quantum states, and physical phenomena, allowing physicists to analyze and visualize complex quantum systems.

✓ **Example**: Physicists use GANs to simulate high-energy particle collisions in experiments like those at CERN's Large Hadron Collider (LHC). Traditional simulations take weeks, but GANs can generate results in seconds.

✓ **Example**: GANs help model fluid dynamics with high precision, improving engineering and aerodynamics studies.

2.2 GANs in Astronomy and Space Science

Astronomers deal with massive datasets collected from telescopes, satellites, and space missions. GANs can:

✓ Enhance astronomical images by removing noise and increasing resolution.

✓ Simulate cosmic structures to study galaxy formation and dark matter.

✓ Predict exoplanet characteristics based on limited observational data.

✓ **Example**: Researchers use GANs to generate realistic simulations of the early universe, improving our understanding of cosmic evolution.

✓ **Example**: GANs assist in classifying celestial objects from telescope images, distinguishing galaxies, quasars, and stars more efficiently than traditional methods.

2.3 GANs in Climate Science and Environmental Research

Climate models require huge computational resources to simulate weather patterns, global warming effects, and natural disasters. GANs can:

✓ Predict climate changes by generating synthetic weather data for future trends.

✓ Simulate extreme weather events, such as hurricanes or droughts, to improve disaster preparedness.

✓ Enhance satellite imagery to monitor environmental changes, such as deforestation and glacier melting.

✓ **Example**: GANs help predict hurricane paths and intensities, allowing better early warning systems.

✓ **Example**: Climate scientists use GANs to downscale coarse-resolution climate models, improving the accuracy of regional climate predictions.

2.4 GANs in Materials Science and Chemistry

GANs are accelerating discoveries in material design, drug synthesis, and molecular simulations by generating new materials with desired properties.

✓ Generate novel molecular structures with optimized chemical properties.

✓ Predict chemical reactions to accelerate new drug discoveries.

✓ Design new nanomaterials for applications in electronics, medicine, and energy storage.

✓ **Example**: IBM researchers use GANs to generate new polymers and materials with specific thermal, electrical, and mechanical properties.

✓ **Example**: Chemists use GANs to predict crystal structures, enabling the discovery of stronger and more efficient materials for batteries and superconductors.

2.5 GANs in Biomedical Research and Genetics

GANs are transforming biology and medicine by generating synthetic medical images, predicting genetic variations, and modeling disease progression.

✓ **Example**: GANs generate realistic MRI and CT scans for training AI-powered diagnostics.

✓ **Example**: GANs help in gene sequence prediction, aiding in personalized medicine and genetic engineering.

3. How GANs Improve Computational Efficiency

One of the key advantages of using GANs in scientific research is the significant reduction in computational costs. Traditional simulations often require:

✓ Supercomputers to process data-intensive calculations.

✓ Long processing times, sometimes weeks or months.

✓ Huge storage capacity for high-resolution simulations.

GANs act as highly efficient approximators that can generate realistic simulations in seconds instead of days, allowing researchers to:

✓ Run more simulations in less time.

✓ Explore a wider range of scenarios before conducting physical experiments.

✓ Optimize hardware usage, reducing energy costs.

✓ **Example**: Researchers at MIT and NVIDIA used GANs to generate high-resolution fluid dynamics simulations, reducing computation time by 90% while maintaining accuracy.

4. Challenges and Limitations of GANs in Scientific Research

Despite their benefits, GANs have some limitations when applied to scientific research and simulations.

4.1 Accuracy and Reliability Issues

✓ GAN-generated data may contain artifacts or inaccuracies, making results less reliable than traditional methods.

✓ **Solution**: Hybrid approaches combining GANs with physics-based models can improve accuracy.

4.2 Interpretability and Transparency

✓ GANs operate as black-box models, meaning scientists cannot always explain how they generate specific results.

✓ **Solution**: Using explainable AI (XAI) techniques to interpret GAN outputs.

4.3 Data Bias and Ethical Concerns

✓ GANs rely on training data, meaning biased or incomplete datasets can lead to misleading results.

✓ **Solution**: Curating high-quality, unbiased datasets before training GAN models.

5. The Future of GANs in Scientific Research

The future of GANs in scientific research is promising, with advancements leading to:

✓ AI-powered autonomous labs, where GANs design and run simulations without human intervention.

✓ Integration of GANs with quantum computing, enabling even more powerful scientific simulations.

✓ AI-assisted space exploration, using GANs to process data from telescopes and space missions.

✓ Personalized healthcare breakthroughs, with GANs tailoring treatments based on simulated patient data.

GANs are revolutionizing scientific research and simulations, enabling faster, more efficient, and cost-effective discoveries. From simulating cosmic evolution and climate change to designing new materials and predicting drug interactions, GANs are proving to be an indispensable tool for researchers across multiple disciplines.

While challenges remain in ensuring accuracy and transparency, hybrid AI approaches combining GANs with physics-based models are paving the way for the next era of AI-driven scientific breakthroughs. The future holds immense potential, with GANs continuing to push the boundaries of what is possible in scientific exploration. 🚀

19.4 Applications in Astronomy and Climate Science

Generative Adversarial Networks (GANs) have emerged as powerful tools in astronomy and climate science, revolutionizing how researchers analyze vast datasets, enhance images, and make predictions. Traditional methods in these fields rely on complex models, extensive computations, and manual data processing. GANs accelerate research by generating synthetic data, improving image quality, and enabling more accurate simulations of celestial and climatic phenomena.

This chapter explores how GANs are transforming astronomy and climate science, offering innovative solutions to some of the most pressing challenges in these fields.

1. GANs in Astronomy

Astronomers collect vast amounts of data from telescopes, satellites, and space probes. Analyzing this data is often challenging due to factors like low resolution, noise, missing information, and limited observational time. GANs address these issues by:

✔ Enhancing telescope images by denoising and improving resolution.

✔ Simulating cosmic structures to study galaxies, exoplanets, and dark matter.

✔ Predicting missing astronomical data from incomplete observations.

✔ Classifying celestial objects more efficiently using AI-based recognition.

2. Enhancing Astronomical Images with GANs

One of the biggest challenges in astronomy is capturing clear, high-resolution images of distant celestial objects. Many images suffer from:

✔ Atmospheric distortion (for ground-based telescopes).

✔ Low-light conditions (for deep-space observations).

✔ Instrument limitations and noise interference.

GANs can remove noise, sharpen images, and even reconstruct missing details, providing clearer insights into the universe.

2.1 Super-Resolution for Space Images

GANs, such as Super-Resolution GANs (SRGANs), enhance the quality of low-resolution telescope images.

✓ **Example**: Researchers at NASA use GANs to improve images from the Hubble Space Telescope and James Webb Space Telescope (JWST), revealing more details about distant galaxies.

✓ **Example**: GANs help refine exoplanet surface imaging, allowing astronomers to analyze atmospheric compositions with greater accuracy.

2.2 Restoring and Enhancing Historical Astronomical Data

Historical astronomical images taken decades ago often lack the clarity of modern technology. GANs can restore and colorize old images, providing new insights into past observations.

✓ **Example**: AI-enhanced images of the Moon and Mars from past missions are helping scientists reassess old data with modern tools.

3. GANs in Exoplanet Discovery and Classification

Finding Earth-like exoplanets is one of astronomy's most exciting frontiers. However, most exoplanet images and spectra are incomplete or noisy. GANs help by:

✓ Generating realistic simulations of exoplanet atmospheres.

✓ Filling in missing data to improve exoplanet classification.

✓ Detecting faint planetary signals in telescope observations.

✓ **Example**: GANs assist in classifying exoplanet light curves, improving the accuracy of planet detection from telescopes like Kepler and TESS.

4. GANs for Simulating the Universe

Simulating the evolution of the universe requires massive computational resources. GANs can:

✓ Generate large-scale simulations of galaxies and dark matter.

✓ Predict gravitational lensing effects for astrophysics research.

✓ Model star formation and supernova explosions to study cosmic evolution.

✓ **Example**: Researchers at MIT developed cosmology GANs, which simulate realistic galaxy distributions, saving computation time in astrophysics research.

5. GANs in Climate Science

Climate change research depends on large-scale simulations, satellite imagery, and historical climate models. GANs enhance climate science by:

✓ Predicting climate patterns and extreme weather events.

✓ Enhancing satellite images for environmental monitoring.

✓ Simulating future climate scenarios.

6. Climate Prediction and Extreme Weather Forecasting

6.1 GANs for Hurricane and Storm Prediction

Predicting hurricanes, typhoons, and tornadoes requires analyzing satellite and radar data. GANs help by:

✓ Improving short-term and long-term storm forecasts.

✓ Generating synthetic storm paths to train weather models.

✓ Enhancing resolution in satellite images for better storm tracking.

✓ **Example**: GANs were used to simulate hurricane intensities based on historical data, improving prediction accuracy.

6.2 Downscaling Climate Models with GANs

Most global climate models (GCMs) operate at low resolution due to computational limitations. GANs enhance these models by downscaling coarse climate data to high-resolution predictions, leading to more precise regional climate forecasts.

✓ **Example**: GANs help predict localized climate changes, such as rising sea levels in coastal cities and desertification trends.

7. Environmental Monitoring with GANs

GANs assist in environmental science and conservation efforts by processing and analyzing satellite images.

7.1 Tracking Deforestation and Habitat Loss

✓ **Example**: GANs analyze Amazon rainforest satellite images to detect illegal deforestation.

✓ **Example**: AI-powered GANs help monitor wildlife populations in remote areas.

7.2 Monitoring Glacier Melting and Ocean Changes

✓ **Example**: Scientists use GANs to track glacial retreat in Antarctica by enhancing satellite imagery.

✓ **Example**: GANs predict coral reef bleaching events by analyzing ocean temperature data.

8. Challenges and Limitations of GANs in Astronomy and Climate Science

Despite their transformative impact, GANs have challenges:

8.1 Accuracy and Data Bias

✓ GANs generate synthetic data, which may not always reflect real-world observations.

✓ **Solution**: Hybrid AI models combining GANs with traditional simulations.

8.2 Ethical and Reliability Concerns

✓ GAN-generated climate predictions must be validated against real-world data to avoid misleading results.

✓ **Solution**: Human-AI collaboration in research and decision-making.

9. The Future of GANs in Astronomy and Climate Science

The future of GANs in astronomy and climate science is promising, with advancements leading to:

✓ AI-powered space telescopes capable of real-time image enhancement.

✓ Autonomous climate models that continuously learn from new data.

✓ Integration of GANs with quantum computing for high-speed simulations.

✓ Better disaster preparedness, using GAN-generated models to predict extreme weather.

GANs are revolutionizing astronomy and climate science, enabling researchers to generate, enhance, and analyze complex data with unprecedented accuracy. From improving telescope imagery and discovering exoplanets to predicting extreme weather and monitoring climate change, GANs provide scientists with powerful tools to push the boundaries of human knowledge.

As AI technology advances, GANs will continue to drive breakthroughs in space exploration, climate research, and environmental conservation, shaping our understanding of the universe and our planet. □✦

19.5 The Role of GANs in Robotics and Automation

Generative Adversarial Networks (GANs) have transformed various fields of artificial intelligence, and their impact on robotics and automation is particularly significant. Robotics has traditionally relied on rule-based programming, reinforcement learning, and supervised learning to develop intelligent behaviors. However, GANs introduce a new paradigm by enabling robots to learn from synthetic data, enhance sensor inputs, and generate realistic simulations for training.

This chapter explores how GANs are revolutionizing robotics and automation, from simulating realistic environments and improving robotic vision to enhancing decision-making and motion planning.

1. How GANs Enhance Robotics

Robots rely on visual perception, sensor data, and decision-making algorithms to interact with their environments. GANs improve these capabilities by:

✓ Generating high-quality synthetic training data for robots.

✓ Improving robotic vision through image enhancement and noise reduction.

✓ Enabling robots to simulate and predict real-world scenarios.

✓ Optimizing robotic control policies without real-world risks.

By leveraging these advantages, GANs help develop autonomous robots that adapt better to real-world challenges.

2. GANs for Robotic Perception and Vision

2.1 Enhancing Computer Vision in Robots

Most robots rely on computer vision to navigate and interact with their environment. However, real-world images often suffer from poor lighting, motion blur, and occlusions. GANs enhance robotic vision by:

✓ Denoising images for clearer recognition of objects.

✓ Super-resolving low-quality images captured by robotic cameras.

✓ Improving object detection and segmentation in cluttered environments.

✓ **Example**: Autonomous drones use GANs to enhance low-light images, allowing better navigation at night or in foggy conditions.

2.2 Synthetic Data Generation for Training Robots

One major challenge in robotics is obtaining high-quality training data. GANs generate realistic synthetic datasets, reducing the need for expensive real-world data collection.

✓ **Example**: Self-driving cars use GAN-generated synthetic street scenes to train perception models without requiring millions of real-world miles.

3. GANs for Robotic Simulation and Training

3.1 Creating Realistic Virtual Environments

GANs enable robots to learn in virtual environments before deployment in the real world. Instead of expensive and time-consuming physical testing, robots train in AI-generated synthetic worlds.

✓ **Example**: AI-powered robots use simulated factory floors to learn industrial automation tasks before real-world deployment.

✓ **Example**: GANs create photo-realistic 3D indoor environments for training household robots in tasks like cleaning and organizing.

3.2 Domain Adaptation – Bridging the Gap Between Simulation and Reality

Training robots in simulation is useful, but simulations often lack real-world variability (e.g., lighting changes, unexpected obstacles). GANs improve domain adaptation, making robots trained in virtual environments perform better in the real world.

✓ **Example**: Autonomous cars trained in simulated cities use GANs to adapt to real-world road conditions, improving their ability to navigate urban environments.

4. GANs for Motion Planning and Control

4.1 Predicting Movements and Enhancing Dexterity

GANs help robots predict and generate realistic movement patterns, improving their dexterity and control.

✓ **Example**: Humanoid robots use GANs to generate human-like walking patterns, making their movement more natural.

✓ **Example**: Industrial robotic arms use GAN-generated motion trajectories for better precision in assembling delicate components.

4.2 Reinforcement Learning with GAN-Generated Data

Reinforcement learning (RL) is widely used in robotics, but training RL agents requires massive amounts of interaction data. GANs generate synthetic interaction experiences, accelerating RL training.

✓ **Example**: Robots use GAN-generated reinforcement learning data to practice grasping objects in simulation before real-world trials.

5. GANs in Industrial Automation

Industrial robots are widely used in manufacturing, logistics, and quality control. GANs improve industrial automation by:

✓ Detecting product defects in manufacturing through AI-enhanced vision.

✓ Predicting equipment failures before they happen (predictive maintenance).

✓ Optimizing warehouse layouts for faster and more efficient automation.

✓ **Example**: GANs help detect faulty components in electronic manufacturing, reducing defects and increasing production efficiency.

6. Challenges and Future of GANs in Robotics

6.1 Data Bias and Ethical Concerns

✓ GANs trained on biased datasets can produce unfair or unsafe outcomes in robotics.

✓ Solution: Use diverse and well-curated training data.

6.2 Computational Challenges

✓ Training GANs for real-time robotic applications requires high computational power.

✓ Solution: Using edge AI and cloud computing to optimize performance.

GANs are transforming robotics and automation by enhancing perception, improving simulation training, and optimizing robotic motion. From self-driving cars and industrial robots to autonomous drones and robotic assistants, GANs enable machines to adapt and learn from synthetic data, making them smarter and more efficient.

As AI continues to evolve, GAN-powered robots will become even more autonomous, capable, and adaptable, shaping the future of automation across industries. 🚀

20. The Future of Synthetic Intelligence

As Generative Adversarial Networks (GANs) and AI creativity continue to evolve, they are shaping the foundation of synthetic intelligence—AI systems capable of generating, adapting, and innovating like never before. In this final chapter, we explore the future of GANs, deep learning, and AI-generated content, from advancements in self-improving AI models to the emergence of fully autonomous creative agents. We'll discuss how synthetic intelligence will impact industries like entertainment, design, healthcare, and the metaverse, as well as the challenges of AI ethics, regulation, and human-AI collaboration. With rapid progress in AI research, the line between human and machine creativity is becoming increasingly blurred. By the end of this chapter, you'll gain insights into what the future holds for GANs, AI-driven innovation, and the next generation of intelligent systems. □🚀□

20.1 Next-Generation GANs: What's Coming Next?

Generative Adversarial Networks (GANs) have made remarkable progress since their introduction in 2014, transforming fields like art, gaming, medical imaging, and autonomous systems. However, as AI research advances, next-generation GANs are emerging with better efficiency, stability, and creative potential.

In this chapter, we explore the future of GAN technology, discussing upcoming improvements in training methods, architectural innovations, and potential real-world applications that will redefine synthetic intelligence.

1. Solving Current GAN Limitations

1.1 Addressing Mode Collapse

Mode collapse is one of the most common GAN training issues, where the generator produces limited variations of output instead of diverse, high-quality samples.

✓ Future GANs will integrate new loss functions, such as contrastive divergence and energy-based learning, to ensure greater output diversity.

1.2 Enhancing Training Stability

GAN training often suffers from instability and sensitivity to hyperparameters. Future models will:

✓ Use self-supervised learning to reduce dependency on labeled datasets.

✓ Leverage adaptive optimizers to dynamically adjust learning rates.

1.3 Making GANs More Efficient

Current GANs require massive computational power, limiting their accessibility. Next-generation GANs will focus on:

✓ Lighter architectures that run efficiently on edge devices.

✓ Quantization techniques that reduce memory usage without sacrificing quality.

2. Emerging Architectures in Next-Gen GANs

2.1 Transformer-Based GANs

Transformers have revolutionized natural language processing (NLP), and researchers are now exploring their use in GANs. Transformer GANs can:

✓ Improve long-range dependencies in image synthesis.

✓ Enhance video and text-to-image generation by understanding complex patterns.

2.2 Diffusion GANs – A New Alternative?

Diffusion models (e.g., DALL·E 2, Imagen) have recently outperformed GANs in some areas. Next-generation GANs may integrate diffusion-based approaches to:

✓ Improve image coherence and texture quality.

✓ Generate realistic, high-resolution visuals without artifacts.

2.3 Self-Supervised GANs

Self-supervised learning allows AI to train on unlabeled data, reducing the need for massive labeled datasets. Future GANs will learn from raw data, improving efficiency in:

✓ Medical imaging (MRI synthesis without labeled scans).

✓ Realistic 3D object modeling (training GANs on unlabeled 3D scans).

3. Expanding the Creative Capabilities of GANs

3.1 AI-Generated 3D Content for Virtual Worlds

With the rise of the metaverse and AR/VR applications, GANs will:

✓ Automate 3D model creation for virtual worlds.

✓ Generate realistic human avatars with fluid animations.

✓ Improve AI-powered world-building tools for game designers.

3.2 Advancements in Text-to-Image and Video Synthesis

Next-gen GANs will refine text-to-image models like DALL·E and MidJourney by:

✓ Producing higher-resolution, more photorealistic images.

✓ Supporting real-time AI video generation from text descriptions.

4. Ethical Considerations for Future GANs

As GANs evolve, so do ethical concerns. Future developments must address:

✓ Deepfake detection technologies to combat misinformation.

✓ Fairness in AI-generated content to reduce biases.

✓ Watermarking AI-generated content to ensure transparency.

The future of GANs is incredibly promising. With new architectures, improved training techniques, and greater creative potential, next-generation GANs will push AI to new heights of realism and intelligence. As synthetic intelligence advances, GANs will play a crucial role in art, gaming, robotics, medicine, and beyond, shaping the future of digital creativity. 🚀

20.2 The Merging of GANs with Reinforcement Learning

Generative Adversarial Networks (GANs) and Reinforcement Learning (RL) are two of the most influential advancements in artificial intelligence. While GANs specialize in generating realistic data through adversarial training, RL enables AI agents to make decisions by interacting with environments and learning from rewards. The combination of GANs and RL is paving the way for groundbreaking developments in robotics, game AI, self-driving cars, and adaptive AI systems.

In this chapter, we explore how GANs enhance RL and vice versa, leading to AI systems that can generate realistic environments, simulate human-like behaviors, and adapt to dynamic real-world challenges.

1. Why Combine GANs and Reinforcement Learning?

GANs and RL have distinct yet complementary strengths:

✓ GANs generate realistic data that RL agents can use for training.

✓ RL optimizes GANs by improving the generator's ability to produce high-quality, goal-driven outputs.

✓ Together, they enable more intelligent, adaptable AI systems that can both create and make decisions.

By merging GANs with RL, AI can simulate, adapt, and learn more efficiently, making it ideal for autonomous systems, robotics, and dynamic game AI.

2. How GANs Improve Reinforcement Learning

2.1 Generating Synthetic Training Environments

Training RL agents requires massive amounts of interaction data. GANs help by generating synthetic environments, allowing RL agents to learn in simulated worlds before real-world deployment.

✔ **Example**: Self-driving cars use GAN-generated virtual roads for training, reducing reliance on expensive real-world data collection.

✔ **Example**: Robots train in GAN-simulated environments to perfect their movements before real-world testing.

2.2 Enhancing State Representation

RL agents rely on state representations (the way they perceive the world) to make decisions. GANs improve state representation by:

✔ Denoising and enhancing sensor data in robotics.

✔ Filling in missing environmental details, helping agents navigate more effectively.

✔ **Example**: GANs enhance low-resolution drone footage, allowing RL-based drones to navigate better in complex environments.

3. How Reinforcement Learning Improves GANs

3.1 Adaptive GAN Training with RL

Traditional GANs often suffer from mode collapse, where the generator produces limited variations of data. RL optimizes GANs by:

✔ Introducing reward-based training, encouraging the generator to explore diverse outputs.

✔ Helping GANs generate goal-driven content instead of random outputs.

✔ **Example**: RL-based GANs generate game levels that adapt to a player's skill level, making AI-driven game design more dynamic.

3.2 Reinforcement Learning for GAN Discriminator Optimization

The discriminator in a GAN is responsible for distinguishing real from fake data. RL can:

✔ Improve discriminator training by dynamically adjusting difficulty levels.

✔ Help GANs evolve over time, continuously improving output quality.

✔ **Example**: RL-based GAN discriminators detect deepfakes with higher accuracy by adapting to new types of generated images.

4. Applications of GAN + RL in Real-World AI Systems

4.1 Game AI and Procedural Content Generation

GANs + RL are transforming gaming by automating content creation and making AI more adaptive to player behavior.

✔ **Example**: OpenAI's Neural MMO uses GAN-generated environments where RL-trained AI agents evolve strategies over time.

✔ **Example**: AI-powered NPCs adapt to player actions using GANs for character animation and RL for behavior learning.

4.2 Autonomous Vehicles and Robotics

Self-driving cars and robots benefit from GAN-enhanced simulations and RL-based decision-making.

✔ **Example**: Tesla's Autopilot trains using GAN-generated traffic scenarios to improve safety.

✔ **Example**: AI-powered robotic arms use RL to refine movements and GANs to generate training scenarios.

4.3 AI-Powered Virtual Assistants

Future AI assistants will be more conversational and personalized by merging GANs and RL.

✔ **Example**: GANs generate human-like speech and facial expressions, while RL enables assistants to learn from user interactions for improved responses.

5. Challenges and Future Directions

✓ **Computational Complexity** – Training GANs and RL models together requires significant computational resources.

✓ **Ethical Concerns** – AI-generated content must be monitored for bias and ethical issues.

✓ **Generalization Issues** – RL agents trained on GAN-generated data may not always generalize well to the real world.

Future research will focus on efficient training methods, ethical safeguards, and more robust AI models that combine the best of GANs and RL.

The fusion of GANs and Reinforcement Learning is creating AI that can simulate, create, and adapt in ways never before possible. From self-driving cars and adaptive game AI to robotics and virtual assistants, this combination is shaping the next generation of synthetic intelligence. As AI continues to evolve, GAN + RL systems will become smarter, more creative, and increasingly autonomous, pushing the boundaries of what machines can achieve. 🚀

20.3 AI-Human Collaboration in Art and Science

The intersection of art, science, and artificial intelligence is unlocking new possibilities in human creativity and innovation. While AI-generated content is becoming more sophisticated, true breakthroughs come from collaboration between AI and human intelligence rather than AI replacing human creativity. Artists, scientists, and researchers are now leveraging AI as a powerful tool to augment and expand their capabilities.

In this chapter, we explore how Generative Adversarial Networks (GANs) and other AI models are being used to push the boundaries of artistic expression, scientific discovery, and technological advancements. From AI-assisted paintings to drug discovery, the collaboration between humans and AI is reshaping creative and analytical fields alike.

1. AI as a Creative Partner in Art

While traditional artists have relied on their intuition, skills, and imagination, AI now provides new tools that enhance and expand creative possibilities. Instead of replacing artists, AI acts as a co-creator, offering inspiration, automating tedious tasks, and generating novel ideas.

1.1 AI-Generated Art and Human Curation

✓ **AI-generated paintings** – Artists use GANs like StyleGAN and DeepDream to generate digital art, which they then refine and curate.

✓ **Example**: The artwork Edmond de Belamy, created by an AI trained with GANs, was sold at Christie's for $432,500, demonstrating how AI can influence the fine art market.

✓ **Collaboration** – While AI generates the artwork, human artists refine compositions, add emotions, and decide what makes the final cut.

1.2 Music Composition with AI

✓ **AI-assisted music creation** – GANs like MuseGAN and OpenAI's Jukebox generate melodies, harmonies, and even entire songs.

✓ **Example**: Artists like Taryn Southern have co-produced albums with AI, using it to compose melodies while adding human vocals and mixing.

✓ **Human role** – Musicians fine-tune AI compositions, making creative choices that AI alone cannot.

1.3 AI in Film, Animation, and Visual Effects

✓ **GANs for film restoration** – AI enhances old film footage, increasing resolution and restoring missing details.

✓ **AI-generated special effects** – Studios use GANs for realistic CGI, reducing manual work in movie production.

✓ **Example**: Deepfake technology is being used in cinema to digitally recreate actors, but human oversight ensures ethical and creative integrity.

2. AI in Scientific Discovery and Innovation

AI is accelerating scientific research by analyzing massive datasets, automating experiments, and even proposing new hypotheses. GANs are particularly useful for simulating and generating scientific data in fields such as medicine, physics, and materials science.

2.1 AI in Medicine and Drug Discovery

✓ **GANs for medical imaging** – AI enhances MRI scans, X-rays, and CT scans, improving early disease detection.

✓ **AI-assisted drug discovery** – Generative models predict molecular structures, speeding up drug development.

✓ **Example**: AI helped develop COVID-19 treatments by analyzing protein structures faster than human scientists alone could.

2.2 AI in Climate Science and Environmental Research

✓ **GANs for climate modeling** – AI generates high-resolution climate simulations, helping predict extreme weather events.

✓ **Example**: AI-assisted satellite image analysis detects deforestation patterns and ocean pollution for conservation efforts.

2.3 AI in Space Exploration

✓ GANs enhance astronomical images, revealing distant galaxies and cosmic structures.

✓ AI processes massive amounts of space data, identifying exoplanets and black holes.

✓ **Example**: NASA uses AI to sift through data from the Kepler telescope, identifying thousands of potential new planets.

3. Ethical and Philosophical Considerations of AI-Human Collaboration

While AI enhances both art and science, it also raises ethical questions about authorship, bias, and the role of human intuition in creative and scientific endeavors.

3.1 Who Owns AI-Generated Art and Discoveries?

✓ If AI creates a painting or composes music, should the algorithm, its creator, or the AI itself get credit?

✔ Legal frameworks are evolving, but currently, human creators retain ownership of AI-assisted works.

3.2 The Risk of AI Replacing Human Creativity

✔ AI is a tool, not a replacement for human artists and scientists.

✔ The best outcomes emerge from AI-human synergy, where AI handles repetitive tasks, and humans focus on intuition and innovation.

3.3 Ethical AI in Scientific Research

✔ AI-generated medical solutions must be tested and validated by human experts to ensure safety.

✔ AI predictions in climate science and medicine require transparency to avoid biases in results.

4. The Future of AI-Human Collaboration

4.1 AI-Generated Content as a New Medium

✔ Just as photography and digital art revolutionized traditional art, AI-generated content is becoming a new medium for artists, musicians, and filmmakers.

4.2 AI-Augmented Scientific Discovery

✔ AI will become an essential research assistant, helping scientists uncover hidden patterns and generate new theories faster.

4.3 AI and Humans: Co-Creators, Not Competitors

✔ Future AI systems will be designed to work alongside human experts, rather than replace them, fostering greater innovation across fields.

The future of AI-human collaboration is not about replacing human creativity and intellect but enhancing them with AI-powered tools. From generating breathtaking art and music to accelerating scientific breakthroughs, GANs and other AI models are becoming partners in innovation.

As AI becomes more sophisticated, the challenge will be to balance automation with human intuition, ensuring ethical, meaningful, and impactful contributions to both the creative and scientific worlds. 🚀

20.4 Can GANs Evolve into Artificial General Intelligence?

Artificial General Intelligence (AGI)—the concept of AI systems that can perform any intellectual task that a human can—has long been the ultimate goal of AI research. While Generative Adversarial Networks (GANs) have revolutionized AI creativity by generating realistic images, music, and even human-like text, the question remains: Can GANs evolve into AGI?

In this chapter, we explore the potential and limitations of GANs in the pursuit of AGI. While GANs excel in generating and mimicking patterns, they currently lack fundamental elements of intelligence, such as reasoning, adaptability, and self-improvement beyond their training data. However, hybrid approaches combining GANs with reinforcement learning, meta-learning, and self-supervised learning may push AI toward more generalized intelligence.

1. The Strengths of GANs in AI Development

GANs have transformed many fields of AI, particularly in creativity and data generation. Their unique architecture—where two neural networks (the generator and the discriminator) compete—enables them to produce highly realistic outputs. These abilities position GANs as a potential component of future AGI.

1.1 The Power of GANs in Data Generation

✓ GANs can generate hyper-realistic images, videos, music, and text that mimic human creativity.

✓ They improve over time through adversarial training, a key component of self-improvement in AI.

1.2 Unsupervised Learning and Pattern Recognition

✓ Unlike traditional AI models that require labeled data, GANs learn without direct supervision, making them highly scalable.

✓ They can recognize and synthesize patterns in vast datasets, which is a foundational skill in intelligence.

1.3 Creativity and Imagination in AI

✓ GANs generate new, unseen data rather than just making predictions based on existing information.

✓ Creativity is an essential aspect of human intelligence, and GANs mimic aspects of it in art, storytelling, and design.

2. The Limitations of GANs in Achieving AGI

Despite their impressive abilities, GANs alone are not enough to achieve AGI. They lack fundamental traits of general intelligence, such as reasoning, memory, and adaptability.

2.1 Lack of Reasoning and Understanding

✓ GANs generate synthetic data based on probability distributions but do not understand what they create.

✓ They do not perform logical reasoning, causal inference, or problem-solving, all of which are essential for AGI.

2.2 No Long-Term Memory or Knowledge Retention

✓ GANs are trained on a specific dataset and cannot retain or recall information beyond that training.

✓ True intelligence requires an ability to store knowledge, learn from past experiences, and apply it in new situations.

2.3 Fragility and Mode Collapse

✓ GANs often suffer from mode collapse, where they produce limited variations of data instead of truly diverse outputs.

✓ AGI would need adaptability and self-correction, which GANs currently lack.

3. Combining GANs with Other AI Models for AGI

While GANs alone may not lead to AGI, integrating them with other AI approaches could bring us closer to generalized intelligence.

3.1 GANs + Reinforcement Learning (RL)

✓ Reinforcement Learning (RL) allows AI to learn from experience by maximizing rewards, a key step toward AGI.

✓ Hybrid models like GAN-RL systems could enable adaptive learning beyond simple data generation.

✓ **Example**: AlphaStar (DeepMind) used RL to master StarCraft, a complex game requiring long-term planning and adaptation.

3.2 GANs + Meta-Learning

✓ Meta-learning ("learning how to learn") allows AI to generalize knowledge across different domains.

✓ GANs could be combined with meta-learning techniques to enable more flexible adaptation to new problems.

3.3 GANs + Symbolic AI for Reasoning

✓ Symbolic AI focuses on logical reasoning and rule-based intelligence, areas where GANs are weak.

✓ Combining GANs with knowledge graphs and symbolic reasoning could enhance AI's ability to understand and explain concepts.

4. The Future of GANs in AGI Research

While GANs are not AGI, they will play a crucial role in the development of more advanced AI systems.

4.1 AI Self-Improvement and Evolution

✓ Some researchers propose "self-improving GANs" that generate better AI architectures over time.

✓ Future GANs may evolve into AI that designs new AI, reducing human intervention in model development.

4.2 GANs as a Step Toward Creative and Emotional AI

✓ GANs demonstrate rudimentary creativity, which is a step toward AI systems that understand and express emotions.

✓ Advanced AI systems could generate emotionally aware content, leading to breakthroughs in human-AI interaction.

4.3 The Role of GANs in the AGI Timeline

✓ Experts predict AGI may emerge within the next few decades, but GANs alone are unlikely to achieve it.

✓ Instead, GANs will be a powerful component in multi-model AI architectures that eventually lead to general intelligence.

GANs represent one of the most exciting advancements in AI, pushing the boundaries of creativity and data generation. However, they lack reasoning, memory, and generalization abilities, making them insufficient for AGI on their own.

The future of AGI will likely involve hybrid AI models that integrate GANs with reinforcement learning, symbolic AI, and meta-learning. While GANs won't single-handedly create AGI, they will play a key role in shaping the next generation of intelligent systems. 🚀

20.5 Final Thoughts: Where Do We Go from Here?

Generative Adversarial Networks (GANs) have revolutionized artificial intelligence, unlocking new possibilities in creativity, automation, and problem-solving. From generating hyper-realistic images and music to aiding in scientific discoveries and game development, GANs have pushed AI beyond simple automation into the realm of synthetic intelligence—machines that can create, innovate, and even inspire.

Throughout this book, we explored the fundamental mathematics, architectures, training techniques, and real-world applications of GANs. We also tackled their challenges, including mode collapse, ethical concerns, and computational constraints. Most importantly, we looked at how GANs might evolve—not just in creative domains but as part of a larger AI ecosystem that could one day lead to Artificial General Intelligence (AGI).

The Future of GANs and AI Creativity

While GANs have made tremendous strides, they are still just the beginning of AI-generated creativity. Here are a few key trends shaping the future:

1. GANs Will Become More Efficient and Scalable

✓ Researchers are working on faster, more stable training techniques to reduce computational costs.

✓ New architectures like StyleGAN3 and BigGAN are already improving realism and control in image synthesis.

✓ Techniques like self-supervised learning and few-shot learning will make GANs more generalized and adaptable.

2. AI and Human Creativity Will Merge

✓ Artists, musicians, and writers are collaborating with AI to enhance their work rather than replace it.

✓ AI will serve as a creative assistant, helping designers generate new ideas, refine concepts, and push artistic boundaries.

✓ Future tools will integrate GANs with virtual reality (VR), augmented reality (AR), and 3D modeling, leading to entirely new creative industries.

3. Ethical AI Will Be a Priority

✓ As AI-generated content becomes indistinguishable from human work, misuse risks will rise (e.g., deepfakes, misinformation).

✓ AI developers must implement responsible AI frameworks to ensure transparency and prevent bias.

✓ Governments and tech leaders will need to establish legal protections around AI-generated content and copyright laws.

GANs as a Stepping Stone Toward Synthetic Intelligence

GANs have already proven their ability to generate and imitate reality, but can they evolve into something more? While they alone may not lead to true intelligence, they will be a crucial building block in the pursuit of self-improving, adaptive AI.

In the coming decades, GANs will likely merge with reinforcement learning, neuromorphic computing, and quantum AI, leading to smarter, more autonomous AI models. These advancements may eventually pave the way for Synthetic Intelligence—machines that think, create, and learn beyond their training data.

Final Words: The AI Revolution Is Just Beginning

We are standing at the edge of an AI-driven creative revolution. GANs have already reshaped art, music, storytelling, and science, but their true potential is yet to be realized. The journey from simple pattern recognition to machines that can dream, imagine, and reason is underway.

As a reader, whether you are a developer, researcher, artist, or AI enthusiast, you are part of this movement. The knowledge and skills you've gained from this book are not just theoretical—they are tools for building the future.

The next great AI breakthrough could come from you. Keep exploring, keep experimenting, and keep pushing the boundaries of what AI can do. The future of synthetic intelligence is in our hands. 🚀

GANs & AI Creativity: Building Synthetic Intelligence takes you on an in-depth journey into the world of Generative Adversarial Networks (GANs)—one of the most groundbreaking advancements in artificial intelligence. From foundational concepts to hands-on implementation, this book equips you with the knowledge and skills to understand, build, and apply GANs in various creative fields, including art, music, storytelling, and game design.

Through step-by-step coding tutorials, real-world applications, and discussions on advanced architectures like StyleGAN, CycleGAN, and 3D GANs, you'll gain a comprehensive understanding of how GANs generate synthetic data and push the boundaries of AI creativity. Additionally, this book explores the ethical implications, legal challenges, and future of AI-generated content, ensuring that you not only master the technical aspects but also develop a responsible perspective on synthetic intelligence.

Whether you're a beginner, developer, data scientist, or AI enthusiast, this book provides a structured, practical, and insightful guide to mastering GANs. By the end, you'll be ready to create AI-generated content, experiment with new GAN architectures, and explore the limitless possibilities of AI creativity.

Artificial intelligence is no longer just a tool—it's becoming a creative force. Are you ready to be part of this revolution? 🚀

To all my readers,

From the very first book in the AI from Scratch series to this latest journey into GANs & AI Creativity, your support, curiosity, and passion for artificial intelligence have been the driving force behind my writing. Whether you are a beginner taking your first steps into AI or an experienced professional pushing the boundaries of machine learning, I am deeply grateful that you chose this book as part of your learning journey.

AI is evolving rapidly, and with each breakthrough comes new opportunities and challenges. Your dedication to understanding and mastering these concepts inspires me to keep sharing knowledge in the clearest, most practical way possible. It is because of you—students, researchers, developers, artists, and AI enthusiasts—that this book, and indeed this entire series, exists.

I also want to extend my heartfelt thanks to the open-source AI community, whose contributions continue to fuel innovation and make advanced AI accessible to everyone. To my family, friends, and mentors, your encouragement and patience throughout this writing process mean the world to me.

Finally, if this book has helped you, I would love to hear from you. Your feedback, thoughts, and success stories motivate me to keep improving and exploring new frontiers in AI. If you've enjoyed this book, please consider sharing your experience, whether through a review, a discussion, or by applying what you've learned to create something amazing.

Thank you for being part of this journey. Keep learning, keep experimenting, and keep pushing the limits of AI creativity! 🚀

With gratitude,

Gilbert Gutiérrez

<u>GANs & AI Creativity: Building Synthetic Intelligence</u> takes you on an in-depth journey into the world of Generative Adversarial Networks (GANs)—one of the most groundbreaking advancements in artificial intelligence. From foundational concepts to hands-on implementation, this book equips you with the knowledge and skills to understand, build, and apply GANs in various creative fields, including art, music, storytelling, and game design.

Through step-by-step coding tutorials, real-world applications, and discussions on advanced architectures like StyleGAN, CycleGAN, and 3D GANs, you'll gain a comprehensive understanding of how GANs generate synthetic data and push the boundaries of AI creativity. Additionally, this book explores the ethical implications, legal challenges, and future of AI-generated content, ensuring that you not only master the technical aspects but also develop a responsible perspective on synthetic intelligence.

Whether you're a beginner, developer, data scientist, or AI enthusiast, this book provides a structured, practical, and insightful guide to mastering GANs. By the end, you'll be ready to create AI-generated content, experiment with new GAN architectures, and explore the limitless possibilities of AI creativity.

Artificial intelligence is no longer just a tool—it's becoming a creative force. Are you ready to be part of this revolution? 🚀

To all my readers,

From the very first book in the AI from Scratch series to this latest journey into GANs & AI Creativity, your support, curiosity, and passion for artificial intelligence have been the driving force behind my writing. Whether you are a beginner taking your first steps into AI or an experienced professional pushing the boundaries of machine learning, I am deeply grateful that you chose this book as part of your learning journey.

AI is evolving rapidly, and with each breakthrough comes new opportunities and challenges. Your dedication to understanding and mastering these concepts inspires me to keep sharing knowledge in the clearest, most practical way possible. It is because of you—students, researchers, developers, artists, and AI enthusiasts—that this book, and indeed this entire series, exists.

I also want to extend my heartfelt thanks to the open-source AI community, whose contributions continue to fuel innovation and make advanced AI accessible to everyone. To my family, friends, and mentors, your encouragement and patience throughout this writing process mean the world to me.

Finally, if this book has helped you, I would love to hear from you. Your feedback, thoughts, and success stories motivate me to keep improving and exploring new frontiers in AI. If you've enjoyed this book, please consider sharing your experience, whether through a review, a discussion, or by applying what you've learned to create something amazing.

Thank you for being part of this journey. Keep learning, keep experimenting, and keep pushing the limits of AI creativity! 🚀

With gratitude,

Gilbert Gutiérrez